The Oxford

Catch

Anna Farkas is an American citizen who has lived in the UK for over 10 years. She is an experienced freelance writer and researcher, whose other books include (as contributor) *The Hutchinson Guide to the World* and *The Hutchinson Encyclopedia*.

Oxford Paperback Reference

The most authoritative and up-to-date reference books for both students and the general reader.

The Oxford Dictionary of
Catchphrases

Compiled by
ANNA FARKAS

OXFORD
UNIVERSITY PRESS

OXFORD
UNIVERSITY PRESS

Great Clarendon Street, Oxford OX2 6DP

Oxford University Press is a department of the University of Oxford.
It furthers the University's objective of excellence in research, scholarship,
and education by publishing worldwide in

Oxford New York

Auckland Bangkok Buenos Aires Cape Town Chennai
Dar es Salaam Delhi Hong Kong Istanbul Karachi Kolkata
Kuala Lumpur Madrid Melbourne Mexico City Mumbai Nairobi
São Paulo Shanghai Singapore Taipei Tokyo Toronto

Oxford is a registered trade mark of Oxford University Press
in the UK and in certain other countries

Published in the United States
by Oxford University Press Inc., New York

© Oxford University Press 2002, 2003

The moral rights of the authors have been asserted
Database right Oxford University Press (maker)

First published 2002
First issued as an Oxford University Press paperback 2003

All rights reserved. No part of this publication may be reproduced,
stored in a retrieval system, or transmitted, in any form or by any means,
without the prior permission in writing of Oxford University Press,
or as expressly permitted by law, or under terms agreed with the appropriate
reprographics rights organization. Enquiries concerning reproduction
outside the scope of the above should be sent to the Rights Department,
Oxford University Press, at the address above

You must not circulate this book in any other binding or cover
and you must impose this same condition on any acquirer

British Library Cataloguing in Publication Data
Data available

Library of Congress Cataloging in Publication Data
Data available

ISBN-13: 978-0-19-860735-9
ISBN-10: 0-19-860735-0

3

Designed by Jane Stevenson
Typeset in Argo and Swift
by Kolam Information Services Pvt. Ltd
Pondicherry, India
Printed in Great Britain
by Clays Ltd, St Ives plc

Contents

Introduction

IF SOMEONE SAYS TO YOU 'Eat my shorts', or 'Follow your dreams…
BEEFCAKE!', or 'Gotta catch 'em all', are you instantly on their
wavelength, or do your eyes glaze over? If the latter, then how about
'Left hand down a bit', 'Beautiful downtown Burbank', or 'Bernie, the
bolt'? And if those fail to press any buttons, try 'Can I do you now,
sir?', 'Can you hear me, mother?' or 'The day war broke out'.

Those are all catchphrases, and the chances are that one or more of
them will be familiar to you. Which ones you know, however, will
depend to a great extent on your generation. If you grew up in Britain
during the Second World War, the last group will raise a smile of
recognition. The middle three are more likely to ring a bell with post-
War baby-boomers. And to make head or tail of 'Eat my shorts' (from
the animated cartoon *The Simpsons*), it probably helps to be under 35.

This illustrates the curious duality of catchphrases. There is an
undeniable ephemerality about them—David Crystal has
characterized them as language 'on the wing'. But for people exposed
to them at an impressionable time of life—generally speaking, in
youth or early adulthood—they stick in a corner of the mind, and
cataloguing someone's mental hoard of catchphrases is almost as
reliable a diagnostic of their age and interests as counting the growth-
rings is in determining the age of a tree.

The term 'catchphrase' dates back to the middle of the nineteenth
century, but at that time it was far from complimentary. It denoted a
phrase with sufficient plausibility to appeal to or persuade the
unsophisticated (etymologically, the idea behind the word is that it
'catches' people's attention or interest). The memorable catchphrases
of the latter part of the nineteenth century are mostly hucksterish
slogans (for instance, 'the greatest show on earth'). But gradually, over
the first half of the twentieth century the term shed its implications of
speciousness and opportunism (although political catchphrases, such
as 'You've never had it so good', can put a strain on credence), and
came to have the meaning we associate with it in today's popular

culture: a phrase (or occasionally a word—'Pass!' (*Mastermind*),
'perfick!' (*The Darling Buds of May*)) which, through repeated usage, has
come to be identified with a particular individual, organization,
product, or cultural entity.

Catchphrases spring out of a variety of spheres, including literature,
sport, and politics, but by far the most effusive sources are advertising
(of which more anon) and popular entertainment—both individual
performers (notably comedians) and radio and television programmes,
films, etc. This latter trend was accentuated from the late 1930s
onwards by developments in radio comedy. On programmes tailored
specifically for radio, catchphrases provided predictable recognition
points for audiences, and almost guaranteed a laugh (the main pioneer
in Britain was Arthur Askey's *Bandwagon*, first broadcast in 1938,
whose contributions to the genre included 'Ay thang yew', 'Doesn't it
make you want to spit?', and 'Hello, playmates!'). A memorable
catchphrase became vital to the success of a comedian (Jack Benny
had his 'Now cut that out!', Jimmy Wheeler his 'Aye, aye, that's yer
lot!', Hilda Baker her 'She knows, you know!', Bruce Forsyth his 'I'm in
charge!', and so on, and on), and scriptwriters would be hired to dream
new ones up (this phase in the history of the catchphrase was guyed in
BBC TV's *The Fast Show*, with the spoof 1940s comic Arthur Atkinson's
'How queer!').

As television moved away from stand-up towards situation-based
comedy drama, catchphrases tended to be linked more with fictional
characters than with real performers (Cpl. Jones's 'Don't panic!',
Mr. Humphries's 'I'm free!', Basil Fawlty's 'Don't mention the war',
Baldrick's 'I have a cunning plan'). Nor did the drama have to be
comic; cop and crime shows have made a significant contribution too,
from PC George Dixon's 'Evening, all' through Kojak's 'Who loves ya,
baby?' to Arthur Daly's 'nice little earner'.

For a slogan to become a catchphrase—free word-of-mouth—is the
adman's holy grail. And over the past century scores of these gems
have passed from the billboard and the television screen into common
(if temporary) parlance, from 'Drinka Pinta Milka Day' (which
bequeathed *pinta* to the English language) to 'I'm only here for the

beer' (Double Diamond), from 'Tell Sid' (for gas privatization) to Kentucky Fried Chicken's 'It's finger-lickin' good'.

This last reminds us that the pervasiveness of US media culture has familiarized British people with large numbers of catchphrases of American origin: 'What's up, Doc?', 'Hi-ho, Silver!', 'Tomorrow is another day', 'Yabba-dabba-doo!', 'the kind mother used to make', 'You cannot be serious!', to mention only a tiny proportion. Migration westwards has been much rarer, although the success of the BBC's *Monty Python's Flying Circus* in the US did introduce one or two catchphrases into American English, such as 'And now for something completely different' and 'Nudge nudge, wink wink'.

Catchphrases are self-validating, and we must take them or leave them, but it has to be admitted that some of the best known of them are less than 100 per cent genuine. Sherlock Holmes never actually said 'Elementary, my dear Watson!', for instance, nor Rick Blaine (played by Humphrey Bogart in *Casablanca*) 'Play it again, Sam', nor yet Tarzan 'Me Tarzan, you Jane'.

The *Oxford Dictionary of Catchphrases* explains the origin of over 800 catchphrases, and puts them in their cultural and historical context. They are presented in alphabetical order, but in addition, in order to provide the reader with an alternative point of access to the material in the book, there is an index at the end which brings together all the catchphrases from a particular source (e.g. *The Fast Show*, *Seinfeld*, Kelloggs products). Brief descriptions are also given at the back of the dictionary of all television programmes, films, and books that have contributed three or more catchphrases to this collection. If you want to look up a half-remembered catchphrase that is part of your personal map, or browse among the diverse range cherished by others, this is the place to do it.

JOHN AYTO

London 2002

Aaaay!

From the US TV series *Happy Days* (1974–84) set in the 1950s; popularized by the cool, motorcycling Arthur 'Fonzie' Fonzarelli, also known as the Fonz (Henry Winkler) who, when combing back his bouffant hairstyle in the mirror, could never refrain from pausing to appreciate his own reflection with both thumbs up and this sound of approval. The producers of *Happy Days* had not originally conceived of the show as centring on the Fonz, but he soon became the star of the show, when suddenly kids all across the country were popping their thumbs in the air and saying 'Aaaay!', and the big-hearted Italo-American—originally introduced as the local hoodlum—became a new national hero.

absolutely fabulous (or AbFab)

A somewhat exaggerated exclamation which has become associated with the BBC TV comedy series *Absolutely Fabulous* 1992–6 (1994–7 in the US). The series centred around the life of Edina Monsoon, played by Jennifer Saunders, Edina's daughter Saffron (Julia Sawalha), and best friend Patsy Stone (Joanna Lumley). The show—with its role reversal of mother and daughter, new age trends, free use of drugs, and predominantly female cast—struck a special chord with a large segment of the 1990s TV audience. Also used as the title of a 1997 Pet Shop Boys single, the expression has become common currency, entering the language of business as well: 'Computer Corp. CEO Michael Capellas closed a quiet first day at the Windows 2000 Conference & Expo here by pitching his company's "absolutely fabulous technology"' (in ZDNet: Windows 2000 Special Report, 5 February 2001).

accidento bizarro

From the popular BBC TV comedy series *The Fast Show* (1994–7), created by Paul Whitehouse and Charlie Higson. The words, meaning simply 'bizarre accident' (usually leading to a death—'tuto morte'), form part of the vocabulary used in one of the show's most popular regular sketches, featuring a TV news studio set in a fictitious South American country. The news programme's sportcaster (played by Simon Day) uses the phrase frequently as a joke, when he has in fact no news to report.

action pumpo!

A recurring term in the fictitious language employed in 'Chanel 9' sketches on the BBC TV comedy series *The Fast Show* (1994–7). The phrase usually appears in the commercial or 'Mesago sponsoro' breaks during the show's regular TV news programme—'Chanel Nine's Republica presente...' set in a fictitious South American country whose citizens speak a bizarre hybrid language combining English with Spanish/Italian/Greek-sounding words. The words usually describe the latest 'auto-gizmo' featured in the advertisement, as in this one presented by Charlie Higson: 'Beneres? Nikko fuerto tippo magico—"auto-gizmo". Novello proboscis multo multo kinagrophos. Tefaselos action-pumpo!'

after all, tomorrow is another day

Scarlett O'Hara's final words of optimism and belief in a better future form the closing line of both the 1936 novel *Gone with the Wind* and the 1939 film version. Known since the early 16th century in the form 'tomorrow is a new day', the version with 'another' became commonly used from the early 20th century, finally becoming popularized by Margaret Mitchell's best-selling, Pulitzer prize-winning novel telling a story of the US Civil War. The words, already associated with Scarlett in the novel, became even more widely identifiable following the release of the film starring Vivien Leigh as Scarlett and Clark Gable as Rhett Butler.

after you, Claude!|no—after you, Cecil!

Spoken by Horace Percival and Jack Train, playing two over-polite handymen (Cecil and Claude) on the BBC radio show *ITMA*, the most popular radio series of the 1940s (starring Tommy Handley and written by Ted Kavanagh). A kind of mutual deference that can easily become comic as it can be potentially never-ending and therefore inconclusive. The phrase has come to be used often in sports reporting to describe how players sometimes back off from taking the ball in a way that is detrimental to their team's efforts, as in 'Lomu had run through virtually unchallenged in an after-you-Claude sort of way as the defence backed off' (in the *Guardian*, 1 November 1999).

ahhh, Ricky...

Used by Lucille Ball in the US TV situation comedy series *I Love Lucy* (1951–61), referring to Ricky Ricardo, her on-screen husband, played by her off-screen husband, Desi Arnaz. The popular show offered television audiences hour-long stories of the misadventures of the Ricardos and the Mertzes (Fred and Ethel, played by William Frawley and Vivian Vance). With her *I Love Lucy* series Lucille Ball, probably US television's most famous redhead, helped create what would be the blueprint for future sitcoms. The show's premiss was simple: Ball played Lucy Ricardo, wife of Cuban bandleader Ricky Ricardo, and all she wanted was to be a part of Ricky's act. In some ways, the show began the era of pop culture, spawning catchphrases—such as this one and 'Vitameatavegamin'—and was widely imitated. At the end of the 1990s the catchphrase began to be commonly used with reference to another Ricky. Namely, by fans of the highly popular US Latin singer 'ahhh, Ricky Martin'.

I Love Lucy was so popular during the 1950s that in 1953, more people watched the famous episode in which Lucy gave birth to Little Ricky than would watch Eisenhower's inauguration which occurred the following day.

ah, gee whiz, pop!

A juvenile interjection indicating mild surprise, amazement, or enthusiasm, that was popularized by its frequent use on the US children's game show *Choose Up Sides* (1956) and other 1950s children's programmes. The show was produced by Mark Goodson and Bill Todman (responsible for the game shows *What's My Line* and *The Price is Right*), and pitted two groups of four children—the 'Bronco Busters' and the 'Space Pilots'—against each other. The two teams competed in various stunts, doing their best to earn 200 points.

ain't I a stinker?

Aren't I a dishonourable or objectionable person—spoken without any sign of remorse. Originally a tag line used by US comedian Lou Costello of the popular comedy duo Abbott and Costello, who moved from burlesque to feature films for Universal Pictures in the 1940s, gaining their own radio show in 1942. The phrase was also popularized by cartoon-film character Bugs Bunny, who first began using the phrase frequently during the 1940s, as in *Hare Force* (1944) and *A Hare Grows in Manhattan* (1947). The carrot-crunching, ever-impervious laid-back rabbit was named in 1940 after West Coast mobster Bugsy Siegel, probably because Bugs Bunny's character rarely displayed any scruples—in other words, he was a real 'stinker'.

ain't it a shame, eh? ain't it a shame?

Associated with a character played by Carleton Hobbs on *ITMA*, the most popular British radio comedy series of the Second World War; that aired weekly 1939–49. Hobbs (who later played radio's Sherlock Holmes 1960-3) joined *ITMA* as part of the show's post-war new look in 1945. This catchphrase belonged to Curly Kale, the chef who hated food but loved terrible puns.

ain't nobody here but us chickens! (, there)

Spoken mainly in social situations, where the phrase is used to let newcomers know fewer people than expected are present, and generally implying that the gathering or venue is not a terribly attractive one. It is also associated with the dumb, instant give-away response of the chicken thief (usually a fox in cartoons), given to the farmer asking 'Anybody there?' upon hearing someone rustling about in his chicken coop. The phrase, which originated in the US in the late 19th century, was popularized during the late 1940s and 1950s after Louis Jordan recorded a rhythm & blues song entitled 'Ain't Nobody Here But Us Chickens' (1947, written by Alex Kramer and Joan Whitney). It was through the song—later recorded by many others, including BB King and Lisa Stansfield—that the expression gained currency in the UK.

all dressed up and nowhere to go

From the title of a song written by US songwriter Benjamin Hapgood Burt in 1913 ('When you're all dressed up and no place to go'), and popularized by US stage comedian Raymond Hitchcock in musical shows 1914–16. *The Beauty Shop*, on the New York stage in 1914, featured Hitchcock with what became 'his' song. He returned with the song in 1916 during the run of the musical play, *Mr Manhattan* at the Prince of Wales Theatre, London.

A song entitled 'When you're all dressed up and have no place to go', written by US songwriter George Whiting in 1912 provides a slight variation on the wording, but the version that became most widely used came from US journalist William Allen White in late 1916. White, a member of the Progressive Party, said 'All dressed up, with nowhere to go', after the party's presidential nominee, Theodore Roosevelt, withdrew from consideration and threw his support behind the Republican candidate, Charles Evans Hughes.

all human life is here

Used as an advertising slogan for the *News of the World* during the late 1950s. The expression is from a quotation in Henry James's novel *The Madonna of the Future* (1879): 'Cats and monkeys—monkeys and cats—all human life is there.'

The line comes up in a rather sinister context in the 1994 US film *Interview with the Vampire*, when Louis, played by Brad Pitt, says 'All human life was here, for the taking. And we took, all three of us, in our different ways.'

all jam and Jerusalem

A British phrase, originating in the 1920s, commonly used to describe the Women's Institute (WI) and its members. The WI's reputation for making jam and producing good cooks was reinforced during the Second World War when the national organization was allocated sugar by the government for jam making, and equipment for canning fruit and vegetables to help in the effort to feed the nation. Although the WI is not associated with any religious faith or political party, its members were mistakenly and mockingly portrayed as God-fearing women who sang the 1916 Blake/Parry arrangement 'Jerusalem' when they weren't busy making jam or generally keeping house. In recent years the WI has tried to shed the mistaken image associated with this phrase (believed to be responsible for a drop in numbers) in order to attract younger women. *Jam and Jerusalem: A Pictorial History of Britain's*

Greatest Women's Movement is the title of a book by Simon Goodenough about the WI published in 1977.

all I know is what I read in the papers

One of US cowboy humorist Will Rogers's most popular sayings. The phrase, suggesting that the speaker knows no more or better than the next guy, was very much in tune with ideas and attitudes of the self-made man which Rogers represented so successfully. Will Rogers, also known as the 'Cherokee Kid', started telling jokes while working in wild west shows and vaudeville. He began an additional career as a syndicated columnist in 1922, and started writing a daily column 'Will Rogers Says' in 1926. Although he dropped out of school he never stopped trying to learn in whatever way he could, and soon became recognized as a well-informed, sharp philosophizer who could convey truths in a simple and accessible way. This particular phrase, as well as his other well-known saying 'I never met a man I didn't like', both clearly illustrate the simple wisdom Rogers became so famous for.

all is well—and all will be well—in the garden

Associated with Peter Sellers in the role of Chance, the slow-witted gardener and hero of the 1979 film *Being There*, based on the 1971 satirical novel by Jerzy Kosinski. Chance, who has only had two pursuits in his life—gardening and watching television—is mistaken in America's most influential political circles for a businessman whose comments are invaluable. Chance innocently comes out with simple truisms from the garden, such as 'all is well in the garden' (with reference to the changing of the seasons) and 'Spring is a time for planting', and these are taken as metaphors about economics.

Having lived all of his life inside the walls of an elegant Washington town house, devoting himself to gardening and watching television, the ingenue Chance has no notion of the workings of the real world. One day the master of the house dies and the household staff is disbanded. Impeccably dressed in his employer's tailored suit, and equipped with only his TV's remote-control, Sellers wanders out into the city. He stumbles into Washington's political and social upper crust, and is immediately mistaken for Chauncey Gardiner, an aristocratic businessman. Thanks to a series of mistaken assumptions, this illiterate, ignorant, yet gentle, person quickly becomes the closest confidant of a dying billionaire industrialist (Melvyn Douglas), who is in turn the closest confidant of the president.

all lies lead to the truth

One of the maxims popularized by *The X-Files* (1993–2002), a US cult TV series that delves into the rich world of the paranormal. The line appeared in the opening episode of the fifth season, *Redux*. As with the show's other major dictum, 'believe the lie' (see below), the belief presumably embodied by this phrase is based on the premiss that the government is out to mislead and lie to the public to successfully conceal certain truths. There are no lies without the truth so, on the *The X-Files* at least, there can be no truth without lies. FBI Special Agents Fox Mulder (David Duchovny) and Dana Scully (Gillian Anderson) are forever wading through streams of lies to reach truths that can never be thoroughly ascertained.

all systems go!

Everything is functioning properly and is ready to proceed. The phrase originated in the US in the late 1950s and 1960s, used mainly by space flight controllers just before the launch of a spacecraft. Thanks to its dramatic potential, the phrase was included in the scripts of numerous live-action and animated TV shows and other media featuring space travel. It has more recently appeared in business (and particularly computing) pep talks and promotional material.

all the news that's fit to print

Advertising slogan for the *New York Times*, which first appeared on the newspaper's editorial page on 25th October 1896. From February 1897 to the present it has appeared on the paper's masthead logo. In 1896, Adolph S. Ochs gained control of the then financially ailing paper, and devised the slogan to highlight what he believed to be the benevolence of the newspaper's owners. He promised that the *New York Times* would 'give the news impartially, without fear or favor' and that it would discuss all issues of public importance.

The Ochs-Sulzberger family are still the principal owners, and the concept or premiss that some people are in a position to know and determine what news is or isn't 'fit to print' continues to hold true.

The 1997 Proxy Statement of The New York Times Company explains the special voting rights that assure family control in terms of the desire for 'an independent newspaper, entirely fearless, free of ulterior influence and unselfishly devoted to the public welfare.'

all we want is the facts, ma'am (or: just the facts, ma'am)

From the highly stylized and much parodied US TV series *Dragnet* (1952–9 and 1967–70) about life on the beat for two detectives in Los Angeles. Originally a black-and-white half-hour series, starring Jack Webb as the crusading cop, Sergeant Joe Friday. Created and produced by Webb, *Dragnet* episodes would begin with a prologue stating 'the story you are about to see is true; the names have been changed to protect the innocent', and in the mid-1950s the series was applauded for its realism. Webb returned to TV screens as Friday in 1967 with a new partner, Officer Bill Gannon (Harry Morgan), but the new series' conservatism and out-dated moralism eventually led to its cancellation in 1970.

One of the show's 'realistic' elements was its emphasis on the technical aspects and drudgery of police work, which inevitably included questioning witnesses. Whenever Friday would interview someone and that person would start to tell his or her story he would remind them: just the facts. What the seasoned detective understood was that when someone told a story they were always giving his or her interpretation of the facts. The facts of a situation never change, but how they are perceived and then spoken about would depend on who was telling the story.

all you add is love

A maxim popularized by a 1960s advertising campaign for Ralston Purina Dog Chow. One poster showed a boy lovingly stroking a puppy on his lap, with the caption: 'One dog food so complete…all you add is love.' Purina Dog Chow's long-running string of 'all you add is love' TV commercials were narrated by B-movie cowboy actor and singer Rex Allen. The phrase is often used with reference to cooking and to recipes, deemed so complete that a bit of loving care is all that is missing. It is also the title of a 1969 country song by Lynn Anderson. The similar-sounding Beatles' hit single 'All You Need Is Love' was released in 1968 (*Yellow Submarine*).

alrighty then!

A catchphrase belonging to Ace, played by Jim Carrey, in the 1994 US film *Ace Ventura: Pet Detective* (and sequels). In this whacky comedy Ace Ventura, a pet detective, is searching for a kidnapped dolphin called Snowflake (a mascot of the Miami Dolphins football team). This phrase, a loud (and usually superfluous) confirmation, is delivered at the end of an exchange or a joke, becoming a recurring punch line in itself.

always merry and bright

The sarcastic epithet associated with British comedian Alfred Lester, who was known for his consistently rueful demeanour on stage. In the original production of the musical comedy *The Arcadians*, which ran from 1909 to 1911 in London, Lester played Doody, a jockey, and sang 'My Motter' in the final act. The words that had come to describe the actor were incorporated into the song's lyrics as the character's personal maxim. The phrase has been used to describe attempts to cover up what were in reality grim or sad situations, as in a Mr McGilligan's statement during a debate on a finance bill in the Dáil Éireann (Irish parliament) in June 1935: 'Deputy Corry's attempt to-night to sing "Always Merry and Bright" and to persuade the House that everything was in a flourishing state, did not indicate the plight to which that particular Deputy has been brought by the action of the Ministry whom he follows.'

The phrase has also been associated with US writer Henry Miller, who claimed it was his family's doomed slogan. The four-word statement first appears in the foreword of the first, 1935, edition of Miller's *What Are You Going to Do About Alf?* Jay Martin's biography of Henry Miller is entitled *Always Merry and Bright* (1978; 1979 UK).

always remember To Tell the Truth!

One of Bud Collyer's catchphrases on the US TV game show *To Tell the Truth*, which he hosted 1956–69. During the time the game series was on the air, the phrase became a familiar part of popular culture and language. See also 'goodbye...and God bless you'.

America's story teller

A registered trademark of Kodak, manufacturers of cameras and film, since 1979, and a slogan utilized in an advertising campaign that ran through to 1981. Kodak Eastman, which started in 1888 with the slogan 'you push the button, we do the rest', put the first simple camera into the hands of a world of consumers, and in so doing made what had been a cumbersome and complicated process easy to use and accessible to nearly everyone. The result was close to a complete and comprehensive documentation of American life, based on the notion that 'every picture tells a story', and, more importantly, almost everyone is taking pictures. The phrase has been used to describe numerous US writers, songwriters, and musicians, considered to have a documentary value, including folk singer and songwriter Woody Guthrie, writer James Michener, and jazz legend Ken Burns.

Anaheim, Azusa, and Cuc-ca-monga

A regular comic feature on the US TV series *The Jack Benny Show* from 1950 to 1965 (and on radio 1932–55). The line was spoken by Mel Blanc playing a Union Depot train caller who announced via megaphone or loudspeaker system the trains arriving and departing from the station. After announcing the departure of this train several times, Blanc might say 'Look we're not asking much. Two of ya, or even one of ya…just somebody to keep the engineer company'. And later into the show, 'Please, please! I'll get fired if I don't get somebody on the train for Anaheim, Azusa, and Cuuuu-ca-mon-gaaa!' To add some comic suspense, there would often be a degree of playfulness with the phrase's famous pause, placing it between 'Cuuu' and 'ca-mon-gaaa'. Once a whole comedy skit was completed during the pause. Having been made famous by this long-running joke, the town of Rancho Cucamonga, in California, erected a statue honouring Jack Benny in 1993.

ancient Chinese secret

Originally from an advertising slogan in the US for Calgon detergent, aired 1972. In the TV commercial, a woman walks into a Chinese laundromat (launderette) and asks the owner how he gets her laundry so fresh. He replies: 'ancient Chinese secret.' One then hears a woman in the back room say 'We need more Calgon'. The customer looks at the man and says 'ancient Chinese secret, huh?' The phrase became an all-purpose excuse for not telling somebody something. Whether you are too lazy or it's too complicated to explain or you don't actually know yourself, 'ancient Chinese secret!' was the simplest way to say 'I'm not going to tell you' without being offensive. It also became a catchphrase associated with the computer game *Shadow Warrior.*

and awa-a-aay we go!

A catchphrase used in show business popularized by *The Jackie Gleason Show*, a US TV variety show which ran from 1952 to 1970. 'The Great One', as Jackie Gleason was often referred to, would open each show with a comic monologue and then lead into the first sketch with 'and awa-a-aay we go!' as he left the stage. Gleason, a popular comedian of the 1950s and 1960s and one of TV's early stars, was best known as the scheming bus driver Ralph Kramden in *The Honeymooners*. Although this TV series ran only from 1955 to 1956, Gleason's role as the loud-mouthed, blue-collar philosopher Kramden helped it achieve cult status in endless reruns. His other well-known catchphrase was 'How sweet it is!'

and for the life of me, I don't know why...

Associated with US comedian David Letterman, who has used the phrase repeatedly as host of the popular TV talk show *Late Night with David Letterman*. Letterman employs the idiomatic phrase, 'for the life of me'—meaning no matter how hard I try—to add comic stress in the many absurd and bizarre situations and subjects featured on the show.

and I'm spent!

A conclusive declaration meaning I'm all worn out or thoroughly tired of some activity. The expression was popularized by Austin Powers, 'International Man of Mystery', played by Mike Myers, who uttered it repeatedly in the 1999 'psychedelic' spy spoof film *Austin Powers: The Spy Who Shagged Me.*

and it's goodnight from me—and it's goodnight from him

The regular sign-off ending episodes of the TV comedy-variety show *The Two Ronnies* which ran on BBC1 from 1971 to 1987. Starring for the first time in their own joint series, the two Ronnies, Ronnie Barker and Ronnie Corbett, created a consistent formula that prevailed throughout the programme's long run. Each show started and finished with the pair seated behind a desk reading spoof news items. In between there were sketches, musical extravaganzas where the Ronnies danced, sang, or marched, adventure serials such as 'Death Can be Fatal', a Ronnie Barker monologue/sketch, the inevitable rambling anecdote from Ronnie Corbett (seated in his chair) and, finally, the closing 'newsreader' slot: 'It's goodnight from me—and it's goodnight from him.'

and knowing is half the battle

Words of wisdom following a piece of advice popularized by the action/adventure US TV cartoon series *G.I. Joe* (1985–92, syndicated). G.I. Joe was one of the first 'action figures' designed by toymaker Hasbro as a boy-friendly rival to Mattel's successful Barbie line. The man-doll debuted in 1964, shot to instant popularity, and the syndicated weekday *G.I. Joe: A Real American Hero* animated TV series began in 1985. By then G.I. Joe had been joined by a multitude of good and evil characters, but regardless of the mayhem involved in each episode, none of them ever died, and at the end of each half-hour episode, a member of the Joe team would educate home viewers on some important safety tip, ending with '...And knowing is half the battle.'

During the late 1980s, the US government had passed a law requiring any TV show made with the intention of selling toys to have a public service announcement (PSA) at its end. Almost every *G.I. Joe* episode consequently ended with a message from a member (sometimes two) of *G.I. Joe*. The PSAs showed children in different situations, doing something wrong or potentially dangerous, in response to which the Joes gave them advice. The term 'And knowing is half the battle' implied that some of the key knowledge a child needed to know in life could be learned from these endings. One example of a PSA from the series' first season was: '*Mutt—Don't pet strange dogs*: Don't run! Walk away slowly. Never try to pet an animal you don't know. He might be lost, sick or scared. If we don't know, we leave 'em alone.'

and loving it!

A phrase popularized by Maxwell Smart, Agent 86, on the wacky US TV comedy series *Get Smart* (1965–70), a show spoofing James Bond and the spy craze of the time. Max (Don Adams) would use this line whenever the Chief (Edward Platt), head of CONTROL, would explain how this latest mission would place Max in immense danger. For example, in *Mr. Big* when Chief says 'Max, you realize you'll be facing every kind of danger imaginable', Max replies: 'And loving it!' The initial ideas of the show, including Max's recurring spy gadget—the shoe phone—were conceived by its two writers, Mel Brooks and Buck Henry.

and now for something completely different...

Phrase enabling a speaker to shift to an entirely new subject or activity which originated in, and became associated with, the BBC TV sketch comedy series *Monty Python's Flying Circus* (1969–74). The line was used in the show's first episode on 5 October 1969 (spoken by Eric Idle), which immediately signalled the Pythons' intention to disconcert viewers expecting to see programmes typical of the times. The opening scene featured a farmer discussing the properties of his sheep—which believed they were birds—as they nested in the trees. This was followed by two Frenchmen discussing the commercial potential of aviation by sheep. Then, as viewers were just beginning to understand the direction of the sketches, the camera cut to a shot of a man behind a news desk announcing, 'And now for something completely different...' In subsequent episodes the announcer was usually John Cleese, in a dinner jacket sitting at a desk positioned in the most incongruous locations available. It was also the title of the Python team's first feature film in 1971.

On the subject of this catchphrase, Michael Palin (one of the Pythons) recalled that 'a lot of the newspaper articles would have the headline "And Now For Something Completely Different", which I think was John and Graham's catchphrase...The great thing was, it was said so often anyway, normally, on television, that we just found ourselves saying it. By that time, we'd identified it as a silly catchphrase, and now no one can say it without really being aware of Python.'

and so to bed!

A recurring phrase in Samuel Pepys's *Diary* (1660–9), which so often ends the day's entry and first appeared a journal entry dated 20 April

1660. *The Diary of Samuel Pepys*, a unique record of the daily life of the period, was written in cipher, a kind of shorthand, and was not decoded until 1825. The phrase consequently became a catchphrase in the 19th century, and it was further popularized by James Bernard Fagan's successful play *And So to Bed* (1926) which had Pepys as its chief character. A musical, adapted from Fagan's play by Vivian Ellis, opened at the New Theatre in London in 1951 and featured a song entitled *And So to Bed*.

One example of Pepys's many uses of the phrase in the *Diary* appears in his journal entry for 9 March 1667: 'I have got a great cold, so home late and drank some buttered ale, and so to bed and to sleep. This cold did most certainly come by my staying a little too long bare-legged yesterday morning when I rose while I looked out fresh socks and thread stockings, yesterday's having in the night, lying near the window, been covered with snow within the window, which made me I durst not put them on.'

and so we say farewell . . .

A phrase that was originally associated with cinema travelogues made by James A. Fitzpatrick during the late 1920s and early 1930s, for which it always formed part of the closing line. Fitzpatrick's 1930s 'Traveltalks' were produced by MGM as pre-feature shorts, and included as their subjects Rio, Prague, Mazatlan, Capetown, Cairo, Honolulu, and Hong Kong. The brief documentaries—with titles like 'Los Angeles, Wonder City of the West' and 'Dutch Guiana, Land Of The Djuka'—provided movie audiences with glimpses of distant parts of the world. Viewed today, the shorts make their subjects look all the more exotic and unreachable. They have become important and fascinating documents of the past, with images, for example, of the virtually traffic-free streets of 'Charming Ceylon' and an unknowingly poignant portrait of pre-war Japan.

The phrase was parodied in a radio sketch—a hilarious spoof travelogue on a district of South London entitled 'Balham—Gateway to the South'—written by Frank Muir and Denis Norden in the late 1940s. The phrase was repopularized when the sketch was later performed by Peter Sellers in the late 1950s and early 1960s (first recorded in 1958). More recently, a review of an episode of the BBC1 soap opera *EastEnders* began: 'And so we say farewell-ish to Peggy

Butcher, the bijou landlady of the Queen Vic, who is moving in with her son, Phil. The implausible thing about this is that Phil shows no signs of resenting the sudden arrival of his mother, her large wardrobe of wigs (including my favourite, That Ginger Tom From Next Door) and a large bust of Queen Victoria' (in the *Guardian*, 23 May 2001).

and that's the way it is

Trademark sign-off phrase of US TV news anchorman Walter Cronkite, who delivered the world's most important events on the CBS Evening News over three decades. Prized and admired for his objectivity and authoritative delivery, independent polls over the years (one as recent as 1995) established Cronkite as one of the most trusted men in America. Affectionately nicknamed 'Old Iron Pants' for his unflappability under pressure, Cronkite first uttered his trademark catchphrase on 16 April 1962, and spoke it for the last time on 6 March 1981.

Two other catchphrases associated with Cronkite are 'you are there' and 'and you were there'. He hosted the historical documentary series *You Are There* (1953–7), introduced always with: 'The time...the place...all things are as they were then, except...you are there!' In each of the episodes Cronkite would travel back in time to witness a major event in world history and interview its participants. The programme would always end with the following words: 'What kind of day was it? A day like all days, filled with those events that alter and illuminate our times. And you were there.'

and the best of luck!

A catchphrase belonging to British comedian Frankie Howerd, and what he would wish his audiences from the late 1940s. He very quickly established himself as one of the nation's favourite performers, distinctly recognizable by his exaggerated expressions. This and his other frequent catchphrases 'Ooh er Missus' and 'Titter ye not', rapidly caught on and became his trademarks, and part of everyday vocabulary. Although Howerd claimed in his 1976 autobiography *On the Way I Lost It*, to have coined the phrase while appearing as a regular on the 1940s and 1950s BBC radio series *Variety Bandbox*, the phrase was already in usage by the Second World War, if not earlier, and could often be spoken sarcastically.

and the next object is...

Words spoken by the Mystery Voice in *Twenty Questions* (1947–76), a BBC radio celebrity panel game in which panellists had twenty tries to identify a word or phrase ('animal, vegetable, mineral, or abstract'). Before the panellists began, the Mystery Voice would inform listeners of the object in question, prefaced always with this phrase.The series' the original panel was Richard Dimbleby, Anona Winn, and Jack Train, and the celebrity Mystery Voice was pianist Norman Hackforth until he became a panellist in 1965 and was replaced by a new Mystery Voice. From December 1950 the series also ran on Radio Luxembourg, and was transferred to television during the 1950s and early 1960s.

and there's more where that came from!

A phrase already established by the mid-19th century among music-hall comedians, it appears in Charles Dickens's *Martin Chuzzlewit* (1843), where it is used to reassure those concerned there would be no shortage of drink. The phrase was more recently popularized by the BBC radio *Goon Show* (1952–60), on which it was uttered by various characters; *And There's More Where That Came From!* was also the title given to audio cassette compilations of *Goon Show* episodes published 1996. Although often used, especially in music-hall or comedy contexts, to mean more jokes, laughs, or gags are bound to follow, the phrase can also refer to disasters as in 'There's More Where Honeywell Came From', the title of an article predicting more economic woes for investors (www.TheStreet.com, 22 June 2000).

and with that, I return you to the studio!

A common line given by an on-the-scene broadcaster, signalling the end of the report and serving as a cue to his or her studio counterpart. The phrase was popularized in the late 1950s and early 1960s by the BBC man, played by Hugh Paddick, on the BBC radio series *Beyond Our Ken* (1958–64). The series featured Kenneth Horne, Kenneth Williams, Hugh Paddick, and Betty Marsden (with Bill Pertwee joining in the second series) performing short sketches.

another fine mess

See 'here's another fine mess you've gotten me/us into'.

any time, any place, anywhere

The phrase, meaning positively without restrictions or limits, was used in a song entitled 'I Love To Cry at Weddings', featured in the musical *Sweet Charity* which premiered on Broadway in 1966. But the line was then made truly popular when it became an advertising slogan for Martini in Britain from 1970. A slight variation on the catchphrase appears in Blondie's 1980 hit single 'Call Me' (also the theme from the US film *American Gigolo*): 'Any time, any place, anywhere, anyway/Any time, any place, anywhere, any day.'

The Martini ad's famous words quickly entered the language of popular culture, cropping up in TV shows such as *Doctor Who*. In an episode entitled *Dark Universe* Romana (the first regeneration of Romanadvoratrelundar, played by Mary Tamm 1978-9) says to the Doctor: 'Could be anywhere Doctor. You know that as well as I do. Any time, any place, anywhere', to which he responds with a smile and 'You sound like a Martini advert'. The doctor found it difficult to get along with Romana, although she usually came up with answers long before he could. The phrase has more recently become a favourite within the lexicon of finance and commerce. As in 'Consumers will demand "Martini Finance"—access any time, any place, anywhere—from any access device' (www.cnn.com, 11 August 2000).

anyone for tennis?

A question that came to typify characters in light, drawing-room comedies of the 1920s and 1930s, and was then much associated with Humphrey Bogart, who, so rumour had it, had delivered it as his first line on stage. It probably originated with George Bernard Shaw's play *Misalliance* (1914), in which the question, 'Anybody on for a game of tennis?' appears.

Eric Clapton wrote a mellow, melodic song called 'Anyone For Tennis' which was included on Cream's 1968 album *Wheels of Fire*.

apology is policy

A motto that replaced 'The Truth Is Out There' as the tagline for the third season's two-part episode, entitled *731*, on the popular US cult TV series *The X-Files* (1993-2002). It neatly sums up what FBI Special Agent Fox Mulder (David Duchovny) sees as the government's agenda, and its overall doctrine of excusing itself from revealing and taking responsibility for the truth. By apologizing, the government can continue to conceal information from the public without having to justify or take responsibility for its actions if and when these truths are revealed. The phrase was first uttered by agent Dana Scully (Gillian Anderson) in the same episode.

are we down-hearted?—no!

A question or phrase (when the answer 'no' is provided by the same person) used to provide encouragement or uplift spirits in difficult times. It was associated with the early stages of the First World War, when the expression was taken up by British soldiers. A 1914 song, 'Here we are! Here we are again!' by Charles Knight and Kenneth Lyle, encapsulated this unsuppressible fighting spirit: 'When there's trouble brewing, When there's something doing, Are we downhearted? No! Let them all come!' Once more, in the context of war and resilience, the phrase made a dramatic impact in a speech given by Winston Churchill during the celebrations on 8 May 1945 following the announcement of the end of the war in Europe. Churchill and his principal colleagues appeared on the balcony of the Ministry of Health in Whitehall, and made two brief speeches to the vast crowd. In the second speech Churchill said (of Londoners during the Blitz): 'There we stood, alone. Did anyone want to give in? [The crowd shouted "No".] Were we down-hearted? ["No!"]'

An earlier version of the phrase was used in a 1906 speech made by Joseph Chamberlain, referring to a constituency which had remained unaffected by an electoral landslide—'We are not downhearted. The only trouble is we cannot understand what is happening to our neighbours.' The phrase also appears in the refrain of a 1909 Irving Berlin song entitled 'Someone's Waiting For Me (We'll Wait, Wait, Wait)'. It had been picked up in America by the end of the First World War, appearing as the title of an article in a 1919 issue of the *Cleveland Advocate*.

are yer courtin'?

A question that was popularized by British actor and presenter Wilfred Pickles on his BBC radio quiz show *Have a Go* (1946–67), in which he interviewed ordinary people and gave cash prizes for simple questions. The very first question asked on the first broadcast from Bingley on 4 March 1946 was 'Are yer courtin'?' and it became a recurring one on the popular series that 'brought the people to the people'. A Yorkshireman, Pickles, with his regional accent, broke the 'BBC English' mould when he read the news in the 1940s, and became a household name as presenter of *Have a Go*.

are you a man or a mouse?

Do you have what it takes? A question asked of a person whose courage is in doubt, and one which rarely receives a serious answer. Its current use may have indirectly sprung from the title of John Steinbeck's 1937 classic *Of Mice and Men*, which in turn points to earlier uses, as in Robert Burns's poem 'To a Mouse' (1786)—'The best laid schemes o' mice an' men / Gang aft a-gley'. In any event, the expression was common in the US by the late 1930s, appearing in films such as *Made For Each Other* (1939), in which Carole Lombard asks Jimmy Stewart 'What are you, a man or a mouse?' and to which he replies, without hesitation, 'A mouse!' The phrase has also cropped up a lot in cartoons since the 1940s, where it is usually a trick question, as the wits of men are rarely a match for those of most of the mischievous, wily rodents involved.

are you experienced?

From the title of a Jimi Hendrix song and the legendary guitarist's first album (1967), which was interpreted as referring to experimentation with drugs, an activity that characterized a lot of the youth culture of the 1960s. The phrase was adopted by young people, and hippies in particular, to determine just how 'hip' a person might be. It was repopularized in 2001 when it became the advertising slogan for Microsoft Windows XP and Office XP. The slogan—'Windows XP and Office XP: Are you experienced?'—makes uses of XP (as in eXPerienced).

are you out of your Vulcan mind?

Spoken by Dr Leonard 'Bones' McCoy (DeForest Kelley) of the Starship *Enterprise* on the original US TV series *Star Trek* (1966–9) to his half-human half-Vulcan friend and favourite verbal sparring partner, Commander Spock (Leonard Nimoy). A witty extension of the well-worn idiomatic phrase 'out of your mind', used to express disbelief in someone's foolishness or lack of mental stability; 'out of your tiny mind' is another more recent variation. McCoy, who frequently finds occasion to lament or poke fun at Spock's Vulcan attributes, used this phrase most memorably in the 1982 film, *Star Trek II: The Wrath of Khan*, when he tries in vain to stop Spock from sacrificing his life to ensure the survival of the starship's crew, numbering over four hundred. When Spock strides toward the 'main reactor roto-door' McCoy gets up quickly, blocks Spock's path and says 'Are you out of your Vulcan mind?! No Human can tolerate the radiation in there!' To which Spock calmly replies: 'As you have so often pointed out, Doctor, I am not Human.'

are you sitting comfortably? Then I'll|we'll begin

Preamble to BBC children's programme *Listen with Mother* (1950–82), spoken by the story-tellers Julia Lang and Daphne Oxenford. It became a popular catchphrase during the 1950s and the 1960s and was also employed as a double entendre. The daily 15-minute programme of simple songs and stories for under-fives became a national institution until it was dropped in September 1982; its disappearance caused a national outcry. A sub-series started in 1954, *Listen on Saturday*, introduced by Franklin Engelmann.

are you threatening me?

Popularized by Beavis (as the Great Cornholio) in the 1990s US animated TV series *Beavis and Butt-head*, which centres on the two eponymous adolescent characters, also described as 'two little weinerheads'. Created by former musician Mike Judge, the series debuted on MTV in 1992 and ran until 1997. Beavis and Butt-head have quite different personalities, Beavis being very much the follower, doing whatever Butt-head tells him to do, which usually leads to trouble of one sort or another. Beavis has an alter-ego, 'The Great Cornholio', a wild and insane version of Beavis who appears whenever he's had too much sugar. Claiming to come from Lake Titicaca and speaking a jumble of bits of Spanish, and behaving very oddly, the Great Cornholio responds defensively whenever spoken to with 'Are you threatening me?'

are you up for it?

An idiomatic phrase, meaning are you ready (or have the energy/will) for an activity or venture, that was popularized during the 1980s when it was used as an advertising slogan for 7-Up soft drink. The phrase was chosen for the drink's advertising campaign because it was perceived as appropriately energetic and positive while incorporating a component of the product's brand name.

The citrus soda 7-Up was created in 1929; while most sources concur that '7' was selected because the drink's original containers contained 7 ounces, it seems that 'Up' was chosen either because it indicated the direction of the bubbles or because it stood for 'bottoms up'. 7-Up's earliest advertising slogan was 'It takes the ouch out of grouch'.

are your friends living beyond your means?

An advertising slogan for Chivas Regal Scotch (early 1980s), that plays on the well-known phrase, 'living beyond one's own means'. In its advertising campaigns, the Chivas Regal brand, which is owned by Seagram Spirits and Wine Group, has always positioned its scotch whisky as 'an icon of the good life', and has aimed at 'discriminating whisky drinkers'. Chivas Regal only began to cast off its 'for formal occasions' image in recent years, but continues to use the appeal of expense and 'the finer things in life' to sell a measure of status along with its product. Another similar slogan for Chivas Regal which has tongue-in-cheek 'snob-appeal': 'Isn't that a lot for a bottle of Scotch? Yes.'

as every schoolboy knows

A somewhat condescending and, nowadays, out-dated way of commenting on a fact or item of supposedly common knowledge. It has become a cliché that is often completed in the form of a highly dubious statement, and was used by the English philosopher Robert Burton in *The Anatomy of Melancholy* (1621), an analysis of depression and compendium of medical and religious opinions of the time. Another common form is that used by British clergyman and devotional writer Jeremy Taylor: 'Every schoolboy knows it' in *The Real Presence in the Blessed Sacrament*, section 5 (1654). 'Every Schoolboy

Knows' is also the title of a song by Aviator, released on a 1997 CD called *Aviator*.

as if!

Sarcastic remark, similar to 'right!', employed when the opposite is clearly correct. The response was associated with and popularized by the 1995 film *Clueless*, and in particular its central character, Cher Horowitz, a popular Beverly Hills teenager (Alicia Silverstone). The film, a comedy about teenage matchmaking and romance with a plot that was apparently based largely on Jane Austen's novel *Emma*, and has been therefore summarized as 'Jane Austin's Emma meets Beverley Hills 90210 in California teen lifestyle parody'. A pure fantasy, the film comes across as written, and certainly acted, by Valley Girls for whom 'as if!' is a well-established component of their language (know also as Valley-speak).

as if I cared...

A catchphrase of Sam Fairfechan, the self-contradictory Welshman played by Hugh Morton, on the popular weekly BBC radio series *ITMA* (1939–49). Morton and his character joined *ITMA*'s team in their first post-war series, when it was decided that most of the familiar characters would be dropped and the series given a new look. Sam Fairfechan would often utter his catchphrase right after having greeted someone politely with: 'Good morning, how are you today?' The contradictory Welshman would also say things like 'I'm as fit as a fiddle, Vic Oliver's'.

as it happens

Associated with Jimmy Savile, miner, wrestler, cycle racer, dancehall manager, marathon man, Britain's first DJ, Mensa member, book reviewer, *Top of the Pops* presenter, and charity fundraiser, for which he was honoured with an OBE, then a knighthood. Best known as a DJ and as the person who presented BBC TV's very first *Top of the Pops* in January 1964, Savile used the phrase practically unconsciously as a filler or form of punctuation in his speech. Aware and unashamed of his syntactic habit, Savile made it the title of his 1974 autobiography (full title *As it Happens: Jimmy Savile, O.B.E*). Perhaps he did later tire of the association, as the book was published in 1976 under a new title (*Love is an Uphill Thing*).

— as we know it

See 'end of civilization as we know it'.

ay, caramba!

Popularized (most recently) by Bart on *The Simpsons* (1989–), the longest-running cartoon on US prime-time network television. The series chronicles the adventures of Homer Simpson and his wildly dysfunctional family. Bart, who is forever stuck in the fourth grade, is the Simpsons' oldest child. The sassy 10-year-old and borderline juvenile delinquent (voice by Nancy Cartwright) provided the early focus of the show. This, one of Bart's favourites, is a Spanish interjection denoting surprise or astonishment, and has no particular meaning in that language (similar in ways to 'wow!'). It has been associated with Latin America and particularly Latin American personalities and performers, such as dancer and singer Carmen Miranda. 'Ay, Ay Caramba' is the title of a well-known Brazilian samba tune, and it is quite possible the expression had its origins in the music for this Latin American ballroom dance.

ay oh, oh ay!

An expletive bringing attention to or heralding a problem with consequences ranging from the unpleasant to the calamitous, belonging to Tony Micelli (Tony Danza) on the US TV series *Who's the Boss?* (1984–92). The show's success was largely due to the chemistry between Tony and his boss, Angela Bower (Judith Light) and the special bond their such seemingly disparate families held.

ay thang yew

A catchphrase belonging to British comedian Arthur Askey, popularized on the BBC radio show *Bandwagon* (1938-9), which he co-hosted with Richard Murdoch. Askey claimed that he had picked up this particular pronunciation of 'I thank you' from London bus conductors. See also 'doesn't it make you want to spit?'

aye, aye, that's yer lot

Recurring words of farewell delivered by British music-hall comedian Jimmy Wheeler. The South London comic would invariably finish his act wielding a violin and saying 'Aye, Aye that's your lot', usually preceded by 'Ta-ta for now, folks'. His stage act catchphrase later carried over to television when he hosted a stand-up series called *The Jimmy Wheeler Show* (BBC, 1956–7). The expression 'And that's your lot' on its own, to mean that is all you'll be getting, don't expect to receive any more, had been in use in the UK since 1920, if not earlier.

Bb

●●●●●●●●●●

baby baby baby, you can't bottle love!

An early 1990s advertising slogan for Good Seasons Salad Dressing, in which a rabbit, sounding just like Barry White, tells the woman in the commercial to 'loooove' her salad. The bunny then hops towards the camera singing, 'baby baby baby, you can't bottle love!' implying the product is perfect as long as you add this last ingredient (see also 'all you add is love'), while bringing to mind the well-known Beatles' lyric, 'can't buy me love'. Alternatively, the slogan could be taken to mean that the dressing itself is like love, in that it cannot be contained.

be a Pepper

The title of an advertising campaign for Dr Pepper soft drink that ran during the late 1970s and early 1980s. The drink's slogan during the 1960s had been 'The Most Misunderstood Soft Drink', while in the 1970s it was, 'The Most Original Soft Drink in the World'. Following, in a quirky way, its established image as the soft drink that is 'different' and therefore makes one stand out, in 1977 Dr Pepper launched its 'Be a Pepper' campaign. The commercial featured David Naughton dancing and singing the silly jingle 'I'm a pepper, he's a pepper, she's a pepper, we are peppers, wouldn't you like to be a pepper too?'

be all that you can be

Recruitment slogan for the US Army introduced in the post-Vietnam era and dropped only in 2001. It was based on the idea that Uncle Sam was the only employer that would house and feed young Americans, while providing basic skills training. The army was saying 'even if corporate America won't give you a job, we will', and you will be allowed to fulfil your potential. The highly successful slogan lasted 20 years; *Advertising Age*, an industry information leader, ranked the campaign as the second best of the 20th century. By 2000, however, corporate America was providing more jobs than ever, and the campaign began to lose its appeal. It was replaced in January 2001 by 'an army of one'.

The phrase has been used by many US companies as a challenge and incentive to employees to be their best. Variations on the phrase also became popular, as in 'Buy All That You Can Buy', the title of an article about military personnel using Pentagon credit cards for spending sprees (www.abcnews.com, 27 July 2001).

be cool, stay in school

The popular slogan from a 1980s US public service announcement (PSA) encouraging pupils to attend school and avoid leaving early. The TV commercial involved a group of penguins and the following, catchy song: 'If you want to be cool then do what I say/You've got to go to school every school day/Cause if you want to get a job it's a very simple rule/You got to get an education got to go to school/You got to get it all together if you want to make it pay/you've got to stay in school til graduation day. So be cool stay in school.' The announcer would conclude: 'If you want to be cool stay in school', after which one of the penguins would take off his sunglasses and say 'ohh!' The current PSA in the US on this issue is 'stay in school—give yourself a chance'.

beam me up, Scotty

Often used to mean 'get me out of here', or away from a particular situation. Request to Chief Engineer Montgomery 'Scotty' Scott (played by James Doohan) to be transported—dematerialized and rematerialized—in the classic original *Star Trek* TV series which ran in the US from 1966 to 1969. Although this has become one of *Star Trek*'s best-known catchphrases, these exact words were never actually spoken in the series. The closest were 'Beam us up, Mr Scott', and 'Two to beam up, Scotty', both spoken by Captain Kirk (William Shatner) to his chief engineer.

Star Trek's special effects were not terribly complex or technically impressive, but they were notable, became quickly familiar, and also had substantial linguistic influence. Phasers, photon torpedoes, and warp drive all became integral parts of the show and the language of the time. It was, however, the 'transporter', used to 'beam' members of the crew down to nearby planets (and hopefully back again) that was the show's best-known device or special effect. The now so familiar effect to show dematerialization was in fact enhanced by studio technicians throwing aluminium dust into a beam of light.

beanz meanz Heinz!

Heinz Baked Beans slogan (UK, 1967–97). The line was created in a pub in 1967 by Young & Rubicam's then deputy creative director, Mo Drake. The jingle went 'A million housewives every day, pick up a can of beans and say, Beanz Meanz Heinz'. The slogan was only dropped after thirty years when Heinz decided it wanted to ensure its brand was identified with more than just baked beans. However, during the 1970s, Heinz's new advertising campaign, including the refrain 'Don't be mean with the beans, mum, Beanz Meanz Heinz', quickly became a classic. In 1977 *The Goodies* (BBC comedy series, 1970–82) produced a rival jingle: 'Beanz Meanz Fartz'.

beautiful downtown Burbank, this is

Spoken with irony by Gary Owens, the outrageously over-modulated announcer on the fast-paced, free-form US comedy TV series *Rowan and Martin's Laugh-in* (1968–73). A sarcastic note directed at the show's network, Burbank being the area in Los Angeles where NBC studios are located. The highly popular show mixed topical satire and shtick, and comic routines. Black-outs, one-liners, sketches and cameo appearances by famous celebrities—including Sammy Davis Jr., Zsa Zsa Gabor, and John Wayne, and even national politicians— were all edited into the show. Meanwhile, Gary Owens, facing the microphone—hand cupped to ear, held the show together with his pronouncements from 'beautiful downtown Burbank'. Many catchphrases came out of *Laugh-in*, and quite a few of the more popular phrases, including this one, became national bywords. *Laugh-in*'s trademark mannerisms and catchphrases were repeated over and over until they were associated closely with particular performers and became part of everyone's consciousness.

because I'm worth it!

Slogan from a L'Oréal hair care and cosmetics advertisement campaign from the mid-1980s, appealing to the 'new woman's' sense of self-worth. The claim, made by a series of beautiful, successful celebrity women, including Andie MacDowell and Jennifer Aniston (and men, such as footballer David Ginola), has transcended the brand, becoming a social phenomenon. Having been a presence in US advertising without interruption for over 15 years, the slogan has become a national catchphrase that can rarely be spoken without bringing to mind one of the well-known TV commercials. Although the slogan might at first sound a bit shocking or pretentious, it simply suggests that each woman should take care of herself, that she is someone important, who deserves the best. Veering away from a conceited image, more recently the tag-line has been changed to 'because you're worth it'.

because it's there...

A reason or, at times, a defiant reply, given for doing something which cannot be easily justified. It is the simple existence of the thing or challenge that motivates the doer and justifies the action. Chiefly associated with the British mountaineer, George Leigh Mallory (spoken in a 1923 interview, in response to 'why do you want to climb Mount Everest?'); the phrase was re-popularized by the New Zealand mountaineer Edmund Hillary who repeated it in 1953, the year in which he reached the summit of Mount Everest. It was also the title of a play by Jonathan Holloway (2000), based on the story of Mallory's 1924 expedition.

Beep! Beep!

Often used to let others know they should make way, as one is coming through, or simply a onomatopoeic 'excuse me!' Associated with the Road Runner, a popular cartoon character, created by Chuck Jones and featured on a variety of Warner Bros. animation series from 1949. The constant (and constantly elusive) prey of the monomaniacal Wile E. Coyote, the Road Runner's *beep-beeping* was largely a cipher, since the character never speaks and only occasionally uses signs to communicate with either the audience or the Coyote. A road runner is a crested terrestrial bird of the cuckoo family that is native to North America and can actually run at a speed of 15mph/25kph.

believe it or not!

Exclamation stressing the veracity of what may appear bizarre, unreal or incredible; popularized by the compendium of bizarre facts *Ripley's Believe It or Not* (from 1923). The long-running syndicated newspaper feature, and radio and TV series began in the US and later ran in the UK and other countries. US cartoonist Robert LeRoy Ripley, creator of the syndicated column, became a sports cartoonist for the *New York Globe* in 1913 and later began to present sports records in the series called 'Believe It or Not!' He then moved from sports to all kinds of oddities and obscure facts, taking his column to the *New York Evening Post* in 1923 and later to national syndication. Ripley, master of the bizarre, became a household name in America. More than 50 years after his death, the *Ripley's Believe It or Not* cartoon is still wildly popular around the world.

believe the lie

This phrase, associated with the US cult TV series *The X-Files* (1993–2002), replaced the show's usual tagline, 'The Truth Is Out There' (see below) for the episode *Gethsemane*, and is, quite succinctly, what the government told Fox Mulder (David Duchovny), as well as what it hopes the public will do. Although ostensibly about aliens, conspiracies, and monstrous creatures, the themes that the series really examines are subjects that are perhaps far more frightening: trust, faith, security, freedom, belief, and truth. The show's numerous catchphrases, such as 'Believe the Lie' and, most famously, 'The Truth Is Out There', successfully emphasize these central themes. The series often fails to delineate between fact and fiction, never actually answers the questions and speculations it raises, thus challenging viewers to question what may or may not be 'the truth'.

believe to understand

One of the sayings popularized by the US cult TV series *The X-Files* (1993–2002) that investigates the mystery-filled world of the paranormal. The maxim, suggesting belief in the possibility of what is normally unbelievable—including the existence of aliens—first appeared as the tagline to an episode called *Closure*, in February 2000. This episode, in which FBI Special Agent Mulder (David Duchovny) finally finds closure with regard to his young sister's disappearance almost 20 years earlier, centres on an investigation of a series of graves containing the bodies of children (see also 'everything dies'). Toward the end of this episode Fox Mulder walks through a clearing in the woods and sees a group of ghostly children happily playing, which turns out to include his sister, Samantha. She runs to Mulder and jumps into his arms, and the happy reunion brings him to tears. In this case, his 'belief' finally allows him to find closure, and a little later, he reassures Scully, his concerned partner, saying calmly 'I'm fine ... I'm free'.

Bernie, the bolt!

Instruction given on the British Saturday night skill game show *The Golden Shot* (1967–72, then 1974–5). The contestants would mostly be telephone callers on the live show, and would play the game by instructing a blindfolded cameraman to adjust their aim in order to fire a 'telebow' (a crossbow tied to the camera) at targets. The bow was loaded by the show's feature character, 'Bernie the Bolt', who was originally a studio technician. The original Bernie had to be replaced when the programme changed its studio, and there had been three 'Bernies' by the time the show came to its end. The programme also had a number of different hosts, including Bob Monkhouse twice. The show's other catchphrase was 'Left a bit, right a bit, fire!'

The catchphrase has come in handy for a number of Bernies, as in 'Bernie the Bolt—Comprehensive nut/bolt/screw supplier' (online classic car directory), and guitarist and songwriter (formerly of Suede) Bernard Butler, has been referred to by many as Bernie 'the Bolt'.

best a man can get, the

A rather macho assertion made by an advertising slogan for Gillette razors. Gillette proclaimed its product's superiority confidently, without the slightest hint of embarrassment at the unabashed sexism in the slogan. After years of scant advertising on the women's market front, in the 1990s, Gillette eventually launched a brand-new female campaign with the bold, far less catchy slogan, 'Gillette for Women: Are You Ready?' *Best A Man Can Get* is the title of a book by John O'Farrell, published in 2000.

best part of waking up is Folger's in your cup, the

A US advertising slogan for Folger's coffee, featured in a 1980s campaign centring on 'feel good' and 'homey' situations. In one TV commercial a young woman (of university age) enters her parents' house. Realizing that everyone is still asleep, she makes some Folger's coffee. They all wake up from the presumably wonderful wafts of coffee aroma, come downstairs, and are thrilled to see their daughter. The spot ends with the family drinking coffee and the voice of Canadian singer and songwriter Diana Rae comes on, reminding viewers that the 'best part of waking up is Folger's in your cup!'

best to you each morning, the

An advertising slogan for Kellogg's breakfast cereal since 1953, which proved to be such a defining phrase that it became practically a trademark and consequently a part of the vocabulary of cereal eaters across America. Almost half a century later, the cereal company continued to affectionately cling on to its successful slogan: 'As we enter a new millennium, Kellogg Company remains committed to bringing "the best to you each morning" and throughout the day' (Kellogg Company website).

betcha can't eat just one

An advertising slogan for Lay's potato chips (crisps) coined in 1963 that became the brand's registered trademark. A cross between a boast and a dare, the slogan implied that if you have eaten one, you will eat another, and probably another. The line has come to be used in the US to describe a number of 'addictive' or 'moreish' food products and other items. The approach has since been echoed by advertising campaigns for a number of other products, including Pringles in the late 1990s, with 'once you pop, you can't stop'.

better red than dead

Slogan used by pacifists and campaigners for nuclear disarmament from the late 1950s onwards, and the reversal of the conservative, cold-war slogan 'better dead than red' current in the early 1950s. The latter argued that nuclear war was preferable to the prospect of life under Communist rule and was held by those who believed that nuclear deterrence formed an essential key to world peace and security. While those against nuclear deterrence, who argued that the consequences of the existence of nuclear weapons and their potential use were too horrible to contemplate, threatening the very existence of mankind, rallied behind the slogan, 'better red than dead', thus indicating the strength of their convictions. Despite the ending of the cold war, both versions of the phrase continue to be used by some politicians, as when US Rep. James A. Traficant reported he had been 'well received by supporters of the opposition political parties and his slogan "better dead than red," caught on even among Albania's school children' (in *The Business Journal Online*, 4 May 2001).

Beulah, peel me a grape

Mae West's famous request, addressed to her maid in the 1933 film *I'm No Angel*, where it marked her complete lack of concern after an infuriated man friend had just stormed out of her home. West, who wrote her own dialogue, set herself up as a provocative sex symbol and the virtuoso of verbal innuendo. 'Peel me a grape', one of the actress's lines that have entered the American vocabulary, also came to express ultimate luxury or extravagance, the sort that could easily befit the sensual hedonist Mae West portrayed in her films. In the mid-1930s, this utterance became one of her most frequently imitated phrases. *Peel Me a Grape* (1975) is the title of a book by Joseph Weintraub (originally published as *The Wit and Wisdom of Mae West*), a compilation of the best of West's saucy expressions.

BFN

An abbreviation of 'bye for now' that was popular in the UK by the late 1960s and became a catchphrase of British singer and BBC radio presenter Jimmy Young. Young joined Radio 2 in 1973, where he has stayed ever since presenting his daily programme, known to its millions of listeners (in its abbreviated form) as 'The JY Programme'.

Big Brother is watching you

A phrase which has come to sum up the act or sensation of surveillance, and particularly that carried out by the state or corporations. The line is from the 1949 futuristic novel *Nineteen Eighty-Four* (part 1, chapter 1) by George Orwell, and refers to the main leader of the government of Oceania, known as Big Brother. In the book, it appears as the caption to a government, or INGSOC (English Socialism), poster. The poster itself is described as 'one of those pictures which are so contrived that the eyes follow you about when you move'. The novel portrays the catastrophic excesses of state control over the individual, a totalitarian state where Big Brother rules and citizens' lives are constantly monitored—watched and heard by the Thought Police through Telescreens or Choppers that occasionally hover around the buildings peeping into the windows. Many of the other concepts and words coined by Orwell in this novel, such as newspeak, doublethink, and thought police, have also passed into common usage.

The phrase was popularized in Britain by the award-winning 1954 BBC TV dramatization of novel, and then internationally, and more recently, by the highly popular fly-on-the-wall TV game show *Big Brother* (2000–   ) in the USA, UK, Australia, and seven European countries, including Germany, Belgium, and Italy. *Big Brother*, which became one of the most-talked-about television programmes in years, had been shown in 18 countries by the end of 2001. It features 10 recruits who must spend 70 days in a house which is cut off from the rest of the world without television, radio, or the Internet, but with a battery of cameras following their every move. The residents are under permanent surveillance by cameras recording their activities for television and the Internet. Viewers are privy to their rows and frustrations and can vote to expel residents, with the last one remaining taking a cash prize.

big-hearted Arthur that's me!

One of Arthur Askey's best-known catchphrases, used in comedy sketches on the BBC radio show *Bandwagon* (1938–9). This was the first of the series' numerous catchphrases, appearing in the first show broadcast 5 January 1938 and, as Askey later revealed, it was a phrase he had been using in real life for many years.

big-time show bidness

Associated with US comedian David Letterman, host of the TV talk show *Late Night with David Letterman*. A silly, comic play on the word 'business' and a familiar phrase (big-time show business)

describing the glamour and power of the entertainment industry—
often the butt of Letterman's jokes.

billions and billions served

A boastful, and still unsubstantiated, claim made by an advertising
slogan for McDonald's fast food chain, which rapidly became a
catchphrase in the 1990s. It has since been aptly used by web sites and
search engines, as in: 'the Netscape site is a very busy one, receiving
well over ten million hits per day (billions and billions served!)...'
(*View Source*, online). The sheer magnitude of the claim was treated
humorously in a *New Yorker* cartoon showing a boy who reads 'Billions
and Billions served' over the trademark Golden Arches and muses,
happily and reminiscently, 'I wonder how many million I've eaten?'
While in 1996, Vegan Action in the US produced T-shirts using the
McDonald's 'M' and altered their 'billions and billions served' slogan to
'billions and billions saved'.

bit of a cock-up on the — front

A favourite excuse employed by Jimmy (Major James Gordonstoun
Anderson), Reggie's brother-in-law, on the BBC TV comedy series *The
Fall and Rise of Reginald Perrin* (1976–9). The eccentric Jimmy, played by
Geoffrey Palmer, was always making a mess of his attempts to start a
secret army, mistakes he explained by originally saying: 'bit of a cock
up on the catering front' (no food to feed his army cadets). The use of
'cock-up' to mean a blunder or error was originally British military
slang dating from the 1920s, an expression befitting Jimmy—a
forgetful old former army officer who was totally confused by civilian
life and would either forget to buy any food, or run out of money to do
so. Catering is the front he most frequently manages to cock up,
though other blunders include 'cock-ups' on 'the explosives front'
(arm in sling), on 'the judgement of men front' (partner ran off with
project money), and 'the author-sexing front' (calling George Eliot a
man and Evelyn Waugh a woman).

Making the most of its name, a vegetarian Indian restaurant in
Plymouth, England, called 'Veggie Perrin's', boasts 'no cock-up on the
catering front' on its premises. It also makes a reference in its
advertising to another famous catchphrase from the same TV series
with: 'I didn't get where I am today by eating meat!'

blondes have more fun

From the advertising slogan used in Clairol's 'Blondes' campaign from 1957. 'Miss Clairol' gave American women the ability, for the first time, to colour their hair quickly and easily at home, and to find out for themselves whether the claim about blondes was true. US advertising copywriter Shirley Polykoff, one of only five women so far inducted into the US Advertising Hall of Fame, was responsible for Clairol's extremely successful advertising campaigns. The 'Blondes' campaign encompassed Polykoff's idea that every woman should be whatever she wanted to be, including being a blonde. Considered a cutting edge slogan at the time, 'Is it true blondes have more fun?' was, after some hesitation, accepted by Clairol. For television, Polykoff wrote the following jingle:

Is it true blondes have more fun?
Is it true blondes have more fun?
A Lady Clairol blonde . . . that's silky, shiny blonde . . .
A Lady Clairol blonde . . . that's silky, shiny blonde . . .
Is it true blondes have more fun?

This jingle became known around the world and was even a hit in Russia. Polykoff's campaign enticed numerous women to go blonde and the positive publicity quickly spread across the media, with comedians and television personalities even commenting on the continued success of the Clairol products. Also the title of a 1978 album and song by Rod Stewart.

blow some my way

Let me have some of that too. The words came from an advertising slogan for Chesterfield cigarettes, introduced in the late 1920s, and aimed at women. A 1926 Chesterfield ad showed a woman encouraging her date to 'Blow some my way', intimating that she enjoys the smoke and possibly that her date might offer her one. In 1923, women consumed only 5% of all cigarettes sold in the US, but by 1929, the number had grown to 12%, and it jumped to 18.1% by 1933. In 1928, another Chesterfield ad featured an attractive couple in a romantic moonlit, outdoor setting. The man is smoking while the woman looks longingly (almost lovingly) at the cigarette smoke with the slogan forming the ad's caption. The ads reflected the attempts by women in this era to assert their independence and freedom to choose, and although it caused a public outcry, the campaign continued and was even imitated by Lucky Strike.

boldly go where no man has gone before, to

Often used ironically, to add a comic note or tinge to a proposed endeavour or task. It forms part of the mission of the Starship *Enterprise*, restated at the start of each episode of the US TV series *Star Trek* (1966–9): 'to explore strange new worlds, to seek out life and new civilizations, to boldly go where no man has gone before'. This, like other catchphrases from the series, became so familiar—even to many who weren't even born when it was first transmitted—that the split infinitive which at first offended many purists is now taken for granted. In fact, the idea of changing the word order of the phrase would undoubtedly destroy the emphasis and so the grammar was never altered in subsequent series. The show's producers did change it slightly for the show's second series, *Star Trek: The Next Generation* (1987–94), going 'PC' to make it 'to boldly go where no one has gone before'.

bono estente

From the 1990s BBC TV comedy sketch series *The Fast Show*, created by Paul Whitehouse and Charlie Higson, together with a team of actors and writers including Caroline Aherne, Arabella Weir, and Mark Williams. The phrase would precede one of the show's regular sketch settings—the news programme in a TV studio of a pseudo-South American network, and was presumably a form of greeting, or equivalent of 'good evening'.

book him, Danno!

Catchphrase of the deadpan, tight-lipped Detective Steve McGarrett (played by Jack Lord) on the US TV police series *Hawaii Five-O* (1968–80), shot entirely on location in Hawaii. The strait-laced McGarrett, who made 'Book him, Danno' a fixture of American slang, was the head of an elite state police investigative unit on what became the longest running police drama in television history. The instruction to formally arrest someone was spoken triumphantly and was directed at McGarrett's assistant, Detective Danny Williams, who was played until the show's penultimate season by James

MacArthur. According to Hawaiian government officials, the show did much to enhance the Hawaiian economy and to foster significant increases in tourism.

boom, boom!

Used by comedians to highlight and punctuate a punchline or comic note within a narrative, like the little drum beat often added by an off-stage band member to aid a comedian or simply make a silly joke sillier. The device probably originated with British comedian and music-hall star Billy Bennett, and has since been employed by many British and US entertainers and comedians.

It was also associated with Ivan Owen's furry fox glove puppet, Basil Brush, who commanded a prime-time spot from 1970 until the early 1980s. Basil released at least one album entitled *Boom! Boom! It's Basil Brush*. These were not recordings of the show but a selection of tunes with such titles as 'Mah-Na, Mah-Na' and 'Why Can't We Have The Sea In London?' Basil, whose famous 'boom, boom' catchphrase was played to TV audiences in 14 countries, including Australia and Japan, is expected to be brought back again to the small screen.

boop-boop-a-doop

A catchphrase of the 1930s cartoon character Betty Boop that became a trademark component of her songs (voice of May Questal). Betty Boop was first created as a dog character by Grim Natwick and appeared as the girl friend of another dog named Bimbo in a Fleischer Studios Talkartoon little film called *Dizzy Dishes* in which she showed off her musical talents, singing 'I Have to Have You' to Bimbo, which contains many a 'boop-boop-a-doop'. The song was also recorded by Helen Kane, the original 'boop-boop-a-doop' girl. Betty finally came into her own with *Betty Co-Ed* in 1931 when she shed her dog identity and the long ears became earrings. While her singing style was taken from Helen Kane, Betty's voluptuous figure was modelled after Mae West's. By 1932 Betty was considered to be the first and only female animated screen star; her last film, *Yip Yip Yipee* was released in 1939.

Helen Kane became a hit on Broadway and in early talking pictures because of her flapper-like demeanour and trademark 'boop-boop-a-doop' vocals. When Max and Dave Fleischer came out with Betty Boop in 1931, Kane felt that the cartoon character looked and sounded

suspiciously like her and, in 1934, Kane sued the Fleischers for
damages. However, the Fleischers' lawyers persuaded the jury by
presenting a 1928 film clip of a little-known black singer named 'Baby
Ester' who also employed the 'boop-boop-a-doop' line in one of her
songs, insinuating that Kane had perhaps stolen the line herself. Years
later, animator Grim Natwick admitted in *The Fleischer Story* (1988) by
Leslie E. Carbaga, that Dave Fleischer had in fact asked him to pattern
the new cartoon character after a sheet music photo of Kane.

booyakasha!

All right, very good! A catchphrase of Ali G, a 'black gangsta' played by
British comic Sacha Baron Cohen. Ali G first became a popular
television figure as a sketch on Channel 4's satire comedy series *The
11 O'Clock Show* (1998–) and then in two series of *Da Ali G Show*
(2000–1). The phrase was often used by Ali G as a form of greeting or to
emphasize approval.

Børk! Børk! Børk

The favourite expression of the 'Swedish Chef' on *The Muppet Show*,
(1976–80), created by puppeteer Jim Henson for US television. The
character, also known as 'Ze Swedish Chef', was always crisp and clean
in his white apron, striped shirt, and pink bow-tie. Armed with a
wooden spoon, he spoke his particular version of mock Swedish
and was always happiest when 'Køokin' der yummee-yummers'.
A typical quote might be: 'Vergoofin der flicke stoobin mit der børk-
børk yubetcha!'

In April 2001 Google, an Internet search engine, introduced
'BorkBorkBork' as one of the new language interfaces on its new
page translation option. In addition to traditional languages,
'BorkBorkBork' is fully active, making Google speak a language
based on the speech patterns of the Swedish Chef from the
Muppets.

boutros, boutros gali

Although sounding precisely like the name of the former UN
secretary-general Boutros Boutros-Ghali, these words were
popularized by the BBC TV comedy series *The Fast Show* (1994–7),

where they were uttered as a closing salutation, or sign-off, in the fictitious hybrid language employed throughout the show's regular 'Chanel 9' sketch settings. Paul Whitehouse and other newscasters participating in the news programme, set in the TV studio of a pseudo-South American network and entitled 'Republica presente', would use the phrase to bring a story or report— invariably carrying no news or 'naya neus' whatsoever—to an end, and always to bid farewell to viewers at the end of the news programme. Viewers could in fact still see them and perhaps hear one of the newscasters propose an after-work trip to the beach, an idea which is, however, most often abandoned in favour of a 'drinko'.

boy ain't right! the

Popularized by cartoon Texan Hank Hill, the head of the principal family featured on the US animated TV sitcom *King of the Hill* (1997–   ), delivered as a concerned, but fond, assessment his only son, the rather chubby Bobby. Bobby is a 12-year-old boy scout who plays Little League baseball, but shows little interest in either activity, thus causing his father a degree of worry and embarrassment. Hank, a suburban husband and father who makes a living selling 'propane and propane accessories', is a gruff former college football player—a slow-talkin' man's man who is not at all comfortable with the emotional demands of family life, including showing his son affection. However, compared to his friends and neighbours, Hank is remarkably sensitive and sensible. The series was written and created by Mike Judge and former *Simpsons* producer Greg Daniels.

Hank often feels that Bobby is a little 'left of centre', and uses this phrase to summarize his frequent forebodings, as in this scene from an episode entitled *King of Horde Hill*, in which Hank is shocked to see Bobby in a kilt:

Hank: I don't care WHAT you call it, it's a dress! Now take it off before the neighbours see you!
Bobby: OK . . .
Hank: What?!? Boy, where is yer underwear!?
Bobby: But he said you're supposed to wear it RESIDENTIAL.
Hank: Well, don't change here, go into the tent. [pause] That boy ain't right.

boy, is my face red!

A way of announcing one's complete embarrassment in a situation. Of American origin, but recently popularized by US comedian David Letterman, host of the TV talk show *Late Night with David Letterman* (1982–). The phrase has become particularly associated with Letterman, who uses it frequently and seems to specialize in gaffes and generally embarrassing comments, while also having the sort of complexion that is easily prone to blushing. He used this catchphrase most famously in 1995 when, after doing a less-than-wonderful job of hosting the Academy Awards, he said 'I had no idea this thing was televised. Boy, is my face red'.

breakfast of champions

A phrase, used as an advertising slogan for Wheaties cereal from 1933, that has since been used as a running gag—now a rather lame one—delivered by waiters when they serve martinis. It is also still used less sarcastically to describe a hearty breakfast. The slogan came from Wheaties' association with sports, which began in 1933 with the sponsorship of baseball broadcasts. The now familiar words, coined by Knox Reeves, an advertising executive for Wheaties' Minneapolis-based agency, first appeared on a large advertising signboard at the ball park that was home to the Minneapolis Millers. *Breakfast of Champions* is the title of a novel by Kurt Vonnegut published in 1973, and of a 1999 film based on the book, starring Bruce Willis, Albert Finney, and Nick Nolte.

bring out your best

An early 1980s advertising slogan for Budweiser Light, that gained currency when it was taken up as the unofficial theme for the 1984 summer Olympic games held in Los Angeles. In the mid-1980s Hellman's mayonnaise came out with a slogan that played with a similar wording, but a slightly different message—'Bring out the Hellman's and bring out the best'.

buck stops here, the

Words printed on a sign that sat on US President Harry S Truman's desk in his White House office. The sign was made in the Federal

Reformatory at El Reno, Oklahoma, and mailed to President Truman on 2 October 1945, appearing at different times on his desk until late in his administration. The saying derives from the slang expression 'pass the buck' which means shifting the responsibility for something to someone else. The latter expression is said to have originated with the game of poker, in which a marker or counter (frequently in frontier days a knife with a buckhorn handle), was used to indicate the person whose turn it was to deal. If the player did not wish to deal he could pass the responsibility by passing the 'buck', as the counter came to be called, to the next player.

President Truman referred to the desk sign in public statements on quite a few occasions. For example, in an address at the National War College on 19 December 1952 Truman said, 'You know, it's easy for the Monday morning quarterback to say what the coach should have done, after the game is over. But when the decision is up before you— and on my desk I have a motto which says "The Buck Stops Here"— the decision has to be made.'

bulging lallies

A Cockney phrase meaning muscular legs, as in 'vada them bulging lallies'—'take a look at those muscular legs'. Popularized by Julian and Sandy, two camp actors from London played by Hugh Paddick and Kenneth Williams, in their regular sketches on the BBC Radio 4 comedy series *Round the Horne* (1965–9). The pair, who became the programme's favourite characters, would make their appearances on a more or less weekly basis, and were always found to be 'filling in' between acting jobs. Julian and Sandy spoke in 'Polari', a bizarre mixture of languages and a diction used to great effect within the gay community in the UK in the 1960s. With talk of 'bulging lallies' and catchphrases like 'I'm Julian, and this is my friend Sandy', the pair soon attained cult status.

business as usual

The normal course of some activity, despite disruptions or damages stemming from any number of problems, whether caused by humans or acts of God. This term originated as an announcement that a commercial establishment was continuing to operate in spite of fire, reconstruction, or some similar interruption. It became a slogan during the First World War after it was extended to take on a broader sense in November 1914, when Winston Churchill said in a speech at the Guildhall: 'The British people have taken for themselves this motto—"Business carried on as usual during alterations on the map of Europe."' He was later traditionally quoted as saying: 'The maxim of the British people is "Business as usual"', which became the wording of the slogan for the rest of the war.

Today it may be used in this positive sense but also pejoratively, as in 'Ignoring the mounting violence on the streets and the ensuing death toll, the government claims its job to be business as usual'. US President George W. Bush made use of the phrase on several occasions in 2001, to describe his administration in the wake of the 11 September terrorist attacks.

but I'm all right now

A catchphrase associated with Hattie Jacques on the popular wartime BBC comedy radio series *ITMA* (1939–49) that entered the language. The show starred Tommy Handley and his regular *ITMA* team which originally included Jack Train, Vera Lennox, and Sam Costa. Hattie Jacques joined the team later into its run, making her debut on the show in 1947 as Sophie Tuckshop, the greedy schoolgirl, whose bouts of gluttony were invariably followed by a giggle and 'but I'm all right now'.

I Used to Be an Animal, But I'm All Right Now is the title of a 1986 book by rock musician Eric Burden. The music memoir of the former Animals member documents his encounters with the likes of Chuck Berry, The Rolling Stones, John Lennon, The Who, The Doors, and others, and his survival through a series of rock 'n' roll excesses.

... but we don't want to give you that!

Words spoken by Chris Tarrant, host of the popular TV quiz show *Who Wants to Be a Millionaire?* (1998–; US 1999–   ), to urge a contestant to gamble their winnings once more, rather than play it safe. When the money starts getting really serious (£32,000 and over), the host will reach for the appropriate cheque and sign it. Whilst this is mainly used as a theatrical device, the cheques can be cashed in by the contestants for real. It is with reference to one of these cheques that Tarrant will teasingly say this phrase.

The tactics of the Chancellor of the Exchequer Gordon Brown, when discussing plans to subsidize heating bills for the elderly, have been comically compared to those of the famous quiz show host. It would seem that Brown sounded 'like Chris Tarrant—"But I don't want to give you £150, I want to give you..."'—and the Labour benches cheered like a studio audience grateful for their free tickets and the chance to keep warm' (in the *Guardian*, 9 November 2000).

but you can't get them in the shops!

The phrase was popularized by Private Joe Walker (James Beck), a 'spiv' who dealt in black-market goods, on the long-running BBC TV comedy series, based on the Home Guard during the Second World War, *Dad's Army* (1968–77). Private Walker, who was discharged from the Army because he was found to be allergic to corned beef, was well known in Walmington-on-Sea for being able to obtain almost anything on the black market. These items were, however, naturally sold at inflated prices. But whenever a customer complained, Walker would reply with his ever-handy catchphrase.

by golly, he won't die!

One of the many catchphrases associated with Dr Leonard McCoy (DeForest Kelley) of the Starship *Enterprise* on the original *Star Trek* TV series (1966–9). Despite the many years McCoy had spent as Chief Medical Officer and the countless bizarre and initially inexplicable cases he had encountered aboard the *Enterprise*, he remained, at heart, the simple country doctor who first left earth years earlier. Hence this exclamation, appropriate to the many instances in which McCoy finds himself shocked, yet again, by the 'unnatural' behaviour of organisms/ beings from other planets, with other natures.

by gum, she's a hot 'un

An expression that was associated with British music-hall comedian Frank Randle, who achieved his greatest popularity during the 1930s and 1940s. The phrase, spoken in his brash Northern (he was from near Wigan) working-class accent, was used to note a woman's

attractiveness or sex appeal, and usually appeared in a sketch in which
he played a character celebrating his hundredth birthday. Despite his
age, the character's sex drive was comically portrayed as youthful as
ever. When an old girl friend, long past her prime, arrived on stage he
would chase her off, reappearing with her undergarments in his
hands. His stage wife would glare at him accusingly, while he would
innocently insist 'They just came off in my hand, love'.

by Jove, I needed that

British expression usually uttered immediately after downing an
alcoholic beverage, especially in moments of stress. Associated with
British comedian Ken Dodd during the 1960s and 1970s, as well as
with the the BBC radio *Goon Show* (1952–60).

byeee!

One of the famous catchphrases used by Ed Stewart (also known as
'Stewpot') while fronting *Junior Choice* on BBC Radio 1 during the
1970s. Commanding an audience of 17 million—one of the
largest-ever radio audiences—'Stewpot', with his trademark
'Byeee!', was also known for having had the unusual honour of
getting a request from Princess Margaret to play 'Car 67' for the
Queen Mother's 80th birthday. When asked about the origins of
his distinctive sign-off, he said, 'Well, "Byeee!" is just the way
you say it, isn't it?' (BBC Online interview).

Cc

· · · · · · · · · ·

calling all cars!

Alerting all available police in cars to go to a crime scene or to apprehend a criminal. The line was standard script for US radio shows from the 1930s as well as on 1950s police and gangster films and TV series. *Calling All Cars* was the title of a 1935 film featuring the Three Stooges (and of one of the songs included in the film), an indication of just how quickly the phrase became a potentially comic cliché. In 1939, the Three Stooges followed this up with a short entitled *Calling All Curs*.

can I do you now, sir?

From the 1940s BBC radio programme *ITMA*; associated with 'Mrs. Mopp', who would invariably say her famous catchphrase whenever she entered the office of the Mayor (played by Tommy Handley) of Foaming at the Mouth, a seedy seaside resort. It was in October 1941, during the programme's fourth series, that Dorothy Summers introduced 'Mrs Mopp', the cheerful office charlady with the raucous Cockney voice, sent by the 'Corporation' to clean the Mayor's office which she did rather noisily, brandishing bucket and brush. (She later progressed to her own series, *The Private Life of Mrs Mopp*, in 1946.)

can you come back every night? That would be great!

Associated with US comedian David Letterman, host of the TV talk show *Late Night with David Letterman* (1982–). Besides Johnny Carson, who hosted *The Tonight Show* for 30 years, no other television personality comes near Letterman's impressive run on late night network television. This line—flattering the audience while sarcastically making fun of it—is typical of Letterman's sardonic, sometimes slightly juvenile, but consistently 'fun-and-games' sense of humour. It has earlier, possibly vaudeville, origins, used by performers or comedians to ingratiate and encourage their audience. See also British entertainer Bruce Forsyth's 'can you come back next week?'.

can you come back next week?

A catchphrase belonging to British entertainer Bruce Forsyth, used while hosting *Sunday Night at the London Palladium* (1958–71 and 2000). As compère, Forsyth would be there for most weeks of the year, introducing new acts and new talent, pulling out this line to flatter and amuse his audiences. A way of showing appreciation of an audience's reception, the line undoubtedly predated Forsyth, and variations on it are still popular.

can you hear me, mother?

Catchphrase of the popular British comedian Sandy Powell. Powell made his radio debut in the late 1920s in a BBC variety show, and appeared in such shows regularly from then on. During one of these shows, in the early 1930s, he dropped his script just after saying the line 'Can you hear me, mother?' (he was trying to say something to his mother, who he thought would be listening to the broadcast), and was reduced to ad libs while he struggled to retrieve all the sheets of paper. In the meantime, he kept repeating the phrase over and over, thus unintentionally creating one of the earliest radio catchphrases. It became such an audience-pleaser that he included it in his act from then on.

During the Second World War, Powell toured extensively, entertaining allied soldiers abroad and, it seems, wherever he went his famous catchphrase was soon to be heard among the troops. While touring with ENSA in Naples, he had barely disembarked from the ship in Naples harbour, with men and munitions moving all around him, when those in his immediate vicinity stopped and the cry went up, 'Can you hear me, mother?' When Powell was touring in such places as South Africa and New Zealand it was apparently quite common to hear his well-known catchphrase; the saying had truly entered the international comedy lexicon.

can't pay, won't pay!

A political catchphrase in the UK, adopted as a slogan by those protesting against the government's community charge, or 'poll tax', in 1990. The poll tax's unpopularity led to widespread opposition and regional demonstrations, notably the central London anti-poll-tax rally in March 1990, which culminated in violent clashes between demonstrators and police, and high-street looting, and ultimately contributed to the downfall of the then prime minister Margaret Thatcher. The slogan came from the title of a play by the Nobel prize-winning Italian dramatist Dario Fo, *Non si paga, non si paga* (1974), which had a strong political message and was first translated in 1978 as *We Can't Pay? We Won't Pay!* It was published in English under its current title, *Can't Pay? Won't Pay!*, in 1981.

captain, I see no reason to stand here and be insulted

Spoken by Commander Spock (Leonard Nimoy) on the original *Star Trek* TV series (1966–9), created and produced by Gene Roddenberry. As Captain James T. Kirk's (William Shatner) first officer, Mr Spock was one of the principal heroes of the Starship *Enterprise*. A half-human, half-Vulcan with pointed ears and arched eyebrows who was ruled by logic, Spock was both intriguing and touching as a character who wrestled with the human side of his nature and was both drawn to and afraid or disdainful of his human 'feelings'.

Star Trek was scripted and produced by Gene Roddenberry who conceived it as an adult science fiction series through which he 'could make statements about sex, religion, Vietnam, unions, politics and intercontinental missiles', messages which were being sent and which fortunately 'all got by the network'.

captain, I sense something

Comment popularized by Counsellor Deanna Troi (Marina Sirtis) who serves as ship's psychologist on the US science fiction TV series *Star Trek: The Next Generation* (1987–94), spoken as a warning to Captain Jean-Luc Picard (Patrick Stewart). Troi is particularly suited to her job as Counsellor, being of mixed human and Betazed heritage. The latter race is known (in the 24th century) for its inter-species telepathy and its emotional empathy with most other species whether on board the ship, in a ship at close proximity, or on the planet below. Such abilities clearly heightened her counselling skills, while also aiding Captain Picard's command mission decisions on numerous occasions, including hostile encounters, negotiations, and first-contact missions. This phrase is often the first signal Troi might give to indicate she is on to something.

captain's log...

Used jokingly to create a pause and describe or sum up a situation or plan of action. Associated initially with Captain James T. Kirk (William Shatner) of the Starship *Enterprise* on the original *Star Trek* TV series (1966–9), and then with successive captains responsible for the progressively more technologically advanced vessels featured in subsequent *Star Trek* series from 1987 onwards. The phrase, spoken as a voice-over by the captain, follows the show's well-known preamble (see 'boldly go...') and provides the specific background or setting to each episode's storyline that is about to unfold. An example of how the phrase might be employed is: 'Captain's Log, Stardate 3754.1: (We are) currently en route to the planet Vegga in the Flora cluster. We are responding to a distress call from a Cultural Contact Team dispatched by the Federation to establish peaceful relations with the inhabitants of that planet.'

carry on, —

A format phrase that had its origins among the armed forces, where it might be uttered by an officer as an instruction to someone of lower rank to continue what they were already doing. It was first popularized during the long-running BBC radio programme *In Town Tonight* (and the television version), which always ended with the announcer commanding 'Carry on London!' *In Town Tonight* was first broadcast in 1933 and ran for 27 years. In the US, the phrase was used by President Roosevelt as a re-election slogan in 1936. 'Carry on, Roosevelt!' proved to be the right ticket as the 1936 election was in fact won entirely on the record of the New Deal.

'Carry On', as a style, was made famous by a series of British comedy films (as well as television and stage shows) that sprang from the old music-hall theatrical tradition, and was marked by an emphasis on the unsubtle double entendre. A total of 31 of these low-budget Carry On films were produced between 1958 (*Carry On Sergeant*) and 1992 (*Carry On Columbus*). Regular stars included Kenneth Williams, Charles Hawtrey, Sid James, and Joan Sims. Conceived in the sexually repressed 1950s, the films flowered in the 1960s, becoming ever ruder, until, finally in the 1970s, sexual frankness rendered the double entendre redundant, and many viewers began to find tits, bums, and toilets less funny. However, the British public's love of the Carry Ons has carried on, making them prime candidates for stage adaptations and tributes. The most recent, *Cleo, Camping, Emmanuelle & Dick*, won a 1998 Olivier Award.

chase me, Charley|Charlie!

Originally from the title of a song, an Irish jig popular by 1900, and meaning 'come on boys, I'm ready to be courted'. It could also be used an an adjective as in this late 19th-century American song: 'The girls stood up when the buggy came in sight./"Look, she's wearing pink dimity," one cried in admiration./I can tell it's trimmed with real Val lace./ "That's a Chase-me-Charley" hat she has on.' *Chase Me, Charlie* was the title of a 1917 silent film starring Charlie Chaplin, and the phrase also appears in the works of James Joyce—in *Ulysses* (1922) and *Finnegans Wake* (1939).

The phrase was repopularized as one spoken by a man and with a subsequent gay connotation after it was used as the title of a 1950 Noel Coward song. 'Chase Me, Charlie', a song about two flirtatious cats, numbered among the songs in Coward's musical play *Ace of Clubs*, which opened at the Cambridge Theatre in July 1950. In the 1980s, 'Chase me' became the catchphrase associated with camp British comedian Duncan Norvelle, known for his endless innuendo. His catchphrase has been copied by many comedians and impressionists throughout the UK. A Chase-me-Charlie competition is also an equestrian event, and can be used to describe scuffles, such as those often occurring at football matches.

cheeky monkey!

Lancashire dialect, an affectionate reprimand usually applied to the brash, precocious, or unruly child. Betty Turpin (played by Betty Driver), the longest serving barmaid at the Rover's Return on the ITV soap opera *Coronation Street* (since 1969), has made frequent use of

the phrase. A variation on the expression was popularized in the 1950s
by British comedian Al Read, whose catchphrase was 'Right, Monkey!'
Al Read, a sausage maker from Salford, made his radio debut in 1950,
and his humorous 'pictures of life' were based on his working-class
Lancashire experiences.

cheesy peas

Popularized by comedian Paul Whitehouse as the star of a series of
fictitious advertisements for the culinary concoction—usually
pronounced 'cheezy peaz'—shown between sketches during the BBC
TV comedy series *The Fast Show* (1994–7). The first of these ads
featured Whitehouse reeling out the following sales pitch: 'Do you like
cheese? D'you like peas? Well, you'll *love* these: *Cheezy Peaz!* A
combination of *cheese* an' *peas* to form *Cheezy Peaz!* They're great for
your *teas!* Come on Mam—think *cheese*, think *peas*, think *Cheezy
Peaz!* It's *easy-peasy* with *Cheezy Peaz! Pleeease!*'

— City, Arizona!

Used by Tony Webster (Trevor Adams) on the BBC TV comedy series
The Fall and Rise of Reginald Perrin (1976–9) to describe just about
anything. Webster, a Sunshine Desserts employee, introduced this
inane catchphrase in the show's second series, alternating it at times
with '—ville'. A few examples are 'Success City, Arizona' (lying to
Reggie Perrin about his new job), 'Aggression City, Arizona'
(commenting on boxing matches) and 'Gatheringville, Arizona' (when
Reggie's friends and family gather at Christmas). Tony Webster's other
well-known catchphrases are 'Great!' and 'Knockout!'

Come alive! You're in the Pepsi generation

An advertising slogan for Pepsi Cola introduced in 1963, aimed
specifically at a commercially and socially significant demographic
event—the post-war baby boom. This was the generation being referred
to in the ad campaign, including the jingle, sung by Joanie Sommers, and
broadcast on the radio throughout the 1960s. The jingle quickly became
as familiar as one of the great pop hits of the time. It was one of the
earliest instances, in advertising history, that a product was identified,
not so much by its attributes, as by its consumers' lifestyles.

come on down

Associated with US TV game show *The Price is Right* (NBC 1956–63; ABC 1963–5). Repeatedly spoken by its host, initially Bill Cullen (1956–65), then Bob Barker from 1972 when it premiered as a CBS daytime game show to the present. Contestants sitting in the studio audience would be instructed to 'come on down!' and try their luck at guessing the prices of things. Used also in the UK (ITV) version (1984–8), hosted by Leslie Crowther, and later versions, notably *Bruce's Price is Right*, hosted by Bruce Forsyth since 1995.

The expression was used in the 1987 US film in *Raising Arizona*, spoken by 'Nathan Arizona' in a TV commercial—'So come on down to Unpainted Arizona for the finest selection in fixtures and appointments for your bathroom, bedroom, boudoir!' It is also featured in the title song to the US animated series *South Park*: 'Come on down to South Park.'

come to where the flavour is

Advertising slogan that has invited smokers to 'come to Marlboro country' since 1963. The ad campaign was symbolized by the Marlboro Man, a cowboy, and the prototypical 'guy's guy', at home in the saddle, seen driving cattle across the sagebrush. The caption or the voice-over entreats us to 'Come to where the flavour is…Come to Marlboro country'. With sales growing at 10% a year after it was introduced, the slogan quickly became one of the most successful slogans ever. And despite curbs on tobacco advertising, the campaign's slogan and style—atmospheric, enticing, and seemingly irrelevant to the product being pushed—has endured. According to Philip Morris, 'Years of consistent execution of the campaign have made Marlboro Country a very real place in the minds of millions of people'.

come up and see me sometime?, why don't you

A saucy, suggestive invitation coined by Mae West which was associated with her first starring role in *She Done Him Wrong* (1933), and quickly entered the American lexicon. In the mid-1930s, her line 'come up 'n' see me sometime', in its shorter and catchier form, became the most-repeated phrase of the day. What Mae West actually said in the film to Captain Cummings (a very young Cary Grant) was: 'I always did like a man in uniform. And that one fits you grand. Why don't you come up sometime and see me? I'm home every evening'.

This famous line was first used by Mae West in the Broadway hit *Diamond Lil* (1928), upon which *She Done Him Wrong* was based. She played the show's star, Lil, a swaggering saloon singer pursued by a host of male admirers, who became the prototype for all future Mae West characters. Her famous adage infuriated censor Will Hays, who hounded her unsuccessfully from one movie to the next in an effort to save the 'morals of America'.

come with me to the Casbah!

Often attributed to Charles Boyer in the 1938 film *Algiers*, but the actor never actually spoke the line. *Algiers* was based on Julien Duvivier's French screen adaptation of *Pepe le Moko*. Boyer plays Pepe, a master criminal forced to remain in the sanctuary of the sinister Casbah quarter of Algiers, where policemen dare not enter. He falls in love with a wealthy tourist (Hedy Lamarr), to whom he purportedly spoke this line. It became a trademark film for Boyer—much to his chagrin—and presented a parody of the actor as the 'great lovair' saying, 'Come wiz me to za Casbah...' that he became famous for. He believed it created the impression that he was not a serious actor. 'In America', he said, 'when you have an accent, in the mind of the people they associate you with kissing hands and being gallant. I think this has harmed me, just as it has harmed me to be followed and plagued by a line I never even said'.

It became a true catchphrase when the Warner Brothers cartoon character Pepe Le Pew, appropriated it. Based on Boyer's Pepe Le Moko character, Pepe Le Pew first appeared in Chuck Jones's 1945 cartoon *Odorable Kitty*. This French, incurably romantic skunk was forever schmoozing and chasing after consistently indifferent females (who usually turn out to be cats). Quite surprisingly, given his crass image, Yosemite Sam, another Loony Tunes character, says in one cartoon, 'Come with me to the Casbah. We'll make beautiful music together'. A 1966 episode from the US spy series *The Man From U.N.C.L.E.* was entitled 'The Come With Me to the Casbah Affair'.

confidentially, she stinks!

Originally said by Boris Kolenkov, the boisterous Russian ballet master in the 1936 comedy *You Can't Take It With You*, a two-act play, by Moss Hart and George S. Kaufman, about an eccentric group of relatives sharing a home near Columbia University. The phrase was popularized by the 1938 film version (by the same title) in which Kolenkov, played by Mischa Auer, says it when asked how one of his students is doing. The film won Academy Awards for best picture and for Frank Capra as best director. It then became a catchphrase used in various 1940s Warner Bros. cartoons, including *A Gander at Mother Goose* (1940), in which it is spoken by Mistress Mary voiced by Katherine Hepburn, *Robinson Crusoe, Jr* (1941), and in *Hare Conditioned* (1945) in a slightly modified form.

correctomundo

From the US TV series *Happy Days* (1974–84); associated mainly with 'Fonzie' (or 'the Fonz'), played by Henry Winkler, and meaning right!, absolutely correct, or 'A-OK'. Formed by combining the Spanish words for 'correct' and 'world', the expression was meant to sound good or 'cool' while getting the message clearly across. The show, which initially had mediocre ratings after its debut on 15 January 1974, quickly became one of the most popular programmes of the late 1970s.

Happy Days was set in the 1950s in Milwaukee, the heart of middle-class America, and told the story of the Cunningham family. The Cunninghams' son, Richie (Ron Howard), hung out at Arnold's Drive-In diner with his friends, trying to be as cool as the coolest greaser in town, 'the Fonz'. Although cast as a local hoodlum, Arthur Fonzarelli was also made a benevolent companion to Richie and his pals, and soon became the sitcom's central character. The character of Arthur Fonzarelli was so popular, there was talk of changing the title to 'Fonzie's Happy Days'.

The catchphrase crops up in the dialogue of Quentin Tarantino's 1994 film *Pulp Fiction*:

Jules: We're all going to be like three little Fonzies here. And what's Fonzie like? Come on Yolanda, what's Fonzie like?
Yolanda (quietly): Cool.
Jules: What?

Yolanda: Cool.
Jules: Correctomundo!

coughing better tonight

Catchphrase belonging to British variety and music hall artist George Formby Sr. From Ashton under Lyne, Wigan, and Warrington, he was known as The Wigan Nightingale and The Wigan Sprinter (because of one of his stage sketches), but suffered from bronchitis that had plagued him since childhood. When he began performing as a child, if he had a coughing attack, whilst singing, he would challenge anyone to out-cough him for a shilling, making his audience think he was joking. He later made his bronchial cough a feature of his act—his catchphrase, 'Coughing better tonight' (or sometimes, 'Coughing well tonight') struck a chord with his audience, many of whom would probably die from the same disease, as did Formby himself, aged 45.

could we get you a moist towelette?

A favourite with US comedian David Letterman, host of the TV talk show *Late Night with David Letterman* (1982–   ). This line, usually underlining the nervousness experienced by a member of the audience or guest, was guaranteed to get laughs as it expresses one of Letterman's trademark comic combinations of concern and ridicule. *Late Night with David Letterman* quickly became a staple of American late-night TV viewing, with favourite one-liners, such as this one, being repeated the next morning at workplaces across the country.

covers a multitude of chins

An advertising slogan for Williams's Shaving Cream introduced in 1921, which succeeded in catching consumers' attention with its humour. This approach was made more successful by the slogan's mild reference to a then probably better-known proverb and earlier biblical entry—'Charity shall cover a multitude of sins' (Peter 4:8).

cowabunga!

An expression of excitement or surprise that originated on one of US television's most popular children's programme, *The Howdy Doody Show* (1947–60), which combined humans and marionettes. Eddie Kean, who wrote scripts and more than 2,000 songs for the show (1947–56), created the famous 'Cowabunga' cry of Chief Thunderthud, one of the much-loved characters in the town Doodyville, USA. Also written 'kawabonga' or 'kowa-bunga', it indicated 'bad things'. Its companion word, 'kawagoopa', indicated 'joyful things'.

It became a part of surfers' slang in the 1960s after it was used in *Gidget*, a US TV series about surfers, as a cry of exhilaration when cresting a wave in. 'Cowabunga' would be shouted out by the surfer played by Jody McRae as he ran with his surfboard across the beach into the water. In the 1970s it was used in the children's TV show *Sesame Street*, and was more recently re-popularized in the 1990s by the Teenage Mutant Ninja Turtles and the animated TV show *The Simpsons*.

crazy way to travel spreading a man's molecules all over the universe

Phrase associated with Chief Medical Officer Leonard McCoy (DeForest Kelley) of the Starship *Enterprise* on the US TV series *Star Trek* (1966–9). McCoy is referring to travel by 'transporter', the preferred and probably quickest way to travel to and from the Starship *Enterprise* for an individual or small groups. This, one of McCoy's many catchphrases, also underscores his basic, down-to-earth, 'country doctor' image and his readiness to question some of the 23rd century's technological achievements. See also 'beam me up, Scotty'.

— cry all the way to the bank

An expression, meaning criticism can easily be shouldered when one has already been rewarded with financial gain, which was popularized, and probably coined, by US pianist and entertainer Wladziu Valentino Liberace. The words became a regular part of his stage act from the 1950s. The flamboyant Liberace, with his gold or diamond encrusted piano and candelabra, wildly extravagant wardrobe consisting of gold lamé suits, furs, huge robes, tuxedos covered with sequins, and top hat and canes, became one of the biggest television stars of the 1950s and 1960s.

He became the first of the most highly paid performers to play Las Vegas (even before Elvis Presley or Frank Sinatra), asking for, and getting, $50,000 per week, an unheard-of sum at that time. Asked whether he was ashamed to collect all that money just for playing a piano, Liberace replied: 'Oh yes . . . I cry all the way to the bank!' In his 1973 autobiography—*Liberace: An Autobiography*—he wrote: 'When the reviews are bad I tell my staff that they can join me as I cry all the way to the bank.'

customer is always right, the

An early 20th-century catchphrase, believed to have been coined by H. Gordon Selfridge, the US entrepreneur who in 1909 founded Selfridges in London, the first large department chain store in Britain. The same premiss for excellence in customer service had perhaps already been established by Swiss hotel proprietor Cesar Ritz, who had famously declared 'Le client n'a jamais tort'/'The customer is never wrong', in *Piccadilly to Pall Mall* (1908), by R. Nevill and C. E. Jerningham.

cut . . . it . . . out!

Please stop or 'quit it'. A catchphrase associated with Joey Gladstone, played by Dave Coulier, on the US sitcom *Full House* (1987–95). The series is about Danny Tanner and how he copes bringing up three young daughters after his wife's death, with help from Jesse, his brother-in-law, and Joey, his best friend. Joey would say his catchphrase at least once each episode, always accompanying the words with corny, snipping hand gestures.

Dd

·············

da nose knows

A favourite among comedians—especially those with prominent
snouts, the phrase, meaning 'you can trust me on this', was
popularized by US comedian Jimmy Durante. Known also as the
great 'Schnozzola', Jimmy Durante began his career as a piano
player at parties on the Lower East Side of New York. From there he
played in Harlem, co-owned a speakeasy during the 1920s, and
finally ended up in vaudeville, pretty much an overnight sensation.
Radio shows, television series, and film appearances soon followed,
and those who saw him in the 1950s and 1960s recall him as the
raspy voiced, big-nosed, song–dance, and joke man.

daily diary of the American dream, the

Billing of the *Wall Street Journal*, a daily financial newspaper founded by
Wall Street news agents Charles H. Dow and Edward D. Jones in 1889,
that was devised by the Fallon McElligitt advertising agency in 1985. It
is the most influential business-oriented newspaper in the US and one
of the most respected daily papers in the world. The slogan refers to
coverage of the potential for success or monetary gain, and the
customarily optimistic approach to business embodied in the
'American dream', sometimes referred to as the 'American daydream'.

damn fine coffee

From the cult (and largely surreal) US ABC TV series *Twin Peaks*
(1989–91) created and written by Mark Frost and David Lynch and
directed partly by David Lynch. The phrase is associated with FBI
Special Agent Dale Cooper (also referred to as 'Coop'), played by Kyle
Maclachlan, who is very partial to doughnuts and strong, black coffee.
Usually: 'Damn fine coffee . . . And hot!' Often together with 'damn fine
cheese cake (or damn fine pie)'.

damn it Jim, what the hell's the matter with you?

Spoken in anger or frustration on several occasions by Dr McCoy (DeForest Kelley) to his friend and commander Captain James T. Kirk (William Shatner) of the Starship *Enterprise* on the US TV series *Star Trek* (1966–9) and the *Star Trek* films. In *Star Trek II: The Wrath of Khan* (1982), McCoy wishes Admiral Kirk a happy birthday, to which Kirk replies: 'I don't know what to say', and seems completely uninterested. McCoy, annoyed by his attitude eventually loses patience, and says 'Damn it, Jim, what the hell's the matter with you? Other people have birthdays, why are we treating yours like a funeral?'

damn(ed) clever these Chinese! (or dead clever chaps/devils these Chinese!)

An expression referring, half-jokingly and half-grudgingly, to the reputation for ingenious inventiveness enjoyed by the Chinese, as well as to their presumed under-handedness. The expression was in use in America by the 1930s and was picked up in Britain during the Second World War. It was the popularized by its use as a catchphrase on the BBC radio *Goon Show* (1952–60), in the form of 'fiendish clever these Chinese!'

day war broke out ... , the

From the war-time radio monologues of Liverpudlian comedian Robb Wilton, which actually became known as the 'The Day War Broke Out Monologues'. Wilton started his comedy sketches with 'The day war broke out...' and would often continue with 'my wife/the missus said to me...' and thus lead on to funny comments or jokes. For example: 'The day war broke out, my wife, she said to me, "You know, you should get a job." Eee—she's got a wicked tongue.'

Wilton first appeared on the stage in Liverpool in 1899, and made his London debut at the 'Royal', Holborn in 1909. He then presented a long series of sketches—'The Fire Station', 'The Magistrate', etc.— together with his distraught wife ('the missus'), Florence Palmer. One of these sketches led to the creation of his funniest and best-known character, the befuddled Mr Muddlecombe JP, who featured in several radio series.

deadbeats and ne'er-do-wells

Saying associated with US comedian David Letterman, who has used it frequently while hosting the popular TV talk show *Late Night with David Letterman* (1982–). A comically out-dated and incongruous way of giving a compact and blanket description of all freeloaders and failures. Letterman utters the phrase with sarcasm, rather than as a serious judgement.

deceive, inveigle, obfuscate

This phrase replaced the usual tagline of 'The Truth is Out There' for the fourth season episode *Teliko* in the US cult TV series *The X-Files* (1993–2002). It is associated with Special Agent Dana Scully (Gillian Anderson), and is best explained in the context of Scully's field journal entry: 'What science may never be able to explain is our ineffable fear of the alien among us; a fear which often drives us not to search for understanding, but to deceive, inveigle, and obfuscate. To obscure the truth not only from others, but from ourselves'.

dee plane! dee plane!

Tattoo's catchphrase on the US TV series *Fantasy Island* (1978–84). The surreal romantic drama series starred Ricardo Montalban as Mr Roarke, and Hervé Villechaize as Tattoo, Roarke's faithful dwarf sidekick. Whenever an aeroplane, carrying guests destined to land on Fantasy Island, became visible, Tattoo, always dressed in his flashy white suit, would let the island residents know by gleefully exclaiming: 'Dee plane! Dee plane!' Villechaize starred in a 1992 Dunkin' Donuts TV commercial in which he asked for 'Dee plain! Dee plain! Donuts'.

deefeecult for you; easy for me!

Catchphrase belonging to Johnny, a character composed of master ventriloquist Señor Wences's hand, with a mouth drawn over the thumb and index finger and a tiny blonde wig draped over the top. Señor Wences, known for his strongly Spanish-accented English and whose catchphrase was 'S'Awright!' or 'S'OK?', often appeared on TV programmes during the 1950s and 1960s, including *The Ed Sullivan*

Show (1948–71). Wences would sometimes puff on a cigarette while stuffing a handkerchief in Johnny's mouth, all the while creating Johnny's muffled voice. Then he would give Johnny a puff, making his own hand look like it was smoking. Wences and Johnny would inevitably end up arguing over some trivial matter and the arguments would peak with this catchphrase, as in:

Wences: Is difficult
Johnny: Is easy
Wences: Difficult
Johnny: Easy
Wences: Dee-fee-cult
Johnny: Deefeecult for you. Easy for me!

deny everything

One of a series of maxims featured on the US TV series *The X-Files* (1993–2002), the words 'Deny Everything' describe FBI Special Agent Fox Mulder's (David Duchovny) view of government policy. When 'The Cigarette-Smoking Man'—Mulder's worst enemy and one who seems to constantly have his hand in the affairs of the X-Files—meets Bill Mulder (Mulder's father) in *Anasazi*, his suggested retort to any of Mulder's questions about his father's work for the state department is: 'Deny Everything'. In this episode, we learn that the two worked together on a secret project whose exposure they both fear, and that the guilt-ridden Bill Mulder is terrified that his son will learn of his involvement in a secret cover-up. He is about to confess his role to his son, when double agent Alex Krycek assassinates him, thereby framing Mulder for his own father's murder.

The other character to utter the phrase was the enigmatic and dangerous (Mr) X, who alternately warns and informs Mulder. Although a later episode revealed that X worked for The Cigarette-Smoking Man, it seemed that he might have his own agenda. In *Herrenvolk*, X is tricked into revealing his betrayal, which leaves him shot to death on Mulder's doorstep. His dying words, however, are a message for Mulder that leads him to a new player in the game, and to yet more questions. The two words also replaced the show's usual tagline 'The Truth is Out There' in the opening titles of the episode entitled *Ascension*. Mulder continues to hunt the causes of paranormal goings-on, while the government relentlessly denies any evidence that could help him substantiate his findings.

diamond is forever, a

The phrase was popularized as the immortal slogan in a successful De Beers ad campaign from 1948 onwards. The diamond cartel, now operated by De Beers Consolidated Mines Limited, was set up by the South African mining magnate, Sir Ernest Oppenheimer, in 1934. It is now the vehicle through which over 80% of world sales of rough diamonds is administered and marketed. The slogan, developed by the Ayer advertising company for De Beers, became one of the longest-running advertising slogans ever (named the No. 1 advertising slogan of the century in a special edition of *Advertising Age* published in March 1999).

Mary Frances Gerety, a part of the Ayer team working on the account, coined the famous slogan which became so much a part of American culture that many people were not even aware of its place within a marketing strategy aimed at the ritual of engagement. The phrase developed from the traditional idea of a diamond's hardness and durability. By capitalizing on this tradition through the development of its slogan and strategically designed advertisements, De Beers has done much to help maintain the diamond's symbolism of love and commitment, with almost 80% of all American marriages beginning with the gift of a diamond ring.

A similar concept appears in a famous quotation from the 1925 novel *Gentlemen Prefer Blondes* by US novelist and screenwriter Anita Loos: 'I really think that American gentlemen are the best after all, because kissing your hand may make you feel very, very good but a diamond and a safire bracelet lasts forever' (Lorelei Lee's entry for 27 April, ch. 4). This comic classic, shaped as a diary of two best-friend show girls on a transcontinental cruise searching for the right man, became the basis of a popular play, but was best known as a 1953 film adaptation—a musical comedy directed by Howard Hawks (featuring Marilyn Monroe's famous rendition of 'Diamonds are a Girl's Best Friend'). Parodying her image as portrayed in the 1953 comedy classic, Marilyn Monroe once said: 'I always say a kiss on the hand might feel very good but a diamond tiara lasts forever.'

A variation on the catchphrase (in its plural form) also became popular after it appeared as the title of a James Bond novel by

Ian Fleming, published in 1954, and a 1971 film. *Diamonds Are Forever* (1954), the fourth book in the James Bond 007 series, put Bond in the path of malicious diamond smugglers.

diamonds are a girl's best friend

Title of a song written by Leo Robin in 1949 and made famous by Marilyn Monroe who sang it in the 1953 US film *Gentlemen Prefer Blondes*, a musical comedy directed by Howard Hawks. The film was an adaptation of Anita Loos's 1925 novel (see also 'a diamond is forever'), in which the concept that diamonds, and precious stones and metals generally, are more reliable and enduring than the average gentleman, is clearly professed. As the song claims, 'A kiss on the hand may be quite continental, But diamonds are a girl's best friend.' Ultimately, and quite predictably, the two show girls in the film, played by Monroe and Jane Russell, never completely lose their romantic notions while searching for Mr Right.

did I do that?

Uttered frequently by Steve Urkel (Jaleel White) on the US TV comedy series *Family Matters* (1989–98). The show was originally about the Winslows, a middle-class African-American family living in Chicago, composed of Harriette, her policeman husband Carl, and their three children—15-year-old Eddie, 13-year-old Laura, and 9-year-old Judy. Other live-in relatives were Carl's mother Estelle, Harriette's widowed sister Rachel, and Rachel's son Richie. Steve Urkel, a goofy-looking teenager who wore thick glasses and had a terrible crush on Laura, was their neighbour. Never originally intended to be a recurring character, Urkel—everyone's favourite nerd—soon became the star of the series. He would visit the Winslow's home regularly, never failing to break something or inadvertently cause a problem, to which he would always respond with an apologetic and rather pathetic 'Did I do that?' Cartoon-like Urquel's popularity quickly turned his predictable line into a national catchphrase.

did I ever tell you about the time I was in Sidi Barrani?

From the BBC radio comedy series *Much-Binding-in-the-Marsh* (1944–54) which, like *ITMA* before it, was filled with catchphrases. This one belonged to Kenneth Horne and was directed at Richard Murdoch, the show's other principal star. It was always used to introduce yet another tedious story about his military exploits in North Africa during the Second World War, and thus became a familiar signal to the listener to find a way to change subject or find some other urgent matter to attend to.

did she want it, sir? Did she want it?

Bawdy and insistent prodding aimed at discovering whether a woman has actually agreed to have sex with the person being questioned. The phrase was popularized by the two lewd, 'dodgy' tailors played by Paul Whitehouse and Mark Williams on the popular BBC TV comedy sketch series *The Fast Show* (1994–7), who enunciate the words with a great deal of insinuation. They never actually get an answer, something which seems to be hardly missed as its significance is completely outweighed by the unrelenting innuendo. These words are often combined with the duo's other favourite catchphrase, 'suits you, sir' (see below) as in this sketch from the first series:

PW: Ooh, suits you sir. Were you out with a *lady* last night, sir? *Ooh*, did she want it, sir?
MW: Did she, sir?
PW: Did she? Did she want it, sir? *Ooh*, suits you, sir.
MW: Suits you, sir.
Both: *Ooh!*

didn't he (or she or they) do well?

Popularized by the jaunty British comedian Bruce Forsyth as the original host of BBC TV's *The Generation Game* (1971–), who used it to encourage those participating in the games that made up the show. The show involves four couples, each of which have to be related and of different generations (eg. Son and Mother, Stepfather and Stepdaughter). The teams play two heats each, two couples go through to the semi-final, one team wins out of this and goes on to play the conveyor belt game, at the end of which the winning pair leaves with many prizes and possibly a holiday. Their tasks or games are generally quite ridiculous and nonsensical, including acting out farcical sketches, making omelettes or clay kangaroos, so that Forsyth's line would often be delivered with comic, yet ever-cheerful, sarcasm. Forsyth hosted the elaborately produced show until 1978, when he was replaced by Larry Grayson, but returned to host the show again from 1990 to 1995. Jim Davidson has co-presented the show— renamed *Jim Davidson's Generation Game*—with Melanie Stace since 1996.

dingbat

An empty-headed or silly person; an insult popularized by loud, often vulgar, blue-collar worker Archie Bunker (Carroll O'Connor) on the US TV sitcom *All in the Family* (1971–83). The word has had many meanings since it was first recorded in 1838, but was never used as an insult until *All in the Family*. It has meant an object, such as a brick or stone, used as a missile, or an unspecified gadget or other small article, while in the printing industry, it has come to mean a typographical ornament or symbol. But it has become most popularly known as what Archie Bunker commonly called his wife Edith (Jean Stapleton), who was actually sometimes referred to by fans and in the press as Edith 'Dingbat' Bunker. When interviewed after the series ended, Jean Stapleton remarked that she was extremely glad to move on from her role as the dingbat. See also 'meathead' and 'stifle yourself!'

disco baby sexy baby HOTTTT!!!

A phrase that parodies the language associated with 1970s disco-fever phenomenon. Spoken by hot disco singer Mikki Disko, played by Charlie Higson, on the BBC TV comedy sketch series *The Fast Show* (1994–7). Mikki's act is featured frequently on the show's pseudo-South American/Greek 'Chanel 9' sketches. (See also 'accidento bizarro' and 'scorchio'). Higson enters the studio stage in 1970s garb, wearing a silk shirt and topped with an obvious perm, singing (à la the Bee Gees) 'Ohh-ohh! Disko baby! Sexy baby! Hot! Hahh! Hahh!'

do the right thing

Conduct yourself ethically, with consideration for what is morally correct. Although already current in the US, the phrase was popularized when it was used as the title of a 1989 US film, directed by

Spike Lee, about flaring racial tensions on a summer day in Brooklyn, New York. During the 1990s it became the name adopted by a number of non-profit organizations and programmes across the US aimed at helping children. The Do The Right Thing programme started with the Miami Police Department in 1990 when the community volunteers witnessed the impact of rewarding a student who had fought crime and drug abuse in his or her inner city school. The New York and St Louis police departments are among the many in the country involved in Do The Right Thing programmes, working with schools, media, and businesses to recognize and promote the positive social behaviour of school-age children in their regions.

The February 1990 issue of *Harper's Weekly* published statistics showing that the number of times the phrase 'do the right thing' had appeared in the Congressional Record since the release of Spike Lee's film totalled 53; of this total, the phrase appeared 16 times in reference to the Congressional pay rise, while it was used only once in reference to racial issues.

do you come here often?—only in the mating season

Often spoken by British comic actor and writer Spike Milligan on the 1950s BBC radio *Goon Show*. The second part of the catchphrase became a popular response to the classic chat-up line which had already become common by the 1940s and which, by the 1950s, had even become a film cliché.

do you know —?|no, but if you hum it ...

A popular format for jokes on TV and radio variety programmes that was common in the US and the UK by the 1960s. The comic stock phrase also became a favourite included in bar joke repertoires, as in 'The man walks over to the piano player and says "Do you know your monkey just pissed in my beer?" The pianist replies "No, but if you hum it I'll play it."' The catchphrase was first popularized in the UK by the BBC radio comedy series *Round the Horne* (1965–9) which featured it frequently in its sketches. It was employed by US Vice-President Hubert Humphrey when he appeared on the ABC TV variety show *Happening '68* (later re-titled *It's Happening*; 1968–9) as part of his presidential campaign. When one of the presenters asked him 'Do you know it's been a pleasure to have you on the show?' Humphrey replied: 'No, but if you hum a few bars I can fake it.'

do you mind?

Associated with Carry On stalwart Kenneth Connor in the BBC radio comedy series *Ray's a Laugh* (1949–61), and expressing indignation or reproach. The phrase belonged to Sydney Mincing, one of Connor's classic creations for this catchphrase-based radio series. Sydney was a gloomy, wheezy, pinched voiced North Londoner who, according to Connor 'was inspired by this itinerant librarian who used to call from door to door when I was a youngster'. In the same interview, Connor recalled, 'Sydney also came from a distressed cleric who lived in the same area. He had the most extraordinary sour view of life. Doom-laden, really. He was a staunch believer in poverty and knowing your place. I once got a pet dog and when he saw it in the garden he simply said, in the most disapproving tone, "Spreading yourself, aren't you?"'

do you think that's wise?

Popularized by Sergeant Arthur Wilson (John Le Mesurier) on the BBC TV comedy series *Dad's Army* (1968–77), about the weekly crises of a group of misfit characters making up a village Home Guard platoon during the Second World War. Wilson, an upper-class ex-public schoolboy, often had disagreements with Captain Mainwaring (Arthur Lowe), who was his boss at the bank where he was Chief Clerk. Mainwaring had achieved his position as bank manager through hard work and merit, but was always being frustrated and annoyed by Wilson's upper-class education and manners, including Wilson's tendency to always question his decisions with his classic catchphrase—'Do you think that's wise, Sir?' Lacking any power of command, Wilson is not able to shout out orders, frequently using the rather less military phrase 'would you mind?'

does my bum look big in this?

Associated with comedienne Arabella Weir in the 1990s BBC TV comedy series *The Fast Show*. Weir shot to fame on this show with her character 'The Insecure Woman', who never made an appearance without uttering this catchphrase. The phrase was based on Weir's own past phobia about her weight—and is one most women can identify with. In the case of 'The Insecure Woman', the phobia has reached a level of frenzied obsession, as this monologue from the show illustrates: 'Look, does my bum look big in this? Do these earrings make me look fat? Can you see my tits from here? Are they a bit saggy? Can you see that my tummy's fat from here? Do I look all, do I look all right? Does my jacket hide it?' and so on. In 1997, Weir made the most of her catchphrase by publishing a bestseller entitled *Does My Bum Look Big In This?*

does not compute

Phrase associated with 'Robot', the B-9 Environmental Control Robot (Dick Tufeld and Bob May), who accompanies the Robinson Family on the US TV science-fiction series *Lost in Space* (1965–8). The Robot, one of TV's best-loved science fiction robots, was designed by art director Robert Kinoshita and prop builder Bob Stewart. Standing 6′4″ in his web-track feet, he has a bubble head of clear plastic, accordion-style arms and legs, claw hands and a body of aluminium, rubber, and plastic. Other features are numerous intricate computer systems, radar-antennae 'ears', and a 'heart' that glows when excited.

The Robinson family and their Robot found themselves 'lost in space' after their Jupiter II craft, originally on a five-year voyage of the Alpha Centauri star system, was thrown off-course by the evil stowaway and saboteur Dr Zachary Smith (Jonathan Harris). It is usually the Robinsons' extremely brainy youngest son, Will (Bill Mumy), who joins forces with his robot companion to undermine the villainous Dr Smith's nasty schemes. The Robot's other catchphrases include: 'Logic error', 'Data incomplete', and 'Danger! Danger Will Robinson!' In 1997, the series was made into a feature film, also entitled *Lost in Space*, in which Robot states: 'Friendship does not compute'.

does she ... or doesn't she?

From a landmark 1955 Clairol ad, written by US copywriter Shirley Polykoff, which changed an entire generation's attitudes toward hair colour and helped sales go up by 413% in six years. By suggesting the product's results were so natural-looking that no one would know for sure, the phrase successfully challenged women to colour their hair. Research at the time showed that women did not detect any possible sexual innuendo in the phrase, so it remained a trademark Clairol slogan until 1973. The response accompanying the line—'Only her hairdresser knows for sure'—also became a popular catchphrase.

doesn't it make you want to spit?

Remark made with reference to something that should induce disgust or scorn. The line was popularized by British comedian Arthur Askey on the BBC radio show *Bandwagon* (1938–9). Askey, whose background had been mainly in music-hall, and compère Richard Murdoch provided the comedy spots that came to dominate the show. Another catchphrase from this popular radio series was 'Ah, happy days', sighed by Askey and Murdoch (who in many of their sketches shared a top floor flat in the BBC's Broadcasting House in London) when reminiscing about the past. Murdoch's comment about Arthur—'You silly little man'—became his catchphrase on the show.

d'oh!

Associated with Homer J. Simpson in the animated TV show *The Simpsons* (1989–), who uses the expression at least once in almost every episode. A father who gives bad advice, Homer is a slightly dim safety inspector for the local nuclear power plant in Springfield, the show's fictional location. His trademark 'D'oh' developed out of a general exclamation to indicate anger, and has therefore always been referred to in the show's scripts as 'Annoyed Grunt'. The sorts of occasion in which Homer uses this exclamation include: when the candy machine wouldn't take his screwed-up dollar (used twice); when he pulls the phone down, by tripping over the lead; and when he says that TV respects him, then turns the TV on, and the man on the TV is laughing at him.

don't be ridiculous

Exclamation popularized by Balki Bartokomous (Bronson Pinchot) on the US TV comedy series *Perfect Strangers* (1986–93). Balki, a wacky shepherd from the Mediterranean island of Mypos, moves to Chicago to live with his distant cousin, Larry Appleton (Mark Linn-Baker). The sitcom focuses on their adventures as flatmates and eventually, best friends. Balki, intrigued and enthralled by everything American has, however, some difficulties with American expressions (e.g. 'Cousin, are you going to have a nervous breakdance?'), and his linguistic errors often land him and Larry in a lot of trouble. The show relied heavily on silly dialogue (made possible largely by Balki's English), slapstick pratfalls and Balki's useful catchphrase, usually prefaced so: 'But of course not, don't be ridiculous...' (pronounced 'don be reedeeculous').

don't force it, Phoebe!

A piece of alliterative advice given by British comedian Charlie Chester to a character called Phoebe on the BBC radio show *Stand Easy* (1946–50), that became a national catchphrase during the 1940s. The show had developed directly from *The Charlie Chester Show*, making a successful transition into a series which immediate post-war BBC Light Programme listeners first got to know, and love, with all its overtones of demob-suits, Dads' home-comings, and protracted rationing. Chester always had a little political rhyme for each show, such as, 'Down in the jungle, living in a tent, better than a prefab. No rent!'

don't forget the diver!

One of the more baffling of the many catchphrases from the 1940s BBC radio show *ITMA* that entered the language. Spoken by 'Deepend Dan the Diver', played by Horace Percival (based on a man that Tommy Handley once saw diving off the pier at New Brighton and collecting money from ferry passengers), whose other main catchphrase was his doleful: 'I'm going down now, sir', spoken with a brisk bubbling as he submerged. It was taken as the title of the 1958 book by C. A. Chard, a veteran diver (more than ten thousand 'dips' in some thirty years), and was the title of a 1974 *Dad's Army* TV episode (adapted for radio in 1975 and originally broadcast on BBC Radio 4).

don't forget the fruit gums, mum!

An advertising slogan for Rowntree's fruit gums launched in 1956 and successfully promoted through television commercials in the UK during the late 1950s. The authorities then forced Rowntree's to change the slogan because of unfair pressure on mothers. The company quickly and cleverly came up with 'don't forget the fruit gums, chum' instead.

The Advertising Standards Agency's code now prohibits advertising based on a 'direct' appeal to children. In particular, section 47.4 states that advertisements and promotions addressed to children 'should not make a direct appeal to purchase unless the product is one that would be likely to interest children and that they could reasonably afford'. This old slogan was an example of just such an appeal.

don't get mad, get even!

A late 20th-century saying often attributed to US tycoon and diplomat Joseph P. Kennedy, father of President John F. Kennedy, Robert F. Kennedy, and Senator Ted Kennedy. The phrase has at times also been attributed to his sons John and Robert, and it seems that the whole Kennedy clan shared this motto. When John F. Kennedy was elected president in 1961 he had many scores to settle, for his treatment during the campaign, for the many mistakes of the CIA over the years, and for the bitterness that arose immediately after the votes had been counted, showing he had won the presidency by one of the narrowest margins ever recorded. It became known that Kennedy frequently stated among his associates: 'It has long been a Kennedy tradition…Not to get mad, but to get even. I fully realize that I shall not be able to "get even" during my first term in office; but during the second term you are going to see some important changes.'

An adapted version of the famous maxim—'Don't Get Mad. Get Everything' was used as the advertising slogan for the 1996 US film *The First Wives Club*, starring Bette Midler, Goldie Hawn, and Diane Keaton. The film is about three well-heeled New York ex-wives who decide to embark on a mission to wreak revenge on the husbands who had coldly dumped them for younger 'trophy' wives.

don't have a cow, man!

One of the catchphrases popularized by plucky 10-year-old Bart on the immensely popular animated TV show *The Simpsons* (1989–). Bart's bad-mannered retort is similar in meaning to 'don't have a fit', urging the person being addressed to remain calm and refrain from over-reacting. This and his other trademark put-down, 'Eat my shorts', (see below), were faithfully mimicked by millions of schoolchildren across America, much to the horror of teachers and parents. Many elementary schools banned Bart Simpson T-shirts, especially those with the slogan, 'Under-achiever, and Proud of It'. Preachers, the religious right, and former US president

George Bush all censured *The Simpsons*. Bush and former Secretary of Education William Bennett publicly criticized the programme for its subversive and anti-authority tendencies. In fact, by the mid-1990s, the show had softened somewhat, and Homer and Bart's depravity is in any case always thwarted or ultimately turned to good. Bart actually stopped (for five or six seasons, at least) using the catchphrases 'Don't have a cow, man' and 'Eat my shorts'.

don't leave home without it

The indispensable; a phrase that has been applied to a number of items—both in jest and with serious concern. The words are a slogan from an long-running advertising campaign for the American Express credit card created by Ogilvy & Mather Agency in 1975. Companies often keep their slogans for years at a time, and even play off them when times change. In 1999, to suit the changing times, American Express cleverly twisted its longtime slogan into 'Don't leave homepages without it', to get across its message that American Express cardholders would not be responsible for any unauthorized charges from shopping online.

don't mention the war

Spoken repeatedly by Basil Fawlty (John Cleese) in a 1975 episode of the BBC TV situation comedy series *Fawlty Towers* (1975–9). Basil Fawlty is based on a real hotel manager—Mr Sinclair who ran a hotel in Torquay—where Cleese and the rest of the Monty Python team stayed while filming. The catchphrase, which came from an episode in which Cleese challenged the bounds of acceptability in British comedy by breaking into SS-style goose-stepping before a party of Germans, became one of the most famous lines from a comedy and passed into common currency. Although Basil keeps telling everyone 'Whatever you do, don't mention the war', he seems to be unable to control himself, infuriating his guests by referring to the Second World War at every opportunity. In July 2001, producers of a German remake of *Fawlty Towers* decided to drop this episode. Fawlty's comments—he mistakenly orders 'a prawn Goebbels, a Hermann Goering, and four Colditz salads'—were deemed too controversial for a modern German audience.

Although there were only two series ever made, comprising 12 episodes, it became one of the most revered sitcoms ever. Cleese, together with Connie Booth (who played the waitress Polly), wrote the entire series which featured an ill-mannered hotelier with a compulsive desire to verbally brutalize his guests. Basil Fawlty is an inveterate snob who is abusive to everyone, particularly Manuel (Andrew Sachs), the keen but clueless Spanish waiter, and is kept in check by his domineering wife Sybil (Prunella Scales). *Fawlty Towers* has been shown in more than 60 countries. *Don't Mention the War!: A Shameful European Adventure* was the title of book by Stewart Ferris and Paul Bassett published 2000. *Don't mention the war* is also the title of a review of the book *Master Georgie* by Beryl Bainbridge written by Anne Chisolm, *Guardian*, 5 April 1998.

don't panic!

A generally futile, if not counter-productive piece of advice. The admonishment was popularized by BBC TV comedy series *Dad's Army* (1968–77), associated with Lance Corporal Jack Jones (Clive Dunn), the elderly local butcher who likes to remind everyone of his experiences during the Boer War, when he served with General Kitchener in the Sudan. Despite these experiences, his parade drill is very poor—even in comparison with the other members of the platoon. He remains nonetheless very keen, volunteering his services at every opportunity and offers the platoon his butcher's van as a means of transport.

These two words were popularized again in the late 1970s and early 1980s by Douglas Adams's *The Hitchhiker's Guide to the Galaxy*, which began as a BBC radio show, was published as a novel in 1979, and then serialized for television in 1981. The words 'DON'T PANIC' are inscribed in 'large, friendly letters' on the cover of the best-selling intergalactic reference book, *The Hitchhiker's Guide*, which is often consulted, especially in emergencies, by the heroes in this satirical invention.

don't some mothers have 'em?

A Lancashire expression meaning the person referred to is dumb or empty-headed. It was British comedian Jimmy Clitheroe's most famous catchphrase, sometimes amended to 'Don't some twits' mothers have 'em'. Jimmy Clitheroe was a star of variety, films, radio, and television in a career that spanned five decades. His radio show, *The Clitheroe Kid*, ran from 1957 to 1972 and became the principal vehicle for an early 'Carry On' brand of humour. Another of his catchphrases was 'I'm all there with me cough drops', a Lancashire expression denoting someone quick-witted. When he got into a scrape—which he frequently did—his catchphrase was 'Ooh, flippin' 'eck'.

A variation on the phrase, 'some mothers do 'ave 'em', with the same meaning, was also popular and was used as the title of a BBC TV situation comedy (1973–8). The series' central character was Frank Spencer (Michael Crawford), a walking disaster area who was guaranteed to get it wrong, whatever it might be.

don't try this at home! Go to a neighbour's house

Popularized by US comedian David Letterman, host of the highly popular TV talk show *Late Night with David Letterman* (1982–   ). A comic take/twist on the verbal warnings sometimes issued on television at the beginning or end of commercials, demonstrations, or documentaries to discourage imitation or 'copy-cat' behaviour which could lead to injury or damages and thus avoid costly legal suits.

don't worry, be happy

Popularized in 1988 as the title of the catchy Grammy-winning song by Bobby McFerrin, and as George Bush's unofficial campaign theme-song. While Governor Mike Dukakis highlighted his ethnic immigrant roots by playing Neil Diamond's 'America' at the 1988 Democratic Convention, at the Republican equivalent then Vice-President Bush surfed a wave of economic contentment by playing McFerrin's hit single. The song's strong 'feel-good factor' ensured its successful permeation of US society, bringing with it a revival of happy, or 'smiley', faces and other emblems of the simpler, 'flower power' tenets of the 1960s. The phrase had in fact been associated during the late 1960s and early 1970s with the Indian spiritual teacher Meher Baba whose smiling face graced posters captioned with the motto 'Don't Worry, Be Happy'. Actually, Meher Baba's full quote was 'Do your best. Then, don't worry, be happy'.

The phrase surfaced again during the 2000 US presidential campaign, when candidates chose to ignore warnings that the economy could be anything less than healthy. An ABC News online article entitled 'Don't Worry, Be Happy' (www.abcnews.com, 29 December 2000) begins: 'Why? Neither candidate, it seems, wants to spoil the party. The economy is humming along and there is little upside to warning voters about a looming crisis'.

don't you just love being in control?

A slogan from a British Gas TV advertising campaign during the early 1990s. The television commercial, first shown in 1991, would end with the featured person saying the phrase, just after producing a flame in the place of their thumb with a click of their fingers. The advertisement was based on the idea that gas appliances could be controlled more efficiently than electric ones, thereby giving the consumer full control. The phrase has often been used with a comic tone and/or sexual innuendo. A sketch featuring 'The Lovely Randy Old Ladies' (played by Harry Enfield and Kathy Burke) in a 1994 episode of the BBC TV comedy series *Harry Enfield and Chums* ends with the ladies overpowering the gas man who had called to check a non-existent gas leak. Finally, seemingly about to have her way with him, one of the ladies sits on the man, turns to face the camera, 'lights' her left thumb, à la British Gas commercials of the time, and says: 'Don't you just *love* being in control?'

don't you know there's a war on?

Reproach or chastisement to someone behaving as though unaware of the pressures or seriousness of a situation. The phrase and its variant 'remember there's a war on', were used during the First World War, but became more popular both in the UK and the US during the Second World War. An oral account, contributed by Betty Griffis (b. 1934) to the Museum of London's Blitz Exhibition, clearly recalls the circumstances in which the phrase found its popularity during those years: 'Making a run for it, and our air raid warden telling us to hurry up me duk don't you know there's a war on...our rules were, "grab your gas mask and make a run for it." No back lip for the quotation of the day was "don't you know there's a war on!" The Brits can find the time for humour, it kept us going.'

The catchphrase has continued to be popular in films, television, comics, and other media since 1945. It turns up in Frank Capra's

1946 classic film *It's A Wonderful Life*, starring Jimmy Stewart and Donna Reed, when George (Stewart) says admonishingly: 'All right, now, hold on, hold on, hold on, now. Don't you know there's a war on?' The phrase is also employed by the coolheaded Colonel Robert Hogan (Bob Crane) on the US TV series *Hogan's Heroes* (1965–71), set in a German prison camp during the Second World War. More recently, the line and variants of it have been used by various characters on the US TV series *Star Trek: Deep Space Nine* (1993–9), notably by Lieutenant Ezri Dax (Nicole deBoer) to reporter Jake Siskow (Cirroc Lofton), with reference to the ongoing Dominion War. *Don't You Know There's A War On?* is the title of two children's books, one by James Stevenson (1992) and the other by Avi (2001).

doomed I am, doomed

From the popular radio comedy series *Round the Horne*, which was broadcast on BBC radio (1965–9) and was written by Barry Took and Marty Feldman. The phrase was associated with Spasm the butler, played by Kenneth Williams. Also: 'we be doomed, we all be doomed'.

drinka pinta milka day

An advertising slogan for milk featured in a UK Dairy Council advertising campaign from 1958, that plays with orthography, and the strong-weak syllabic rhythms of the language. The popular poster campaign was created by the National Milk Publicity Council, established in 1920 to promote milk and dairy products. The 'Drinka Pinta Milka Day' campaign was still going strong in 1969, when 'Pinta Girl is Popular' became a more modern version of the well-known slogan. The National Milk Publicity Council's other memorable advertising campaigns for milk include 'Gotta Lotta Bottle' and, more recently, the image of dancing milk bottles.

duh ... I heard that!

Phrase associated with Barth, of Barth's Burgers (played by Les Lye), on the Canadian children's TV programme *You Can't Do That On Television* (1979–90, on the cable TV network Nickelodeon). The show had a revolving cast, with over a hundred children appearing on the show at some point. Les Lye played all the adult male parts, including Barth, Ross, and Blip. Barth was one of the principal, and most popular, of skit-based comedy series' characters. The sloppy, unshaven burger chef, with bandages on his hands and arms, and wearing a grimy apron, prepared truly awful food. He would always be heard saying 'Duh, I heard that!' whenever someone criticized his cooking. Barth's diner sketches often ended with someone asking 'What do you think is in the burgers?' In the 'opposite sketches' always shown half-way through each episode, Barth's cooking would be edible, if not actually good.

DWAHHH!

Trademark cry of Duckman (voiced by *Seinfeld*'s Jason Alexander), star of the eponymous critically-acclaimed US animated TV series, which ran from 1994 to 1997. Duckman is a crabby, hard-boiled, tough talking, cowardly, selfish duck detective who scrapes along, taking on cases that no respectable detective would stoop to accept. The series also features the voices of Nancy Travis as Duckman's deceased wife's identical twin Bernice, Dweezil Zappa as Ajax, Duckman's goofy teenage son, Tim Curry as King Chicken.

dy-no-mite!

Fantastic, absolutely the best. A catchphrase belonging to J. J. Evans, played by then little known stand-up comic Jimmie Walker, on the US TV sitcom *Good Times* (1974–9). J.J. would use the phrase to describe both himself and situations. The hit series, set in a high-rise on the South Side of Chicago, starred Esther Rolle as the sardonic maid Florida Evans (a part she originated on the hit show *Maude*); John Amos played her husband, Henry, while their three children were played by Walker (the eldest), Ralph Carter as Michael, and Bernadette Stanis as Thelma. It tackled daring topical issues—including prejudice, black on black crime, gangs, President Nixon, and the oil crisis—with a degree of humour and from an Afro-American perspective. J.J., with his beanpole body, was immediately perceived as the show's most comic character, and from the time he first used his famous exclamation during the second episode on, he was known as 'Kid

Dy-no-mite!' He became the star of the series and 'dy-no-mite!' became a national catchphrase in the USA.

Walker went on to perform stand-up in Las Vegas, released a bestselling comedy album entitled *Dy-no-mite!* as well as all sorts of merchandising items, including a talking doll that says 'dy-no-mite!' when its string is pulled.

Ee

· · · · · · · · · · ·

eat my shorts!

Defiant and slightly tasteless phrase popularized by Bart, the Simpson family's oldest child on the animated TV show *The Simpsons* (1989–   ). Bart used his famous 'eat my shorts' catchphrase again in 2000, after having dropped it during the preceding five or six seasons, presumably in response to criticism received from religious groups, educational bodies, and conservative politicians in the US.

ee bah gum!

'Ee!'—a north of England exclamation expressing surprise or dismay— together with 'bah gum', to mean: 'Well, I never!' Associated with a variety of well-known characters and media, from the cartoon strip hero Andy Capp to the long-running British TV soap opera *Coronation Street*, set in Manchester, the phrase has become a part of the modern English lexicon.

ee, it was agony, Ivy

From the highly popular BBC radio comedy series *Ray's a Laugh* (1949– 61) starring Ted Ray. The two funniest and best-known characters were Mrs Hoskin and Ivy, played by Bob Pearson and Ray respectively. The two old ladies were based on real-life characters Ray had met in Morecambe. The phrase was spoken repeatedly by Mrs Hoskin, a somewhat overweight woman with a never-ending range of ailments, to describe her latest pain or malady.

elementary, my dear Watson!

A supposed quote by Sherlock Holmes, though the line does not appear in any of Sir Arthur Conan Doyle's stories about the great detective. Holmes does say 'Elementary', as in 'The Crooked Man' (in *The Memoirs of Sherlock Holmes* 1894), and 'My dear Watson' (for example, 'It was very superficial, my dear Watson, I assure you' in 'The Cardboard Box'), but never the two together in any of the original 60 stories written by Conan Doyle. The phrase does appear in the closing lines of the first Sherlock Holmes 'talkie', *The Return of Sherlock Holmes*, released in 1929, and became popularized through subsequent film versions starring Basil Rathbone. It is Sherlock's response to an inquisitive Dr Watson, his sidekick, and means to consider the simple or elementary answer to a problem or, in other words, the obvious.

eleven minutes late...

Reggie's habitual excuse for his train's delays in BBC TV comedy series *The Fall and Rise of Reginald Perrin* (1976–9). Monday to Friday, Reginald Perrin, played by Leonard Rossiter, would leave his home for his work at Sunshine Desserts and head for the station to catch the train to London's Waterloo station. Without fail, every working day, his train would be late. Reggie himself would inform his secretary of each of these delays and their myriad causes (for example, 'Eleven minutes late . . . signal failure at Vauxhall', or 'somebody had stolen the lines at Surbiton').

There was an American version of the series starring Richard Mulligan as Reggie Potter broadcast by ABC in 1983, which was essentially similar to the first British series except that C. J. was a young whizzkid, Reggie worked at the Funtime Ice Cream Co. and he lusted after his son's girlfriend.

end of civilization as we know it, the

The collapse of society and familiar, established ways of life. The phrase became considered a cinematic cliché, often referring to the effects of enemy or alien invasions, and is at times used sarcastically to suggest a person is over-reacting or being unduly alarmist about a problem or inconvenience. It was used by Orson Welles in *Citizen Kane* (1941): 'a project that would mean the end of the world as we know it'.

The catchphrase appears as part of the title of a 1977 British comic film, *The Strange Case of the End of Civilization As We Know It*, starring John Cleese as the descendant of the legendary Sherlock Holmes in a modern-day detective drama of international power and intrigue. Naturally, the character played by Cleese is completely inept, bungling all his crime-solving efforts. More recently, worries about 'the precipice of Y2K disaster—and the end of civilization as we know it' were voiced in an article entitled 'It's the End of the Internet As We Know It' (*ClickZ Today* (www.clickz.com) 31 December 1999). President George W. Bush accused Osama bin Laden and his al-Qa'ida network in early November 2001 of attempting to develop nuclear, biological, or chemical weapons 'to try to harm civiliztion as we know it' (*Independent*, 7 November 2001).

energizer, the

Anything that gives strength, stamina, and vivacity. From the advertising slogan for Duracell batteries, embodied by a battery-run toy rabbit known as the 'Energizer Bunny' (a registered trademark), who became a pop culture icon and a familiar character to millions of Americans. Duracell's ever-popular Energizer Bunny made his television advertisement debut in 1989, first appearing in a parody of the brand's 'Toys' campaign in which he not only lasted longer than toys not powered by Duracell batteries, but kept 'going, and going, and going...' From the start the commercial set out to interrupt other commercials for imaginary products. Much of the commercials' success was rooted in their unpredictable nature—no one ever knew when or where the Energizer Bunny was going to pop up.

In the business world, the Energizer Bunny has come to represent sought-after characteristics and values that many companies aim to create in their own brand imaging—'Brands do well if they are championed by the image of a friendly and authoritative figure, for example the company CEO, a personality spokesperson, or a character, like the Energizer Bunny' (*Business Leader* (online version), August 1999). On its own, 'the energizer' has been used to promote a wide range of products—such as 'Ginseng, the natural energizer'—and treatments, including one against hair loss.

enter Bluebottle!

A favourite catchphrase of Bluebottle (Peter Sellers), one of the regular characters on the surreal BBC comedy radio *Goon Show* (1952–60). Bluebottle, a primary school boy scout from East Finchley, London, has the habit of reading out his own stage directions. The best friend of Eccles, Bluebottle often ends up being blown up, or 'deaded', as he describes it. See also 'you dirty rotten swine, you'.

even better than that!

Catchphrase associated with Mark Williams on the BBC TV comedy series *The Fast Show* (1994–7), created by Paul Whitehouse and Charlie Higson. Williams invariably uses the phrase to introduce preposterous or bizarre notions during the show's 'Interesting Life' sketches in response to questions from Eryl Maynard. For example, when Maynard asks: 'Now, did you get the eggs, the butter and the potatoes?' Williams replies: 'Even better than tha-a-at! I got some biscuits shaped like radios, a map of Cairo AND an ice-pick!'

even your best (or closest) friends won't tell you

Slogan from the well-known advertising campaign for Listerine mouthwash that was launched in the 1920s, and broached the somewhat taboo subject of halitosis, or bad breath. The ad, which referred to one's 'closest friends', spelled out the truth of the matter when it came to people's basic embarrassment and fear of offending when it came to this subject. The catchphrase, most often with 'best' replacing 'closest', has been used to describe a number of situations in which friends dare not be truthful. In the 1937 US film *Stage Door* (about show business and the lives of aspiring, rival actresses who are looking for a break, hoping to appear on the New York stage), when Terry (Katharine Hepburn) says 'At least I'm gonna have a try at it. If I can act, I want the world to know it. If I can't, I want to know it', the wisecracking Eve (Eve Arden) quips: 'Even your best friends won't tell you.'

evening (or evenin'), all

Associated with PC George Dixon, played by Jack Warner, the chief character in the BBC TV police series *Dixon of Dock Green* (1955–76). The remark/salutation would be accompanied by a salute to the helmet from the ordinary 'bobby' on the beat with the inevitable heart of gold. The series was principally set in a suburban police station in the East End of London and concerned uniformed police dealing with routine tasks and low-level crime. The character of PC Dixon was already known to the British public as he had first appeared (played by Warner) in the 1949 Ealing film *The Blue Lamp*, towards the end of which the warm and amiable policeman was shot and killed by a young thug, played by Dirk Bogarde. A spin-off of the character and circumstances became the television series *Dixon of Dock Green*, created by writer Ted Willis.

every day, and in every way, I am getting better and better

Maxim employed by French pharmacist Émile Coué who promoted his ideas on the value of positive thought through this one-size-fits all approach to autosuggestion. In 1920, Coué introduced at his clinic in Nancy a novel method of psychotherapy characterized by frequent repetition of this formula. He encouraged people to repeat this saying over and over again until it became a part of their philosophy of life, and at the height of his career in the 1920s he had almost everyone in Europe and America going around chanting, 'Every day, and in every way, I am getting better and better'. The fact that some of those people really did report getting 'better and better' proved how effective the power of suggestion could be, and increased the appeal of this method of autosuggestion which came to be known as 'Couéism'.

every home should have one!

A phrase that can apply to almost anything or anyone considered to be a must in the average, 'modern' household. Originally a popular advertising slogan, which was current in the US by the 1920s, its variant—'no home should be without one'—was being used to promote products in the UK by the beginning of the 20th century. The phrase, and its use as an advertising tool, still crops up frequently. It was the title of a 1981 album released by Patti Austin, and of a 1970 comic film about an advertising man (Marty Feldman) relaunching a 'boring' product—his job is to make Scottish porridge sexy.

everybody out!

A cry calling on workers to strike that had became familiar in the UK by the 1960s. It remained—on the docks and in the mines and car plants—quite a regular event until the 1980s. The command, usually issued by a trade union official, was popularized by the BBC TV sitcom *The Rag Trade* (1961–3 and 1977–8) which followed the exploits of a group of women working at Fenner Fashions garment factory.

The rundown East End sweat-shop was owned by the beleaguered Harold Fenner (Peter Jones), but was run by feisty shop steward Paddy

(Miriam Karlin), forever ready to shout 'Everybody out!', threatening to bring production to a standstill, when Fenner failed to comply with her demands. The call became so popular that it was adopted as a national catchphrase. The helpless, despondent, and groaning Fenner came to symbolize the plight of bosses who struggled to maintain production in that era of trade union militancy.

The phrase still retains its trade union connections, as an article entitled 'Everybody out now' about sex workers in Holland forming their own union shows (BBC News Online, 2 October 2001). The title carried two double meanings, as the prostitutes were 'outing' their sexual activities/services as well as their earnings, as 'the downside is now they have to declare their dealings to the taxman'.

everybody wants ta get inta da act

Popularized by US entertainer Jimmy Durante, the 'Schnozzola', who constantly lamented 'Everybody wants ta get inta da act!' making it one of his trademark phrases. He would usually utter it in a mock-furious tone whenever another performer adopted his techniques.

everyday story of country folk, an

Introduction to and sub-title of the extremely popular BBC radio serial *The Archers* (1950–   ). The Archers' address is Brookfield Farm, Ambridge, and their signature tune 'Barwick Green'. The series originated in Birmingham with Godfrey Baseley, who produced farming programmes and acted as editor, and Tony Shyrane, producer. It was designed as a vehicle for the Ministry of Agriculture to inform farmers about the latest practices and methods as the country tried to get back on its feet after the Second World War. When *The Archers* was launched on the BBC's nationally networked Light Programme in 1951, it was billed as 'an everyday story of country folk', and has remained so ever since.

The power of the serial was demonstrated on the night of 22 September 1955, when the BBC stole all the attention from ITV's opening night by 'killing' Grace Archer in a fire. The serial maintains a loyal following, despite considerable character and cast changes. There have also been endless variations on this catchphrase, such as 'Just an everyday story of Microsoft folk' (in *Computergram International*, 24 February 1999), 'James: An Everyday Story of Pop

Folk' (in *New Musical Express*, 16 March 1985), and 'An everyday story of complacent folk' (in the *Guardian*, 11 February 2000).

everything dies

Associated with the Alien Bounty Hunter in the US TV series *The X-Files* (1993–2002), and one of a series of home-truths popularized by the series. In the episode entitled *Herrenvolk*, when Special Agent Fox Mulder (David Duchovny) asks the alien bounty hunter to save a mysterious man and the clone of Mulder's sister Samantha, the square-jawed bounty hunter responds: 'everything dies.' The phrase replaced 'The Truth Is Out There' in the opening titles sequence.

After 8-year old Samantha disappeared from the Mulder family home, Mulder searched for her for almost ten years, abandoning a dazzling FBI career for the dusty realms of the X-Files. He finally finds proof in *Closure* that the young Samantha was abducted for alien testing, but was eventually saved by a 'walk-in', a spiritual intervention that rescues children from horrible situations by transporting their souls through starlight. When Mulder finally accepts that his sister is dead, he is relieved, telling his partner Scully, 'I'm free'.

everything you always wanted to know about — but were afraid to ask

From the title of the highly popular 1969 book *Everything You Always Wanted to Know About Sex, But Were Afraid to Ask*, written by US psychiatrist and noted sex expert Dr David Reuben. Reuben's manual reflected the time's new spirit of 'free love', and the generally more open attitudes towards sex. The book received an amazing response— becoming a No. 1 bestseller in 51 countries, read by more than 100 million people, according to publisher HarperCollins. The phrase was further popularized by Woody Allen's satirical film by the same title which was released in 1972.

Just about every subject and concept has been inserted within this familiar phrase. To provide just one example, in mid-2001 a Joseph 'Jofish' Kaye was offering a week-long course at MIT entitled 'Everything You Always Wanted To Know About Smell But Were Afraid To Ask', that had been taught in January 2001.

In 1999 Dr Reuben published a new edition to *Everything You Always Wanted to Know About Sex*, and like his first book, it attempts to reflect the times and how the art of making love is viewed.

exit stage left!

Signature line of Hanna-Barbera cartoon character Snagglepuss, a pink lion who was also a frustrated actor—hence this stage direction, delivered to himself with a dramatic flair. The sartorially elegant lion would cock his arms, ready to dash off the screen, when he would invariably say this catchphrase and disappear with accompanying sound effects. Snagglepuss first appeared as a minor character in 1959 on a number of cartoon shows and, in 1960, he met Major Minor the hunter, the character who would always be his arch-enemy. The cool cat was given his own segment on *The Yogi Bear Show* when it premiered in 1961, and from then on Snagglepuss, voiced by Daws Butler, enjoyed a successful career into the 1980s. See also 'heavens to Murgatroyd!'.

Usually employed simply to announce an imminent departure from the scene, the catchphrase can also have an added comic effect, thanks to its political connotations, as in a BBC News Online article entitled 'Exit-Stage...' (7 March 2001). The article reported on the decision of Labour MP Tony Benn, who 'has been branded a dangerous left-winger', to stand down from the House of Commons at the general election.

exterminate! exterminate!

Spoken by the Daleks in the BBC TV series *Doctor Who* (1963–89), the world's longest-running TV science fiction series. *Doctor Who* was first broadcast on 23 November 1963, and the Daleks debuted in December of the same year. The fearsome Daleks, encased in their pepperpot-shaped travel machines, were mutant monsters from the planet Skaro whose only thoughts were of conquest. Convinced that they were the most superior race in the Universe, the Daleks would ensure that all other species, including humans, would either be subjugated or destroyed. According to many of the series' fans, it was when the Doctor encountered a gaggle of Daleks, with their mechanical cry of 'ex-ter-min-ate! ex-ter-min-ate!', that the show really took off. By 1964, the Daleks had practically eclipsed *Doctor Who* itself to become one of the great British success stories of the early 1960s. The entertainment industry quickly latched on to them, seeing how profitable they and their spin-offs could be. In 1965, the first of two feature films, *Dr Who and the Daleks*, was released, as were an array of toys and games, and the first Dalek stage play, *The Curse of the Daleks*, opened at Wyndham's Theatre in London.

extinct is forever

Advertising slogan for Friends of Animals, Inc., an international, non-profit, membership organization founded in 1957. The organization works to protect animals from cruelty, abuse, and institutionalized exploitation, and is involved in efforts to protect and preserve animals and their habitats around the world. The slogan—ironically reminiscent of the familiar De Beers ad slogan, 'a diamond is forever' (see above)—was coined by Dr Kurt Benirschke when writing on his work with endangered species at San Diego Zoo (*Christian Science Monitor*, 29 May 1980). Benirschke, a professor of pathology and reproductive medicine, was director of the Center for Reproduction of Endangered Species (founded 1975). Friends of Animals have often combined the rather depressing slogan with a more hopeful one— 'Extinct is forever; endangered means there's still time'.

Ff

fab, fantabulosa

Fantastic, fabulous; an exclamation forming part of the rich 'parlare' (speech) or Polari language spoken by Julian and Sandy (played by Hugh Paddick and Kenneth Williams) in their sketches on the BBC radio comedy series *Round the Horne* (1965–9). (See 'I'm Julian and this is my friend Sandy'.) By far the programme's most popular characters, the effete, 'fantabulosa' Julian and Sandy spoke in a sort of homosexual street code, and their likeable, chirpy personas probably had a beneficial effect on popular attitudes towards homosexuality in Britain in the mid-1960s, when it was still illegal (it ceased to be illegal over the age of 21 in 1967) and few listeners could claim to know personally any openly gay men. 'Fab, fantabulosa' (emphasis on the fourth, elongated syllable), was popular during the late 1960s and early 1970s among homosexuals, people in show business, and 'hip' circles in Britain.

fabulous, sweetie!

From the cult BBC TV comedy series *Absolutely Fabulous* (1992–6; –97 in the US). Often uttered by Edina (Jennifer Saunders), the manic PR guru who is obsessed with keeping up with the times, and her best friend Patsy (Joanna Lumley), becoming a standard response within the language of their whirling world of fashion and the media. The award-laden and internationally acclaimed comedy series was written by Jennifer Saunders, and developed out of a sketch on *French and Saunders* called 'Modern Mother and Child'.

famous for fifteen minutes

Phrase associated with the US pop artist Andy Warhol, who used it in a 1968 exhibition catalogue. The full phrase was: 'In the future everybody will be famous for fifteen minutes', and apparently sprang from the evolving art scene of the time, with its volatile nature allowing for overnight successes and failures, and for the artist to combine creativity with being a successful celebrity and business person. Seemingly tired of being tagged with this catchphrase, Warhol later wrote: 'I'm bored with that line. I never use it any more. My new line is, "In fifteen minutes everybody will be famous"' (*Exposures*, 1979).

The line appears in a stanza in Duran Duran's song 'Pop Trash Movie' (2000):

I'm living in a Pop Trash Movie
We star together in every scene
We'll all be famous for fifteen minutes
Part of a celluloid dream.

fascinating

One of Commander Spock's (Leonard Nimoy) recurring remarks on the original *Star Trek* TV series (1966–9). Spock, the Starship *Enterprise*'s half-Vulcan first officer, would pronounce his trademark judgement with intense scientific excitement or appreciation. Very often, what he found utterly 'fascinating' from a scientist's point of view would in fact prove to be a dangerous threat to the *Enterprise* and/or its crew. Typical examples of Spock's use of his catchphrase are: 'Fascinating, a life form, totally alien to our galaxy' or 'Fascinating. Pure energy. Pure thought. Totally incorporeal. Not life as we know it.' Questioned once about his use of the word, Spock replied: 'Fascinating is a word I use for the unexpected' (from the episode entitled *Squire of Gothos*).

faster than a speeding bullet

One of a set of superhuman traits attributed to Superman, the first comic-strip superhero, from the 1940s onwards. Created in 1938 in the US by writer Jerome Siegel and artist Joseph Shuster, Superman later featured in radio serials, television, and films. When Superman proved his popularity in the comic books, leading to the first ever comic book devoted to a single character, DC Comics decided to find another medium in which to promote him. So, in February 1940, the first episode of what would become a popular radio serial went on the air complete with the first version of what would soon become the most famous opening signature in history: 'Faster than an airplane! More powerful than a locomotive! Impervious to bullets! Up in the sky— look! It's a giant bird! It's a plane! It's...SUPERMAN!' By 1942 Superman was flying over the airwaves daily, and he continued to do so until 1951.

Superman, the TV series filmed in black-and-white, starring George Reeves, ran from 1953 to 1957. By then, the aeroplane had already been replaced by the speeding bullet and the entire voiced-over opening went as follows: 'Faster than a speeding bullet. More powerful than a locomotive. Able to leap tall buildings in a single bound—Look! up in the sky! It's a bird, It's a plane. It's Superman!...Yes, it's Superman—strange visitor from another planet who came to Earth with powers and abilities far beyond those of mortal men. Superman—who can change the course of mighty rivers, bend steel with his bare hands, and who, disguised as Clark Kent, mild-mannered reporter for a great metropolitan newspaper, fights the never-ending battle for *Truth, Justice and the American Way*.' A more up-to-date use of the phrase appeared in a 1999 newspaper headline: 'How the Internet moves faster than a speeding bullet' (23 September, *The Canadian Press*).

feel the velvet

From an advertising slogan for Canadian Black Velvet Whiskey during the mid-1980s, that became popular largely due to its notoriety. While the wording seemed to refer simply to the smoothness of the drink on one's palate, the accompanying ad was far more suggestive, drawing so much criticism that it was eventually pulled. In the ad, the Black Velvet whiskey bottle is placed under an attractive young woman in a strapless, black velvet evening gown. The caption, 'Feel the Velvet Canadian' is positioned over the figure in such a way that the words, 'feel the', are squarely over her breasts.

finish him|her!

An exclamation popularized by a series of Nintendo computer games, Game Boy, and PlayStation called *Mortal Kombat*. In the game, players choose one of a number of fighters to fight in a random realm against a human player or the computer. With fighters engaging in martial arts/supernatural combat to the death, the tournament known as *Mortal Kombat* has advanced progressively from the original 1992 version to the fourth instalment (2000) in this ultra-violent series. Players must use a series of special moves, including projectiles, to defeat their opponent twice in three rounds of fighting. After the opponent is defeated, the fight MC announces 'Finish Him!' The player then has a few seconds to perform a special sequence of joystick positions and button combinations to have his or her character 'perform a fatality'. Two films—*Mortal Kombat* (1995) and *Mortal Kombat II: Annihilation* (1997)—and an animation series have been based on the game.

flavour of the week|month|day

A US ice-cream parlour advertising phrase familiar by the 1940s, which would single out a particular ice cream flavour for the week or month for special promotion. The phrase became mainly associated with the Howard Johnson's chain which was extremely popular up until the 1980s. Each restaurant was topped with a bright orange roof so the traveller would immediately recognize the restaurant. This became a beacon to the travellers as Howard Johnson's became known not only for its reasonable prices but also its added lure of ice cream in 28 flavours. The phrase later became an idiom for the current fashion or craze, or someone who enjoys a short period of great popularity.

flippin' kids!

Associated with British comedian Tony Hancock on the early 1950s BBC radio show *Educating Archie*, scripted by comedian Eric Sykes. Hancock appeared alongside Hattie Jacques but surprisingly (for radio) the stars of the show were a ventriloquist's dummy called Archie Andrews and its operator, Peter Brough. Hancock's catchphrase—'flippin' kids!' caught on with the public at large, increasing his popularity and helping him to move on to television and his own shows.

flobbadob

A patois used by the puppets Bill and Ben in the BBC children's programme *The Flowerpot Men* (1952–4). It was the second *Watch with Mother* programme after *Andy Pandy* and the work of the same team. Bill and Ben, the Flowerpot Men, lived in flowerpots near a potting shed at the bottom of a garden owned by a sinister but unseen gardener. The characters were designed as identical twins, their bodies shaped like flowerpots, their legs made of small pots stacked one on top of the other, and their playthings were man-sized. Their companion was a weed—called Little Weed, also known as 'Ipple Weeb'—who told them when it was safe to come out and play or when the gardener was returning.

Those 'flobbadobs' and 'flibbadobs', which some parents claimed were impairing their children's speech development, were created by Peter Hawkins, who later put words into the mouths of Captain Pugwash and the Daleks. The series returned to TV screens in January 2001 with a 26-part series. The pair, with their friend, Little Weed, received a 21st-century makeover, which replaced their strings with stop-frame animation, and made their faces bigger and more expressive, to appeal to modern children. However, Bill and Ben continued to converse in their own dialect, 'flobbadob', which is translated by a narrator.

fly the friendly skies

Advertising slogan for United Airlines introduced in 1965. By 1970, the airline's identity became tied to this slogan which, in its full form was: 'fly the friendly skies of United'. Created by the giant Chicago agency, Leo Burnett, and dropped only in the mid-1990s, it became one of the longest-running and most memorable advertising campaigns in aviation history. With attitudes about air travel undergoing major changes, United eventually opted for a shift in its advertising. As a report in *Time* magazine's Business section (16 June 1997) notes, even though United 'was enjoying a record year financially', the airline decided to sack Burnett in October 1996 because 'today's hate-to-fly passengers hardly regard the skies as friendly'.

follow your dreams... BEEFCAKE!

From the US TV cartoon series *South Park* (1997–), spoken by Eric 'Beefcake' Cartman. Eric Cartman is the overweight, obnoxious son of a single mother who spoils him dreadfully with high-fat junk food. The obscenity-spouting Cartman often sings insulting songs, but his favourite is 'Come Sail Away', which he insists on finishing whenever someone starts singing it. He seems to have an unknowing sense of the surreal and outrageous, dressing up as Hitler for a Halloween party and using his somewhat absurd and self-deluding, but immensely popular, line: 'Follow your dreams, you can reach your goals, I'm living proof, beefcake! BEEFCAKE!!!'

The show, created by Trey Parker and Matt Stone, features the antics of four foul-mouthed 8-year-olds—Cartman, Kyle, Kenny, and Stan—as well as rest of South Park's inhabitants, including their often dubious parents, the school teacher, chef, bus driver, and many more—debuted on Comedy Central in August 1997. At its peak, in 1999, the show attracted some 6 million viewers. In the UK, *South Park* also hit the nation's TV screens on Channel 4 and Sky in summer 1997, repeating its US success. In 2000, the film *South Park: Bigger, Longer, Uncut* was released. Media Index claimed the movie packed 399 'bad words' and 128 'crude gestures' into just 80 minutes. The film was eventually released in America with an 'R' rating—meaning anyone under 17 had to be accompanied by an adult.

Although it is aimed at adults, *South Park* has built up a cult following among adults and children alike. Fuelled by screenings on Sky and Channel 4, *South Park* has become a playground cult in the UK. The show has been criticized in the UK by schools, at least two of which wrote to appeal to parents to ban their children from watching the show. The King's School in Ely, wrote to parents telling them that the cartoon was 'filth of a most unsavoury nature' and should not be watched by younger children. Although he can at times elicit a little sympathy, if not pity, Cartman is surely one of the show's assortment of consistently 'unsavoury' characters.

for real

Remark, meaning seriously or 'that's something', popularized by Ali G, an uneducated, misogynistic, black man from Staines played by Sacha Baron Cohen—a Jewish, Cambridge-educated white comedian—on Channel 4's *Ali G Show* (2000). Always appearing in his trademark yellow FUBU track-suit, wrap-around shades, chunky gold jewellery, and Tommy Hilfiger hat, Ali G first appeared on Channel 4's topical satire comedy series *The 11 O'Clock Show* (1998–), interviewing prominent politicians and personalities (asking them inane questions which they would try to answer seriously, believing him to be a legitimate, straight-faced TV interviewer). *Da Best of Ali G* (1999) showed highlights of these interviews.

for the man who has everything

Advertising slogan originating in the US in the 1950s, and used by numerous brands and businesses ever since. Just one example was its use by Pulsar, the brand name of The Time Computer Company of Lancaster, Pennsylvania (USA), formerly the Hamilton Watch Company. During the 1970s, one of the corporate advertising slogans for their LED time-only wristwatches was 'the man who has everything won't be happy until he has Pulsar'. Another popular variation was 'What do you give/buy a man who has everything?'

42!

Catchphrase or 'catch-all answer' from Douglas Adams's *The Hitchhiker's Guide to the Galaxy*, which began as a BBC radio science-fiction comedy series, was published as a novel in 1979, and then serialized for television in 1981. *The Hitchhiker's Guide to the Galaxy* was extremely popular during the late 1970s and early 1980s, becoming the source of several catchphrases (see also 'I'm so depressed' and 'don't panic!'). The series follows the exploits of Arthur Dent, who is is rescued by Ford Prefect (a non-belligerent alien) just before Earth is destroyed by an alien fleet to make way for a hyperspace bypass. Dent discovers that Earth was really was an experiment by mice to discover the answer to Life's ultimate question. The Earth's destruction provides the sought-after answer—42—but not the formulation of the question to which it is the answer. The answer is eventually supplied by the computer Deep Thought: 'The Answer to the Great Question Of...Life, the Universe and Everything...[is] Forty-two'. (1979, ch. 27). The catchphrase is employed in Zadie Smith's novel *White Teeth* (2000) to describe how cigarette smoking is viewed by many teenagers: 'Smoking was their answer to the universe, their 42, their *raison d'être*. They were passionate about fags.'

Francisco Franco is still dead

A catchphrase of US comedian Chevy Chase as anchorman on *Saturday Night Live*'s mock news segment, 'Weekend Update'. The TV comedy sketch series first went on the air in 1975, and Spain's Generalissimo Francisco Franco died in November 1975, while Chevy Chase was playing the cheeky anchorman. Chase was so clearly elated by the death of the Europe's last fascist dictator that, for weeks afterward, he kept announcing the news of Franco's death. A typical example of the start of a Chevy Chase-anchored 'Weekend Update' during that period would begin (after Chase is caught by the camera in the middle of an intimate phone conversation): 'Good evening, I'm Chevy Chase, and you're not! Our top story tonight: Generalissimo Francisco Franco is still dead. Secretary of State Henry Kissinger stated today that he is tired of using his silly accent in public, and will speak in English…' (13 December 1975).

Frankie Says Relax

A catchphrase of the early 1980s, when it appeared on T-shirts across Britain and then the US after the song, 'Relax (Don't Do It)' by the British band Frankie Goes to Hollywood hit it big in 1983. What really distinguished the group was not their music, but their marketing campaign, which focused on a series of slogans, T-shirts, and homoerotic videos. Everyone in the music video produced for this song wore T-shirts with big bold letters crying out for you to relax. The gist of the entire marketing campaign, devised by former music journalist Paul Morley, was an intentionally bold command, one which was eventually seen as offensive or pretentious. 'Relax' shot to number one in the UK charts in January 1984, but the Frankie sensation was virtually over by 1986. The song is featured in an episode of the US animated series *The Simpsons*, in which one of the boys on the school bus wears a T-shirt with, 'Frankie Says: Relax' written on it.

Frasier has left the building

A concluding voice-over for the *Frasier* theme song (sung by Kelsey Grammer), played at the end of each episode of the award-winning US TV comedy series since 1993. Some of the theme song's lyrics vary every episode, and this particular line is one that appears periodically, as in: 'But I don't know what to do with those tossed salads and scrambled eggs. They're callin' again. Frasier has left the building!' The phrase, playing on the earlier catchphrase 'Elvis has left the building', parodies the pompous Dr Frasier Crane's often inflated sense of self-importance.

The phrase involving Elvis Presley has become so much a part of American pop culture that it may show up in anything from a documentary on Elvis Presley to a science fiction movie. In the US alien invasion film *Independence Day* (1996), a hero speeds away from an exploding alien mothership with the announcement, 'Elvis has left the building'. Various persons associated with 'the King' have claimed responsibility for the phrase's coinage. The expression is said to date from Elvis's 1950s performances on the old Louisiana Hayride show in Shreveport, Louisiana, and was a way to get people out of the building at the end of a concert. The minute Elvis left the stage he ran to a waiting car to speed away before the crowds could catch up with him; the announcer then used the phrase to disperse the crowd. Al Dvorin, band director and booking agent for Elvis in the early years, and his stage announcer into the 1970s, became the person most associated with the phrase.

freeze! This is Miami Vice!

Associated with cynical Miami vice detective James 'Sonny' Crockett (Don Johnson) on *Miami Vice*, an NBC police drama which ran from 1984 to 1989, who would accompany the phrase with a menacingly pointed handgun. The stylish, MTV-influenced series (music by rock composer Jan Hammer) was a smash hit, and transformed struggling actor Don Johnson into a 1980s icon. His linen pastel blazers worn over a T-shirt, his famous stubble, no socks, and an angry scowl started a men's fashion revolution. Crockett was TV's first anti-establishment 'narc', and seemed to represent the contradictions of the Reagan era in which drugs figured prominently and were often mixed with politics.

fuhgeddaboutit

Forget about it, spoken with an Italian-American pronunciation. It was popularized in the late 1990s, first through its use in the 1997 US film *Donnie Brasco*, based on the true story of an FBI agent who infiltrates the mob (starring Johnny Depp and Al Pacino), and then by the US TV series *The Sopranos* (1999–   ). The award-winning New Jersey-based mobster series has not only featured 'Italianized' English words or phrases such as this one, but has been credited for creating

'Sopranospeak', or at least popularizing 'mobspeak'—a street
language that employs bastardized Italian-American forms of Italian
words. *Fuhgeddaboutit*, a tongue-in-cheek handbook for becoming a
'wiseguy', by joke-writer Jon Macks, was published in 2001.

fully functional

Words associated with the android Lieutenant Commander Data
(Brent Spiner), the Starship *Enterprise-D*'s science officer, on the US TV
series *Star Trek: The Next Generation* (1987–94). As designed, Data is
programmed not to lie or deceive, recalls everything he has ever been
exposed to, cannot use verbal contractions, and has super-human
strength, dexterity, voice duplication, self-diagnostics, and 'fully
functional' male sexual abilities without the emotional attraction.

While Data has a total linear computational speed rated at sixty
trillion operations per second, he also has an emotion chip, which
Chief Engineer Georgi LaForge (LeVar Burton) helped him install in
2371. Although the chip cannot be forcibly removed, Data can turn it
on and off. In the 1996 film *Star Trek: First Contact*, the chip proved an
Achilles' heel during Data's capture by the Borg Queen, when she
literally tempted him with sensations of the flesh he had never
experienced despite his growing worldliness. When she enquired
about his abilities with regard to certain forms of physical
interaction, implying sexual relations, Data pointed out that he was
'fully functional'. In the end, the emotional data overload was not
enough to overrule his ethics programme.

funny how?

Tense, if not neurotic, questioning employed repeatedly by Tommy
(Joe Pesci) in Martin Scorsese's 1990 film *Goodfellas*, a gritty,
unflinching treatment of a true mobster story about three violent
'wiseguys' (Mafia slang for 'gangsters'). Tommy, one of the 'wiseguys',
exhibits the first signs of his quick-trigger, psychotic, pathological
temper as he entertains other mobsters with hilarious tales of violence
laced with swear words. But when Henry (Ray Liotta) chuckles at his
friend, saying 'You're a pisser. You're really funny. You're really funny'
the cheerful scene immediately turns sour and the tension mounts as
a clearly aggravated Tommy persists in asking in a cold-blooded,
fearsome, yet ambiguous tone: 'Funny how? I mean, funny like I'm a

clown? I amuse you? I make you laugh? I'm here to fuckin' amuse you? How da fuck am I funny? What da fuck is so funny about me? Tell me, tell me what's funny.' Pesci won an Oscar for his performance as the increasingly psychotic full Sicilian Tommy De Vito.

funny thing happened to me on the way to the theatre (tonight), a

A line that has its origins in traditional music-hall and vaudeville acts, where it was used to introduce a joke or move on to a new, unrelated subject. The phrase was a favourite of Lucy (Lucille Ball) and her husband, Desi Arnaz, during the early 1940s. Their appearance together in a vaudeville-style stage revue in New York in 1942 later inspired the successful TV sitcom, *I Love Lucy*. Here's just one instance of the phrase's use in their stage exchanges:

Ricky: Say Lucy.
Lucy : Yeah Ricky.
Ricky: You know a funny thing happened to me on the way to the theatre tonight.
Lucy : What?
Ricky: A tramp came up to me in the street and he said he hadn't had a bite in weeks.
Lucy : What'd you do, bite him?

The phrase, along with its many variations, became popular with comedians who soon made the line itself the butt of jokes, as in a 1954 *Goon Show* episode entitled 'The Canal' which had guest star Valentine Dyall saying 'A funny thing happened to me on my way to the theatre tonight—a steam roller ran over my head. So much for humour—and now pray allow me to tell the story of . . .' By the 1950s, variations on the phrase were being used to add comic levity in diverse situations and professions. After his defeat in the presidential election in 1952, in which Eisenhower won a landslide victory, Adlai Stevenson said, in a speech: 'A funny thing happened to me on the way to the White House.' The phrase was popularized again in the 1960s with the Broadway musical *A Funny Thing Happened on the Way to the Forum* (1962), which was adapted for film in 1966. The frenzied musical farce about a conniving slave in ancient Roman times starred Zero Mostel in what many considered his best comedy role.

future's bright. The future's orange, the

Advertising slogan for the Orange telecommunications company since 1994. A relative latecomer to the UK mobile phone market, Orange made up for lost time by launching an aggressive, avant-garde advertising campaign. Orange's endline goes well with the surreal quality of its advertising and the use of the colour orange. In fact, the incongruity of the brand name within the telecommunications sector helped to make both the name and the slogan more memorable.

The choice of the company name, to begin with, was clearly part of a wider choice of image and potential advertising concepts, including the catchy slogan.

Gg

·········

George—don't do that

A catchphrase associated with British actress and writer Joyce
Grenfell, used repeatedly in her 'Nursery School Sketches' (1953), and
as the title of her 1977 book. Grenfell, who also appeared in many
films including the St Trinian's series, was famous for her hilarious
radio monologues. The one that was most popular with audiences was
'The Nursery Teacher', which developed out of 'How to Talk to
Chidren' on the *How to* radio series. It was never quite clear what
George was actually doing when his teacher would need to pause and
utter warningly: 'George, don't do that!'

get down, Shep!

Spoken by *Blue Peter* presenter John Noakes after he joined the regular
cast on the popular BBC TV children's programme in 1965. Sporting a
Beatle haircut, Noakes became an instant hit with the public as he
undertook a series of daredevil stunts such as scaling Nelson's
Column. He also had a pet of his own—a black and white collie
by the name of Shep. John and Shep became inseparable on the
series, and John's good-humoured admonition became a nationwide catchphrase. It soon became almost a cliché as well as the butt
of many jokes. See also 'here's one I made earlier (or prepared
earlier . . .)'.

get out!

An American expression from the 1980s meaning 'I don't believe it',
or 'you must be kidding'. It was popularized by Elaine Benes (Julia
Louis-Dreyfus) on the highly successful US TV comedy series *Seinfeld*
(1989–98), starring comedian Jerry Seinfeld and his fictional friends.
Elaine (Seinfeld's ex-lover and good friend) would often issue this cry
of disbelief with some physicality, giving the person delivering the

unbelievable information a two-handed push on the chest, sometimes knocking the person over or across the room.

get out of that!

From a running gag on the TV shows of British comedians Morecambe and Wise (1961–83). The tall, bespectacled Eric Morecambe would suddenly stop, clap an out-stretched hand under his partner's chin and say: 'get out of that!' (often followed by: 'You can't can you!'). With the success of their first ATV series from 1961 to 1968, Morecambe and Wise, along with their various catchphrases, became firmly established in the minds of the British television public. As their popularity grew, the quality of their guests also improved and, in December 1963, they recorded a show with The Beatles. During the exchange between the rock band and the show's hosts, Paul McCartney parodied Morecambe's description of Wise being the one with the 'short fat hairy legs'. George Harrison then said, 'We're the ones with the big fat hairy heads. Get out of that!' Harrison put his hand (opened flat, palm down) under Morecambe's chin while uttering the famous catchphrase.

get over here

A catchphrase from *Mortal Kombat*, a series of computer games and other products on the market since 1992, as well two feature films (see 'Finish Him/Her'). The infamous thundering call belongs to Scorpion, one of the fighters against which players or the computer plays. Scorpion is a spectre (having been killed by his rival Sub-Zero), and a professional assassin for the group of Ninjas known as the Shirai Ryu bent on revenge.

get thar fustest with the mostest

The military dictum popularly ascribed to US Confederate General Nathan Bedford Forrest, recommending speed combined with large numbers of men to win battles. Promoted to the rank of brigadier-general in 1862, Forrest led raids against Union forces throughout the South. As his saying clearly suggests, Forrest had little formal schooling. However, he accumulated enough wealth through slave dealing to buy land in Mississippi and establish a cotton plantation, and in 1866 he founded the Ku Klux Klan. *Fustest with the Mostest: The Military Career of Tennessee's Greatest Confederate, Lt. Gen. Nathan Bedford Forrest*, by Edward F. Williams III, was published in 1969.

In more recent years the saying has become a mantra among company managers and directors, and particularly 'commanders' of the Internet economy, where the strategic concept is 'Move fast, occupy territory, win big'.

get your knickers on and make us a cup of tea

Popularized by comedian Simon Day on the BBC TV comedy series *The Fast Show* (1994–7). The catchphrase belongs to TV character Monkfish, played by 'John Actor' (Simon Day), whose sketches were parodies of BBC drama series, with names like 'Monkfish: Undercover Cop', 'Monkfish, MD', and (as a veterinarian) 'All Monkfish Great and Small'. Monkfish's trademark line would find its way into the dialogue of all his sketches as when Inspector Monkfish arrives at the scene of a murder, turns to the wife of the deceased and says: 'Excuse me, I realize this must be a very difficult time for you, so put yer knickers on an' go an' make me a cup o' tea!'

give 'im|'er the money, Barney!

That is correct, you win! One of Wilfred Pickles's catchphrases, delivered on his popular BBC radio quiz show *Have a Go* (1946–67). During the series he visited factories, hospitals, and other venues around Britain and talked to ordinary people, giving small cash prizes for simple questions. (See also 'are yer courtin'?') The Barney referred to in the phrase was Barney Colehan, producer of the series, who, upon hearing these words would be informed (along with the listeners) of the latest winner. Originally, the prizes had been handed out by Mabel, Pickles's wife, and the well-known catchphrase had been 'What's on the table, Mabel?' until she retired from the show and Colehan took over.

give me a hug

Catchphrase of Danny Tanner (played by Bob Saget) on the US sitcom *Full House* (1987–95). The series centres on Danny, an archetypal 'nice guy', and how he copes when he is left to raise his three young daughters by himself after his wife's death. Claims about the therapeutic nature of hugs, including the benefits of 'group hugs', were popular in the US from the early 1980s.

give us a twirl!

Line delivered weekly by Bruce Forsyth to his television hostess Anthea Redfern (later his wife) on BBC's *Generation Game* from 1971 to 1977, and again at the beginning of the 1990s. At its peak, when the TV game show attracted 20 million viewers, this and Forsyth's other catchphrases—'nice to see you, to see you nice' and 'Didn't he do well?'—became familiar in households across the nation.

go ahead, make my day!

A provocation and potentially a warning, suggesting ironically that a certain response would only give pleasure to the issuer. Originally spoken by Detective Harry Callahan (Clint Eastwood) in the film *Sudden Impact* (1983), the fourth instalment in the 'Dirty Harry' series. Eastwood's cool San Francisco cop tries to bring criminals to justice, but when he finds himself being hemmed in at every turn by the rules and regulations dictated by civil liberties, he turns roguish. When an armed thug threatens a hostage Harry is trying to free, the ironic, embittered detective eggs him on with his Magnum. At the end of the film (screenplay by Joseph Stinson), Eastwood says 'Come on, make my day'.

The phrase was reminiscent, in tone and attitude, of another famous line used in the Dirty Harry series: when Harry has a gunman cornered and wondering how many shots he has left, he says, 'You've gotta ask yourself one question: Do you feel lucky? Well, do ya, punk?' In the climate of 1980s Reaganomics, 'Go Ahead, Make My Day' and the angry frustration of the Dirty Harry character, effectively expressed a mood of blue-collar fear and discontent in a country portrayed as being run by bureaucrats, sociologists, and incompetents without any backbone.

In the US, there is a law—the Domestic Protection Bill—called 'Go Ahead, Make My Day', named after Eastwood's famous line. As one might guess, the 'Make My Day' law gives homeowners and apartment dwellers the right to use deadly force against a person who has entered a residence unlawfully, if there is reason to believe the intruder has committed a crime. The occupant also must have reason to believe the intruder intends to use force.

go for gold!

A slogan used as an encouragement to aim for a gold medal or the ultimate reward. It was first used by the US Olympic team at the Lake Placid Winter Olympics in 1980, but by the time of the 1984 Olympics other teams (including the UK) had also taken it up. *Going for Gold* was the title of a 1983 thriller by Emma Lathen and of a BBC TV quiz that began in 1987. The words had actually formed part of a 1832 political slogan—'To Stop the Duke, Go for Gold'—which was intended to prevent the Duke of Wellington, who was unpopular for his opposition to parliamentary reform, from forming a government in the run up to the Reform Bill (enacted that year). The slogan was coined in May 1832 by Francis Place, a radical politician, for a poster campaign apparently aimed at causing a run on gold at the Bank of England.

go on

Words of persuasion popularized by Mrs Doyle (played by Pauline McLynn) on the Channel 4 TV comedy series *Father Ted* (1995–8), written by Graham Linehan and Arthur Matthews. The series is set in and around the Parochial House on Craggy Island, a small island off the west coast of Ireland, home to three priests—the embarrassment prone Father Ted Crilly (Dermot Morgan), the happily oblivious young Father Dougal McGuire (Ardal O'Hanlon), and semi-conscious reprobate Father Jack Hackett (Frank Kelly)—and one housekeeper—Mrs Doyle, who keeps an eye on events over an ever-boiling kettle. Mrs Doyle is endlessly plying the priests and their visitors with cups of tea and biscuits or sandwiches, repeating her catchphrase until they give in, usually simply in order to get her to stop. Her trademark 'Ah, go on, go on, go on' became so well known that McLynn was recruited by the Inland Revenue in 2001 in its TV and radio campaign urging Britons to fill in their tax returns in time and, if preferred, online: 'Go on, go on, go online!'

For Mrs Doyle, tea preparation is a truly special and rewarding activity: 'Father, I LOVE the whole tea-making thing! You know, the playful "splash!" of the tea as it hits the bottom of the cup; the thrill of adding the milk, and watching it settle for a moment, before it filters slowly down through the cup, changing the colour from dark brown to...a lighter brown. Perching an optional Jaffa cake on the saucer, like a proud soldier standing to attention beside a giant...cup of tea!'

go to bed, old man!

Line used by US stand-up comedian Dana Gould in his stage routine during the late 1980s and the 1990s. Gould's trademark angst is often expressed in his painfully realistic impressions of his family, his father often being the target of his insolent catchphrase.

God will get you for that

Catchphrase of Maude Findlay (Beatrice Arthur) on the US TV sitcoms *All in the Family* (1971–9) and *Maude* (1972–8). *All in the Family* focused on the blue-collar household of Archie Bunker (Carroll O'Connor) and his slightly vacuous, but sweet, wife, Edith (Jean Stapleton). Maude Findlay was Edith's progressive-minded cousin, who enjoyed taking Archie to task for his sexist attitudes. Maude eventually became so popular with audiences she earned her own show. She would respond with her menacing catchphrase when she disapproved of something or was angered by someone, most often her husband Walter (Bill Macy).

goit

Insult and favourite saying of Commander Arnold 'Ace' Rimmer (Christopher Barrie) on the cult BBC TV science fiction sitcom *Red Dwarf* (1988–92), directed mainly at Dave Lister (Craig Charles), 'the last human alive'. The show's two central characters have quite low opinions of each other, and Rimmer, on board the Red Dwarf mining ship as a hologram, often ends up arguing with Lister, calling him a 'stupid, ugly goit' or a 'jammy goit'. Reminiscent of both 'git' and 'goitre', or possibly a combination of the two, Rimmer's trademark insult is basically a nonsensical invention with a distinctly offensive ring. See also 'smeg, or smeghead' and 'smoke me a kipper, I'll be back for breakfast!'

good game, good game!

One of British comedian Bruce Forsyth's catchphrases on the BBC TV show *The Generation Game*, which he hosted from 1971 to 1977 and 1990 to 1995. The line, spoken with an exaggeratedly ingratiating tone, was for the audience's benefit, as were many of his other recurring lines, such as 'didn't he (or she or they) do well?' (see above).

good God, man, get out of there!

Words of warning associated with Dr Leonard 'Bones' McCoy on the original US TV series *Star Trek* (1966–9). McCoy directs this phrase at Commander Spock (Leonard Nimoy) in the 1982 film, *Star Trek II: The Wrath of Khan*, when he tries desperately to stop his half-Vulcan friend from sacrificing himself in order to save the lives of the starship's crew. See also 'are you out of your Vulcan mind?'

good idea—son, a

Popularized by Max Bygraves on the BBC radio programme *Educating Archie* (1950–3) and in a song. Spoken in a heavy Cockney accent, these amiable words of endorsement became, along with 'bighead', Bygraves's best-known catchphrases. *A Good Idea—Son!*, a stand-up comedy show with Max Bygraves and written by Eric Sykes was broadcast on BBC TV in 1953. Bygraves became enormously popular on stage and television with his clever mix of song and patter.

good morning, sir, was there something?

From *Much-Binding-in-the-Marsh* (1944–54), one of the most popular BBC radio comedy series spawned from the war years. The series was first introduced as taking place in an RAF station, but by the early 1950s, as the RAF station ceased operating, the former staff ran a newspaper called the *Daily Bind*. The programmes were written by, and starred, Kenneth Horne and Richard Murdoch. Following on from *ITMA*, which was jam-packed with catchphrases, the characters each had their own, this being Sam Costa's. Maurice Denham, who played the upper class Dudley Davenport, was associated with 'Oh, I say, I am a fool!'

good night and may God bless

US comedian Red Skelton used these words to end his TV show from 1951 to 1971. *The Red Skelton Show* was one of America's longest-running comedy/variety series, show-casing Skelton's many original characters. See also 'I dood it'.

good to the last drop

The advertising slogan and registered trademark of Maxwell House coffee since 1907. Joel Cheek, a wholesale grocer in Nashville who specialized in coffee sales, had been hired by the Maxwell House Hotel to develop a new blend of coffee, and eventually came up with a very popular coffee that became known as 'Maxwell House' coffee. In 1907, while on a visit to 'The Hermitage', home of Andrew Jackson in Nashville, President Theodore Roosevelt was served a cup of Maxwell House coffee, and gave the brand its famous slogan by declaring 'It's good to the last drop!' Since this highly respected and youthful president (at 42, he was the youngest person to become president of the USA) liked this particular blend of coffee, no better publicity could possibly be found.

goodbye ... and God bless you

Farewell phrase used by Bud Collyer, US radio and TV personality, as host of the TV game show *To Tell the Truth* (1956–69). Collyer, the first game show superstar and a devout Christian, would send his contestants out with this phrase. As host of *Beat the Clock* and then *To Tell the Truth*, he was responsible for many catchphrases that entered the American lexicon of the late 1950s and the 1960s, such as 'Roxanne, who do we have now?' and 'Maybe next time will be YOUR time to *Beat the Clock*!' See also 'will the real — please stand up?' and 'always remember To Tell the Truth!'

goodness gracious me!

An expression emphasizing astonishment or surprise, associated with Peter Sellers's comic impersonation of an Indian doctor in a 1960 recording. In addition to his film and radio work, Sellers recorded several comedy albums, including the track 'Goodness Gracious Me' with Sophia Loren, based on their roles in the film *The Millionairess*, adapted from the George Bernard Shaw play and directed by Anthony Asquith. Sellers plays the Indian Doctor Kabir to Loren's beautiful Italian heiress. Though less slapstick than his portrayal of the accident-prone Indian actor in Blake Edwards's film *The Party* (1968), Sellers still brings his characteristic humorous fumbling to the role of the devoted doctor. Sellers's Indian impersonation became a classic, later emulated by many comic actors and comedians.

The song, which actually reached number 3 on the UK charts in November 1960, began:

Loren: Oh doctor, I'm in trouble.
Sellers: Well, goodness gracious me.
Loren: For every time a certain man
Is standing next to me.
Sellers: Mmm?
Loren: A flush comes to my face
And my pulse begins to race,
It goes boom boody-boom boody-boom boody-boom
Boody-boom boody-boom boody-boom-boom-boom,
Sellers: Oh!
Loren: Boom boody-boom boody-boom boody-boom
Sellers: Well, goodness gracious me.

Goodness Gracious Me! was also the title of a BBC radio comedy series from 1996 to 1998 which took its name—with the irony which was a hallmark of the show—from Peter Sellers's cod-Indian novelty hit of 1960. Sending up both British and Asian culture, was the team of Meera Syal, Sanjeev Bhaskar, Nina Wadia, and Kulvinder Ghir who created a series of unforgettable characters and a show that became a flagship for British–Asian comedy. Many of the sketches featured regular stock characters, including the Bollywood gossip columnist, 'Smita Smitten—Showbiz Kitten'; the all-Asian superhero, Bhangraman, who is able to avert disaster by practising traditional dance; and the bourgeois Kapoors, who insist their name is pronounced 'Cooper', play golf, and complain about immigration. The television version, also titled *Goodness Gracious Me!*, was shown on BBC2 from 1997 to 2000.

goodnight, children ... everywhere

Closing words normally spoken by presenter 'Uncle Mac', Derek McCullough, in the 1930s and 1940s on the BBC radio programme

Children's Hour (1922–64). Princess Elizabeth made her first broadcast on the programme, introduced by 'Uncle Mac' from Windsor Castle in October 1940. This highly enriching children's programme also helped launch Julie Andrews, James Galway, Brian Redhead, and many others. The popular closing phrase was also the title of a 1942 Gracie Fields song, and of an award-winning 1998 play by Richard Nelson which deals with the aspect of Second World War history that began in 1940 when air raids forced hundreds of thousands of London parents to send their children away to safety.

goodnight Mrs Calabash ... wherever you are

US comedian Jimmy Durante's trademark closing line from about 1940. For years, Durante ended his radio and television shows with this unusual, and somewhat mysterious, sign-off. Most people thought Mrs. Calabash was probably a fictional character that Durante introduced just to tease his audiences. But longtime residents of Calabash, North Carolina, apparently believe otherwise. The people of this town claim that Mrs Calabash was really a local woman named Lucille 'Lucy' Coleman, who ran a restaurant where Durante stopped once in 1940. It seems he met her, promised to 'make her famous', and when he left the restaurant he turned to her and said, 'Good night Mrs Calabash'.

Perhaps it was coincidental, but soon after that alleged encounter the popular entertainer began signing off his radio shows with a similar message. For years, audiences enjoyed this rather light-hearted farewell mystery. By the time of Durante's death, it had become one of his trademarks, one that was almost as distinguishing as his considerable 'schnozzola'.

goody, goody gumdrops!

A catchphrase belonging to Humphrey Lestocq, the host of BBC TV's early 1950s children's show *Whirligig*. One of the first exponents of variety on children's television, *Whirligig* was devised by Michael Westmore and was broadcast as a fortnightly Saturday afternoon treat. The show was actually hosted by a duo—the obnoxious string puppet Mr Turnip and his hapless stooge, Humphrey Lestocq, known to viewers as HL. While HL's catchphrase was 'Goody, Goody Gumdrops', Mr Turnip's was 'Lawky, Lawky, Lum'. 'Goody, Goody Gumdrops' was also the title of a 1968 song and album by the US band 1910 Fruitgum Co., masters of the so-called Bubblegum movement.

got a present for ya!

A positive exclamation from the real-time strategy computer game series *Command & Conquer* (1995–   ), spoken by the 'commando'. The highly popular games focus on the global conflict between the fictional Global Defense Initiative (the 'good guys') and the insidious Brotherhood of Nod organizations, and puts the player in complete charge of fast-paced, squad-level military operations utilizing a wide variety of troops, ground vehicles, base installations, air strikes, and production facilities. The player's commando sprite will unexpectedly shout, 'Got a present for ya!' before slapping a wad of C-4 to a SAM site, followed, a few seconds later by: 'KA-BOOM!'

gotta catch 'em all!

A term first used in the *Pokemon* video game which quickly became a craze among children after it first appeared in Japan in 1998. *Pokemon* began as a video game but soon expanded into cartoon series, comic books, trading cards, dolls, films, and more, around the globe. Part of a video game created by Nintendo for its Game Boy system, *Pokemon* (pronounced POH-kay-mahn) is the American name for 151 Pokemon cards, each with a brightly coloured picture of a cartoon character and geometric symbols which correspond to the powers of the character. The characters—called Pocket Monsters in Japan—each have their own power and personality. Whether one plays the video games or with the trading cards, the core of the Pokemon mission is summed up in its slogan: 'Gotta catch 'em all!' The player is challenged to become a Pokemon trainer, who must train Pokemon for battle and trade them with other trainers in hopes of capturing more Pokemon and becoming a Pokemon master.

This mission, summed up in the 'Gotta catch 'em all!' slogan, has led to criticism that Pokemon entails and fosters gambling. In April 2001, religious committee members in the United Arab Emirates issued a fatwa against Pokemon because of fears that it promotes gambling. The fatwa did not mean the game had been banned, as it has in other Muslim countries such as Saudi Arabia. However, it added to the growing religious resistance in the Middle East to the

game because of its perceived bad influence. The fatwa also warned
that the game promoted violence. Religious scholars in Qatar and
Egypt have also made Pokemon 'haram', or religiously prohibited.
The game has also come under fire in Christian countries such as
Mexico, where the Catholic Church called the game 'demonic'. In the
USA, many schools banned the trading cards because they were
believed to be distracting pupils from their studies. And in the UK,
police have urged parents not to allow children out with the cards,
although in school many have fought to get their hands on them.

government denies knowledge

This phrase, with its grim official stamp-like quality, is associated with
the US cult TV series *The X-Files* (1993–2002), flashing up for a second or
two during the opening titles of each episode. The formula also
succinctly describes FBI Special Agent Fox Mulder's (David Duchovny)
assessment of the high-level conspiracies he seems to meet
everywhere he turns.

grapes, like children, need love and affection

An advertising slogan for US wine manufacturer Almaden Vineyards,
now a product of Canandaigua Wine Company, Inc. The slogan dates
to the early 1980s, when various US wine manufacturers—such as
Almaden, Gallo, Masson, Inglenook, and Taylor—all took their
respective attempts at breaking through to consumers via television
advertising. This spot, though its slogan was both entertaining as a
simile and very catchy, was soon withdrawn, as were the others, when
it became clear money was being wasted on an audience that was
largely uncaring about wine. Interest in wine in the USA came years
later, after the Surgeon General claimed that moderate consumption
of red wine was actually good for one's health.

   Known for its quality wines, Almaden's heritage can be traced to
Etienne Theé, an émigré from Bordeaux, France, who founded
Almaden Vineyards, near Los Gatos, CA, in 1852.

greatest show on earth, the

A catchphrase used to describe a wide variety of spectacles and
events—from the Olympics, to the carnival in Rio de Janeiro, to the

wonders of nature. The billing was originally, and most famously, associated with P(hineas) T(aylor) Barnum and with the Ringling Brothers and Barnum and Bailey Circus. The US showman P. T. Barnum established what he called the 'Greatest Show on Earth' in 1871 (now a registered trademark), featuring a circus, a 'Great Roman Hippodrome', and much more. Barnum merged his business with that of his chief competitor, Bailey, from 1881 to 1885, and then again in 1888. The first performance of Ringling Bros. and Barnum & Bailey was held in New York City's Madison Square Garden in 1919, and this integral part of American culture has continued to entertain audiences to this day under this name.

The 1952 academy award-winning Cecil B. DeMille epic *The Greatest Show on Earth*, starring James Stewart, was produced with the cooperation of the Ringling Bros. Barnum & Bailey Circus. 'Astronomers prepare for the greatest show on earth' was the title of an article published on 17 November 1998 by *Australian Broadcasting News* (online version), about preparations to watch the 10-hour Leonid meteor shower, 'expected to be the century's most spectacular display of shooting stars'.

greatest tragedy is indifference, the

An advertising slogan for the Red Cross since 1961, and a concept which effectively prods the conscience of potential donors. The Red Cross is an international organization concerned with the alleviation of human suffering and the promotion of public health. The Red Cross or Red Crescent flag has become the world-recognized symbol of mercy and absolute neutrality. The phrase has been adopted by those wishing to appeal for action in the face of crises of varying orders.

There are always numerous situations in which groups of people's quality of life or health care and prospects are determined by the delivery or absence of active care. As Dr Robert Taylor pointed out at a Society of Critical Care Medicine (SCCM) Educational and Scientific Symposium on 24 January 1999: 'Continued improvement in the quality of critical care is not only possible, it's obligatory. I firmly believe that the greatest tragedy is indifference.'

greetings, gate!

Trademark greeting of Jerry Colonna, US character actor distinguished by a walrus moustache, wild-eyed expression, and distinctive zany voice. A long-time sidekick of Bob Hope, Colonna appeared as a supporting player on the Hope radio, television, and USO shows. Colonna was caricatured in a number of Warner Bros. cartoons, and many of his catchphrases, including this one, found their way into cartoons produced during the 1940s. It obviously provided inspiration for the title of *Greetings Bait* (1943), a cartoon directed by Friz Freleng, at the end of which Colonna himself makes an appearance as the fisherman. Variations on the greeting appeared in numerous WB cartoon films, including *Slightly Daffy* (1944), where an American Indian says 'Greetings, Gate, lets scalpitate!', and in *The Wise Quacking Duck* (1943), in which Daffy Duck says 'Greetings, Gate, let's osculate!'

Guinness is good for you

An advertising slogan for Guinness Brewery since 1929. The phrase became famous throughout Britain and Ireland, although it would not be allowed under current advertising legislation. Since the years immediately following the First World War through to today, the line has also remained the basis of Guinness advertising overseas. The adage came from a British advertising campaign of the 1920s, which surveyed drinkers, asking why they favoured Guinness. The most common response was 'Because it does me good'. The slogan was discontinued at the beginning of the 1940s because of the disapproval the claim would be met with—it would be considered misleading, if not unethical, to tell consumers alcohol was good for their health when medical findings did not substantiate the claim and actually showed the opposite. It was revived again in the early 1960s, but has not been used since 1963. Although relatively short-lived, it is one of Britain's most familiar slogans, ranking among the top ten slogans voted into the UK's Advertising Slogan Hall of Fame.

guns before butter

A political catchphrase—sometimes 'guns or butter'—attributed to both Joseph Goebbels and Hermann Goering, though its precise origins are unclear. In a speech delivered in Berlin on 17 January 1936, Goebbels, Nazi Minister of Propaganda, said: 'We can do without butter, but, despite all our love of peace, not without arms. One cannot shoot with butter, but with guns.' However, earlier in the summer of that year, in a radio broadcast on the Four Year Plan, Field Marshal Hermann Goering announced, 'Guns will make us powerful; butter will only make us fat'.

In any event, the choice to be made—arms in favour of unnecessary material goods—became a clear element of Nazi ideology and propaganda. German Nazi leader Rudolf Hess, who had signed the decree for the introduction of compulsory military service in March 1935, in a speech that he made on 11 October 1936, took up Goering's cry of 'Guns before Butter' when he said: 'We are prepared in the future, too, if need be, at times to eat a little less fat, a little less pork, a few eggs, since we know that this little sacrifice is a sacrifice on the altar of the freedom of our people. We know that the foreign exchange which we thereby save, expedites the output of armaments'. In fact, Goering's 'Guns before Butter' four-year economic plan (1935–9) boosted armaments and helped ready the country for war.

Hh

· · · · · · · · · · · ·

Ha, ha, ha, I kill me!

A charmingly ungrammatical, somewhat self-lauding, expression
popularized by Alf (Alien Life Form), the furry extraterrestrial star of
the US TV comedy series *ALF* (1986–90). Stranded on Earth, Alf (voiced
by series co-creator Paul Fusco) becomes a part of the Tanner family
and, when he's not getting into trouble, enjoys cracking jokes, often
remarking on his own abilities to amuse or astound, this phrase being
one way of noting just how funny he is. Alf, with his distinctively big,
ridged snout, was a puppet in stationary scenes, while diminutive
actor Micah Maestros would be dressed up as the alien for walking
scenes. Unlike other sitcoms of the late 1980s, *ALF* was highly
popular with children, leading to two cartoon spin-offs. (See
also 'hey, Willie'.)

hang the Kaiser!

Originating probably with remarks made by British First World War
soldiers, intended to vent feelings and put speculation about Kaiser
Wilhelm II and Germany aside from consideration, the words were
taken up as a slogan by British Prime Minister Lloyd George and his
coalition government. It became a popular political slogan in 1918
after Lloyd George, in a series of impassioned addresses, had rallied
his fellow-citizens to this cry, viewed as a fit reply to the German
'Gott strafe England!' (God punish England). Lloyd George
achieved a huge majority in the 1918 elections, and, having a
major role in the Versailles peace treaty in 1919, made sure the
Allies committed themselves to bringing Wilhelm II to justice.
This was, however, not to be, and Wilhelm II died in 1941 of natural
causes.

The anti-Kaiser sentiments embodied by the slogan were
widespread before the end of the war as part of a stanza from an anti-
war poem by Carl Sandburg, entitled 'The Four Brothers', shows:

Eating to kill,
Sleeping to kill,
Asked by their mothers to kill,
Wished by four-fifths of the world to kill—
To cut the kaiser's throat,
To hack the kaiser's head,
To hang the kaiser on a high-horizon gibbet.

Initially published on 29 October 1917 in the *Chicago Evening Post*, where Sandburg was a staff writer, it soon reached thousands of readers via reprints in newspapers and magazines across the country.

happiness is a warm gun

Title of a song written by John Lennon, on the Beatles' 1968 *White Album*. It seems that the song was only indirectly inspired by Charles Schulz's cartoon strip *Peanuts* (1950–2000), as the title, parodying the popular *Peanuts* adage 'Happiness is a warm puppy', was actually taken from an ad in an issue of *Soldier of Fortune* magazine. Lennon, an active pacifist, apparently saw the firearms ad, was both outraged and inspired by the combined sexual/macabre twist to so innocent a saying, and so wrote the tune, which includes these lines:

When I hold you in my arms,
And I feel my finger on your trigger,
I know, I know no one can do me no harm,
Because happiness is a warm gun.

The song's witty sexual imagery and innuendo effectively ridicule and denounce the entire pro-gun mentality.

The *Peanuts* book *Happiness is a Warm Puppy* appeared in 1962, and alternated pages with adages and aphorisms with illustrations matched to those sayings. The great success of this book ensured that there would be many more such prose-and-picture books to follow, including *Happiness is a Sad Song* and numerous revised editions of *Happiness is a Warm Puppy*. The saying spawned countless bumper stickers and ads in the US and the UK, including 'Happiness is a Quick-Starting Car' and 'Happiness is a Cigar Called Hamlet'.

happy da!

A greeting popularized by US comedian David Letterman, while hosting the popular TV talk show *Late Night with David Letterman*

(1982–). Letterman would use this silly salutation at the beginning of his shows, as a recurring feature of his 'intro'.

happy days

An expression, meaning everything's great or 'fine and dandy', popularized most recently by British TV celebrity chef Jamie Oliver. Oliver, or the 'Naked Chef', is known for his juvenile catchphrases and tendency to use slang and Cockney expressions. In 2001, he launched his 'Happy Days Tour'; the same year saw the publication of his latest cookbook *Happy Days with the Naked Chef*. Jamie Oliver's popularity has spread also to America, and the Internet now provides a multitude of 'Naked Chef' websites (see, for example, 'The Cookery Network'), and even a slang dictionary for Americans (see 'Food Network'). *Happy Days* is also the title of a play by Samuel Beckett (1961), and 'Oh Happy Day' is the title of a popular gospel song.

happy happy joy joy

Words of elation popularized by the US TV comedy animated series *The Ren & Stimpy Show* (1991–5). The Nickelodeon show featured the adventures of the animated characters, Ren and Stimpy—a scrawny, headstrong, angry Chihuahua Ren Hoek, and his overweight, gullible feline friend Stimpson J. 'Stimpy' Cat. The catchphrase came from the 'Happy Happy Joy Joy' song (which repeated these words over a dozen times) that could be heard at the beginning of each episode. It would begin: 'Hello, boys and girls, this is your old pal Stinky Wizzleteats. This is a song about a whale—no! This is a song about being happy. That's right! It's the Happy Happy Joy Joy song!'

The fast-paced show, created by animators John Kricfalusi and Bob Camp (Spumco Productions), combined bizarre plots with overblown antics and gags, and pushed the boundaries of the disgusting to new limits, featuring screeching voices, bloodshot eyes, exposed tooth nerves, and whatever else the animators could get away with. *The Ren & Stimpy Show* quickly became a cult favourite among college students, and has spawned a successful merchandising line.

hasta la vista, baby

Until we see each other again; a phrase one might expect from a gringo trying to speak Spanish. These words of farewell were popularized by Arnold Schwarzenegger in the 1991 US film *Terminator 2: Judgment Day*. In this sequel (see also 'I'll be back!') Schwarzenegger returns as one of the good guys, helping a mother (Linda Hamilton) do everything possible to protect her son who is destined to save the human race in the apocalypse of the future. The robot played by Schwarzenegger is eager to pick up new sayings and uses this one with a certain self-congratulatory relish.

An article published in *Global Food Quarterly* (Summer 1999) adds a touch of humour to its title by using the catchphrase with reference to 'so-called "terminator" or "suicide seeds"'—'Biotech Companies Say "Hasta la vista, baby!" to So-called "Terminators"'.

have a Coke and a smile

One of Coca-Cola's most successful advertising slogans. The 'Have a Coke and a Smile' campaign, emphasized the reliability and reward in drinking Coca-Cola, and was launched in 1979 in commercials featuring Bob Hope and Bill Cosby, who explained the idea of the slogan and encouraged viewers to watch for the new advertising. The TV commercials consisted of dozens of vignettes featuring people from many walks of life drinking Coca-Cola while working or relaxing. One of these, known as 'Mean Joe Greene' released on 1 October 1979, became one of the most famous Coke commercials. It featured the 'Mean'-looking lineman of that nickname from the Pittsburgh Steelers professional football team and a 12-year-old boy, Tommy Okon. The ad proved to be immensely popular, winning the 1979 CLIO award. The ad's concept was adapted to other countries of the world, including Brazil, Argentina, and Thailand, with versions featuring renowned football (soccer) players from each country. 'Mean Joe Greene,' also inspired a made-for-TV movie (1981).

have gun, will travel

The title of a US Western TV series (1957–64), in which Richard Boone played an atypical professional gunfighter called 'Paladin'. The unique title survives today, in countless incarnations in advertising and other media, where any number of products or activities have filled the space in 'Have —, Will Travel.' The half-hour show was aired on Saturday evening, just before another popular western, *Gunsmoke*, and ran for six successful seasons. Its dramatic opening had Paladin aiming his gun and his words directly at the audience, and the series always featured an intelligent, no-nonsense approach—a bit of a rarity on the small screen in those years.

A far cry from the stereotypical hired gun, Paladin is a cultured Renaissance man. He is a well-dressed, articulate West Point graduate who appreciates the arts, fine food, brandy, and good cigars. After the Civil War, he settles in San Francisco in a first class hotel with his Chinese cook and valet 'Hey Boy'. His business card reads, 'Have Gun, Will Travel—Wire Paladin, San Francisco', charging a flat fee of $1,000 for his services, a small fortune in the late 1800s. He wears black but is the good guy, typically helping the oppressed and the wronged. Series co-writer Gene Roddenberry went on to achieve fame with *Star Trek*.

Have Gun Will Travel: The Spectacular Rise and Violent Fall of Death Row Records is the title of an investigative report by Ronin Ro published 1998. 'Have Gun, Will Travel' is also the name given by Handgun Control, Inc. (renamed the Brady Campaign to Prevent Gun Violence in 2001), the leading US gun control body, to Amendment 218, which was approved by the House Judiciary Committee by voice vote in early August 1998. H.R. 218, the Community Protection Act, would permit gun owners licensed to carry concealed weapons in their state to carry them across state lines in many cases, and would also exempt off-duty law enforcement officers from state laws prohibiting the carrying of concealed firearms.

have it your way

An advertising slogan for the Burger King fast food chain introduced in 1974. Although the phrase can also mean 'I give in, you win', in this case the advertiser is 'giving in', inviting the customer to create their own product. When Burger King introduced its now long-running slogan, the company was battling the pre-moulded image of assembly-line fast food restaurants by positioning itself as the chain where burgers were made to order. Its largest competitors at the time (McDonald's) sold their hamburgers pre-made and wrapped, but Burger King's promise was to allow diners to customize their burgers by asking counter staff to 'hold the pickle, hold the lettuce', etc. The novel way Burger King allowed its customers to choose how they wanted their meals prepared was directly reflected in this memorable slogan, which can be applied to any number of situations.

have mercy

Catchphrase of Jesse (played by John Stamos) on the US sitcom *Full House* (1987–95). The series focuses on Danny Tanner (Bob Saget) as he tries to bring up his three young daughters after his wife's death. Jesse, his soppy, guitar-playing brother-in-law, tries to help out, but most often ends up either singing to Michelle (the youngest of his nieces) to gain her forgiveness and calm her down or simply intoning his recurring catchphrase.

have you had your iron today?

An advertising slogan for Ironized Yeast in the 1940s, which was popularized by Daffy Duck and other Warner Bros. cartoon characters who gave the phrase a sarcastic twist. The line is used by one of the Goofy Gophers in *The Goofy Gophers* (1947), just before striking a dog over the head with a shovel, and indirectly by Daffy Duck in *Dripalong Daffy* (1951), just after Nasty Canasta has eaten part of his revolver.

have you read any good books lately?

Used by Richard Murdoch in the BBC radio comedy series *Much-Binding-in-the-Marsh* (1944–54). Often used as a conversation opener, Murdoch popularized the phrase (and gave it a comic twist) as a means of changing the subject in a conversation, especially when he was unable to think of an answer to a question posed by co-star and co-writer Kenneth Horne. A classic example was when Horne said: 'One of the nicest sandwiches I've ever had. What was in it, Murdoch?' And Murdoch replied: 'Well, there was—er—have you read any good books lately?'

he ain't heavy, he's my brother!

The phrase, expressing brotherly sacrifice and good 'Christian' values, has its origins in an exchange Father Flanagan had with one of the boys at Boys Town, the famous home for troubled children in Omaha, Nebraska, Flanagan founded in 1917. He apparently encountered a young man hoisting a boy on his back and carrying him for quite a while. When confronted, he remarked to Flanagan, 'He ain't heavy, he's my brother!' The phrase summarized the philosophy behind the organization or 'town' built for homeless boys and run by them—a set-up that could succeed only through loyalty and a brotherly spirit.

The phrase was popularized by the 1938 film *Boys Town*, starring Mickey Rooney and Spencer Tracy. Tracy won his second consecutive Oscar for his portrayal of Father Flanagan who dedicates his life to helping juvenile delinquents go straight. The successful film gave the actual orphanage a huge boost, eventually catapulting it into a multi-million dollar organization that helps young people throughout America.

King George VI quoted a former US president as using the same anecdote attributed to Father Flanagan, as well as the catchphrase itself, in his 1942 Christmas radio broadcast. Which president he was referring to, however, was not clear. The song, 'He ain't heavy, he's my brother', was recorded first by the Everly Brothers, but became popular when it was later released as a single by the Hollies in 1969.

he can run, but he can't hide

Words of US boxer Joe Louis (Joseph Louis Barrow) spoken to a reporter, with reference to his opponent, the fast-moving Billy Conn, before a world heavyweight title fight on 19 June 1946 (from *Louis: My Life Story*). Louis's assessment of the situation appears to have been correct, as he did in fact win. The saying has become commonly used as a threat or warning directed at those whose wrong-doings must, in public opinion, inevitably be exposed. US President Ronald Reagan employed the phrase in October 1985, as a warning to international terrorists and to stress his country's tough stance on this issue.

he don't know me vewy well, do he?

One of the catchphrases belonging to 'Junior, the Mean Widdle Kid', a character created by US comedian Red Skelton. Junior, an offensive little boy, first appeared on Skelton's radio show in the late 1930s, and was developed further his TV show that ran from 1951 to 1971. Junior typically responded with this catchphrase when someone had misjudged his devilish nature. (See also Junior's other catchphrases—'I/ he dood it' and 'you bwoke my widdle'.) During the 1940s, the phrase was popularized further when it was uttered by Warner Bros. cartoon characters, including Daffy and Chloe as Junior at the end of *The Impatient Patient* (1942), and Bugs Bunny in *Hare Trigger* (1945).

he look-a like a man

Stating the obvious, while suggesting there could be doubts. One of Ms Swan's (Alex Borstein) trademark lines on the US TV comedy series *Mad TV* (1995–), inspired by *Mad* magazine. Ms Swan is an oriental lady who has recently moved to America and doesn't speak much English. Among the handful of phrases she has mastered are this one and 'I tell you everyting'. Chris Hogan, who plays opposite Ms Swan and fails to realize the limits of her grasp of the language, always becomes annoyed by what he believes to be her reluctance to answer his questions more specifically. The series features parodies of films and TV series, combining two different films or series, as in 'Gump Fiction' and 'Get Smarty', and all productions are written by Alfred E. Neuman, with his surname appropriately substituted, as in Alfred E. Tarantino for 'Gump Fiction'.

he's caring. He's connected

A catchphrase belonging to US comedian David Letterman, host of the TV talk show *Late Night with David Letterman* (1982–). One of Letterman's slightly tongue-in-cheek statements, poking fun at the often dubious claims men make regarding their sensitivity, and being 'in touch' with both their own feelings and those of others. Many of Letterman's recurring sayings entered the American lexicon of the late 1980s and 1990s simply because he consistently reached a wide public. *TV Guide* chose him as one of the '50 Greatest TV Stars of All Time', one of the most influential television legends in the history of the medium.

he's dead, Jim!

Spoken by Chief Medical Officer Leonard 'Bones' McCoy (DeForest Kelley) of the Starship *Enterprise* in many an episode of the US TV series *Star Trek* (1966–9) to his friend and commander, Captain James T. Kirk (William Shatner). As the ship's doctor, McCoy, an opinionated Southerner who insists he is 'just a simple country doctor at heart', would often be called on to

determine—using a 23rd-century gizmo—the state of a
being's—human or other—vital signs.

he's fallen in the wa-ter!

Used by 'Little Jim' (Spike Milligan) on the surreal, catchphrase-filled
BBC comedy radio *Goon Show* (1952–60). Little Jim was believed to be
Eccles's (also played by Milligan) nephew and to live in his boot. His
beautifully timed declaration following a loud splash was the only line
the squeaky-voiced boy ever said. Little Jim is the name of the subject
of Edward Farmer's a poem, 'The Collier's Dying Child'—'I have no
pain, dear mother, now'. As the poem was quite well known, it
probably inspired Milligan's naming, if not the creation, of this
child-character.

he's from Barcelona

A phrase used apologetically or by way of explanation by Basil Fawlty
(John Cleese), when referring to Manuel, and especially his poor
command of English, on the BBC TV situation comedy series *Fawlty
Towers* (1975–9). Manuel (Andrew Sachs) is the hotel bellboy/waiter and
is from Barcelona. One of the running jokes within *Fawlty Towers* is that
Manuel can't speak English very well—as he puts it 'I can speak English
good, I learn from a book'—something which leads to many comic
moments as well as countless forms of abuse from Basil. Manuel's most
frequent reply to basic instructions is 'Que?' Basil overcomes this by
speaking broken Spanish to him, which usually adds to the confusion,
and so Basil would often find the need to say: 'Please excuse him, he's
from Barcelona.' When *Fawlty Towers* was dubbed into Spanish, Basil's
common line was changed to 'He's from Rome'.

he's loo-vely, Mrs Hoskin . . . he's loo-vely!

From the BBC radio comedy series *Ray's a Laugh* (1949–61) starring Ted
Ray. The phrase was associated with 'Ivy' (played by Ray), Mrs Hoskin's
(played by Bob Pearson) squeaky-voiced friend. The two elderly ladies
became the programme's best-loved characters. Ivy was forever
talking about (and secretly pining for) the never-seen Dr Hardcastle
and when Mrs Hoskin would say 'I sent for Dr Hardcastle' Ivy would
invariably reply excitedly with this phrase.

he's on the jazz

An expression that was popularized by B.A. (Mr T) and others on the US action/adventure/comedy TV series *The A-Team* (1983–7), about four Vietnam veterans and their secret adventures as mercenaries. The phrase probably dates to the 1920s or 1930s and refers to an earlier usage of jazz, meaning full of vigour and energy, if not to its other contemporary usage to mean copulation. See also 'I love it when a plan comes together'.

he's very good, you know!

A slightly insincere compliment tinged with condescension that was popularized by a number of the regular characters on the insane and inspirational BBC radio comedy *Goon Show* (1952–60).

head for the mountains

Leave the gritty city and the rat race behind, and get back to nature. The principal advertising slogan for Busch Beer since 1979, it brings to mind the mountains, their cool, refreshing springs (which presumably supply the water used in producing the beer) and the concept of the 'great outdoors'—an American institution in itself. When Anheuser-Busch introduced Busch Ice, its advertising featured 'Brave The Cold' theme to complement the company's already familiar 'Head for the Mountains' slogan.

heavens to Murgatroyd!

A catchphrase of Snagglepuss, the Hannah-Barbera cartoon lion created in 1959. This pink, well-dressed, witty feline featured in his own segment on *The Yogi Bear Show* from 1961, and on other shows into the 1980s. The expression, used as 'oh my goodness' might be, was not apparently coined by Snagglepuss, but was an old-fashioned half-nonsensical American phrase, similar to 'Heavens to Betsy'. See also 'exit stage left', Snagglepuss's other favourite saying.

heere I Yaaam!

Inane announcement associated with 'Clem Kaddidlehopper', the country bumpkin character created by US comedian Red Skelton, who was featured on his radio show in the late 1930s, and then on his TV show that ran from 1951 to 1971. Clem's long, drawn-out greeting was also employed by Warner Bros. character Bugs Bunny in numerous cartoon films, including *Buckaroo Bugs* (1944) and *Stage Door Cartoon* (1944). His other catchphrase was the equally drawn-out, distinctively rustic-sounding 'W-e-e-e-l-l-l Daaaisy June!'

heeere's ... Johnny!

Introduction provided by Ed McMahon, Johnny Carson's second fiddle co-host, on the NBC TV *Tonight Show* every week night from October 1962 until May 1992, when the legendary Carson retired. McMahon's instantly recognizable elongated rendition—'and now ladies and gentlemen, heeeeeere's ... Johnny!'—apparently came from earlier days, when he would call the races at carnivals with a typical drawn-out intonation of the words. The status of this catchphrase grew considerably when Jack Nicholson used it in the 1980 classic horror film *The Shining*. In one of the film's most frightening moments, Nicholson, armed with a fireman's axe, chops a hole in the door of the bathroom which his wife has locked herself in to save herself from her insane husband. Once the hole in the door is large enough, he sticks his head through, and with a deranged expression on his face, cries maniacally 'Heeeeeere's ... Johnny!'

The US comedian 'Weird Al' Yankovic recorded a song entitled 'Here's Johnny' (on his 1986 album *Polka Party*), which parodies 'Who's Johnny' by El DeBarge. All about Ed McMahon, it begins: 'There he goes, he drives me crazy/When he says "Here's Johnny"/ That's his job, it's so amazing/All he says is "Here's Johnny".'

hello birds, hello trees, hello clouds, hello sky!

A joyful, juvenile expression celebrating nature and life. Although its precise origins are unclear, it was in use in the US by the late 1930s, and was spoken in a Warner Bros. 1941 cartoon film. The phrase, and variations on it, was popularized by the four Molesworth books published in the 1950s, written by Geoffrey Willans and illustrated by Ronald Searle. The narrator is schoolboy Nigel Molesworth, 'the curse of st custard's which is the skool i am at'. Among the principal characters with whom Molesworth is forced to mingle is the inimitable Basil Fotherington-Thomas, who is 'utterly wet and a sissy' and skips about saying 'Hullo clouds, hullo sky'. More recently, the expression appeared in the 1979 Monty Python film *Life of Brian*, when Brian miraculously ends Simon the Holy Man's 18-year vow of silence by stepping on his foot. Simon just wants to sing and shout, bursting out with: 'Hava Nagila! Hava Nagila, ha ha ha! Look out. Oh, I'm alive! I'm alive! Hello birds! Hello trees! I'm alive!...'

hello darlin'

A greeting that was popularized by Ed Stewart (who became known as 'Stewpot'), particularly on BBC Radio 1's *Junior Choice* programme, which he presented during the 1970s. When asked in an interview how he had come by his famous catchphrase, Stewart replied: "Hello darlin'" came about when I was doing *Junior Choice* and I was going round hospitals interviewing kids. I went to one of the wards in Guys Hospital in London and this little boy said it. I didn't play the tape for six months, by which time I'd completely forgotten who it was and still don't know to this day. People have claimed he was a boy in Guernsey but I maintain he emigrated soon after I interviewed him and he still has no idea he became a star!' (BBC Online). 'Hello Darlin'' is also the title of a love song and an album recorded by country crooner Conway Twitty.

hello, folks

See 'hello, playmates!'

hello, good evening, and welcome

Used by British broadcaster/interviewer David Frost, particularly in opening *The Frost Programme* (Rediffusion, 1966–7; LWT, 1972–3; BBC1, 1977). The programme presented a series of hard-hitting interviews including the 1967 confrontation with Dr Emil Savundra shortly before the latter's arrest. Frost's treatment of Dr Savundra, former head of a car insurance company who had been charged with conspiracy to defraud his customers, became an oft-quoted instance of 'trial by television'.

hello, it's-a me, Mario

Greeting popularized by Mario, star of a series of home video games (including *Super Mario 64* and *Paper Mario*) produced by Nintendo Co.

Ltd., of Kyoto, Japan, since 1985. Players in games such as *Super Mario 64* take control of Mario, Nintendo's famous mascot video game character, and literally leap, bound, swim, and even fly their way through Princess Toadstool's castle. The object is for players to collect Power Stars along their adventure which will ultimately lead to a battle between Mario and Bowser, another principal character. The diminutive plumber is of Italian origin, as his name and his particular way of introducing himself suggest.

hello, John, got a new motor?

A phrase that was popularized by British comedian Alexei Sayle in the early 1980s, when he began using 'John' as a way of referring to the average Englishman. His seminal single, ''Ullo John, Got a New Motor?' reached No. 15 in the UK singles chart in 1984, and he performed the song on the TV show *Top of the Pops* with a Ford Cortina in the studio. The song was seemingly nonsensical while parodying many different songs and films, and included lines like 'Is there life in Peckham?' and 'I keep tropical fish in me underpants', and with each lyric being sung twice. The song inspired another— ''Ullo Tosh, Gotta Toshiba?'—featured in a late 1980s Toshiba TV commercial, which was along the same lines, but about Toshiba products, and was sung by Ian Dury.

hello, me old pal, me old beauty!

Greeting used by 'rustic yokel' character Walter Gabriel in the BBC radio soap opera *The Archers* (1950–   ). Life in the village of Ambridge, in the fictional county of Borsetshire, still continues to draw 4.5 million listeners after over 50 years, surviving in spite of competition from TV soaps, and accusations of political bias and political incorrectness. In recent years the series' biggest challenge has been appealing to the young, as the majority of listeners are aged over 40. That need has spawned a new generation of teenagers, allowing the series to cover current youth-related issues as well as questioning the advisability of GM crops. The plots in the late 1990s were a far cry from its post-war beginnings as an educational agriculture programme which was nearly called Little Twittington, and Walter Gabriel's greeting 'doh, me old pal, me old beauty' has long gone. In fact, Gabriel died in 1988 at the ripe old age of 92.

The catchphrase was also used by Joshua, played by Tony Hancock, in *The Bowmans*, a TV parody of the popular radio series.

hello, Newman!

The greeting—spoken with obvious insincerity—of stand-up comic Jerry Seinfeld to his neighbour Newman (Wayne Knight) on the US TV comedy series *Seinfeld* (1989–98). Newman, an overweight postal worker who lives in Seinfeld's apartment building, first appeared on the series in January 1992. Seinfeld believes Newman to be completely evil, and although the reasons for their mutual loathing are not given, they try their best to avoid each other. When these odd arch-enemies do meet, and must greet each other, they do so reluctantly and with visible contempt.

hello, playmates!

A catchphrase associated with British comedian Arthur Askey on the BBC radio music/comedy show *Bandwagon* (1938–9). This popular weekly radio show was the first of its kind to make considerable use of catchphrases, helped along by the studio audience's enthusiastic response. 'Hello, playmates' was one of the show's earliest catchphrases and actually started out as 'hello, folks' but was changed when Tommy Handley, a well-known Liverpudlian comedian, complained that the latter was his catchphrase.

Handley's 'hello, folks' was picked up and parodied by Neddy Seagoon (Harry Secombe) on the BBC radio *Goon Show* (1952–60). Seagoon would often use a megaphone (or 'the new aluminium voice cone projector') to call everyone's attention with: 'Hello, folks! Hello, folks! Calling, folks! It's Neddy again!' or, more calmly, with 'Hello, folks of world'.

hello, sailor!

Originally, an expression that was traditionally associated with prostitutes, greeting sailors fresh off their boats. It was apparently a part of the chorus in Noel Coward's song 'Matelot' (*Sigh No More*, 1945), and appeared in a BBC radio *Goon Show* in December 1959, in which the bumbling, geriatric Minnie Bannister (Spike Milligan) greets Neddy Seagoon (Harry Secombe) with a puzzling 'Hello, sailor'. During the 1970s it became a well-established camp saying, and a popular greeting between gay characters generally in the media. *Hello, Sailor* was the title of a book published in 1975 by actor and Monty Python member Eric Idle. More recently, the greeting has become part of computer programming jargon (as has 'hello, world', the 'canonical minimal test message in the C/UNIX universe') and is used in a computer game called *Zork* (which also includes 'hello, aviator' and 'hello, implementor').

hello, Shoil!

How Laverne greets Shirley on the US TV comedy series *Laverne and Shirley* (1976–83). The series was about these two young women who worked as bottle-cappers at the Shotz Brewery in Milwaukee during the 1950s and shared an apartment, following their daily lives as they tried to improve their respective stations in life and looked for true love. *Laverne and Shirley* was a spin-off from the hit series *Happy Days*. Laverne DeFazio (Penny Marshall) and Shirley Feeney (Cindy Williams) were first introduced to TV viewers on a late 1975 episode of *Happy Days* which had Fonzie and Richie going on a double date with the two women. The series relied heavily on slapstick humour, comic timing, and its popularity had much to do with the fact that its blue collar stars were portrayed as underdog heroines.

hello, strenzer!

Greeting associated with 'Schlepperman' (Sam Hearn) on the popular US comedy radio programme *The Jack Benny Show*, which ran from 1932 to 1955. The comic tag line ('stranger' pronounced with a strong Yiddish accent) was quickly picked up by Warner Bros. who put it in the mouths of Owl Jolson, a jazz-singing owl, in *I Love to Singa* (1936)—a parody of the 1927 film *The Jazz Singer*, starring Al Jolson (stage name of Asa Yoelson), and of Professor Mockingbird in *I Only Have Eyes for You* (1937). In *The Jazz Singer*, the first talking picture, Jolson played the son of a Jewish cantor who chooses to become a jazz singer.

hello, we're Cockneys!

How 'The Posh Cockneys', played by Paul Whitehouse and Arabella Weir, introduce themselves in their sketches on the BBC TV comedy sketch series *The Fast Show* (1994–7). The Posh Cockneys, intent on finding a pie and mash shop in the area and jellied eels on pub menus, always proudly present themselves with this greeting, whichever part of the country they find themselves.

hep me! Hep me! I been hyp-mo-tized!

One of US comedian David Letterman's many catchphrases, used on his TV talk show *Late Night with David Letterman* (1982–   ). Guaranteed to get a laugh, the line is used as a satirical comment on instances or events in which the protagonist has clearly been lacking in judgement or common sense.

here come de judge

The 'here comes the judge' vaudeville routine written and performed by blacks for black audiences dates to the early part of the century, and particularly the 1920s. The catchphrase was more recently revived and popularized by Pigmeat Markham in a series of sketches on the US comedy TV series *Rowan and Martin's Laugh-in* (1968–73). Markham was black vaudeville's greatest sketch comedian, starring at the Apollo for several decades where he revived the old vaudeville catchphrase. He was a regular cast member on *Laugh-in* from 1968 to 1969 where his career skyrocketed again due to his appearances with Sammy Davis Jr. His 1968 album, entitled *Here Comes the Judge*, includes the title song and comedy sketches. 1968 also saw the release of a recording by Shorty Long, by the same title.

Since 1968, *Here Come the Judge* has also been the name given to a square dance call; the moves to *Sock it to Me* (see below)—another *Laugh-in*-inspired square dance call—are the mirror image of the former.

here come the pet shop boys!

Wisecrack popularized by Jim Royle (played by Ricky Tomlinson) on the popular BBC comedy series *The Royle Family* (1998–2000). The line is spoken with reference to his teenage son, Antony (Ralf Little) and his mate Darren (Andrew Whyment), and has no real message or significance in relation to the British rock band The Pet Shop Boys, but merely sounds funny and mildly clever (spoken in a self-satisfied tone). The only real connection is that Anthony and Darren are 'boys' and Jim, sitting dishevelled in his worn-out armchair, is always ready to seize an opportunity to exercise his wit.

Written by Caroline Aherne, Craig Cash and Henry Normal, this multi-award winning sitcom features terrifyingly realistic characters who never stray far from the sitting room of their unglamorous Manchester home. Occasionally making it into the kitchen, the Royles receive visits from neighbours and non-live-in family members such as 'Nana' (grandmother), amid overflowing ashtrays, constant mugs of tea and their all-time favourite, bacon butties (sandwiches). Ricky Tomlinson won best TV actor at the 1999 British Comedy awards for his portrayal of flatulent, wisecracking Jim, the patriarch in the series.

here we are again!

The entering cry of Joey the Clown (Joseph Grimaldi), one of the greatest and best-loved figures in the history of English pantomime. The line has come down as the catchphrase of all clowns to this day, and is often used in greetings, as in 'so we meet again!'

Grimaldi, the clown from whom all clowns have come to be known as 'Joey', could, according to his contemporaries, achieve with one look more than any of his rivals could achieve with the most elaborate transformations. He seldom spoke on stage but, as in mime, was fully expressive through the use of his body and movements. When he did speak it was usually no more than one word or a monosyllable and it was as if some overwhelming sensation had forced the word from his mouth.

here's another fine mess you've gotten me|us into

This famous catchphrase featured in various Laurel and Hardy films, always spoken by Oliver Hardy to Stan Laurel. It became Hardy's most predictable response to the series of failures and disasters the popular team seemed to court or create. The earliest use of the phrase was in their 1930 film *The Laurel-Hardy Murder Case*. Generally misquoted as 'another fine mess', which was the title of a Laurel and Hardy 30-minute short released in 1930, this form was actually only used in *The Wedding Night* (1938).

Stan Laurel was the creative force in the comedy team and is credited with most of the script-work (including this phrase). He also directed many of the films, and in 1960 he was awarded a Special Oscar for 'his creative pioneering in the field of cinema comedy'.

here's one I made earlier (or prepared earlier...)

The phrase originated with live TV cookery demonstrations in the 1950s, and was popularized by presenters of the popular children's BBC television programme *Blue Peter* from 1963 onwards. *Blue Peter*, one of British television's longest-running programmes, has regularly reached 5 to 6 million children and teenagers. The show's studio items often involve presenters cooking, trying new hobbies, or making home-made toys from household rubbish, such as empty washing-up liquid bottles, wire coat hangers, and egg cartons. The phrases from their scripted cookery demonstrations ('here's one I made earlier') and characteristic expressions (see 'get down, Shep!') became almost clichés and were parodied in pop songs.

hey!

Exclamation favoured by foul-mouthed, overweight ('big-boned') Eric Cartman, one of the principal characters on the US TV cartoon series *South Park* (1997–). (See also 'follow your dreams...BEEFCAKE!') Most of his friends use 'hey', but usually to simply draw the listener's attention as when Stan says to Cartman: 'Hey, that's sick dude!' With Cartman, it becomes a powerful admonishment, as in 'Hey! I am a cop and you will respect my authori-tie', or 'Hey! I'll blow your friggin' head off!'

hey, Boit! Ca-mmeeere!

Catchphrase of Warner Bros. cartoon character Hubie to his 'partner in crime', Bertie. 'Hubie and Bertie' were a pair of mischievous mice who specialized in making cats look silly, and featured in a number of Chuck Jones cartoons during the 1940s and early 1950s, including the Oscar-nominated *Mouse Wreckers* (1949). Hubie was voiced by Mel Blanc, and had a strong Brooklyn accent—most obvious in his pronunciation of his friend's name, while Bertie was voiced by Stan Freberg.

hey, hey, hey!

Catchphrase of Dwayne Clemens (Haywood Nelson) on the US TV sitcom *What's Happening!!* (1976–9), and *What's Happening Now!!* (1985–8). *What's Happening!!*, based loosely on the 1975 film *Cooley High*, was about three black high school students growing up in Los Angeles. The series centred on Roger 'Raj' Thomas (Ernest Thomas), who lived at home with his divorced mother and younger sister. Raj, the studious dreamer, was joined on his escapades by his two best friends, Freddie 'Rerun' Stubbs (Fred Berry), a happy, overweight clown, and 'Hey, hey, hey!' Dwayne, the shy one, who tagged along, doing his best to appear 'cool'.

hey kids, it's only television!

Remember not to take television and the entertainment world too seriously. A recurring line of jocular reassurance delivered by US comedian David Letterman, host of the TV talk show *Late Night with David Letterman* (1982–). Hosting a show that tends to include a number of bizarre items and characters, Letterman likes to periodically remind his audiences that there is a real world outside the TV studio, as well as make sure they understand that he should be able to get away with the occasional gaffe or misbehaviour while doing his job.

hey, Willie

Preface to almost every remark or question spoken by Alf to Willie Tanner (Max Wright) in the US TV comedy series *ALF* (1986–90), as in 'Hey Willie, wouldn't a pizza look good on my tongue about now?' Alf, short for Alien Life Form, is a wisecracking, 229-year-old furry extraterrestrial, who was taken in by the Tanner family after he accidentally crashed his spaceship into their garage. As his home planet, Melmac, had exploded, Alf finds himself stranded on Earth with no real choice but to live in Los Angeles with Willie, Kate, and their children, Lynn and Brian. Willie, a mild-mannered social worker, was often frustrated by his visitor's rash behaviour—including his overwhelming desire to devour the family cat—but continually bailed him out of trouble.

hi-ho

An expression associated with Kermit the Frog on *The Muppet Show*, created by puppeteer Jim Henson. Kermit and the other Muppet characters, including Miss Piggy and Fozzie Bear, quickly became popular figures, if not celebrities, among both young and adult audiences around the world. The ever-charming Kermit would use this cheerful greeting to introduce or bring attention to himself as in 'Hi-ho. This is Kermit'. Other recurring Kermit expressions were: 'Yaaay!' and 'Sheesh'.

hi-ho, Silver!

The Lone Ranger's hearty cry to his trusty white steed from 1933 to 1957, as the daring and resourceful masked rider of the plains set out again to lead the fight for law and order in the early west. Silver, who often managed—sometimes just in the nick of time—to ingeniously help the Ranger out of trouble, gave rise to the celebrated introduction to each half-hour episode: 'A fiery horse with the speed of light, a cloud of dust and a hearty "Hi-ho Silver!"—the Lone Ranger'. This was followed by galloping bars from Rossini's William Tell Overture, instilling a sense of mounting excitement in the programme's largely youthful audience. Other memorable features of the show included the name Tonto, the Ranger's faithful Indian companion, had for him—'Kemo Sabe' (faithful scout)—and the unchanging final line of each episode: 'Who was that masked man?', as the ever-anonymous hero reared up on Silver and rode into the sunset.

The *Lone Ranger* began as a wireless serial on a Detroit station in 1933 and had already been twice filmed when Clayton Moore was cast in the part in 1949 by ABC, then the smallest of America's TV networks. Moore played the character from 1949 to 1951, when he was replaced by John Hart, but in 1954 Moore reclaimed the part and stayed until the series ended, after 169 episodes, in 1957. After his success on television, Moore twice played the masked hero on the big screen, in *The Lone Ranger* (1956) and *The Lone Ranger and the City of Gold* (1958).

hi ho Steverino

Famous cry delivered by comedian Louis Nye on *The Steve Allen Show* (1956–61) that became a national catchphrase. The popular comedy variety TV programme was engaged, during its run, in the most famous ratings war in US television history, shown on CBS from 1956 opposite *The Ed Sullivan Show*—an established television institution. Steve Allen came across as innovative and funny, with a preference for improvisation and ad-libbing. He also launched the careers of several comedians, including that of Louis Nye, who was a regular performer on the show and was known for his ability to reduce Allen to helpless giggles with in-joke ad-libs. Nye created many well-known characters, including the effete and cosmopolitan Gordon Hathaway whose chipper 'Hi Ho Steverino' became a trademark of the programme. *Hi Ho Steverino* was the title of Steve Allen's autobiography published in 1992.

hiiiiiiiideeehoooo!

Distinctive call uttered by 'Mr Hankey' (the Christmas Poo) on the US TV comedy cartoon series *South Park* (1997–). Mr Hankey, a talking turd and a friend of Kyle's, comes out once a year and 'gives presents to all the little boys and girls who have fibre in their diets'. Kyle, the 'smart kid' among the show's main four 8-year-old characters, is often made fun of because he is Jewish. Feeling this most acutely at Christmas time, Kyle plays with his 'imaginary friend', Mr Hankey. As a result of this friendship, Kyle is admitted to a psychiatric hospital in *Mr Hankey, The Christmas Poo*; in this episode he is made a South Park outcast, expressing his dejection through his 'lonely Jew' song. Meanwhile, Mr Hankey and his catchphrase remain decidedly up-beat.

his Reverence won't like it

A phrase indirectly expressing disapproval popularized by Maurice Yeatman (Edward Sinclair), the obsequious verger of St Aldhelm's Church, on the BBC TV comedy series *Dad's Army* (1968–77). Yeatman spends much of his time spreading rumours and reporting to the Vicar (Frank Williams) with stories of wrong-doing committed by Captain Mainwaring (Arthur Lowe), leader of Walmington-on-Sea's bumbling Home Guard platoon.

hiuck, hiuck

Unsophisticated expletive popularized by Scooby-Dum on *Scooby-Doo*, a US TV cartoon series featuring a Great Dane called Scooby that ran from 1969 to 1986. Scooby-Dum, was introduced to the series in 1976 when the series moved from CBS to ABC. He was presented as

Scooby's 'hick' cousin and, as his name suggested, his rustic ways were matched by his charmingly slow wits. His sense of humour was, however, always on the ready and marked by this catchphrase.

hi'ya, Jackson!

A snappy greeting popularized by bandleader Phil Harris on the US TV series *The Jack Benny Show* from 1950 to 1965 (and on Benny's radio programme from 1936 to 1955). A singer, bandleader and comic, Harris was famous for his loud, boisterous, and tipsy image. His entrances on the shows were always conspicuous; most often he would simply burst in with his trademark 'Hiya, Jackson!' or interrupt a conversation Benny was involved in.

ho ho, very satirical!

A sarcastic acknowledgment of what is meant to be a satirical quip or witticism. The phrase has been associated with the British satirical magazine *Private Eye* which was first published in February 1962. The magazine's first cover photo, taken by Lucinda Lambton, was of the Albert Memorial. At the time, the US astronaut John Glenn was about to be fired into space, and it was thought this could be shown as a British equivalent. Queen Victoria was drawn beside it and a bubble came out of her mouth with the words 'Ho, ho. Very satirical!' British comedian Peter Cook, who was running The Establishment Club, and had not yet become directly involved in the magazine, has been credited with coming up with the idea of using a photograph on the cover, and a joke in a bubble attached to it, having seen it in America.

The Albert Memorial analogy had actually already been picked up on, as a 1958 *Goon Show* episode entitled 'The Albert Memorial (aka: The First Albert Memorial to the Moon)' indicates. 'Ho-ho! Very Satirical!' (1998) is the title of the fourth volume in a series of 'The Best of Private Eye—Golden Satiricals' albums.

hold the onions

A catchphrase of unknown origin that appeared in many Warner-released cartoons over the years, including *Pigs is Pigs* (1937), *Polar Pals* (1939), *Porky's Café* (1942), *French Rarebit* (1951), and *Muscle Tussle* (1953). Considered by many to be the key to a perfect sandwich or hamburger, the phrase was popularized further during the late 1970s through Burger King's 'have it your way' advertising campaign (see above), which not only allowed, but actually encouraged, fast food customers to make requests such as 'hold the onions' or any other ingredient. This use of 'hold' to mean stop or restrain (as in the expression 'hold your horses') is used in a number of contexts, becoming something of a format phrase, as in 'hold the sympathy', 'hold the sob story', and so on.

holy —!

Exclamation favoured by Robin the Boy Wonder, superhero Batman's sidekick, in *Batman* comic books, 1940s film serials, the 1960s TV series, and a number of films over the decades. While Batman was always poised and in control of his emotions, Robin was a highly excitable young man. Throughout their exploits, Robin would frequently find some event, thing, or comment completely unbelievable. His reaction on these occasions would be to exclaim: 'Holy (insert words here), Batman!' Just a few of the hundreds of such outbursts are: 'Holy hood-wink', 'Holy crystal ball', 'Holy contributing to the delinquency of minors', and 'Holy Sherlock Holmes'.

The comic-strip character Batman was created in 1939 by US cartoonist Bob Kane and his collaborator Bill Finger. Batman, disguised by a black mask and cape characterized by stylized bat-like shapes, would, together with his youthful assistant Robin, combat the criminal activities of an array of bizarre evil foes, including the Joker, the Penguin, and Catwoman. Adam West and Burt Ward played Batman and Robin in the Pop-art-inspired TV series (1966–8).

Homey don't play dat!

Catchphrase belonging to Homey the Clown (Damon Wayans) on the US TV comedy sketch show *In Living Color* (1990–4). In the spirit of *Saturday Night Live*, the structure of the programme consisted principally of numerous sketches, some of them with recurring characters, being performed in front of a live studio audience. Homey (a word defined in Rap dictionaries as 'close friend' or 'homeboy') is actually an ex-convict who has had to resort to performing on the streets, to make money. Dressed and made-up like the classic clown, including the oversized shoes, Homey the

Clown works the streets and occasional party, but is always frustrated, rebellious, short-tempered, and prone to pummel people with a sock. He would utter his catchphrase to show his disapproval of something—in Rap, to 'play' means to go along with—and Homey found much to disapprove of.

Homey the Clown and his catchphrase are featured in a Rap song by EPMD entitled 'Who Killed Jane' on their 1992 album *Business Never Personal*. The end of the song's fourth verse shows just how thoroughly this catchphrase has become a part of youth, and particularly black youth, culture:

E—Easy partner, chill put the gun down
P—Oh now you tryin' to play me out like Homey the Clown
And you know Homey don't play that
E—Play what?

honest injun!

I swear, it's the absolute truth; used as a rejoinder when one's truthfulness has been questioned. The phrase—popularized by Mark Twain's two classic novels, in American dialect, *The Adventures of Tom Sawyer* (1876) and *The Adventures of Huckleberry Finn* (1885)—has been traced back to 1851, but it is probably much older than that. 'Injun' is a corruption of 'indian' and implies a 'red indian' in particular. It is not clear whether the phrase originally referred to the notion that American Indians were honest compared to Europeans who were prone to lying ('White man speak with forked tongue'), or an expression of sarcastic derision. In any event, it came to be used as a pledge of truth and honesty, similar in meaning to 'scout's honour' or the British 'honour bright'.

An example of Twain's use of this phrase from *The Adventures of Huckleberry Finn* (chapter XXXIII) appears when Tom Sawyer sees Huck after he thought he had been murdered: 'He [Tom] says: "Don't you play nothing on me, because I wouldn't on you. Honest injun, you ain't a ghost?" "Honest injun, I ain't," I says.'

honey, I just forgot to duck

Famous quip of US boxer John Dempsey, spoken to his wife after losing the World Heavyweight title on 23 September 1926 (*Dempsey*

1977, by J. and B. P. Dempsey). The line became a popular excuse and, when US President Ronald Reagan was shot and seriously injured not long after his presidency began in 1981, he reportedly asked his doctors, 'Please assure me you are all Republicans', then later joked about his close call with his wife, Nancy, saying 'Honey, I forgot to duck'. At the time, Reagan's use of Dempsey's line heartened Americans about their president's calm under pressure. There have also been slightly more distant variations on the phrase, as in *Honey I Shrunk the Kids*, the title of a 1989 US comedy film and 1997 TV show.

hoo-ah!

An exclamation expressing approval or appreciation used repeatedly by Frank Slade, a character played by Al Pacino, in the 1992 US film *Scent of a Woman*. Al Pacino's Oscar-winning performance as a bitter, blind, retired lieutenant-colonel who is bent on having a wild, and perhaps final, trip to New York is characterized throughout the film by Slade straightening himself up and bursting out with 'Hoo-ah' For example: 'Tits. Hoo-ah! Big ones, little ones. Nipples staring straight at ya, like secret searchlights'. The catchphrase has become as much Al Pacino's as Slade's. When the actor strode up to the podium in Yale's Whitney Humanities Center to give a Master's class, he 'did his trademark "Hoo-ah," and then launched right into the questions' (*Yale Herald* 3 December 1999).

It would seem that the expression does in fact have its origins in the US armed services. In an address by US President George W. Bush to Marines at Camp Pendleton in California, he said 'I've been looking forward to this trip, and looking forward to being able to extend a proper Marine Corps greeting: Hoo-ah!' To which the audience replied: 'Hoo-ah!' (*Washington Post* (online version) 29 May 2001).

hooligans!

Insult popularized by Chief ARP Warden William 'Bert' Hodges (Bill Pertwee) on the BBC TV comedy series *Dad's Army* (1968–77). Hodges, the local greengrocer, was Captain Mainwaring's main rival authority in Walmington-on-Sea, home to the inept Home Guard platoon the latter is in charge of. While the two men battle over use of the church hall and the Vicar's office, Hodges annoys his rival by calling him 'Napoleon' and his men 'hooligans', if not 'ruddy hooligans'. As chief air-raid warden, Hodges is in charge of checking the village's blackouts and his other catchphrase is consequently 'Put that light out!', a cry that always puts the villagers on edge.

how bona to vada your eek

A phrase in Polari, a strange mixture of the Romany language and homosexual street code, that was popularized during the 1960s by the Julian and Sandy skits on the BBC radio comedy series *Round the Horne* (1965–9). Julian and Sandy (played by Hugh Paddick and Kenneth Williams), would often begin their sketches with some variation on this greeting, meaning 'How good to see your face again'. In Polari, 'vada' (see), from the Italian 'guarda', can at times also be spelt 'varda'. See also 'I'm Julian and this is my friend Sandy'.

how do you do?

An enquiry/greeting associated with US comic Bert Gordon's Mad Russian character on the Eddie Cantor radio programme during the 1930s. The phrase, which was spoken with emphasis on the first 'do', was adopted and further popularized by several Warner Bros. cartoon characters during late 1930s and early 1940s, including the Whim-Wham Whistling Shark in *Fresh Fish* (1939) and one of the Gremlins when greeting Hitler in *Russian Rhapsody* (1944).

how queer!

An exaggerated catchphrase—or parody of a catchphrase—used as a running gag in the blathering sketches of spoof 1940s comic Arthur Atkinson, played by Paul Whitehouse, on the BBC TV comedy series *The Fast Show* (1994–7). This tagline, pronounced ''ow queer', and some mention or use of his favourite comic prop—'me washboard'—are fixed elements in Atkinson's routine.

how rude!

Juvenile comeback, popularized by Stephanie Tanner (Jodie Leanne Sweetin) on the US family sitcom *Full House* (1987–95). Stephanie, who was in kindergarten when the series began, was one of three sisters being brought up by their widowed father (Danny), with some help from his brother-in-law (Jesse), and his best friend (Joey). Stephanie's recurring catchphrase was spoken with an irritation or annoyance that seemed to rub off on viewers.

how sweet it is

Popularized by the corpulent US comedian Jackie Gleason, who used the melodious phrase to express how harmonious or lovely he felt things were. The exclamation would always be included in his conversations with his studio audiences at the opening of each episode of his TV comedy variety show, *The Jackie Gleason Show*, which ran from 1952 to 1970. (See also 'and awa-a-aay we go!')

how tickled I am

I am so pleased or delighted. A phrase associated with the British buck-toothed comic Ken Dodd, whose stage routine involved waving his tickling sticks, talking to Knotty Ash's Diddy Men, and rambling on about how 'tattyfilarious' life is. Dodd would always try to include his audiences, walking onto the stage through the audience, and using opening lines like 'How tickled I am to be here with you this evening' to give off a warmth and charm intended to relax and win over those watching him. When taking his final bows, he would always toss one of his tickling sticks to the delighted fans, and then retreat behind the falling curtain, waving and uttering another of his catchphrases: 'Tatty bye, everybody. Tatty bye.'

Principally a stand-up comedian, Dodd has also had a successful recording career, and, during the 1960s and 1970s, also hosted numerous television series, including *The Ken Dodd Show*, *Doddy's Music Box*, and *Ken Dodd's Showbiz*. *How Tickled I Am: A Celebration of Ken Dodd* was the title of a 1977 biography by Michael Billington.

how you doin'?

A phrase traditionally associated with Italian-Americans, and Mafia members in particular, but more recently popularized by Joey Tribbiani (Matt LeBlanc) on the ensemble US TV series *Friends* (1995–), about six friends living in New York City. Joey is an actor (usually out of, or in search of, work), who does his best to embody the Casanova image the countrymen of his roots are known for, and whose favourite pick-up line is the surprisingly unsophisticated 'How you doin'?'

The line was further popularized by two TV commercials for Budweiser beer that featured a group of Italian Mafiosi meeting at a bar and using their standard greeting. In a parody of the US New Jersey-set TV gangster series *The Sopranos*, a chain of 'How you doin''s are rhythmically repeated by a group of 'wiseguys' in their best New Jersey accents. As the men take their seats at the bar, the camera pulls away, revealing a hidden microphone on top of a light fixture and then an agent with headphones in a van taking everything down. The camera then cuts back to the men in the bar, who are passing around the microphone, repeating the greeting. The advert ends with the men yelling the line into the microphone in unison, practically deafening the FBI agent, and Budweiser's ad campaign's familiar tagline—'True'—appears across the screen.

how'm I doing?

Trademark line associated with Ed Koch, mayor of New York from 1977 to 1989. Famous for his craving for critique, Koch would ask his constituents 'How'm I doing?' again and again over the course of his three terms as mayor, intent on getting feedback from the people he served. The phrase, recognized as a useful tool in gauging performance in other fields, became a favourite among many US businesses and marketing firms. Among the former mayor's non-fiction works is the title *How'm I Doing: The Wit and Wisdom of Ed Koch*, published in 1981.

how's your father?

British slang for sexual intercourse, as in 'Fancy a bit of how's your father, Doreen?'; now also used as penis. It was a popular catchphrase during the early 20th century when it was used by British music-hall performers, notably the comedian Harry Tate. During that period, the phrase had not yet acquired its sexual meaning, and was use to simply mean 'nonsense'. Several of Tate's catchphrases went into the English language for a period of time, including 'Goodbye-ee', and the expression 'I don't think', used ironically (as in 'He's a nice chap em. I *don't* think'). His 'How's your father?' was said as a get-out for not being able to answer something, and in this form is now obsolete.

The phrase appears in numerous British comedy sketches, including Monty Python's 'Banter Sketch' in which the Squadron Leader (Eric Idle) happily embarks on some 'perfectly ordinary banter' with: 'Bally Jerry, pranged his kite right in the how's-your-father; hairy blighter, dicky-birded, feathered back on his sammy, took a waspy, flipped over on his Betty Harpers and caught his can in the Bertie.' Or, as Austin Powers (Mike Myers) puts it, 'Personally before I'm on the job, I like to give my undercarriage a bit of a how's your father!' in the 1999 film *Austin Powers: The Spy Who Shagged Me. How's Your Father?* was the title of a BBC TV sitcom that ran from 1979 to 1980, and was about a middle-aged man (Harry Worth) bringing up his teenage daughter and son.

hubba hubba

An exclamation (in American slang) of liking or approval, with reference to an attractive woman or, more recently, to a man. The expression, already used by the US military in the early 1940s, was popularized by Bob Hope in his shows for troops during the Second World War as well as in his radio shows. His typical comment on a passing beauty would be: 'Hubba, hubba, what a looker!' A rather unlikely object of this appreciative exclamation was Popeye's girlfriend, the stick-figured Olive Oyl, in an episode of the cartoon series called *Beach Peach*, in which a handsome lifeguard's entire body stiffens and points straight out from the tower at Olive Oyl, while the sound effect, 'Boing!' is heard. He says 'Hubba, Hubba!!' and then lets out a loud, long wolf whistle.

hush, keep it dark

A variation on a British and American Second World War security slogan calling on both civilians and armed forces privy to any military information to 'keep it dark!', that was popularized in the UK by Commander High-Price (a character played by Jon Pertwee) on Eric Barker's segment of the forces radio show *Merry Go Round* (1943–8), entitled *HMS Waterlogged*. In 1948 the fictional HMS Waterlogged became the subject of a spin-off show, *The Waterlogged Spa*, and the catchphrase migrated along with the character.

Meaning keep it as a secret from other people, the expression can be traced back to the late 17th century. The phrase was first used as a slogan when the British government launched a 'Keep it Dark' poster campaign in October 1939 (the same message was reinforced the following year with the slogan 'Be Like Dad, Keep Mum'). From April 1942, the US Army also used the phrase to instil a vigilance about military information, with lines like: 'Lives are lost through conversation/So here's a tip for the duration/If you've private information/KEEP IT DARK!'

Ii

······

I am Mr Rock 'n' Roll

One of US comedian David Letterman's catchphrases, popularized on his TV talk show *Late Night with David Letterman* (1982–). Meaning I am 'cool' and a 'party animal', the description is used ironically by Letterman who often quite gleefully ridicules himself.

I am not capable of that emotion

Spoken by Mr Spock (Leonard Nimoy) on the original *Star Trek* TV series (1966–9) on the many occasions in which he found himself unable, as a wholly logical half-Vulcan, to share or even conceive of human feelings which would come to the fore and could deeply affect his closest friend, Captain Kirk, or other shipmates on the Starship *Enterprise*. It is at times said with a twinge of sadness or regret. At others, to suggest subtly that he is perhaps above certain human 'weaknesses', but always semi-masked by a simply informative, matter-of-fact expression. Gene Roddenberry, who created and produced the hugely popular series, had had to fight to keep Spock in the show, as the network feared TV audiences would find him difficult to relate to. It seems, however, his dualistic nature was precisely what made him more charming and intriguing.

I am not fat! I'm big-boned!

Popularized by 8-year-old Eric Cartman on the controversial US TV cartoon series *South Park* (1997–), created by Trey Parker and Matt Stone. Cartman, whose mother spoils him with high-fat treats like 'Snacky Cakes' and 'Cheesy Poofs', is teased ruthlessly by the other kids (his foul-mouthed classmates) about his weight, and he responds by being utterly odious, offensive, and opinionated. This catchphrase, a favourite with the show's fans which has adorned many a T-shirt, is one of Cartman's favourite come backs when he has been insulted. It has practically become a format phrase, as Cartman tends to come up with quite a few variations on its second part, such as 'I'm festively/pleasantly/Christmas plump!' or 'I'm getting fit!'

I am outta here!

A catchphrase of US comedian Dennis Miller as anchorman on *Saturday Night Live*'s popular 'Weekend Update' sketch. Miller joined the popular TV comedy sketch series—which made its debut in 1975—for its 1986-7 season. He would deliver the week's news with acerbic fury, and would invariably end his report by signing off with a trademark pen flourish across his copy and an 'I am outta here!' Usually, and always with a self-satisfied grin, he would announce irreverently: 'Guess what, folks? That's the news, and I am outta here!'

I am Spock

Words of introduction spoken by Commander Spock (Leonard Nimoy), the stoic half-human, half-Vulcan on the original US TV series *Star Trek* (1966–9). *I Am Spock* is the title of Nimoy's latest autobiography, published in 1995—a rejoinder to a slimmer, little-known volume he published in 1975, when *Star Trek* was beginning to achieve super-cult status, entitled *I Am Not Spock*. In his latest autobiography Nimoy comes to grips with the character by which so many define him, while in his earlier work he deals with his concern at being typecast and denied 'non-alien' roles. The 1975 title alienated many fans.

I am the greatest

Self-promotion slogan used by US boxer Muhammad Ali (1942–) from around 1962. Muhammad Ali (adopted name of Cassius Marcellus Clay Jr.) became world professional heavyweight champion in 1964, and was the only man to regain the title twice (in 1974 and 1978). He was known as an extrovert with an arrogant nature, characteristics that seemed to help justify what soon became his catchphrase.

Attempting to make the most of Ali's image of greatness, in 1977, NBC premiered *I Am the Greatest: The Adventures of Muhammad Ali*, an animated series to which Ali lent his vocal talents. It featured him as a modern day Robin Hood, fighting for the under-privileged and solving the occasional mystery. Somehow, the larger-than-life Ali didn't translate well to animated form in the minds of most viewers, and the show was cancelled after only one season.

I asked you not to tell me that!

Popularized by Maxwell Smart (Don Adams) on the US TV comedy series *Get Smart* (1965–70), a wacky James Bond spoof conceived by producer Dan Melnick and writers Mel Brooks and Buck Henry. The phrase did not make an appearance until the show's third season in *Viva Smart*, but quickly became one of Max's favourites. Max, Agent 86, often used it when he didn't want to hear about or be reminded of a mistake or terrible incident. As in:

Max: Don't tell me I fell off the horse.
Agent 99 (Barbara Feldon): You fell off the horse, Max.
Max: I asked you not to tell me that!

I can't believe I ate the whole thing!

A slogan from a 1970s US advertising campaign for the antacid Alka Seltzer that became a national buzzword. One of these still memorable TV commercials showed a man, who had just finished a enormous bowl of pasta, in obvious agony. Looking rather ill, he says 'I can't believe I ate the WHOLE thing'. The voice-over then goes on about Alka Seltzer's efficacy, and the camera returns to the man who now is smiling and says 'the WHOLE thing'. Although the spots were popular, Alka Seltzer's sales went down, as it turned out that people didn't find bloated bellies and popping buttons that amusing after all.

Known for his fondness for food (usually junk food), Homer J. Simpson, the father of the family featured on the US animated TV show *The Simpsons* (1989–   ), is also familiar with this catchphrase. An episode entitled 'The Front' shows Homer's high school yearbook (freeze frame) only entry—beneath a photo of him described as 'a paragon of sloppiness'—to be 'I can't believe I ate the whole thing'.

I didn't get where I am today...

A phrase used to indicate and stress the speaker's self-importance and impatience with the irrelevant or inappropriate. It is the most famous of the numerous catchphrases uttered by Reginald Perrin's boss,

Charles Jefferson (C.J.), played by John Barron in the BBC TV comedy series *The Fall and Rise of Reginald Perrin* (1976–9) and *The Legacy of Reginald Perrin* (1996). This series was jam-packed with catchphrases. In order to emphasize the mundaneness of Reggie's daily life, writer David Nobbs decided the characters surrounding Reggie should have phrases that were uttered on a regular basis, sometimes ad nauseam. With the comic scripts and fast pace of the action, the phrases tripped out until even the viewer became almost unaware of them.

C.J.'s 'I didn't get where I am today ...' was probably the most famous catchphrase of the entire series, and somehow, usually quite quirkily, he was able to use it no matter what the topic of the conversation. For example, in the first series, episode 1, after a tasting session to determine the three most popular flavours of ice cream, the surveys are processed by the computer, which suffers a fault. C.J.'s retort: 'I didn't get where I am today by selling ice cream tasting of bookends, pumice stone and West Germany.'

I do not like this game

Used by Bluebottle (Peter Sellers) in the BBC radio *Goon Show* (1952–60), usually to mean 'I know this will only lead to disaster'. As in this exchange with Neddy Seagoon (played by Harry Secombe): Seagoon: 'Now, Bluebottle, take this stick of dynamite.' Bluebottle: 'No, I do not like this game.' Bluebottle, one of the best-loved characters in the programme, is a young boy scout from East Finchley, London, who is the best friend of Eccles and usually gets blown up or 'deaded', as he calls it. (See also 'you dirty rotten swine, you')

I don't believe it

Associated with the irascible and bored pensioner Victor Meldrew, portrayed by Richard Wilson, in the BBC TV comedy series *One Foot in the Grave* (1990–2000). When Victor Meldrew, who had never been renowned for his patience and tolerance, is forced to take early retirement, he suddenly has plenty of time on his hands to rage against the petty annoyances of life. When he thinks that something is wrong (as he often does) he's never afraid to say so. His long-suffering wife Margaret (Annette Crosbie) just has to grin and bear it. This, his most famous catchphrase, delivered with his trademark intonation, sums up the outrage and indignation that seem to be daily occurrences for him. In one episode, 'The Worst Horror of All', Victor is convinced that the skip he has hired will, in the morning, have an old mattress dumped in it. When he wakes, his familiar cry of 'I don't believe it' reveals that someone has in fact dumped a Citroen 2CV. However, the joke is completed when Victor opens the car door, and out falls the mattress which he had so feared he would find.

Wilson has openly stated, mainly through appearances on the BBC2 programme *Have I Got News For You* (presented by Angus Deayton), that he hated his catchphrase. Wilson appeared as himself in a third season episode of the Channel 4 comedy series *Father Ted*, in which he ends up physically attacking Ted because he can't help saying the catchphrase. The last ever episode of *One Foot in the Grave*, in which Victor Meldrew was run over by a car and killed, was transmitted in the UK on 20 November 2000.

I don't know!

Words popularized by various characters on the Canadian children's TV programme *You Can't Do That On Television* (1979–90). The show, which relied heavily on slapstick, turned 'I don't know' and 'water' into magical words that would instantly and predictably result in one or more of the child cast being slimed or drenched. The use of green slime was one of the show's trademarks, and one accidental 'I don't know' would get on-air personalities doused with a gooey green slop. See also 'duh...I heard that!'

I don't mind if I do

A catchphrase belonging to Colonel Humphrey Chinstrap, played by Jack Train, on the 1940s BBC radio comedy series *ITMA*, to mean yes please, by all means. Colonel Chinstrap made his first appearance when the show returned to the airwaves with its fifth series in September 1942, set in a war factory based at the seaside resort setting of Foaming-at-the-Mouth. The guzzling army officer, who managed to turn almost any innocent remark into the offer of a drink with his catchphrase, rapidly became one of the show's most popular characters.

I dood it

Oft-repeated proclamation of 'Junior, the Mean Widdle Kid', one of US comedian Red Skelton's characters, usually said just before (or after) some bit of mischief or damage. The nasty boy had been developed on Skelton's radio show in the late 1930s, and was later perfected on his TV show that ran from 1951 to 1971. Skelton, who began his career on the vaudeville stage and films, also starred in a 1943 film entitled *I Dood It*. This madcap Second World War-era musical features Red Skelton romping, careening, pantomiming, and pining for the object of his affections—Eleanor Powell. During the Second World War, Skelton performed at many military bases and defence plants. Apparently, when US aviation pioneer James H. Doolittle executed his daring bombing raid over Tokyo in 1942 'I Dood It!' was painted across the nose of his B-52 Bomber.

The phrase was later also used by Bugs Bunny, Daffy Duck, and other cartoon characters. For example, in *Case of the Missing Hare* (1942), Bugs Bunny, just before pasting Ala Bahma's face with a pie, says, 'If I dood it, I get a whippin'. I dood it!' One gag using this phrase was cut from most prints shown today of *The Blitz Wolf* (MGM, 1942). It showed Tokyo being shelled, with a sign reading 'Doolittle Dood It'; the cartoon also showed a newspaper with a reference to the 'whippin'' line.

I forgot the question

A line denoting anything from lack of concentration to lack of intelligence that was popularized by a giggly, bikini-clad Goldie Hawn on the catchphrase-packed NBC TV comedy series *Rowan and Martin's Laugh-in* (1968–73). Hawn, who was a regular performer on *Laugh-in* from 1968 to 1970, was portrayed as the classic, frivolous, blonde airhead, who could scarcely follow any mildly complicated line of questioning—a stereotyping that seemed to carry over into her later film career to some degree as well.

I get no respect

US comedian Rodney Dangerfield's trademark line, both on stage as well as in his many film appearances. Dangerfield's stage act consisted of telling about events in his life, mainly to do with his relationships with people (and animals). By the early 1980s, Dangerfield had became a household name with his 'I get no respect' standup banter and on-screen buffoonery. His jokes centred on the complete indifference and lack of sympathy he continually faced. An example of how he fails to command any respect is made clear in a joke involving what should be man's best friend: 'With my dog I get no respect. He keeps barking at the front door. He don't want to go out. He wants me to leave.' An article reporting on Dangerfield's failure to win additional damages in a libel suit against the *Star* magazine bore the following headline: 'Dangerfield gets no respect in bid for more libel damages' (Associated Press, 6 September 1996).

I go—I come back

Spoken by 'Ali Oop', played by Horace Percival, in the 1940s BBC radio programme *ITMA*. 'Ali Oop', a Middle Eastern vendor of saucy postcards and other dubious merchandise, first appeared in 1941 when the show's setting became that of a seaside resort called Foaming-at-the-Mouth. The popularity of the catchphrases generated by *ITMA* at the time was made clear by a letter which Tommy Handley received from a young girl who had been taken to see the *Tempest* in Manchester. Apparently, when the actor playing Ariel had to say the words 'I go, I go', the whole audience responded by shouting out 'I come back!'

I have a cunning plan

Phrase uttered by Baldrick (played by Tony Robinson) in the BBC TV historical 'situation tragedy' *Blackadder* series (1983–9). *Blackadder*, starring Rowan Atkinson as Edmund (also known as The Black Adder), spans from the 15th century all the way up to the First World War. Baldrick has been in Edmund's service longer than either of them care to remember, and although his master treats him with utter contempt, he remains intensely loyal. However, Baldrick believes his lack of formal education is compensated for by his basic street-wise cunning. Hence his well-known catchphrase, which then inevitably—and always comically—reveals a far from cunning idea.

The Black Adder (1983) is set in 1485, *Blackadder II* (1986) in the early 1560s, *Blackadder The Third* (1987) in the early 19th century, and

Blackadder Goes Forth (1989), the final series, in the trenches of the
First World War. Edmund and Baldrick reappear, as does this
catchphrase, in later series. For example, in one of the later episodes
of the last series, *Blackadder Goes Forth*, Captain Edmund Blackadder
(fighting the hairy Huns in the First World War) comes to know that
there is a spy in the army hospital. While methods of sniffing out the
mole are being discussed, Private Baldrick speaks up: 'I too have a
cunning plan.' His 'cunning' plan turns out to be going around the
hospital and asking everybody, 'Are you a German spy?'

Becoming familiar with the uselessness of Baldrick's cunning plans,
Blackadder would respond with popular lines such as this: 'Baldrick,
you wouldn't recognize a cunning plan if it painted itself purple,
danced on a harpsichord and sang: "Cunning plans are here again".'

I have the power!

Affirmation of strength popularized by the US adventure/fantasy
animated TV series *He-Man Masters of the Universe* (1983 syndicated), one
of the most popular cartoons of the 1980s with a highly successful
merchandising tie-in. The He-Man was the alter ego of the handsome
Prince Adam (both voiced by John Erwin), ruler of the planet Eternia
and overseer of Castle Greyskull. Prince Adam had to protect the castle
from danger, which usually meant threats from the evil Skeletor who
thought that he should be the one to rule the planet. Whenever
called upon to defend his people from Skeletor, Prince Adam would
raise his sword in the air and shout, 'By the power of Greyskull! I have
the power!', thus transforming himself into the mighty hero He-Man.
The show's success reached its peak in 1987 with the release of a
live-action film *Masters of the Universe*, starring Dolph Lundgren as
He-Man and Frank Langella as Skeletor.

I have to write my sermon

A catchphrase belonging to the posturing Reverend Timothy Farthing
(Frank Williams) on the BBC TV comedy series *Dad's Army* (1968–77).
As the vicar or St Aldhelm's Church in Walmington-on-Sea, he is
frequently miffed by Captain Mainwaring's insistence on treating the
church hall, and the office in particular, as his own. The line is often
directed at Mainwaring (Arthur Lowe), leader of the town's inept
Home Guard platoon, as a means of reclaiming what the vicar sees as

his territorial rights. At other times, it provides a ready excuse for exiting from an annoying situation or discussion. See also 'his Reverence won't like it'.

I hear you!

Don't think you are sparing me anything. The line was used repeatedly by Miss Kraus (Inga Swenson) on the US TV comedy series *Benson* (1979–86), directed at Benson (Robert Guillaume) just after he would begin insulting her, thinking she was out of earshot. An unlikely spin-off from the off-the-wall, controversial series *Soap*, *Benson* had Guillaume continuing his role as the acerbic butler who resented working for wealthy, self-centred people. The spin-off found Benson working in the Governor's Mansion, and once again surrounded by inept rich people. The show's highlight was the banter between Benson and Miss Gretchen Kraus, the severe German housekeeper. Vigorously trading insults, their exchanges frequently ended with Kraus exclaiming off stage, 'I hear you!' As the series progressed, their mutual dislike for each other evolved into a sort of semi-tolerance.

I heard you say that, Teddy Boy!

From the popular long-running BBC radio comedy series *Ray's a Laugh* (1949–61) starring Ted Ray that was filled with curious characters and catchphrases. This phrase was spoken by Ted's brother-in-law, Nelson (played by the singer Fred Yule), in domestic situations. Yule, who had been a bass with the Kentucky Minstrels, would enter most scenes with this line.

I kiss you!

An expression that was popularized by the former Turkish journalist Mahir Cagri, the world's first Internet superstar, whose popular homepage helped transform it into a standard Internet greeting. The unassuming Mahir, who lives in Turkey and plays the accordion, suddenly became the most popular man on the Internet in late 1999, even inspiring fan clubs. His website greeted visitors with a warm 'Welcome to my home page!!!!!!!! I kiss you!!!!!' and offered numerous photos of Mahir and his friends. Mahir enthusiastically informs us in dubious English that he is a 'jurnalist' who likes 'to

take foto-camera'. He also writes, 'I like sex', extending an
invitation to all potential friends: 'Who is want to come TURKEY
I can invitate...She can stay my home.'

I know nothing

Don't ask me, I am totally ignorant (and innocent). Popularized by the
corpulent and beef-brained Sergeant Hans Schultz (John Banner) on the
US TV series *Hogan's Heroes* (1965–71), set in a German prison camp in
Düsseldorf in the middle of the Second World War. In constant fear of
banishment to the Russian front, Schultz wishes to hold on to his job as
prison guard at Stalag 13 and so make it home to his wife and children.
He often ignores the antics of Hogan and the other prisoners because, as
he says: 'In war, I do not like to take sides!' Although he claims to
know nothing, his lips can in fact be easily loosened by the promise
of a large portion of strudel. The show's humour is largely dependent
on the idiocy of Schultz and his commander, Colonel Klink, who,
no matter how hard they try, are repeatedly outwitted and
humiliated by the clever American soldier Hogan.

The barracks sitcom's premiss is that, rather than try to escape
from the camp, American prisoners of war would use their superior
intelligence and cunning to help other allies escape, while sticking
out the remainder of the war in surroundings which could gradually
be made as comfortable as a luxury resort. Obviously, to make all this
possible, the Nazis running the camp, which included the
Commandant, Colonel Klink (Werner Klemperer), and his main
prison guard, Sergeant Schultz, would have to be rather incompetent.
As a result of the depiction of these muddleheaded officers, *Hogan's
Heroes* failed to portray the way real-life Nazis behaved. It has
therefore always been seen as quite controversial, and objections
have been raised since the series first aired concerning the treatment
of German soldiers as lovable buffoons. Ultimately, the show's
popularity stemmed really from its characterization of the US
soldiers, particularly Colonel Robert Hogan (Bob Crane) with his
smooth, coolheaded intelligence.

I know you are, but what am I?

A juvenile response to any insult (such as 'You're crazy!') on one's
person. Catchphrase belonging to Pee-Wee Herman, the alter-ego of

I like to watch

US comedian Paul Reubens. Reubens launched the catchphrase in 1981, when the *The Pee-Wee Herman Show* ran for five sellout months at Los Angeles' Roxy night club, and it remained the giggling man-child's trademark line in the 1985 film *Pee-Wee's Big Adventure*, and his live-action children's TV programme, *Pee-Wee's Playhouse* (1986–91). The character, of indeterminate age and sexuality, who possessed a sarcastic enthusiasm for the popular culture of the 1950s and 1960s, drew a substantial audience of adults, who joined his younger fans on Saturday mornings to watch his shows.

I like to watch

A statement uttered repeatedly by Chance, played by Peter Sellers, in the 1979 film *Being There*, based on the 1971 novel by Jerzy Kosinski. *Being There* is a satirical fable about Chance, a reclusive, simple-minded gardener whose only knowledge of the 'real' outside world is through watching television. When Chance's benefactor dies, he wanders aimlessly into the streets of Washington, DC, is struck by a car owned by Eve Rand (Shirley MacLaine), who mistakenly takes him to be Chauncey Gardiner, and takes him to her home for recuperation. (See also 'all is well—and all will be well—in the garden'.) Chance's empty-headed pronouncements are taken to be profoundly intelligent and wisely insightful. His famous line, on watching TV, is always misinterpreted, as when Eve Rand comes on to him in his bedroom. She misinterprets Chance's statement as a kinky desire to watch her masturbate, which she promptly does, while he continues to watch TV.

I love it when a plan comes together

Popularized by Colonel John 'Hannibal' Smith (played by George Peppard) on the US action/adventure/comedy TV series *The A-Team* (1983–7) whenever they completed one of their impossible tasks. With a sly smirk and a cigar jutting jauntily out of his mouth, 'Hannibal' would remark, 'I love it when a plan comes together', right after a tough battle, where somehow he, as the team's leader, had managed to make everything work, and the team emerged unhurt and victorious. *The A-Team* was the name given to a group of four Vietnam veterans (including Hannibal) who were wanted by the government for a crime they did not commit, and worked secretly as soldiers of fortune. The series was considered at one time to be the most violent television show on the air, yet in its trademark way people were rarely hurt by all the gunfire, explosions, fights, etc., that seemed to make up the bulk of the show.

I married him for better or worse but not for lunch

A play on one of the traditional Christian wedding vows, that has become a catchphrase among women's groups and organizations in the USA and the UK, used with reference to adjusting to married life after a husband's retirement, or the onset of memory loss or senility. The exact origins of the phrase are uncertain, but it was popular in both countries by the early 1960s. It has been ascribed to both the Duchess of Windsor, who used it when noting her husband would lunch on his own while she went about her business, as well as to Hazel Weiss, who uttered the line in 1960, after her husband, George Weiss, retired as manager of the New York Yankees.

I must love you and leave you

A witty way of bidding farewell used in casual situations since the late 19th century. One common variation on the phrase is 'love them and leave them', meaning don't get emotionally involved. The saying, 'My daddy always said, love um and leave um is better than keep um', is included in Joseph C. Bridges's *Cheshire Proverbs and Other Sayings and Rhymes Connected with the City and County Palatine of Chester* (1917). 'Love Me or Leave Me' was also the title of a song (words by Gus Kahn and music by Walter Donaldson) from the 1928 Broadway musical *Whoopee!*, recorded by Ruth Etting that year. Since then, the song has been recorded by many artists, including Benny Goodman, in 1934 and 1936, and by Nina Simone in 1957. However, the song was so associated with Etting that it became the title song of her screen biography *Love Me Or Leave Me* starring Doris Day (as Etting) and James Cagney, one of the top-grossing films of 1955.

I pity the fool!

A catchphrase that was as instantly recognizable as the man behind it—Mr T, on the US action/adventure/comedy TV series *The A-Team* (1983–7), and on his own self-titled programme, an animated half-hour framed by live-action inserts (1983–6). The big, tough, Mohawk-sporting Mr T shot to instant stardom as mechanic/tough guy Sergeant B. A. Barracus, one of the four Vietnam veterans forming the 'A-Team', and his catchphrase adorned many a T-shirt during the 1980s. The phrase had already been popularized, to a lesser extent, by the jazz/blues song, entitled 'I Pity the Fool', written by Deadric Malone in 1960 ('I said I pity the fool/She'll break your heart one day/Then she'll laugh if she walks away/Yeah, I pity the fool').

I say, what a smasher!

An expression originating in the UK in the 1940s used to note a particularly attractive woman. Derived from the use of 'smash' to mean a great success or sensation, the phrase was popularized in the early 1950s through its recurring use on the popular BBC radio show *Calling All Forces* that ran from 1951 to 1952. The series was hosted by Ted Ray, until April 1952, when Tony Hancock and Charlie Chester took over as 'co-compères'. Charlie Chester, the Jewish Cockney comic who was most associated with the phrase, also wrote and performed his own weekly single spot. The show carried on for another two years under different titles—it became *Forces All Star Bill*, then *All Star Bill*, and finally *Star Bill!*

I still got it

Self-congratulatory remark popularized by Ralph Malph (Donny Most) on the US TV series *Happy Days* (1974–84), meaning I still have the gift or talent. After Fonzie (Henry Winkler) became the show's central character, Potsie, who had been introduced as Richie Cunningham's best friend, became part of a daft duo with Ralph. And Ralph's character, originally portrayed as slightly more mature and worldly than Richie and Potsie, became a bit of a sissy who would often proclaim, 'I still got it', after making one of his predictably bad jokes. Repeatedly inflicting corny jokes and unbearably obvious puns on an unwilling audience, Ralph would happily ignore the groans of his listeners and follow each of his failed jokes with an enthusiastic 'I got it, I still got it!' Despite his solid optimism and dreams of success as a comedian, he eventually followed in his father's footsteps and became an eye doctor. (See also 'correctomundo'.)

I tawt I taw a puddy tat

The distinctive words and lisp of the little yellow canary bird cartoon character known as Tweety Pie (voice of Mel Blanc) in Warner Bros. cartoon series (1944–). Tweety would typically say, 'I tawt I taw a puddy tat....I did! I did! I did taw a puddy tat!' referring to his enemy, Sylvester, a black and white cat with a red nose. Forever warding off attacks from Sylvester the Cat, Tweety is often helped out by others, such as Granny or one of the generic bulldogs that inhabit Warner Bros. cartoons. At other times, luck would play a part or Tweety would simply take the initiative in protecting himself. Although Tweety, created by Bob Clampett, had a baby voice and a head that looked like a baby's, he actually had quite a mean temperament, and was more than happy to use petrol, clubs, and dynamite to protect himself. Mel Blanc recorded a hit song 'I Tawt I Taw a Puddy-Tat' in 1950. Currently, Tweety is voiced by Joe Alaskey and Bob Bergen.

I think you are getting into the realms of fantasy again, Jones

A gentle reproach urging a realistic approach or view popularized by Captain George Mainwaring (Arthur Lowe) on the BBC TV comedy series *Dad's Army* (1968–77). The recurring phrase is directed at Lance Corporal Jack Jones (Clive Dunn), Walmington-on-Sea's elderly butcher who enjoys telling everyone at length of his experiences during the Boer War. Mainwaring, the seaside town's stuffy bank manager who appointed himself the Home Guard platoon's captain, had little patience with Jones's overly keen and excitable nature. (See also 'don't panic!')

I wanna tell you a story

A catchphrase belonging to British entertainer and comic writer Max Bygraves, accompanied by the trademark loose shaking of his hands, that was mimicked across Britain from the 1950s onwards. It became a one of Mike Yarwood's favourite impressions in his acts during the early 1970s. Bygraves used this distinctive catchphrase as the title of his 1976 autobiography. See also 'good idea—son, a'.

Bygrave's catchphrase has become so much a part of the British lexicon, that it appears in sports contexts, such as: 'After having fifteen minutes to rant, scream and cajole, his charges followed the game plan for precisely ninety seconds before reverting to type, causing the manager to charge onto the field in a manner of Max Bygraves, wringing his hands in a "wanna-tell-you-a-story" manner'. (Newcastle United Football Club match reports, online). It also crops up somewhat surprisingly in a Commons debate about 'the closure of Hunterston A' when Mr Foulkes states: 'I shall use the phrase of the singer Max Bygraves, "I wanna tell you a story", about Hunterston A'. However, when Mr John Home Robertson (East Lothian) asks: 'Will my hon. Friend sing it?' Mr Foulkes replies 'No, I certainly will not sing it. That would empty the Chamber even further' (House of Commons, 5 April 1989).

I want my MTV!

The tag-line—reminiscent of a child's defiant demand—used in a memorable advertising campaign by the groundbreaking music-video channel MTV that debuted on 1 March 1982, and featured various pop stars such as Mick Jagger and David Bowie looking into the camera and saying simply: 'I want my MTV!' MTV, which had been launched on American cable television in August 1981, first etched its way into American teenage consciousness with this now-legendary advertising campaign of the early 1980s, using short, often irreverent commercial spots that always ended with the tag-line, usually uttered by one of a number of rock stars (including Pete Townsend, Stevie Nicks, Adam Ant, Pat Benatar, and the Police) in close-up.

The line successfully invited teen viewers to identify themselves with the stars and consequently the 'I' making the demand. It also had the extra selling point of being spoken defiantly, as though to an imagined authority figure, and implying that this was *not* for a disapproving parent. Now a global phenomenon, MTV is broadcast around the world in a number of national versions in various languages, and its legendary tag-line has been borrowed and adapted to countless products and situations.

I want to be alone

Words strongly associated with, but wrongly attributed to, the Swedish-born US film star Greta Garbo who retired into an enigmatic private life in 1941. Her years of seclusion became associated with this declaration for the rest of her career, but Garbo was not in fact credited with originating the line, and 'I want to be alone . . . I just want to be alone' actually came from her 1932 classic film *Grand Hotel* (screenplay by William A. Drake). Reinforcing the association, in the silent movie *The Single Standard* (1929), she delivered the line (appearing as a subtitle), 'I am walking alone because I want to be alone'.

The phrase was often parodied, and although Garbo insisted that she never said it word for word—'I only said, "I want to be *let* alone." There is all the difference' (*Garbo*, 1955, by John Bainbridge)—it has come to both symbolize and caricature the legendary actress.

I was only obeying orders

A generally lamentable pretext used in films from about 1940 and then associated with the Nuremberg trials (November 1945–October 1946), as the Nuremburg international military tribunal dismissed the 'I was only obeying orders' defence as illegitimate. The phrase has appeared frequently in films that bring up the issue of war crimes and of Nazi war crimes in particular. It has also often been parodied, especially in comedy films directed by Mel Brooks, including *The Producers* (1967).

In Washington, however, the phrase takes on a new twist according to George Will: 'The "Nuremberg defense," used by war criminals, is "I was only obeying orders." Usually it means, "I was only obeying orders I gave myself." Congress' "Nuremberg defense" is, "We were only disobeying orders we gave ourselves" (*Washington Post* Writers Group, online edition, 1999).

I was very, very drunk

The concluding phrase to sketches featuring Rowley Birkin QC (Paul Whitehouse) on the BBC TV comedy series *The Fast Show* (1994–7). The upper-crust barrister was a strange looking old man, with a puffy, reddened nose (from drinking too much), who sat in an armchair, whisky in hand, in an old-fashioned sitting room telling largely unintelligible stories about his past exploits and travels. Some segments of the speech would be understandable, but most of it was an undulating mumble, interspersed with occasional strange noises and hand signals. Only the ends of his sentences come clear ('the whole thing was made completely out of rubber!', '...he didn't get up for three days!'), and he ends his monologues with '...I'm afraid I was very, very drunk', or a variation thereof. In 2001, Whitehouse's rambling character starred in a TV and radio advertising campaign for British Gas, ending his tales praising the gas service with variations on his trademark line, such as 'I was very, very impressed'.

I wish I were an Oscar-Mayer weiner

A slogan and the beginning of a catchy jingle for Oscar-Mayer hot dogs during the 1970s that became familiar to all age groups in the US, and was often sung by adults wishing to appear juvenile and humorous in certain situations. The popular jingle went: 'Oh, I wish I were an Oscar-Mayer wiener; that is what I'd truly like to be. 'Cause if I were an Oscar-Mayer wiener, Everyone would be in love with me.'

I wondered who was going to spot that first!

A sarcastic, but ultimately condescending, remark that was popularized by Captain George Mainwaring (Arthur Lowe) on the BBC TV comedy series *Dad's Army* (1968–77). The grammar school-educated Mainwaring, who was Walmington-on-Sea's bank manager, was put in charge of the seaside resort's inept and bungling Home Guard platoon. Mainwaring's sense of self-importance and middle-class snobbery led him to look down on tradesmen—many of whom made up his platoon—and developed catchphrases such as this one to express his low opinion of their intellectual prowess. See also 'you stupid boy'.

I wouldn't know about that, sor

Slightly embarrassed or awkward response popularized by Ted (Paul Whitehouse) in the 'Ted and Ralph' sketches featured on the catchphrase-filled BBC TV comedy series *The Fast Show* (1994–7) and *Ted & Ralph* (1999). Ralph (Charlie Higson), a well-educated member of the landed gentry, has a mad crush on his loyal Irish handyman Ted, who quietly goes about his business on Ralph's estate. Ralph always tries to make intelligent conversation with Ted, broaching subjects Ted rarely knows anything about or about which he has no opinion. Uncomfortable, if not intimidated, Ted will usually reply with this phrase out of politeness. In one sketch, Ralph tries to convince Ted to come to a Tina Turner concert with him. When Ralph asks 'Do you like Tina Turner, Ted?' he replies simply with 'I wouldn't know about that, sor'. Other recurring variations on Ted's catchphrase are 'I wouldn't really know about that sor', or 'it's not really for me to say, sor'.

I yam what I yam!

A catchphrase belonging to Popeye the Sailor Man, the cartoon character originally created in 1929 by US cartoonist E. C. Segar. Popeye made his first appearance in a newspaper strip called *Thimble Theater* as a feisty, pipe-smoking, spinach-eating sailor, whose motto was 'I yam what I yam!' often followed by 'and that's all what I yam!' He made his first film appearance in 1932; in 1933 a cartoon film entitled *I Yam What I Yam* was released, and between 1933 and 1957, more than 200 animated Popeye cartoons were made. Generations of children have echoed this catchphrase, as well Popeye's other saying: 'They ain't no myskery to life—ya gits borned, an' tha' all they is to it!' The sailor-philosopher's other well-known catchphrase was 'I eats my spinach', which convinced many children to eat their spinach just in case they, too, would be able to grow superhuman forearms that could take the shape of an anvil or jackhammer.

   Popeye: I Am What I Am was the title of a live action film version of the famous cartoon, directed by Robert Altman and starring Robin Williams and Shelly Duval as Popeye and Olive Oyl. The film's score and songs were written by Harry Nilsson, and included a song entitled 'I Yam What I Yam'. The New Jersey group Guiteri incorporated samples of this and other songs from the *Popeye* soundtrack album in their song 'I Yam What I Yam (Popeye Rap)'.

I'd rather fight than switch

Words of utter and uncompromising loyalty, in this case to a brand of cigarettes. The slogan came from an advertising campaign in the US for Tareyton cigarettes during the mid-1960s that featured men (usually blue collar types), and even women, sporting a black eye, proclaiming triumphantly: 'I'd rather fight than switch!' The aggressive assertion quickly became common currency and was used to express views on everything from brands to political parties.

I'll 'ave to ask me Dad

From *ITMA*, the most famous British radio comedy of the war, that aired weekly from 1939 to 1949 and introduced numerous catchphrases, many of which entered the language of the time. This phrase belonged to Mark Time (played by Jack Train), an elderly depraved character who answered all questions with this phrase.

I'll be back!

A combined promise/threat popularized by Austrian-born US film star Arnold Schwarzenegger in the 1984 action epic *The Terminator*. The premiss of this science-fiction thriller is that a future war between man and killer robots could be averted by sending a terminator (a human-seeming cyborg played by Schwarzenegger) to the present to kill the mother of the man who will lead a successful insurrection against their robotic masters. Kyle Reese, a warrior from the future, is also sent to the present to protect her. The time-travelling, muscle-bound robot did, in fact, return in the film's pre-apocalyptic 1991 sequel, and 'I'll be back' appears to be not just a well-worn catchphrase, but his approach to movie-making as plans for a *Terminator 3* were under way in 2001. It was Schwarzenegger's role as Terminator that pushed him to stardom.

'I'll be back' is the title of a review by Marjorie Garber of *Part Two: Reflections on the Sequel* edited by Paul Budra and Betty Schellenberg, which appeared in the *London Review of Books* Vol. 21, No. 16, 19 August 1999. In an example of how popular culture has entered that of the literary world, Garber writes: 'Arnold Schwarzenegger's self-fulfilling prophecy in *The Terminator*, "I'll be back", used as the title for one of the essays here (by Lianne McLarty), hovers over the sequel as— always—something between a promise and a threat.'

I'll drink to that!

Of US origins, in use at least since the 1950s, expressing a hearty approval or agreement in the matter or opinion at hand; sometimes used by comic lushes, trying to seize every opportunity available to have yet another drink. It was popularized by Dick Martin in the popular US comedy TV series *Rowan and Martin's Laugh-in* (1968–73) where he would say it in response to a comic line from Dan Rowan within the show's frenzied pace of one-liners.

I'll get me coat

A phrase used as an admission of being unwanted or undesirable in social situations, popularized by a character (known only as 'I'll get me coat') played by Mark Williams on the BBC TV comedy series *The Fast Show* (1994–7). The character in question is always saying or doing the 'wrong' things, becoming painfully aware that he can't follow discussions or make any acceptable contributions, closing all the sketches with his catchphrase. An interview with Fran Healy (of the Scottish rock band Travis) in *New Musical Express* (14 June 1997) concludes, after the interview became inaudible, with: 'Fran sighs and his eternal catchphrase lingers in the air, unspoken, unacknowledged but always glimmering in his eyes. "I'll get me coat."'

I'll give it five

A polite way of saying one doesn't think very highly of whatever or whoever is in question, and pronounced 'Oi'll give it foive!' by Janice Nicholls on ABC TV's pop music show *Thank Your Lucky Stars* (1961–6). The popular show, hosted by Keith Fordyce and later, by Brian Matthew, was Independent Television's answer to the BBC's *Juke Box Jury*. A weekly panel of young people—including Janice, the lovely clerk/receptionist from Birmingham—chosen by disc jockey Don Moss, gave their views on, and awarded points to, the latest record releases. Thanks to her familiar catchphrase, Black Country accent, general looks, and demeanour, Janice Nicholls probably became the one outstanding memory of the show.

The Beatles made their national television debut on *Thank Your Lucky Stars* in January 1963.

I'll have whatever she's having

Originally a phrase used in restaurants or bars as a sign of deference to or interest in another person, if not out of disinterest in the food or drink itself. It took on a different meaning and became a true catchphrase, however, after it was used in what has become one of cinema's most famous scenes—the 'fake an orgasm in a restaurant' scene from the 1989 US romantic comedy film *When Harry Met Sally*, directed by Rob Reiner, and starring Billy Crystal and Meg Ryan. In an attempt to convince Harry that women can convincingly fake orgasms, the scene featured a virtuoso performance by Sally (Meg

Ryan) which ends with a woman at the next table telling the waiter, 'I'll have whatever she's having'. The line was actually spoken by director Rob Reiner's mother, playing a bit part, and Ryan's ecstatic moans were actually dubbed. The phrase, now often used to express envy or a desire to emulate another person's sexual excitement or satisfaction, has been copied by Herbal Essences in shampoo commercials.

I'll make weapons from your bones!

A catchphrase from *Diablo II*, a computer game published and developed by Blizzard, released in 2000. The threat is spoken by 'The Smith', a demon guarding an enchanted smithing hammer called the Horadric Malus. While all of the dark beasts in the game are dangerous, The Smith is particularly vile and brutal, using the power of the Malus to create weaponry for the minions of Diablo. The player must search for The Smith and kill him in order to grab the Malus and head back to Charsi for his or her reward.

I'll nick anything, I will

Popularized by British comedian Paul Whitehouse, playing Chris the Crafty Cockney on the BBC TV comedy sketch series *The Fast Show* (1994–7). The catchphrase (usually pronounced 'anyfing'), was one of Chris's favourites, spoken proudly by a man who revels in his thieving abilities, describing himself as 'dodgy' and boasting about being 'a one man crime wave'.

I'll thcream and thcream until I'm thick, and I can!

Popularized by Bonnie Langford in the role of Violet Elizabeth Bott on the children's TV drama *Just William* (1977–8), based on books by the English writer Richmal Crompton. The stories, published between 1922 and 1970, told of the exploits of the mischievous schoolboy William and his gang of Outlaws in the 1930s. William regularly had to contend with the attentions of an unwelcome addition to the Outlaws—the lisping Violet Elizabeth, a 'soppy' girl, whose catchphrase was 'I'll thcream and thcream until I make mythelf thick'.

William Brown is perpetually a bright-eyed 11-year-old boy with unruly brown hair, and Violet Elizabeth is the bane of William's life (similar to and possibly the inspiration for Margaret in the comic strip *Dennis the Menace*). Believed by all the adults to be an angelic, model child, Violet Elizabeth is always dressed immaculately and topped with long ringlet curls. William and his mates, the Outlaws, have no time for girls. Nonetheless, Violet Elizabeth has a rather misguided, but soppy, crush on William and he is often forced to play with her. Violet Elizabeth uses her catchphrase as a form of blackmail, threatening to 'thcream' and 'thcream' whenever William attempts to leave her behind on one of his adventures or if it looks like she may not get her way.

BBC1 produced two seasons of the TV drama *Just William* during 1994–5, in which Violet Elizabeth was played by Tiffany Griffiths.

I'm a — person

Format phrase popularized Tom Patterson (Tim Preece) on the BBC TV comedy series *The Fall and Rise of Reginald Perrin* and *The Legacy of Reginald Perrin*. Tom, Reggie's son-in-law, was an indolent and doleful character who would make a point of letting others know what he did and didn't care for, by saying 'I'm a — person' or 'I'm not a — person'. For example, when making coffee, Tom announces 'I'm a coffee person', and when C.J., Tom's boss, tells him he's not pulling his weight, Tom replies 'I'm not a not pulling my weight person'.

I'm a doctor, not a . . . (bricklayer, engineer, mechanic, etc.)!

Associated with Dr Leonard 'Bones' McCoy (DeForest Kelley) on the original *Star Trek* TV series (1966–9), and one of the most familiar and enduring catchphrases of the series. McCoy, whose grumpy exterior barely hid his basic good-hearted, country doctor nature, would frequently find himself in situations that required abilities he was quite sure he didn't have, and would like to point this out by reminding the others what his true abilities in fact were. There were also variations on this theme, such as: 'What am I, a doctor or a moon shuttle conductor?', as well in reverse: 'I'm not a magician Spock, just an old country doctor!' In any case, these moments of assumed 'mistaken identity' would invariably vex McCoy, even though he would always then rise to the occasion as best he could.

I'm a kid. That's my job, that's what I do

A line, spoken by child star Macauley Culkin, in the US film *Uncle Buck* (1989), which was quickly adopted by American youngsters as a witty and handy excuse or explanation for a number of situations, and most often those arising from their mischief. The film starred John Candy as the title character, a big-hearted unemployed softy who receives an emergency call from his brother one night asking him to house-sit and take care of his children for a few days. Buck agrees, and after he arrives at his brother's expensive home in the northern suburbs of Chicago, where he finds three children uneasily waiting for him—a cute little boy (Culkin) and girl, and a glowering 15-year-old—he begins to learn just what kids really do.

I'm a little bit whooor, a little bit whaeey, a bit dodgy, a bit of a geezer

Satisfied self-appraisal popularized by Chris the Crafty Cockney (Paul Whitehouse) on the catchphrase-filled BBC TV comedy series *The Fast Show* (1994–7). Whitehouse exaggerated his own accent to produce this parody of a stereotypically confident, unscrupulous, Cockney character who will happily 'nick anyfing'. (See 'I'll nick anything, I will'.) The description is used to explain why Chris has really no choice but to steal whatever he can: 'Know what I mean? I'm a little bit whooor, a little bit whaeey, a little bit swish-swish-swish! Know what I mean? I'm dodgy. I'm a geezer. Right?' The phrase would be accompanied by little hand and arm gestures to one side then the other, reinforcing the impression that he specializes in fishy transactions.

I'm a sweet little cupcake ... BAKED BY THE DEVIL!!!

I may look all sweet and harmless, but there's more than meets the eye here! Unknown origin, but recently popularized by US comedian David Letterman, host of the TV talk show *Late Night with David Letterman* (1982–). Letterman himself often fits this description, appearing to be well-mannered and wholesome and then suddenly—through his comedic skills—taking a sharp or mischievous jab.

I'm Bart Simpson: who the hell are you?

One of the catchphrases associated with spunky 10-year-old Bart on the critically acclaimed and culturally cynical animated TV show *The Simpsons* (1989–   ). The phrase clearly expresses the boldness and anti-authority stance of Bart's character. 'Daredevil Bart', Homer and Marge Simpson's oldest child, is a borderline juvenile delinquent and provided the early focus of the programme.

I'm dead now. Please don't smoke

Words spoken by US actor Yul Brynner in posthumous anti-smoking TV commercials. The clarity of the words and message combined with the unprecedented nature of the appeal had a strong emotional impact on viewers, and were widely repeated, both seriously and, later on, jokingly. With his distinctive stage presence and trademark shaven head, Brynner was a familiar film star known for his on-screen toughness. When he developed lung cancer in the mid-1980s, he decided to leave a powerful public service announcement denouncing smoking as the cause and appealing to fellow Americans to quit smoking, for broadcast after his death. The Yul Brynner Head and Neck Cancer Foundation was established in his memory.

I'm dreaming of a white Christmas

The first line of 'White Christmas', a song written by Irving Berlin and first recorded by Bing Crosby in the 1942 film *Holiday Inn*, and featured again in the 1954 film *White Christmas*, directed by Michael Curtiz and starring Bing Crosby and Danny Kaye. Crosby had already sold over 25 million copies of the record, so it was not surprising that what was for many years one of the biggest popular hit songs of all time also made for a sizeable hit film. The song has been recorded by many different artists, including Frank Sinatra (1944), Mantovani (1952), and The Drifters (1954), and its opening lines: 'I'm dreaming of a white Christmas, Just like the ones I used to know' are still hummed, if not sung, by many in the US in the weeks preceding Christmas, usually with serious wishfulness.

I'm — fly me!

Advertising slogan for the US company National Airlines from 1972 to 1980. Dick Wolf (more recently executive producer of TV show *Law & Order*) penned the slogan 'I'm Cheryl, Fly Me' which formed the basis for the popular ad campaign featuring pictures of different women (referring to themselves by their Christian names) who viewers were supposed to think were real airlines hostesses. The first airline hostess in the campaign was played by Catherine Hickland who later became well known to US television audiences. National Airlines was taken over by Pan Am in January 1980, and the campaign came to an end. The rock group 10cc had a hit single in 1976 with 'I'm Mandy Fly Me' (on their 'How Dare You!' album), and Britain's Wall's sausages came up with a humorous twist on the phrase with its 1976 ad campaign: 'I'm meaty, fry me'.

The National Airlines campaign aroused anger and protests by US feminist groups which considered it grotesquely sexist. The National Organization of Women (NOW) launched a campaign against National Airlines' offensive advertising campaign, with members of New York NOW picketing National's advertising agency in October 1972.

I'm free!

The frequent cry of the rather camp salesman Mr Humphries in the long-running BBC TV comedy series *Are You Being Served?* (1973–83), written by David Croft and Jeremy Lloyd, creators of *Dad's Army* and *It Ain't Half Hot Mum*, and many more. The series is set in an old-fashioned, fictional London department store called Grace Brothers featuring, in particular, the Ladies' Fashions and Menswear floor, staffed by a loyal, yet highly eccentric, group of people. Grace Brothers is based on Lloyd's experiences at Simpson's in London's West End. The show was originally to centre around Trevor Bannister (Mr Lucas), but the characters of John Inman and Mollie Sugden (who played Mr Humphries and Mrs Slocombe) began to dominate the increasingly popular series, which relied heavily on its outrageous characters and double entendres.

There was also a short-lived Australian version in the early 1980s starring John Inman, the most popular actor of the original series. Writers Lloyd and Croft revived most of the characters in a later comedy series called *Grace and Favour* (BBC1, 1992). *Are You Being Served?* continues to be aired by PBS (by way of BBC America) in the US, by UK Gold (by way of the BBC) in the UK, and by many other stations around the world, and so it still has quite a large following. A feature film version was made in 1977, and an American version was tried out under the title *Beane's of Boston*

I'm in charge

One of the famous catchphrases coined by British entertainer Bruce Forsyth, in this case while hosting *Sunday Night at the London Palladium* (1958–71 and 2000). Forsyth would use the phrase to jokingly remind contestants—especially if they were a bit boisterous—that he was the boss. His abilities a host were put to the test one memorable night in 1961 when a strike by Equity robbed the show of its entire guest list. Luckily, Forsyth was not a member of Equity at the time; he was with the Variety Artist's Federation, as was Norman Wisdom, another very popular entertainer. On this night the two of them carried the entire show for the whole sixty minutes, while winning themselves critical acclaim and many new fans, as well as bolstering Forsyth's catchphrase boast.

Forsyth was an instant hit when he started hosting the show in 1958, thanks largely to his natural ability for ad-libbing and audience participation, and within weeks audience figures rose to over 14 million viewers for the Sunday night spectacular. Never losing his public popularity, Forsyth continued to work throughout the following decades, returning as host of a reborn *Sunday Night at the London Palladium* in the year 2000.

I'm Julian, and this is my friend Sandy

[usually: 'Hallo, I'm Julian, and this is my friend Sandy'.] Associated with Julian and Sandy (played by Hugh Paddick and Kenneth Williams), principal characters in the BBC radio comedy series *Round the Horne* (1965–9). By far the programme's most popular characters, the effete, 'fantabulosa' Julian and Sandy spoke in polari, a bizarre mixture of the Romany language and homosexual streetcode, and were always discovered running odd businesses whilst 'resting' from 'the profession' during their weekly sketches. As male homosexuality was not legalized in Britain until 1967, the boys' 'polari', or way of speaking, was therefore truly an underground argot. Polari could also mean 'a chat', as in 'Go on, get out your ouija—let's have a polari with the spirits!' The Julian and Sandy sketches often began with some variation on the salutation 'How bona to vada your dolly old eek again', meaning 'How good to see your nice old face again'.

I'm Larry. This is my brother Darryl. And this is my other brother, Darryl

Recurring introduction, supplied obviously by Larry (William Sanderson), on the US comedy TV series *Newhart* (1982–90). Larry, his brother Darryl and his other brother Darryl, formed the show's terribly scruffy, strange trio of Vermont handymen bumpkins who would get a wild round of applause every time they made their entrance with what quickly became a theme whine, 'Hi, I'm Larry. This is my brother Darryl. And this is my other brother Darryl'. The series found most of its comedy by putting the relatively normal Dick (Bob Newhart) and Joanna Loudon (Mary Frann) in near-constant contact with the sea of eccentrics around them, including these three yokels. Larry was the talkative one—neither of the two Darryls spoke a word, but made eloquently idiotic faces—but all three were completely inept at the repair jobs they were usually assigned.

The three characters were originally written in by the show's creators to appear in one episode in 1982, but were so well received that they were brought back in the 1983 season for four appearances, and, in 1984, became full-time. Although clearly branded as laughable simpletons, from time to time, Larry would come out with a wonderfully perceptive remark that verged on brilliance. The first Darryl was played by Tony Papenfuss, and the second Darryl by John Voldstad.

I'm listening

Dr Frasier Crane's signature line on his radio call-in show in the highly acclaimed US TV comedy series *Frasier* (1993–   ). The show features the neuroses and weekly trials suffered by Frasier (played by Kelsey Grammer), an insecure, pompous, and snobbish psychiatrist who hosts a Seattle radio advice show. He always answers his first caller with this somewhat affected line: 'This is Dr Frasier Crane; I'm listening.' The priggish, but affable, psychiatrist invariably assumes he can analyse and solve anyone's problem but, more often than not, is completely incapable of following his own or others' advice.

Frasier made history by becoming the first series, comedy or drama, to achieve a record five consecutive Emmy wins for Outstanding Comedy Series. Kelsey Grammer's character is one of the most enduring on the small screen, having originated in the Boston barroom sitcom *Cheers* before relocating to become the star of his own show.

I'm looking for someone to love

A recurring plaintive declaration uttered by Arthur Fallowfield, a character played by Kenneth Williams on the BBC radio comedy series *Beyond Our Ken* (1958–64). The series featured Kenneth Horne with a regular cast performing short sketches, and was principally written by Eric Merriman (with Barry Took for the first two series). The soft-spoken Arthur Fallowfield was a wise Somerset farmer whose answer to everything was 'It lies in the soil'. 'I'm looking for someone to love' is also the title of a 1957 Buddy Holly song.

I'm mad as hell and I'm not taking any more

Words of defiance made famous by newscaster Howard Beale (Peter Finch) in the 1976 US film *Network*. The film, which stirred up much debate about the decaying values of television when it was released, actually centres on Diana Christiansen (Faye Dunaway), an unscrupulous ratings-hungry programming executive. Beale, who was already fed up, an alcoholic, and had just been fired, announces during his final broadcast that he will kill himself because of falling ratings. About to deliver his final farewell the following day, he instead says, 'Well, I'll tell you what happened: I just ran out of bull—'. His frankness works wonders for the ratings, prompting Diana to convince her bosses to keep Beale on. He goes back on the air, and is apparently deep into madness when he utters his famous line. After Beale orders his viewers to 'repeat after me', the film shows shots of people leaning out of their windows and screaming the phrase, all apparently 'mad as hell'. Beale's ratings skyrocket, and a new set is constructed on which he rants and raves after being introduced as the 'mad prophet of the airwaves'.

In 1978, tax crusader Howard Jarvis used the same phrase as a political rallying cry to energize Californians. Jarvis, the father of Proposition 13, California's austere property tax limitation ballot measure, claimed he was leading 'a people's movement' aimed at curbing the power of local governments. Jarvis's measure triggered a series of similar citizen initiatives around the country.

I'm not dead yet

An absurd comic line popularized by its repeated use in the 1975 British film *Monty Python and the Holy Grail*. The film begins with a scene apparently set in a plague-ridden medieval village. A ragged, hunched man is seen pulling a corpse-laden cart through the streets, calling 'Bring out your dead, bring out your dead!' A younger, but still ragged, man (Eric Idle) comes out from a house, with a much older man slung over his shoulder. The older man protests weakly: 'I don't want to go in the cart', and later promises 'I'll be better tomorrow'. Although the man keeps insisting 'I'm not dead', and even the cart puller protests that 'He's not dead yet', the son answers, 'No, but he will be soon and he's just taking up room in the house'. After some negotiation, they both strike the older man on the head, killing him. The cart puller then proceeds down the street, taking up his cry 'Bring out your dead. Bring out your dead'.

The finding of a research team led by Stephen L. Helfand, published in *Science* magazine (14 December 2000), showed that a mutating gene can double the lifespan of fruitflies from 37 days to between 69 and 71 days. The gene complex was named Indy as a joking (abbreviated) reference, and in homage, to the tag line from the Monty Python film—'I'm not dead yet'.

I'm not pissed, you know

Catchphrase shared by the three members of 'The Alcoholic Family'— Derek and Jenny Smashed and their son Simon (Mark Williams, Maria McErlane, and Simon Day) on the BBC TV comedy series *The Fast Show* (1994–7). All hopeless alcoholics (Mr Smashed is so 'smashed' he drinks Listerine and gargles with whisky), everyone in this family will utter this statement when caught in situations when the words are most blatantly and pathetically untrue.

I'm not sure but I think we'll find something here

A modest assumption—usually a correct one—popularized by Freddy, one of the four crime-solving, or 'meddling' teenagers who star along with their Great Dane on the US TV cartoon series *Scooby Doo* that ran from 1969 to 1986 (see also 'scooby-doo'). Freddy is the bravest and smartest of the four friends, and is therefore also the one who usually solves the mystery.

I'm only here for the beer

Meaning my only purpose/reason for being here is to get drunk, have fun, and perhaps take advantage of whatever may be on offer. An advertising slogan for Double Diamond beer, appearing in TV commercials in the UK from early 1971 onwards. Later featured on T-shirts and associated with 'lager louts' who have tended to give Britons a bad name abroad. When the *Sun* reported on the foiled heist of the De Beers 'Millennium Diamond' at the Millennium Dome, London, the words 'I'm Only Here for De Beers' ran across the tabloid's front page (8 November 2000).

I'm so depressed!

From the BBC radio and TV series *The Hitchhiker's Guide to the Galaxy* (also title of 1979 book by Douglas Adams). Associated with Marvin the paranoid Android who also often says: 'I think you should know I'm feeling very depressed.' The unhappy Marvin seems torn between (and deeply saddened by) the two sides of his nature—'Pardon me for breathing, which I never do anyway so I don't know why I bother saying it, oh God I'm so depressed'. The satirical invention of Douglas Adams (1952–2001), *The Hitchhiker's Guide to the Galaxy* originated as a radio play prior to its transformation into a novel, and was finally serialized for TV by Alan J. Bell in 1981.

I'm sorry I'll read that again

An apology customarily supplied by British newsreaders when they muddle their words or commit a gaffe. The phrase was popularized in the late 1960s when it became the title of the BBC radio comedy series, also referred to as *ISIRTA*, that ran from 1964 to 1972. Billed as 'a radio custard pie', the show starred Grahame Garden, Tim Brooke-Taylor, Bill Oddie (these three went on to form the Goodies on BBC TV), John Cleese, Jo Kendall, and David Hatch, and sprang from the undergraduate revues put on by the Cambridge University Footlights Club.

I'm the famous Eccles

How Eccles, an intellectually challenged character played by Spike Milligan, frequently introduces himself on the BBC radio *Goon Show* (1952–60). The naive Eccles, whose other catchphrase is 'Shut up Eccles!', appears mainly together with his friend, Bluebottle (Peter Sellers), who also likes to read out his own stage directions (see 'enter Bluebottle!'). Most episodes of the show would feature an extended scene with the two friends talking nonsense or playing soldiers.

I'm working 365 days a year to entertain America

A satirical take on an American expression of uncertain origin used to stress a person's or a group's dedication and, often selfless, commitment to a community or country. This version of the phrase, aptly describing the lot of the talk show host, was popularized by US comedian David Letterman on his TV talk show *Late Night with David Letterman* (1982–   ). The saying, which is practically a format phrase (the variable word here being 'entertain'), has often been used to describe the services performed by the police force or the armed forces.

I'm worried about Jim

Also: 'I'm a little worried about Jim'. A frequent entry made by Mrs Mary Dale, played (until 1963) by Ellis Powell, about her husband in the BBC radio series *Mrs Dale's Diary* (1948–69). Probably the most famous daily serial of them all, in which Mrs Dale, the doctor's wife, reads the daily happenings in the life of her family. Mrs Dale's classic cliché was created by the programme's first scriptwriter, John Bishop. When the series started the Dales lived in a cosy house in Kenton, Middlesex, where Dr James Dale (Douglas Burbridge) had been GP for 25 years. In March 1963, faded film star Jessie Matthews became Mrs Dale. There was also a new Dr Dale— Charles Simon, and the family moved to Exton New Town. A book version of the series, by Rex Edwards, was entitled *The Dales*.

I've arrived and to prove it I'm here!

Popularized by the BBC radio comedy *Educating Archie* (1958-9), where it was employed by Max Bygraves. It had been Bygraves's catchphrase since the early 1950s, when he began using it in his stage act. Bygraves had also had the show's other best-known catchphrase— 'a good idea, son!'

I've been called worse things by better people

A line first made famous by Canadian Prime Minister Pierre Trudeau, who said it to the international press in 1974 after hearing himself referred to by Richard Nixon on the scratchy Watergate tapes as 'that asshole Trudeau'. The Canadian leader, whose period in office spanned five US presidents, had annoyed his powerful neighbour by recognizing 'Red China' when other countries would not, opposing arms sales to South Africa because of apartheid, and being hosted by Fidel Castro in a house near the Bay of Pigs. When Nixon—whose reputation was then quickly going down the drain—was forced to provide the tapes and this comment was revealed, Trudeau showed no anger, but merely raised his shoulders and brows with a gesture of studied indifference as he dispatched the paranoid president with elegant disdain.

The phrase was more recently popularized by US comedian David Letterman, host of the TV talk show *Late Night with David Letterman* (1982–). The comic play on the familiar phrase beginning 'I've been called worse things', has become one of his more frequently recurring lines.

I've fallen and I can't get up

From an advertising campaign in the US for Life Alert, a handy device for the elderly and/or accident prone worn on the wrist and through which emergency services can be notified. A TV commercial (from 1987), featuring a Mrs Fletcher, showed the elderly woman lying on the floor with groceries strewn around her and saying, 'I've fallen . . . and I can't get up!' The less-than-convincing acting abilities of the actress portraying Mrs Fletcher, together with the commercial's generally unrealistic look, quickly turned her plaintive cry into a national joke and a popular catchphrase. In 1991, when talk show host Jay Leno returned to *The Tonight Show* on crutches after being off for three days with a broken leg, he got his biggest laugh of the evening simply by saying 'I've fallen and I can't get up!' Although still a favourite among comedians, the phrase remains a registered trademark of Life Alert, and has been picked up on by Christian groups, seeing a 'deeper application of the phrase', as in the Bible, where 'we're told that the human race "fell" into sin through Adam's sin' (Cornerstone University, President's Office, online version 2000).

I've started so I'll finish

Associated with Magnus Magnusson host of the BBC TV quiz show *Mastermind* (1972–97), who would say it to contestants when their time ended while he was still asking a question. The phrase became a turn of expression, and was used at times as a double entendre. Magnusson himself seemed to delight in the phrase, using it as often as possible during the show. Once asked by an interviewer why he bothered saying it when everyone knew he would finish anyway, Magnusson replied: 'A lot of people like to hear it at least once during a session so we keep it in....It means that I've got my very own catchphrase, doesn't it?' *Mastermind* was acquired by the Disney/ABC Network in 1999 to be adapted for the US market.

if anything can go wrong, it will

A popular, pessimistic maxim since the mid-20th century, commonly known as Murphy's Law (or, in the UK, Sod's Law), said to have been coined by George Nichols in 1949 and based on a remark made by his colleague, Captain Edward A. Murphy, of Wright Field Aviation Laboratory. Murphy, an engineer working on a US Air Force project designed to see how much sudden deceleration a person can stand in a crash, reportedly cursed a technician one day for an error, saying: 'If there is any way to do it wrong, he'll find it.' Nichols, a project manager with the Californian aviation firm, Northrop, heard Murphy's remark and added it to a list of 'laws' he was keeping, calling this one Murphy's Law. Aerospace manufacturers picked it up and used it widely in their ads during the following few months, and soon it was being quoted in many news and magazine articles, and Murphy's Law entered the language.

if he can, why can't you?

From an advertising campaign for the Internet media company service Excite, Inc., entitled 'You Can Too', launched by the New York based advertising agency Lowe & Partners/SMS in December 1998. The campaign used humour to convey the idea that Excite can help even novices use the Internet to get information, solve daily problems, or just perform tasks. The six TV spots show slow-witted or clumsy people doing stupid things like walking through screen doors. The message is that since even they can use the Internet to get things done, so you certainly can too. Everyone, according to Excite's senior vice president for marketing Fred Siegel, no matter how 'technologically challenged, can do fantastic things on the Web with the help of Excite'.

The satirical commercials feature ordinary people caught during momentary lapses of common sense, such as dropping an air conditioner out of an apartment-building window several stories up as it is being installed, or shattering the window of an overstuffed hatchback car. TV viewers are informed, however, that these same people were able to use Excite to track stock quotes, set up free e-mail accounts, or meet their future spouses in online chat rooms. For example, in the one entitled 'Hatchback' a man is seen trying to close his overstuffed boot in a parking lot. Across the screen appears: 'He met his wife in an Excite.com chat room.' We then see the man make one last attempt to close his trunk. This time, he slams it so hard he breaks the window. The screen then says 'If he can, why can't you?'

if I kiss your butt can I have Carson's job?

Famous words spoken by US comedian Jay Leno, who in fact, did take over from the legendary Johnny Carson as host of the *Tonight Show* in 1992. The job as Carson's successor was heavily contested— one the competing comedians would do 'just about anything' to secure. Consequently, the hefty, jut-jawed Leno took over the show in the face of exceedingly high expectations and from the start tried to give it his own spin, while not alienating the huge Middle American audience Carson had left him. 'This is not your father's *Tonight Show*', quipped Jay Leno after one particularly hip musical act on the NBC late night talk show.

if it feels good then just do it

An advertising slogan for Nike shoes and athletic goods that formed part of the company's 'Just Do It' campaign (see below) during the late

1980s. The phrase, meant by Nike's marketing managers as 'a call to action, a refusal to hear excuses' and as 'a license to be eccentric, courageous and exceptional', was criticized sharply by many US Christian groups at the time for whom it embodied self-centred, self-indulgent, and basically hedonistic values and traits.

if you can't stand the heat get out of the kitchen

Attributed to Harry S Truman, US president from 1945 to 1953. To explain his decision not to run for re-election in 1952, Truman quoted his old friend Harry Vaughan: 'If you can't stand the heat, get out of the kitchen', meaning don't take on responsibilities you're not equipped or able to handle, and in Truman's case, the burden of responsibility was that carried by a US president—perhaps one of the heaviest in the world. A few months later Truman said in a speech: 'The President gets a lot of hot potatoes from every direction and a man who can't handle them has no business on the job. That makes me think of a saying that I used to hear from my old friend and colleague on the Jackson County Court. He said, "Harry, if you can't stand the heat you better get out of the kitchen."' And, in his autobiography, published 1960 Truman wrote 'I used to have a saying that applies here and I note that some people have picked it up: "If you can't stand the heat, get out of the kitchen".'

Whether or not Truman actually coined this familiar adage, he is by now generally considered its author. Truman has also been credited with such quips as 'I don't care what they say about me as long as they spell my name right', and 'It's a recession when your neighbour loses his job; it's a depression when you lose your own', both of which are old maxims that did not originate with Truman, who may not have even said them at all. But, as is often the fate of public figures, the sayings have become associated with and attributed to Truman because they are deemed to 'sound like' him, whether or not he actually spoke them.

if you knows of a better 'ole, go to it

Expressing an indomitable spirit that tries to make the most out of what are clearly adverse conditions, the phrase formed the caption to Bruce Bairnsfather's most famous First World War cartoon (*Fragments of France*, 1915). The British cartoonist served in France with the Royal

Warwickshire Regiment and later was given the title of 'Officer Cartoonist', and toured with the French, Italian, and American armies in France. The cartoon in question, drawn for the *Bystander* magazine, showed two 'Tommies' (soldiers) sheltering in a shell hole amidst a barrage of enemy fire. One soldier, bemoaning his lot, is told by his moustachioed companion: 'Well, if you knows of a better 'ole, go to it.' Old Bill, the cartoon strip's central character, became well known on both sides of the Atlantic, and the play *The Better 'Ole*, featuring this tough soldier, opened in London in 1917 and on Broadway in 1918. Two films based on the play were released in 1918 (UK) and 1926 (US). During the First World War, Old Bill became mascot to the US 8th Air Force.

The Stafford Hotel, in London, is home to The Better 'Ole Club which includes HRH Prince of Wales among its more famous members. On returning from a spell in the United States in 1979, Terry Holmes recalled how on several occasions he had heard Stafford guests saying to non-frequenters—'Well, if you know of a better hotel, go to it'.

illogical

Associated with the half-Vulcan Mr Spock (Leonard Nimoy) on the US TV series *Star Trek* (1966–9). See 'most illogical'.

in a pig's eye!

A chiefly American saying expressing scornful disbelief that was popularized during the late 1960s by Chief Medical Officer Leonard McCoy (DeForest Kelley) of the Starship *Enterprise* on the US TV series *Star Trek* (1966–9). The excitable and often irritable McCoy is always quick to spot and expose untruths or misperceptions. This he generally does with some animation, often calling on modes of expression clearly derived from his Southern, 'simple country doctor' background. The phrase is also an example of rhyming slang, 'pig's eye' being a rhyme for 'lie'.

in my office!

Authoritative order meaning 'we need to talk', and usually implying displeasure with the person being addressed. The expression was popularized by the leather-wearing, tough Arthur 'Fonzie' Fonzarelli, also known as the Fonz (Henry Winkler) on the US TV series *Happy Days* (1974–84) set in the 1950s. Originally intended as a minor character, the Fonz found his popularity soaring as he increasingly took on the role of Richie Cunningham's (Ron Howard) surrogate older brother. These words were in fact usually barked at Richie at Arnold's Drive-In diner, where Richie and his friends normally hung out and where Fonzie's 'office' was located, in the men's room. Fonzie would motion with his thumb towards the men's toilets while uttering the command, and Richie would meekly comply, leaving the two friends he's usually with exchanging worried glances.

in the big inning

A catchy play on words, using a term from baseball, that appeared as the tagline at the beginning of a 1999 episode of the US cult TV series *The X-Files* (1993–2002). In *The Unnatural*, Special Agent Fox Mulder (David Duchovny) investigates the links between a black baseball player, active in the late 1940s, and the government 'conspiracy' to conceal evidence of the paranormal and alien life. (See also 'truth is out there, the'.)

is everybody happy?

A well-worn exhortation aimed at loosening up and winning over an audience. US jazz clarinettist Ted Lewis, whose wild stage antics and crazy clarinet sound brought him fame throughout the 1920s and 1930s, was also famous for always asking the audience, 'Is everybody happy?' At the end of his career he still made appearances with a battered top hat and cane performing old vaudeville routines and delivering songs he had popularized many years earlier when he was billed as the 'High-hatted Tragedian of Jazz' and 'The Medicine Man for Your Blues'. There were three films made about Ted Lewis or starring him entitled *Is Everybody Happy?* The first, made in 1929, starred Tod Todd as Ted, the second was a musical short starring Lewis in 1942, and the third, released in 1943, was a film about Lewis's life (with Larry Parks playing Lewis).

is it bigger than a breadbox?

Phrase coined and popularized by Steve Allen on the US TV panel game *What's My Line?* (1950–67). The show assembled a panel of four famed or semi-famed personalities, who tried to discover the occupations of guests, or the products associated with their jobs. As the panellists were restricted to yes and no questions, they would sometimes need to find ways of being a bit creative in the formulation of their queries. Allen came up with this line when he was a regular guest panellist on the show from 1953 to 1954; many other panellists would employ what had become a popular catchphrase in later shows, certain that the word 'breadbox' would for some reason always be met with some laughs.

is it live, or is it Memorex?

An advertising slogan for Memorex audio cassettes during the 1970s that boasted a recording quality so great that a listener could not tell if what they heard was live or a recording. The campaign was made more memorable when Memorex hired Ella Fitzgerald as a spokesperson, and had her appear in a TV commercial set in a recording studio. The legendary jazz singer shatters a wine glass by singing a long, high note, then the viewers see her voice breaking the glass again, but (asks the announcer)...'Is it live, or is it Memorex?' It has been suggested, quite ironically, that she may have reached her largest audience in this 1970s commercial.

— is like making love to a beautiful woman

From the popular BBC TV comedy series *The Fast Show* (1994–7), written by Paul Whitehouse and Charlie Higson. Although it probably had earlier origins, the phrase was more recently popularized by *The Fast Show* character 'Swiss Toni', played by Charles Higson. Toni, a rather pathetic second-hand car salesman, is always giving advice to younger salesman, using his catchphrase to 'sell' whatever may be the topic of the moment—whether it's making coffee or selling a car. One of Toni's most quoted examples of this phrase is: 'You know, putting up a tent is like making love to a beautiful woman. You undo the zip, pop in your pole and slip into the old bag'. One of Steve Martin's jokes, while hosting the televised Academy Awards ceremony in March 2001 was 'You know what I just realized— hosting the Oscars is like making love to a beautiful woman. It's something I only get to do when Billy Crystal is out of town'.

is she ... or isn't she?

A British advertising slogan for Harmony hair-spray devised in the late 1970s. Suggesting that the quality of the product was so high that one could not tell for sure whether a woman had used any, it was clearly reminiscent of the then already well-known Clairol slogan 'does she or doesn't she?' (see above). This was also one of the earliest examples of sexual innuendo in advertising, referring to a possible ambiguity in a woman's sexual or gender preferences.

is that your final answer?

Chris Tarrant's phrase on the hugely popular ITV quiz show *Who Wants to Be a Millionaire?* (1998–   ). Host Chris Tarrant uses this to add suspense while perhaps introducing doubts in what are often already considerably tense moments for contestants and viewers alike. Since the show began in the UK in 1998 the format has been exported around the globe, with 80 countries and an estimated 100 million viewers regularly giving their final answer. The highly successful US version first aired in August 1999 is hosted by Regis Philbin.

A contestant, chosen from ten qualifiers via a timed question, plays for the £1 million top prize. The contestant must answer 15 multiple-choice questions correctly in a row to win the jackpot. The contestant may quit at any time and keep their earnings. For each question, they are shown the question and four possible answers in advance before deciding whether to play on or not. If they do decide to offer an answer, it must be correct to stay in the game. Hence the significance of the recurring question: 'Is that your final answer?' If at any stage they answer incorrectly, they fall back to the last 'guarantee point'— either £1,000 or £32,000—and their game is over.

'Is That Your Final Answer?' is the trademark name of a computer gameboard based on *Who Wants to Be a Millionaire?*

— is the name of the game

The main goal or most important aspect of a situation or, more generally, of life. The phrase's exact origins are not known, but it was current in the US by the 1950s, and probably had its origins in baseball. At his Hall of Fame induction speech in 1966 US baseball player Ted Williams said, 'Baseball gives every American boy a chance to excel, not just to be as good as someone else but to be better than

someone else. This is the nature of man and the name of the game.'
Williams was signed by the Boston Red Sox and made his major league
debut in 1939, and in 1947 he became the second player ever to twice
win the Triple Crown.

As a format phrase, the line has served many different purposes or
messages, such as *Fame is the Name of the Game*, the title of a 1966 US
made-for-TV film. A US TV series entitled *The Name of the Game* ran
from 1968 to 1971. More recently, 'Tell and sell is the name of the
game' was the title of an article about the effects of the Internet on
the boundaries between news media and corporations (*Guardian*, 20
March 2000).

isn't it delightful?

A catchphrase belonging to Warner Bros. cartoon character Marvin
the Martian, who was created in 1948 by Chuck Jones, and voiced
originally by Mel Blanc. Whatever was being referred to with this
phrase would usually be—from an Earthling's point of view—very
far from delightful. Marvin, clad in a tutu and a Roman helmet and
armed with the dreaded 'Illudium Q-36 Space Explosive
Modulator', made his debut in *Haredevil Hare*, a Looney Tunes
cartoon starring Bugs Bunny. Marvin the Martian (initially
known as 'Commander X-2') went on to have his own show, on
which his single goal in life was to blow up Earth because it
blocked his view of Venus. His other catchphrase was 'Surrender,
Earthling'.

it ain't over 'til it's over

The saying, sometimes quoted as 'the game isn't over 'til it's over', has
been attributed to US baseball player and New York Mets manager
Yogi Berra (who uttered it as a comment on the National League
pennant race in 1973). Sports broadcaster Dan Cook, who coined the
famous line 'The opera ain't over until the fat lady sings' during a
television newscast in 1978, said his line was a takeoff on Yogi
Berra's quote. Cook came up with his phrase after the first
basketball game between the San Antonio Spurs and the
Washington Bullets during the 1977–8 NBA playoffs, to illustrate
that while the Spurs had won once, the series was not over yet.
The quote has often been misattributed to Dick Motta, coach of

the Washington Bullets basketball team. Both Berra and Cook's saying have become modern proverbs, similar to 'don't count your chickens before they're hatched'.

it all depends on what you mean by...

From the BBC radio programme *The Brains Trust* (1941–). Employed in discussions and debates, the phrase became associated with Professor C. E. M. Joad, a regular participant on the programme, who used to say it nearly every time before his response to a question. *The Brains Trust*, a live discussion programme, was first broadcast on 1 January 1941 and became one of wartime radio's most popular programmes. The programme was also televised from 1955 to 1961.

Some of the most eminent people of the time were brought together to answer, spontaneously and without prior knowledge of the questions, some of the issues and questions raised by listeners (or viewers). They would usually deal with six questions during the live broadcast and attempt to be controversial. The scientist and writer Jacob Bronowski, the biologist Julian Huxley, and the philosopher A. J. Ayer appeared regularly on the prestigious programme. The phrase became associated in late 1998 with US President Bill Clinton (and sometimes referred to as a 'Clintonesque' response), specifically with regard to his handling of the Monica Lewinsky scandal and his use of variations of this phrase during his testimony before a grand jury.

it could be you

An initially successful advertising slogan for the UK's National Lottery, launched in 1994. The slogan with the big blue finger pointing out of the sky, devised by Saatchi and Saatchi, was one of the most successful product launches ever, ensuring maximum publicity and Saturday night queues at supermarkets, petrol stations, and corner shops around the country. It seemed to have captured the national imagination. However, in November 1998, the National Lottery operator, Camelot, unveiled an advertising campaign that played down the idea that anyone could scoop the jackpot, featuring the new slogan 'Maybe, just maybe'. Research had shown that players wanted to know more about where the money was going, and had also wised up to the odds against winning the jackpot—about 14 million to one.

it don't arf make you larf!

It sure is funny or makes one laugh. An expression that was popularized in the 1950s by British music hall 'super star' Max Wall. Wall was also famous for his silly walk, a routine which inspired John Cleese's 'Ministry of Silly Walks' character on the BBC TV sketch comedy series *Monty Python's Flying Circus* (1969–74).

it keeps going, and going, and going...

Part of the advertising slogan for Duracell batteries from 1989 in which an 'Energizer Bunny', symbolizing the durability of the product, enabled anything that was Duracell battery-run to keep 'going, and going, and going...' (See 'energizer, the'.)

it satisfies you

An advertising slogan for Snickers chocolate bar from the 1980s (then named Marathons in the UK). Referring to the product's ability to quiet down pangs of hunger and 'satisfy' one's stomach, at least until a proper meal can be had, this phrase came to be used with respect to a variety of other needs. Unsurprisingly, it has also become a favoured, boastful nickname given jokingly by some men to their penises.

it won't bring (or get) the pigs home

A saying from the world's longest-running soap, the popular radio programme *The Archers* (1950–). The series was originally designed to put over serious farming information in a more populist way, and was the brainchild of the BBC, the Ministry of Agriculture, and farmers themselves. Set in a fictitious rural county of Borsetshire, *The Archers*, known as an 'everyday story of country folk' (see above), naturally came up with its share of agrarian-based maxims and words of wisdom. This one, meaning 'it won't solve the problem' or 'do the trick', could be related to the old saying 'till the cows come home'; in both cases, the animals being 'out' suggests we have no or little control over the situation.

it'll play in Peoria

Phrase associated with (but probably not coined by) John Ehrlichman, best remembered for his part in covering up Nixon's role in the 1972 break-in at the Democratic National Committee headquarters in the Watergate complex. The saying, which refers to Peoria, Illinois, as the heartland of 'Middle America', claims the 'average guy' will certainly buy it—whether 'it' is a proposed piece of legislation or a particular policy. First spoken by Ehrlichman when Nixon was running for president in 1968, it was used to indicate how the all-important Middle American would vote and became a campaign gauge. It has been suggested that the phrase came from the fact that Peoria was once a vaudeville haven, where vaudeville entertainers always tested out their acts before taking the show on the road, hence: the phrases 'will it play in Peoria?'/'if it'll play in Peoria, it'll play anywhere' And it has apparently remained a principal test market for many companies trying out new products, based on the 'will it play in Peoria?' saying.

Ehrlichman, who had been President Nixon's top domestic affairs adviser, was convicted in 1975 of obstruction of justice, conspiracy, and perjury—based on his false testimony to a Senate committee and the break-in at a Beverly Hills office of the psychiatrist who had treated Daniel Ellsberg, the former Pentagon aide who leaked the Pentagon Papers to *The New York Times*. After spending 18 months in prison, Ehrlichman later remade himself as a novelist and as an executive of a firm that handled hazardous wastes. Ehrlichman was also known for another phrase—which he did coin and that became part of the country's political lexicon—he used when he advised Nixon to allow acting FBI Director L. Patrick Gray III to become the fall guy for Watergate and to leave him 'twisting slowly, slowly in the wind'.

It's a bird. It's a plane. It's —!

Used jokingly to introduce or mark the arrival of a person or item. The phrase forms part of the well-known introduction to the TV series *The Adventures of Superman* (1953–7)—'Look! Up in the sky! It's a bird. It's a plane. It's Superman!...'—which establishes the vital fact that Superman has the superhuman power to fly. In an earlier version, created for the radio serial which aired from 1940 to 1951, it was a 'giant bird' the citizens of the modern metropolis were peering and pointing at. Aside from the fact that it didn't ring as well, presumably, a giant bird would be testing the credulity of listeners quite prepared to enjoy following the adventures of a non-earthling 'with powers and abilities far beyond those of mortal men'. See also 'faster than a speeding bullet'.

Superman comics have been published by DC Comics since 1938. The career of the first Superman—that is, the version of Superman developed for almost 50 years—ended in September 1986. A new *Superman* series began in January 1987 while the first *Superman* monthly was re-titled *Adventures of Superman*.

it's all done in the best possible taste, (but)

A phrase used to justify the inclusion of morally questionable behaviour, usually nudity on stage or in film. Popularized by the outrageous comic Kenny Everett on the 1980s BBC TV series *The Kenny Everett Television Show*. Everett created a gallery of memorable grotesques, the foremost of which were Sid Snot (a filthy Hell's Angel), Mr Angry of Mayfair, Marcel Wave (a fastidious French hairdresser), the Thora Hird inspired Verity Treacle and, most memorably, the American starlet/drag artiste Cupid Stunt, for whom Everett coined 'all in the best pahssible taste!', as 'she' crossed her legs with an extravagant lack of discretion. Questioned about her latest role, Cupid Stunt, who seemed to be continually required by directors to 'shed' her clothes, would assure viewers of her 'actor's integrity' with this line.

it's all go

A phrase popularized by Kenneth Connor on the BBC radio comedy series *Ray's a Laugh* (1949–61), meaning to get very busy or active. It was associated with one of Connor's many creations for the show— Herbert Toil, a permanently complaining old fellow, whose catchphrase it became. By the end of the series, *Ray's a Laugh* consisted almost entirely of catchphrases.

it's being so cheerful as keeps me going

From the 1940s BBC radio comedy series *ITMA*, a spirited affirmation that is somewhat self-contradictory as well as ironical since the character it is said by—'Mona Lott' (played by Joan Harben)—is invariably gloomy and prone to bad luck.

Miss Lestor, speaking in a debate in the House of Commons on 14 April 1994, tried to shed a misconception of her views, by saying: 'The Government Whip says that it is being so cheerful that keeps me going. I am not cheerful about what I see happening to children and families. If the Honourable Gentleman thinks that this is something to be cheerful about, it is little wonder that the Government are failing as they are.'

it's fingerlickin' good!

So good, you'll want to lick whatever is left of it off your fingers. Advertising slogan for the US fast food chain Kentucky Fried Chicken by the 1950s. The phrase was particularly appropriate to both the 'Down South' origins of Southern-style fried chicken as well as the fact that customers were expected to eat the chicken pieces with their hands.

it's Friday, it's five to five ... and it's Crackerjack!

Start of the children's BBC TV programme *Crackerjack* (1955–84). From 1955, if it was Friday and five to five, that meant only one thing: CRACKERJACK! The popular show offered variety acts, comedy, and competitions in a television theatre. It included corny jokes, pop star guests, a sing-along finale, and 'Double or Drop', a game in which children's arms were piled high with prizes if they answered questions correctly or with cabbages if they got them wrong. And of course there were the celebrated and sought-after *Crackerjack* pencils and pens in exchange for which schoolchildren would willingly have themselves covered in slime and humiliation on national television. The first presenter was Eamonn Andrews; Leslie Crowther and Peter Glaze began a long association with the programme in 1960. Comedian Ronnie Corbett also started out on his long career by appearing in this programme.

it's good to talk

An encouragement to communicate, whether to clear things up or to just chat away for the fun of it. The slogan, from a 1995 British

Telecom advertising campaign starring Bob Hoskins, has been judged one of the most effective pieces of British advertising of that period. According to the Institute of Practitioners in Advertising, the campaign revolutionized telephone usage in the UK, encouraging men to chat on the phone and tackled public misconceptions about the cost of calls. It was estimated that the campaign brought in around £300 million in new revenue, and was so pervasive, and so effective, that it became instantly recognizable as BT's.

One of the TV spots featured a telephone conversation between two young men, college students, discussing a girl, which has all the vagueness and unpredictability of real life. Sam commiserates with Sean, who has a crush on the girl, but it soon becomes clear that they both have a crush on her and she's probably been simply teasing them both. The commercial ends with Bob Hoskins saying: 'And you thought men just talked about football. BT. It's good to talk.'

An article in the *Guardian* (26 September 2000), entitled 'It's good to talk for Bush', uses the phrase wittily to bring attention to a commentary on 'the sudden jump in opinion poll ratings for George W. Bush after he made a few talkshow appearances'.

it's just what the doctor ordered

Precisely what is needed; what is desirable or required under the circumstances. The expression was current in the US by the 1940s, and was (and still is) often used with reference to alcoholic refreshments. It appears in that context in Gore Vidal's *City and Pillar* (1948): 'The waiter brought her a drink. "Just what the doctor ordered", she said, smiling at him'. The phrase was popularized in the 1980s, when it became an advertising slogan for Dr Pepper soft drink.

it's life, Jim, but not as we know it

One of the best-known catchphrases from the original *Star Trek* series (1966–9) created by Gene Roddenberry. Spoken by Dr McCoy (DeForest Kelley) of the Starship *Enterprise* in numerous episodes of the popular US TV series to Captain James T. Kirk (William Shatner), his commander. Because of his medical expertise and general scientific knowledge, McCoy is frequently called upon to diagnose or determine the nature of a whole array of living creatures. These are often neither human nor recognizably alien. McCoy usually accompanies this phrase with a wide-eyed, worried look on his face, invariably a sign of impending trouble for the Starship *Enterprise* and its crew.

A variation on this catchphrase—'They're students Jim, but not as we know them'—opened an article in the *Independent* (19 July 2001) on the anomaly presented by right-wing students demonstrating in favour of US President George W. Bush outside international climate talks in Bonn.

it's me noives

One of the many catchphrases from the popular wartime BBC comedy radio series *ITMA* (1939–49) that entered the language. The show starred Tommy Handley assisted by the regular *ITMA* team which included Jack Train, Dorothy Summers, and Horace Percival. It was the show's liberal use of catchphrases that helped make it so familiar and popular. Characters would knock at the famous imaginary door, enter, rapidly exchange comic lines with Handley, deliver their usual, trademark phrase and exit, one after the other, to roaring applause.

it's morphin' time

A cry associated with a 1990s phenomenon known as Power Rangers. The characters—five earth teens-turned-heroic recruited by an ancient wise man called Zordon—starred in the US TV series *Mighty Morphin Power Rangers* (1993–6) and *Power Rangers Zeo* (1996–7). The teenagers were given special powers and abilities (such as the ability to 'morph'), fancy suits and masks, and powerful assault vehicles called Zords, to fight off the evil sorceress Rita Repulsa, who had escaped from her Moon prison. The series spawned two feature films, *Mighty Morphin Power Rangers: The Movie* (1995) and *Turbo: A Power Rangers Movie* (1997), as well as innumerable action figures, lunchboxes, video games, and other forms of merchandising.

Morphing, or the changing of one object into another over time, had captured the minds of film-goers around the world when the US film *Terminator 2: Judgment Day*, starring Arnold Schwarzenegger, was released in 1991. The film featured impressive sequences of 'morphing', a graphics term used to describe the animated transformation of one image into another by gradually distorting the first image so as to move certain chosen points to the position of corresponding points in the second image.

it's not fancy, but it's good

A slogan, during the 1960s, for Horn & Hardart's chain of 'waiter-less restaurants', which was founded in 1888 in Philadelphia and New York. The restaurants were extremely popular, especially during the 1930s and 1940s because, besides the good cheap food, they had the gimmicky appeal of a mechanized food service and sociable atmosphere. Horn & Hardart, the world's first 'Automat', was initially famous for having 'the best coffee in town', a quality that was immortalized in Irving Berlin's 1932 lyric, 'Let's have another cup of coffee'. By the late 1970s, Automats gave way to fast-food chains; the last New York Automat closed in 1991.

it's not my job, man

Impudent retort popularized by garage mechanic Chico Rodriguez (Freddie Prinze) on the US TV sitcom *Chico and the Man* (1974–8). Chico would predictably provide this excuse whenever he was asked to do anything that wasn't technically part of his prescribed job duties. The catchphrase seems to have become endemic, with activists and journalists complaining of a growing 'it's not my job' attitude. Comedians, such as Dennis Miller, have also seen its comic potential—'You know, nowadays, half the people you ask for help say, "It's not my job, man". And the other half don't have a clue about how in the hell to do their job' (from *The Rants*, published 1996).

Meanwhile, the phrase is also still used as a signal to mobilize for those concerned about employment rights: 'Freddy Prinze may not have planned it as such, but his words, "It's not my job, man!", could well become the rallying cry throughout NYCHA (New York City Housing Authority). Are you being paid less than your position requires?' (*Public Housing Spotlight on NYCHA*, Issue 58, 15 June 2000; online version).

it's not nice to fool mother nature

An advertising slogan for Chiffon margarine featured in TV commercials in the US during the 1970s. Mother Nature was played by

Dena Dietrich, a frequent episodic-TV guest star. When Mother Nature realized that what she had tasted and believed to be butter was in fact margarine, she would be so angered by the deception that she would trigger lightening flashes and earthquakes. Her reaction was summed up by her catchphrase—both an admonishment and a warning. More recently, the catchphrase has been used by those wary of, or against, genetically engineered foods.

it's only a game show

This was sung repeatedly by contestants in Channel 4 TV's fly-on-the-wall game show *Big Brother* (2000–   ). The line would be chanted by Sada, Caggy, Nichola, Tom, Nick, Darren, Andy, Craig, Mel, and Anna—who were placed in a house with no contact with the outside world but with cameras on them 24 hours a day, seven days a week during the summer of 2000—when the tension grew over nominations for evictions, or when the results of public votes on evictions were about to be revealed. It became the show's official catchphrase, and was appropriately ironic, self-referential and invented by the contestants themselves. (See also 'Big Brother is watching you'.)

it's only rock 'n' roll (but I like it)

Enjoy, have fun, without being too concerned about what the source of that enjoyment might be; what's the fuss? It is the title of (and a lyric from) a Rolling Stones song written by British rock musician Mick Jagger, on their *It's Only Rock 'n' Roll* album released 1974. The phrase came to symbolize youth attitudes of the mid-1970s, which included a degree of carefree irreverence. A book on the Rolling Stones, by James Karnbach and Carol Bernson published 1997, was entitled *It's Only Rock 'n' Roll: The Ultimate Guide to the Rolling Stones*.

it's ten o' clock; do you know where your children are?

A long-standing US Public Service Announcement (PSA), periodically shown at the end of the evening news on most television channels (the time therefore varied often to 11), since the 1960s. The question, which presumably puts apprehension in the hearts of some parents, was not taken seriously for long and spawned many jokes in which 'children' would be replaced by 'wife' or 'husband', and so on. In an episode of the animated TV show *The Simpsons* (1989–), Homer J. Simpson is watching TV when the TV announcer says, 'It's ten o'clock. Do you know where your children are?' Homer replies angrily: 'I told you last night, NO!' However, the issue addressed by the PSA is an ongoing one in the US where, in July 2000, Republican Duane Cheney of Indiana promised his constituents emergency legislative action to restore a statewide teenage curfew that had been struck down by a recent federal court ruling. After a passing reference to the old PSA, Cheney added, 'That PSA has been around for so long, it's the subject of jokes. But this court decision is no joking matter. Clearly this is a dangerous situation and the Legislature must act as soon as possible.'

it's that man again!

Late 1930s expression used by press to refer to Adolf Hitler, the acronym of which was taken as the title of popular 1940s BBC comedy radio show *ITMA*. In 1939, Tommy Handley, a well-known Liverpudlian comedian, and Ted Kavanagh decided to name the new show they were devising after a topical catchphrase associated with Hitler who was then beginning to cause quite a stir internationally. Whenever Hitler made some new territorial claim, the newspaper headlines would proclaim 'It's That Man Again'. As it was quite a mouthful to repeat over the microphone, an abbreviated form was adopted—abbreviations or acronyms such as the RAF, the ARP, ENSA, and many others were already very popular at the time. *ITMA* was broadcast between 1939 and 1949 and at its height had over 20 million listeners, becoming an integral part of wartime Britain as well as the ultimate catchphrase comedy. As the show was extremely topical many of the jokes are meaningless today.

it's the real thing

It's the real McCoy, popularized as an advertising slogan for Coca-Cola from 1970 to 1975, which emphasized the drink's genuineness as the oldest, best-established cola on the market. The slogan was introduced when the famous waving ribbon was added to the brand name, to underline Coca-Cola's image, and was used to promote Coca-Cola as a young, dynamic, popular, international drink. The slogan was later echoed and expanded with 'You Can't Beat the Real Thing', introduced by Coca-Cola in 1987.

Jj
······

Jane, stop this crazy thing!

An anxious cry, and practically a format phrase in which any name can be slotted in to replace 'Jane'. The line came from the end-credits of the US animated series *The Jetsons* (1962–76; 1985 syndicated), where George (the bread-winning patriarch of the mid-21st-century family) gets caught on the automatic treadmill while walking his dog, Astro, and calls out to his wife 'Jane! Stop this crazy thing'. The series inspired countless toys and dolls, two television specials, and a feature film, *Jetsons: The Movie* (1990).

Jane, you ignorant slut

From the original *Saturday Night Live* (1975–   ), spoken by Dan Ayckroyd to Jane Curtin, usually ending a point/counterpoint spoof during the show's regular 'Weekend Update', on which they appeared as anchors. The line was particularly funny, not only because of its inappropriate use, but because of the serious, deadpan manner in which it was uttered, and Jane's puzzled and offended look. The 'Weekend Update' was originally anchored by Chevy Chase and Jane Curtin, but was revised for the 1976 season (Chase had moved on after the first) to star Curtin and Ayckroyd and commentary from Gilda Radner's uniquely funny characters Roseanne Rosanna-Danna and Emily Litella (whose catchphrase was 'Never mind').

jeepers!

An exclamation popularized by Daphne Blake, one of the four teenage detectives who solve mysteries on *Scooby-Doo* (1969–86), a US TV cartoon series featuring a Great Dane called Scooby. Also known as 'Danger Prone', as she's the one in the group who inevitably falls through trapdoors or gets locked up somewhere. Whenever the gang finds a clue or figures out a part of the villain's plan, she'll spurt a lively 'Jeepers!' (See also 'scooby-doo'.)

Je-rry! Je-rry! Je-rry!

Chant from *The Jerry Springer Show*, the popular US daily, one-hour TV talk show that premiered in 1991, delivered by the fight-ready and noisy audience. The chanting is obviously for the show's host, Jerry Springer, and is set off when he appears on the stage, or when a fight breaks out. By 2000, the show had become a hit in over 50 countries, and has become America's No. 1 daytime series. Dubbed the current emperor of daytime trash television, Jerry Springer often airs troubling problems or issues, with titles like 'My Daughter Is a Teen Prostitute', 'I'm Pregnant by My Brother', and 'I'm in a Bizarre Love Triangle'. Supplying plenty of material to titillate viewers, the guests tell salacious stories, denounce each other, and engage in violent confrontations on stage.

jolly hockey sticks!

Coined by the schoolgirl 'Monica', played by Beryl Reid, in the 1950s BBC radio series *Educating Archie*. An exclamation associated with a particular type of public school girl or young woman who loves games-playing and is generally excessively enthusiastic, which can also describe a person.

jumpers for goalposts

The phrase is a comic/romantic allusion to boyhood days involving makeshift football pitches. A favourite catchphrase of Ron Manager, a fictional football legend played by Paul Whitehouse on the BBC TV comedy sketch series *The Fast Show* (1994–7). In 2001, Whitehouse's character teamed up with Tommy Stein (Mark Williams) for a weekly comedy quiz show named after Manager's catchphrase, and hosted by Simon Day.

just charge it

Don't worry if you haven't got the cash or can't really afford something, just use your credit card. The slogan, used by the Franklin Charge Account Plan, was developed by William J. Boyle, a banker at Franklin

National Bank in Rockville Center, New York. Introduced in 1951, this was the first bank-issued credit card, the forerunner of the BankAmericard and the MasterCharge card (which later became the Visa and MasterCard). It improved on the Diners Club card, introduced in 1950, which was a charge card requiring full payment each month. Boyle's credit card introduced revolving credit, which allowed monthly payments (with interest), revolutionizing consumer credit, and the Franklin slogan quickly became a national catchphrase.

just do it!

The slogan around which Nike, the athletic equipment company, has built its wildly popular marketing assault since 1988. 'Just do it' has become such a familiar and powerful slogan that TV and print ads rarely need to even name the brand it's associated with. In some ways, it has become not just an advertising slogan, but a philosophy of life, a mantra for strength and achievement. It has helped feed the tendency of people in Western society, particularly in the US, to take pride in pushing themselves to achieve goals no matter what the cost.

The campaign has had at least one embarrassing, if not terribly damaging, moment. In 1989, Nike produced a TV commercial that was shot in Kenya using Samburu tribesmen. At the end, the camera closes in on one tribesman, speaking in native Maa, and the 'Just do it' slogan appears on the screen. A US anthropologist then revealed that the Kenyan was really saying, 'I don't want these. Give me bigger shoes'. Nike spokeswoman Elizabeth Dolan said this was correct, and that Nike 'thought nobody in America would know what he said'.

Bob Dole adopted 'Just Don't Do It' in 1996 as one of his catchphrases in his Republican campaign for president, after receiving Nancy Reagan's blessing. The slogan, which she believed could be 'a tremendous rallying cry' to stop drug abuse, evoked her anti-drug 'Just Say No' (see below) slogan of the 1980s. Borrowing generously from the Nike shoe company, whose 'Just Do It' ads can be found on T-shirts and caps all over the world, Dole told one audience 'Instead of "Just Do It", as Nike says, we say "Just Don't Do It"' (The Associated Press, 19 September 1996).

just like that!

British comedian Tommy Cooper's trademark catchphrase. Cooper had such good comic timing that he was capable of making an audience roll in the aisles without doing anything but stand in front of them, and his catchphrase was one of the most widely imitated in the country. His act relied on a series of bungled tricks delivered with childish simplicity whilst wearing a trademark fez. The fez stemmed from when he was entertaining the troops in the NAAFI in Egypt during the Second World War. Short of a pith helmet prop for his act, he whipped off a nearby waiter's fez and used that instead. It got a laugh, he was a success, and it stayed in the act.

just like your big red conk!

Spoken by Soppy (Peter Sellers), a small boy (who received complaints from Britain's watchdogs for his catchphrase) on the highly popular BBC radio comedy series *Ray's a Laugh* (1949–61) starring Ted Ray. The 23-year-old Peter Sellers was the other main actor in the *Ray's a Laugh* team.

just say no

Take a stand, don't be swayed or pressured by others into doing something. Slogan from a 1980s campaign to teach children to 'just say no' to drugs led by First Lady Nancy Reagan. The 'Just Say No' anti-drug programme began in 1985 in an elementary school in Oakland, California with a simple message: Just Say No, when someone offers you drugs or alcohol. This message spread nationwide when it gained the support of the First Lady. Once Nancy Reagan became spokesperson for the movement, appearing on television and elsewhere in support of the campaign, the words became forever associated with her. Although heavily criticized by some for reinforcing an unrealistic approach to the problems at hand, 'Just Say No' has since become the motto of numerous organizations and support groups for those suffering from alcoholism or drug addiction.

In 1997, a bill called the 'Just Say No' Act, was introduced to the US House of Representatives by Republican Joseph P. Kennedy II. A broad coalition of sixty national, state, and local organizations had joined in a letter to all members of the House of Representatives urging their support for legislation to ban the advertising of distilled spirits on radio and television—to 'stand up for children and "Just Say No" to hard liquor ads in the broadcast media'.

Kk

keep|keepin' it real

A black American expression meaning (in rap) telling it like it is, being honest, but can also mean authentic, true to one's roots or heritage. It has been recently popularized in the UK as a catchphrase of Ali G, a fictional 'black gangsta' (Sacha Baron Cohen), who appeared on Channel 4's comedy series *The 11 O'Clock Show* (1998–), and then starred in two series of *Da Ali G Show* (2000–1). He would often use the phrase to encourage or express admiration for someone in his outrageous interviews.

'Keepin' It Real: Authority and Authenticity in the Performance of African-Americanist Scholarship' was the name given to a conference 'centered on the experience of black scholars and their questions about identity', at the University of Michigan in 1997. As a favoured expression among rap and reggae musicians, it is not surprising that a song by Shaggy, released on his *Hotshot* album in 2000, was entitled *Keep'n It Real*.

keep it under your hat

Keep a secret. An expression, in use by the late 19th century, that alluded to hiding a secret in one's head, covered by a hat. It was popularized through its use in a song by Cicely Courtneidge and Jack Hulbert, recorded in the mid-1920s, and featured in a musical entitled *Under Your Hat*, that opened in London's West End in 1940. It became better known in both the US and the UK during the Second World War as a security slogan appearing on posters, usually with a caption at the bottom, reading 'Careless Talk Costs Lives'. 'Keep It under Your Hat' was also the title of a song featured in the stage and 1953 film version (starring Doris Day) of *Calamity Jane*. More recently, it was used as the title of jazz musician Tam White's 1991 album, the cover of which shows him sporting a hat.

keep on truckin'

Popularized by Robert Crumb in cartoons appearing in his cult underground *Zap Comix* from 1968, and by the song, 'Truckin'', on the Grateful Dead's classic 1970 album *American Beauty*. The phrase—one of encouragement, to persevere, to keep on going and moving ahead even when 'they just won't let you be'—became a popular image of the hippie counter-culture. The origins of the phrase appear to date back to a popular dance step called 'Truckin'' introduced at the Cotton Club in 1933, and to a number of 1920s and 1930s songs, including the blues song 'Keep on Truckin'' and Blind Boy Fuller's 'Truckin' My Blues Away'. It was later featured in a number of Motown songs, including Eddie Kendricks's hit 'Keep on Truckin'', written and produced by Frank Wilson. The dance, associated principally with Black Americans, was described as a 'strutting' two-step which incorporated a 'shuffle step and waving index finger'. 'Truck' could also be used as a slang term for sexual intercourse.

Crumb had moved to San Francisco in 1966 where he began working on *Zap Comix* with other artists in the area. *Zap Comix* No 0, published in 1967, was a smash hit. Crumb and the other artists, including Rick Griffin and Spain Rodriguez, became overnight sensations. For *Zap* No. 1, published in 1968, Crumb created a six panel cartoon which ended with a big-footed character with his foot out saying 'Keep On Truckin''. The image, with its accompanying phrase, struck a note in the collective hip unconscious, and for a while it was everywhere, including in the form of merchandise, most of which was produced without permission. Crumb collected royalties for years, but in the early 1970s a law suit emerged challenging Crumb's copyright which had never been registered and in 1977 a federal judge ruled that Crumb had let the image fall into the public domain.

More recently, the line appeared in the lyrics of a song called 'Novacane' by Beck. The song is included on Beck's 1996 album *Odelay* and begins: 'Keep on truckin' like a novacane hurricane/Blowin' static on the poor man's short-wave'.

keep taking the tablets!

Associated with the 1950s BBC radio *Goon Show*, although it was also the punchline of a joke about Moses and his tablets of stone (1970s). Originally, the phrase summed up what one would expect a doctor to advise to ensure completion of a treatment, but also became a way of saying: 'You're not well yet, and if you don't do as you're told it's no longer my responsibility.'

'Keep taking our tablets (no one else's)' was the title of an article in the *Guardian* (23 July 2000) about the responses of the World Trade Organization and the USA to Africa's Aids crisis and access to cheaper drugs.

keeping up with the Joneses

Trying to live in the style of your affluent neighbours or acquaintances, and in so doing usually straining your resources. The phrase was coined in 1913 by US cartoonist Arthur R. Momand, who used it as the title of a series in the *New York Globe*. The comic strip ran in newspapers until 1931, by which time its title had become a well-established catchphrase.

kick ass!

An American phrase suggesting forceful or aggressive action, most recently popularized by the US TV cartoon series *South Park* (1997–), where it is associated with Eric 'Beefcake' Cartman. Cartman, the 'fat kid' among the four principal 8-year-old characters of the show, is ridiculed for his heaviness, but compensates by claiming that he's 'big boned', by being offensive, and basically, trying to 'kick ass'. These activities would frequently include picking on Pip, the little British kid, and mocking his friend Kyle's overprotective Jewish mother. Cartman's voice is provided by Trey Parker.

kick the baby

One of Kyle Broslovzki's catchphrases on the cult US TV cartoon series *South Park* (1997–), created by Trey Parker and Matt Stone. Kyle, one of the four 8-year-old boys around whom the show revolves, is 'the smart kid', the only one that does well at school. He is also the only Jewish one; his father is a rabbi and consequently—much to his and his friends' dismay—can not celebrate Christmas. He has a baby brother called Ike (who turns out to actually be adopted and Canadian) who he periodically kicks like a football while uttering this phrase.

Ike, who does to some degree resemble an American football in shape, predictably develops his own catchphrase: 'Don't kick the baby.'

kind mother used to make, the

A way of eulogizing authentic home cooking, based on nostalgia. There are several variations on the phrase, with this one being used as a slogan in the US in the early 20th century, when it was a claim made by New England Mincemeat. A perhaps better-known form was 'like Mother used to make', which formed the vital message in a slogan of the 1960s—'Kool-Aid like Mother used to make'. However, with the passage of time and changes in lifestyle, it seems that 'Kool-Aid like Mother used to make' has become ' "Kool-Aid like Grandmother used to make", and most Americans are now one more generation removed from the memory of real food' (University of Illinois Press, April 2000, online version).

kiss my grits!

This exclamation—a more polite way of saying 'kiss my ass'—is associated with Flo (Polly Holliday), the sassy and salacious Southern waitress who immortalized the phrase on the US TV sitcom *Alice* (1976–85). *Alice* was based on Martin Scorsese's 1974 film *Alice Doesn't Live Here Anymore*, and was about a New Jersey single mother who dreams of becoming a singer, but ends up working as a waitress at Mel's Diner in Phoenix, Arizona, to support herself and her 12-year-old son. Florence Jean 'Flo' Castleberry also works at the diner, and her witty remarks and insults, such as 'kiss my grits', are most often directed at her stingy boss, Mel (Vic Tayback). In 1980, Flo left the show to star in her own spin-off series *Flo*, in which she continued to use her trademark response until 1981.

know what I mean, 'arry?

Attributed to English boxer Frank Bruno, who often uttered the phrase in his interviews with BBC boxing commentator Harry Carpenter during the 1980s. Although Bruno did not in reality drop his aitches, this catchphrase became inseparable from him. Bruno briefly held the World Boxing Association (WBA) world from 1995 to 1996, but was better known as a 'lovable loser' rather than a champion. The two men became famous for developing their interviews into a bit of a double act with 'know what I mean, 'arry', becoming part of the act. The congeniality that made their interactions so popular, however, reached less acceptable proportions when Harry cast all objectivity aside during a Bruno–Tyson bout and screamed into his microphone: 'Get in there, Frank'.

Bruno lost his WBA title to Mike Tyson in 1996, and retired from boxing in August 1996. Since then he has pursued his other passion as a performer in pantomime stage shows, and in January 2001 he announced that he planned to stand for the parliamentary seat of Brentwood and Ongar in the county of Essex where he lived. Reporting on the surprise announcement, the *Times of India* (13 January 2001) unsurprisingly began its article with: 'Know what I mean, Tony? Such could be the banter at British Prime Minister Tony Blair's question time if former heavyweight boxer Frank Bruno wins his long-shot bid for a seat in Parliament.'

Ll

....

leave no worm unturned

A 'C.J.ism', in this case a mixed aphorism, popularized by Charles
Jefferson (C.J.), played by John Barron, on the BBC TV comedy series
The Fall and Rise of Reginald Perrin (1976–9) and *The Legacy of Reginald
Perrin* (1996). C.J., Reginald Perrin's boss, was continually mixing up
well-known aphorisms, such as 'leave no stone unturned', and 'the
worm has turned', to come up with this and other comic utterances.
Another bewildering C.J.ism, involving a worm and a mix-up of
sayings, was 'If at first you don't succeed, you'll catch the early worm'.
See also 'I didn't get where I am today...', C.J.'s best-known
catchphrase.

left hand down a bit!

From the BBC radio series *The Navy Lark* (1959–77), an affectionate
spoof on the Senior Service. Set aboard HMS *Troutbridge*, the original
cast included Dennis Price, Leslie Phillips, and Jon Pertwee. Phillips
played the Sub-Lieutenant, a perfect fool whose cry of 'left hand
down a bit' meant impending doom for whichever port they were
entering, or whatever vessel was nearby.

less is (definitely) more

A mid-19th-century proverb, that has been closely associated with
architect German architect Ludwig Mies van der Rohe. The line,
however, had already appeared in Robert Browning's 'Andrea del
Sarto' (1855): 'Well, less is more, Lucrezia.' The association with Mies
van der Rohe was due to his modern views on architecture and
aesthetics, and because he was a leading exponent of the International
Style, which was characterized by simple, almost minimal, geometric,
and especially rectilinear, forms. Later generations of architects
reacted against such notions, such the American Robert Venturi, who

wrote, with a degree of humour, 'Less is a bore', in *Complexity and Contradiction in Architecture* (1966).

It was popularized again in 2000 (with the additional 'definitely'), as the slogan for the Clio, a model of the French car manufacturer Renault. Here, it also involved sexual innuendo, with the related, but ambiguous, slogan 'size matters'.

let me at 'em

An originally menacing expression, meaning don't try to hold me back, I'm going to let them have it. The expression, however, has become associated with Scrappy Doo, Scooby's little nephew, on the US TV cartoon series *Scooby-Doo* (1969–86), giving it a far less menacing and much more sarcastic flavour. Scrappy's other catchphrase is the annoying 'Puppy power!'

let your fingers do the walking

Advertising slogan for the *Yellow Pages* (classified telephone directories) in the US from 1961 to 1998. The walking fingers logo and catchy jingle were created to unite the 21 Bell Telephone companies that made up American Telephone & Telegraph Co. (AT&T), and became one of the most widely recognized advertising campaigns in the US. Around half of the directory publishers still used the logo in 1998, even though AT&T was broken up in 1984. The slogan suggested that the new product/service being promoted enables us to go shopping or access services without having to leave the house, let alone get out of our chair. In 1999, the trade association for telephone directory publishers replaced the 'Let Your Fingers Do the Walking' logo and campaign with a light bulb logo and the slogan 'Get an Idea'.

let's be careful out there

The unforgettable words of police Sergeant Phil Esterhaus (Michael Conrad) on the original 'ensemble drama' *Hill Street Blues* (1981–7). This ground-breaking US television series was about an overworked, under-staffed police precinct in an anonymous inner city patterned after New York. Viewers followed the lives of many characters, from the lowly beat and traffic cops to the captain of the precinct himself. The catchphrase 'let's be careful out there' became part of everyday conversations and a part of popular culture, but the phrase held serious meaning within the context of the show: the Hill Street officers were exposed to a range of dangerous situations.

There was a pervasive sense of a dangerous world, and it was underlined at the end of every morning's roll call as they dispersed to meet the duties of the day, whether it was Sgt. Esterhaus's gentler cautionary tone ('Let's be careful out there') or Sgt. Jablonski's more aggressive intonation ('Let's do it to them before they do it to us'). Sergeant Stan Jablonski (Robert Prosky) replaced Esterhaus in 1984, after the latter died while having sex with his girlfriend in an episode *TV Guide* rated as one of the greatest episodes of all time. The actor, Conrad, in fact died of cancer in 1983.

let's do the show right here! (or let's put on a show...)

A stock phrase from a popular series of films for MGM from the late 1930s to the late 1940s starring the young Mickey Rooney and Judy Garland. It has become a catchphrase used to suggest that happy-go-lucky air of those Garland-Rooney films in which one of them would cry out something like 'my grandmother has a barn, let's do a show!' and the image that would immediately come to mind would be of the two of them dancing down the street picking up more and more kids as they chant, 'Let's do a show!'

The phrase continues to retain the power to conjure up that image, as these first lines of a review of the 1999 film *Cradle Will Rock* indicates: 'A generous dollop of undergraduate earnestness, mixed in with some American Liberalism Lite, and a saucepan of let's-do-the-show-right-here sentimentality has gone into the making of *Cradle Will Rock*, Tim Robbins's new comedy, based on the real-life story of the censorship and uproar surrounding the Federal Theater Program in '30s Roosevelt America.'

let's get busy!

A phrase always used by comedian Arsenio Hall to whip up his audiences' enthusiasm during the introductory section of *The Arsenio Hall Show* (1989–94), the first US late night talk show hosted by an Afro-American. Arsenio was able to compete with Johnny Carson's *Tonight Show* by attracting younger viewers, and his catchphrase—meaning 'it's time to focus on having a good time'—

summed up the aim of his show to create a fun, party atmosphere, and showcase rap and rock and roll bands.

let's go to work

Let's concentrate and get on with it. The phrase was popularized by its use in Quentin Tarantino's 1992 film *Reservoir Dogs*, for which it also served as an advertising slogan, appearing on posters for the film. The phrase also comes up in another Tarantino film, *Pulp Fiction* (1994), spoken by Jules (Samuel L. Jackson) to Vincent (John Travolta) and used to get his mind back on the job, the 'job' in both these films being generally concerned with violence and killing. *Let's Go To Work* was the title of a 1999 album by the Ska band the Kingpins. In the UK, the phrase may indirectly remind some of the famous catchphrase of the 1960s written by author Fay Weldon for the Eggs Marketing Board—'go to work on an egg'.

let's rock!

Let's get things moving, let's start having some fun; a shortened version of 'let's rock and roll', used in the US from the 1950s. This form of the expression was popularized by Al Bundy (Ed O'Neill), the central character in the US TV sitcom *Married With Children* (1987–97). Al, a shoe salesman who enjoys drinking beer and watching sports on TV, actually leads a far from 'rocking' life.

let's roll

An expression used to initiate a group response or action that was popularized after it came to sum up America's resilience after the terrorist attacks of 11 September 2001. They were the final words of Todd Beamer, spoken to a telephone operator, before he and other passengers on United Airlines Flight 93 tackled the hijackers aboard the plane which minutes later crashed into a Pennsylvania field. Although all 45 people on board were killed, the hijackers' presumed plan of flying it into the Capitol or the White House was foiled. The phrase was adopted by US President George W. Bush in a rousing televised address in November 2001, in which he said: 'We cannot know every turn this battle will take. We will no doubt face new challenges, but we have our marching orders. My fellow Americans, let's roll.'

The phrase was also featured in a song by rock and country musician Neil Young. Written and recorded with Booker T. Jones, of the MGs, the single pays tribute to the passengers on the doomed flight—'One standing in the aisle way, two more at the door/We've got to get inside there before they kill some more/Time is running out—Let's roll.'

life is a state of mind

Although spoken only once during the 1979 film *Being There*, this line encapsulated the film's ideas so well and was so memorable that it became a sort of catchphrase or tagline. In the film, based on the 1971 satirical novel by Jerzy Kosinski, Chance (Peter Sellers), a simple gardener, leaves the estate where he has lived and worked his entire life for the first time after his employer dies. His simple, TV-informed utterances are mistaken for profundity, and are taken very seriously by Washington D.C.'s influential political circles, and the president himself. In the final scene—one of the most debated in cinematic history—Chance wanders away from the funeral of a friend, curious about a wilted sapling growing several yards out in a pond of water. Without hesitating, he walks across the water of the pond. 'Life', says President 'Bobby' (Jack Warden), as an oblivious Chance strokes the sapling, 'is a state of mind'. (See also 'all is well—and all will be well—in the garden'.)

life isn't meant to be easy

Words of wisdom popularized by Australia's former Liberal prime minister Malcolm Fraser, which became an unofficial political slogan during his years in office from 1975 to 1983. He had used the phrase to justify his choice of a career in politics, as opposed to a quieter life of comfort and luxury, which he, as a millionaire sheep farmer, could easily have led. Fraser, dubbed the conscience of Australian conservatives, first used the phrase publicly in 1971. He later happily admitted that it came from George Bernard Shaw's *Back to Methuselah* (1921), and that he omitted half of the original piece of wisdom, which read: 'Life is not meant to be easy, my child; but take courage: it can be delightful.' As it is the catchphrase Fraser was best remembered for, it was only appropriate for a 1977 biography by John Edwards to be entitled *Life wasn't Meant to be Easy: A Political Profile of Malcolm Fraser*

life rules

Life is great, the best! A graffiti-style expression of enthusiasm that was one of Arthur 'Fonzie' Fonzarelli's catchphrases on the US TV series *Happy Days* (1974–84). The hip, leather-clad character, also known as the Fonz, and played by Henry Winkler, was responsible for the 'coolest' sayings delivered on this popular 1950s-set series. (See also 'Aaaay!' and 'correctomundo'.)

light the blue touch paper and retire immediately

Words of caution spoken when risk or high tension may be involved, and referring to safety instructions traditionally found on fireworks ('touchpaper' being the twist of paper impregnated with saltpetre that functions as a fuse). The expression was popularized by British comedian Arthur Askey on the BBC radio series *Bandwagon* (1938–9), who used it when retreating from any confrontation with the charlady Mrs Bagwash, one of the regular characters appearing in the comedy sketches that dominated the show.

listen very carefully, I shall say this only once

From the BBC TV comedy series *'Allo, 'Allo* (1984–92), created and written by Jeremy Lloyd and David Croft. This, the most popular of the sitcom's catchphrases, was spoken by the raincoated 'Michelle of the Resistance' (played by Kirsten Cooke) each episode. And it sounded more like this: 'Leesten very carefooly, I weel say this ernly wernce.' The line was used as the title of co-writer Jeremy Lloyd's 1993 autobiography.

One of the most successful BBC comedies over the years, *'Allo, 'Allo* began as a spoof version of the BBC drama series, *Secret Army*, which was broadcast from 1977 to 1979. The series, set in a café in the small town of Nouvion in occupied northern France in 1940, featured café owner René Artois (played by Gordon Kaye) and his various entanglements with German officers and the Resistance who want him to help them to repatriate escaped British airmen. Meanwhile, René just wants to avoid being shot by the Germans and to ''ave it off' with his waitresses without his wife Edith (Carmen Silvera) catching him out.

live from New York, it's Saturday Night!

Since 1975, this line—spoken by a different guest host each week after a short initial sketch—has been the never-changing introduction to the US TV comedy series *Saturday Night Live*. Former *Laugh-in* writer Lorne Michaels was the show's original producer, heading up a collection of comic talent that included several *National Lampoon* magazine writers and a cast of show regulars known as 'The Not Ready for Prime Time Players'—Dan Ayckroyd, John Belushi, Chevy Chase, Jane Curtin, Garrett Morris, Laraine Newman, and Gilda Radner. The idea was that the regulars would present a series of comedy sketches during the 90-minute programme—broken up by musical numbers—while the job of hosting the show would go to a different guest host each week. George Carlin was the first, and literally hundreds more followed, including everyone from semi-regular Steve Martin to folk singer Paul Simon to consumer advocate Ralph Nader to professional athletes Fran Tarkenton, Joe Montana, Wayne Gretsky, and Michael Jordan.

Still going strong after more than a quarter of a century, *Saturday Night Live* has become a TV institution that has entertained several successive generations. During this time it has been a springboard for film comedy careers for many of its regulars—Chevy Chase, Dan Ayckroyd, Bill Murray, Eddie Murphy, Mike Myers, and so on. It has also been a never-ending catchphrase factory, churning out tee-shirt-ready quotes such as 'Consume mass quantities', 'I'm Gumby, dammit!', 'Could it beeeeeeeee...Satan?', 'Not!', and many more. Ideas from the show were less successfully adapted to television in the UK with the BBC comedy series *Saturday Live* (1987–8), and the Channel 4 series *Friday Night Live* (1988).

live long and prosper

Popularized by Commander Spock (Leonard Nimoy), the Starship *Enterprise*'s first officer, on the US TV series *Star Trek* (1966–9). Although reminiscent of a well-worn Chinese proverb, this was a Vulcan salutation which Spock, as a half-Vulcan, would deliver benignly to both fellow Vulcans and non-Vulcans alike, together with his Vulcan hand signal, which neatly formed a 'V' by separating the third digit from the fourth. This formulaic well-wishing suited the good-natured, non-emotional, and therefore pacific, Vulcans.

Lloyd George knew my father

Originally, a proud form of name-dropping by having an indirect connection to the highly-respected Welsh Liberal politician, prime minister of Britain from 1916 to 1922, who died in 1945. The claim was still being made by some in the late 1990s, as attested by this comment made by Mr Tim Boswell in a 1999 House of Commons debate—'I say to Liberal Democrat Members, if they are not aware of it, that I can say with complete accuracy that Lloyd George knew my father, and knew him well enough not to be a supporter of the Liberal party' (13 May). It became a catchphrase after it was used as the basis of a two-line comic song. The song, which consisted of the words 'Lloyd George knew my father, my father knew Lloyd George' repeated endlessly to the tune of 'Onward Christian Soldiers', was possibly by Tommy Rhys Roberts.

Loadsamoney

The name of one of the many popular characters created by British comedian Harry Enfield, who made his name in the BBC comedy series *Saturday Live* (1987–8). He launched his career doing voices on *Spitting Image*, and then in 1988 on the Channel 4 series *Friday Night Live* he introduced a character that instantly swept the consciousness of the nation—Loadsamoney, the archetypal flash, *nouveau riche* Cockney. Loadsamoney was seen as symbolizing the crude mentality of the get-rich-quick Thatcher years, someone who was so busy boasting about his financial success that he couldn't care less about others except to expose what failures they were.

Loadsamoney, who only appeared for a few minutes at a time, became such an immensely popular character that Enfield decided to kill him off a year later, worried he would be typecast. Enfield, the cult comic of 1987, first won over audiences with his character Stavros, a naive and unshaven Greek kebab house owner with a poor command of English and a habit of using 'peeps' as an abbreviation for people—hence his best-known catchphrase 'Cor blimey, peeps'. Aside from Loadsamoney and Stavros, Enfield was famous also for his comic creations Buggerallmoney, You Don't Wanna Do It Like That, Smashie and Nicey, Kevin the Teenager, Tim Nice-but-Dim, The Slobs, and The Scousers.

look for the union label

Buy products and services produced in America by union members; make a political/patriotic statement. An advertising slogan for the International Ladies' Garment Workers' Union (ILGWU), asking shoppers to look for the union label not only because it 'means quality goods and services, but because by shopping they are helping promote justice on the job'. The slogan, usually accompanied by a catchy jingle, had been heard by millions of consumers by the 1960s. It was, however, in the 1970s, after the ILGWU was hit by a huge redundancies amid a devastating economic crisis, that it began lobbying for protectionist legislation and combined its traditional 'Buy Union' promotion with a 'Buy American' campaign of significant proportions, with television ads exhorting shoppers to 'look for the union label'.

look that up in your Funk and Wagnalls

A popular catchphrase from the wacky US comedy TV series *Rowan and Martin's Laugh-in* (1968–73), meaning 'check it out' or look into for youself if you don't believe me or think it's bizarre. Although the comic-sounding name possibly suggested fictitious beginnings, Americans were then, and are still today, looking information up in their 'Funk and Wagnalls', the publishers of a family of English-language dictionaries, encyclopedias, and other reference books distinguished for their emphasis on current usage and for being easy to use. *Funk & Wagnalls New Encyclopedia* has been a reference resource for millions of American families since 1912, while editions of Funk and Wagnalls's equally popular *Standard Dictionary of the English Language* have been published since 1893. But the phrase, repeated by various performers on the show, was so 'funky' sounding and catchy that it became one of *Laugh-in*'s true gems.

lovely jubbly

A descriptive Cockney expression equivalent to 'wonderful' or 'really nice', that was popularized by Derek 'Del Boy' Trotter (David Jason) in the BBC TV comedy series *Only Fools and Horses* (1987–96). Del Boy, voted favourite male TV character in a 2001 *Radio Times* poll, runs, together with his younger brother Rodney (Nicholas Lyndhurst), Trotters Independent Trading Co., which deals in an endless series of suspect sales ventures, from one-legged turkeys to combination briefcases—all with the combination code locked inside. Disregarding his lower class background, Del Boy is forever attempting to appear more cultured and educated than he actually is, thereby providing many of the show's laughs. According to the show's writer, John Sullivan, 'lovely jubbly' was an advertising slogan for a triangular-shaped orange drink he remembered from his childhood. The expression was re-popularized in 2000 by 'Naked Chef' celebrity Jamie Oliver, known for his tendency to use slang and Cockney expressions. The phrase is included in 'The Naked Chef Slang Dictionary', designed as an aid for US fans, which can be found online (Food Network).

Aside from 'lovely jubbly', Del Boy's 'special' vocabulary also includes 'dipstick', thrown in by John Sullivan, and 'cushty', derived apparently from British soldiers referring to a place in India called Cushtabar, purported to be a very 'easy' posting and nicknamed 'Cushty'. His unique toast, uttered suavely and self-assuredly when raising a glass, of 'Bonnet de douche', came from the wording on a shower cap wrapper Sullivan once saw in a hotel catering to French tourists in the Kent seaside resort of Margate.

Mm

make it so

A favourite command uttered by Captain Jean-Luc Picard (Patrick
Stewart), commander of the Starship *USS Enterprise-D* on the sci-fi TV
adventure series *Star Trek: The Next Generation* (1987–94). The words,
usually spoken from the bridge of the *Enterprise*, would set in motion
yet another bold strategy or unavoidable gamble. Of course, all will
work out in the end (or the end of the episode), since the series'
scriptwriters can 'make it so'. Captain Picard's catchphrase comes
from Horatio Hornblower, hero of the classic series of historical novels
(published 1937–62) set during the Napoleonic Wars, written by C. S.
Forester. The novels follow the career—from midshipman to
admiral—of Hornblower, who often makes use of the same command.
The line was suggested by *Star Trek* producer Robert Justman. Horatio
Hornblower was also one of the literary characters upon whom *Star
Trek* creator Gene Roddenberry said he modelled Captain James T.
Kirk.

  Occurrences of this form of command appear to date much further
back. According to a report in *Archaeology* (Vol. 54, No. 1, January/
February 2001), a 'single word, *ginesthoi*, or "make it so," written at
the bottom of a Ptolemaic papyrus may have been written by the
Egyptian queen Cleopatra VII herself'. The papyrus text, apparently
a royal ordinance granting tax exemption to a Publius Actium, an
associate of Mark Antony's, dated to 23 February 33 BC. More
recently, the words are also the registered trademark slogan of the
technology company Stargazer Foundation, which has adopted
Captain Picard's catchphrase as its organization's can-do motto.

make love, not war

A pacifist or 'flower-power' slogan originating in the USA during the
1960s. The maxim summed up the anti-war and anti-establishment
feelings of the 1960s and 1970s, which were also an unprecedented

time of sexual openness in American society, marking what is remembered as the 'sexual revolution'. Coinage has been attributed to Gershon Legman, a sexologist who is credited with first using the phrase 'Make Love, Not War', during a speech in 1963. Others, however, claim that the German political philosopher Herbert Marcuse, who lived in the USA from 1934, actually coined the phrase. His theories combining Marxism and Freudianism influenced radical thought in the 1960s, and his book, *Eros and Civilization* (1955), argued that the tools with which to destroy Western culture were, in effect, sex, drugs, and rock 'n' roll.

make them your own

An advertising slogan for Levi's Jeans since 2000, which refers to their versatility while summing up youth culture's desire to make its own choices. Levi's latest ad campaign has centred on this slogan, hoping to appeal to the 18-to-24 core audience Levi Strauss & Co. desperately needed by addressing that market segment's concern with rugged individualism. To that end, the ad agency handling the campaign, TBWA/Chiat/Day, commissioned a commercial from music video and film director Spike Jonze (*Being John Malkovich*), featuring male and female models trying on the jeans in front of dressing room mirrors, thereby also tapping into the voyeuristic desires that had recently begun to pervade television. The slogan also contrasted with the those being used by Gap, Inc., one of their main competitors —'Everybody in . . .' and the earlier 'Fall into the Gap', which suggested at least uniformity, if not conformity.

makin' copies

Catchphrase belonging to Richard 'The Richmeister' Laymer, created and played by US writer and comedian Rob Schneider on the live TV comedy series *Saturday Night Live* 1989–94. 'The Richmeister', an irritating Accounting Department worker who taunts co-workers 'makin' copies' at the Xerox machine by giving them names (Sandy, for example, was 'Sandita, the Sandstress, Sanditized for your protection').

man you love to hate, the

Billing originally applied to Austrian actor and director Erich von Stroheim whose unmistakable ancestry made him an ideal villain in many propagandistic films produced when America entered the First World War in 1917. The bald-pated, monocled, Teutonic terror was appreciated for his skilful portrayal of stern, autocratic Prussian and Nazi officers in *Sylvia of the Secret Service* (1917), and three 1918 releases, *Hearts of the World* (a D. W. Griffith film on which he also served as technical adviser), *The Hun Within*, and *The Heart of Humanity* (in which he truly horrified audiences by hurling a baby out a window). *The Man You Love to Hate* was the title of a 1979 documentary film, directed by Patrick Montgomery, on the life and career of Erich von Stroheim.

This phrase was often used to describe U.S. President Richard Nixon, especially when his culpability in the Watergate scandal cover-up became clear. Jonathan Frid, who played Barnabas Collins on *Dark Shadows*, a US soap opera that ran from 1966 to 1971, was billed as 'the Vampire America loves to hate'. A dashing leading man, he was at times portrayed as a misunderstood cursed monster, at others a scary monster, depending on the prevailing plot twists. J.R. on the highly popular 1980s soap opera *Dallas* (played by Larry Hagman) was another famous 'man you love to hate'—evil through and through, yet thoroughly captivating.

man's gotta do what a man's gotta do, a

An expression used humorously with reference to a task or obligation that just cannot be avoided, and meaning that you will get the job done even if you don't particularly want to do it. Current in the U.S. by the 1930s, it has practically become a cliché, often spoken by cowboy characters in B feature westerns to show their toughness does not come without a strong sense of duty. Making the most of the line's 'tough guy' connotation, the US Army adopted it as an advertising slogan to urge young people to register for the draft, a process that is presented as a low or no risk proposition—a rite of passage to adulthood, like getting a driver's licence. The well-worn phrase was given this comic twist by actress Rhonda Hansome—'A man's got to do what a man's got to do. A woman must do what he can't'.

Mars a day helps you work, rest, and play, a

An advertising slogan for Mars chocolate bars which ran from 1959 to 1996; the catchy jingle, incorporating the phrase, was introduced in 1973. The original handmade bar, created by the young American

Forrest E. Mars, was such a valuable energy source that it was distributed to armed forces during the Second World War. When rationing ended, the bar was heavily promoted with this slogan. It was used for 37 years, being dropped at the end of 1996, although the company stressed it will continue to appear on the packaging. Long-running campaigns invariably ensure their catchphrases enter everyday language, with even the most anti-advertising consumer becoming familiar with the slogan and brand. Mars successfully achieved brand positioning and presence through the consistent use of this slogan. Murray Walker is thought to have been responsible for devising the slogan in 1959, when he was at the ad agency Masius and Ferguson (now D'Arcy).

The Mars Bar was first sold for two old pence in the UK in 1933 and has often been used as a handy measure of inflation. Forrest E. Mars, a young American nutritionist and the son of an American confectioner, brought his recipe to Britain and began producing the bars, which were an immediate success, at a rented factory in Slough. Back in the late 1920s, Forrest Mars actually believed that chocolate provided a cheap and practical solution to the problem of nourishing depression-ravaged America. He went on to build a global company, eventually moving into the pet food business, before returning to the US to take over his father's old business.

master of your domain

A sly euphemism for remaining celibate—including refraining from masturbation—for a period of time (also: Lord of the Manor, King of the County, Queen of the Castle), that was popularized by its use on the US TV comedy series *Seinfeld* (1989–98), starring comedian Jerry Seinfeld and his friends. One episode involved a 'contest' in which the show's four principal characters place bets on who can remain master of their domain the longest.

may I be excused?

Catchphrase belonging to Private Charles Godfrey (Arnold Ridley) on the BBC TV comedy series *Dad's Army* (1968–77), about the group of men making up the Home Guard in an imaginary seaside resort during the Second World War. Godfrey, a retired gentleman who lived with his two maiden sisters, was often taken short owing to a bladder problem. Hence his frequent request to be excused, and the sometimes troublesome consequences of his absences, as when his visit to the toilet enabled some prisoners that he was meant to be guarding to escape.

may the force be with you!

A cross between an invocation and a blessing, from the phenomenally successful 1977 US film *Star Wars*, written and directed by George Lucas. The line is spoken by Ben 'Obi-wan' Kenobi, played by Alec Guinness, to Luke Skywalker (Mark Hamill). The *Star Wars* films, of which there have been four, are essentially concerned with the eternal struggle between good and evil. The 'force' too, can be either good or evil, and ultimately in the case of the young Jedi Knight Luke Skywalker, it is a matter of finding faith in himself. Whether a person believes in the force or not, he or she would probably like to. Even the macho mercenary Han Solo (Harrison Ford), after dismissing mysticism in favour of a good laser, does not sound insincere when he tells Luke Skywalker with 'May the force be with you', just before Luke's climactic showdown with his father, Darth Vader.

During the *Star Wars* series of films Obi-wan Kenobi and Yoda provided Luke Skywalker with the guidance and tutoring that gave him the strength of character to resist the powers of evil, which he ultimately does. Eventually, Luke uses his new found power to rescue the universe (including his wayward father, Darth Vader) from the clutches of the evil empire. Referring to another, more mundane, sense of the phrase, 'May the force be with you' was the title of a *BBC Online Network* article (12 October 1998) article reviewing the latest crime and police performance figures in England and Wales. The saying is also reminiscent of 'The Lord be with you', from morning prayer in the Anglican prayer book, reinforcing its benedictory intent.

maybe, maybe not!

Favourite retort of Murray Bozinsky (Thom Bray) on the US TV series *Riptide* (1984–6). The series starred Cody Allen (Perry King) and Nick Ryder (Joe Penny), two hip, handsome Southern California detectives who team up with their old friend, computer geek Murray. They set up their own agency, using a cabin cruiser as headquarters. As the 'brains of the outfit', Murray often keeps his friends guessing about the outcome his part in the investigations, and adding some tension or suspense, if not simple annoyance, by uttering this line.

maybe next time will be your time to Beat the Clock!

Catchphrase used by Bud Collyer, US radio and TV personality, as host of the TV game show *Beat the Clock* (1950–61). It was Collyer's enthusiasm that made the frenetic *Beat the Clock*, in which contestants would compete in the popping of balloons with needles in football helmets, or the breaking of cups and saucers against a ticking clock, a hit with viewers and his legendary tagline a part of American conversation. See also 'will the real —, please stand up?' and 'always remember To Tell the Truth!'

maybe the dingo ate your baby

A comic, and therefore possibly irreverent, reference to the true story portrayed in the 1989 film *A Cry in the Dark*, in which Meryl Streep plays a mother accused of murdering her baby, while she contended that dingoes carried her infant daughter off in the night and devoured her. The comment was popularized by Elaine Benes (Julia Louis-Dreyfus) on the US TV comedy series *Seinfeld* (1989–98). During an episode in which a woman at a party keeps mentioning her fiancé, saying 'I have lost my fiancé, what happened to my poor baby?' Elaine, in her best Australian accent, turns to the annoying stranger and suggests 'maybe the dingo ate your baby'. Elaine's line has become a ready and witty response, that quickly highlights the absurdity of the situation/question in which 'baby' is not just an affectionate, but an affected, term. (See also 'get out!')

Oz (Seth Green), a character from the cult TV series *Buffy the Vampire Slayer* (1997–), plays lead guitar in a band called *Dingoes Ate My Baby*.

me main man

A black American slang expression meaning my favourite or most admired/loved person, as in 'my main squeeze' (girlfriend/boyfriend/lover). It has become one of Ali G's catchphrases, popularized on Channel 4's comedy series *The 11 O'Clock Show* (1998–), and *Da Ali*

G Show (2000–1). Ali G, the creation of white Jewish comedian Sacha Baron Cohen, is an outrageous 'black gangsta' from Staines, who uses this phrase when introducing the celebrities he is about to interview, to show his 'respec'' and appreciation. Among those referred to in this way have been Aston Villa football club manager Doug Ellis, David Beckham (''e is one of de best football players in de world'), and, with a slight variation, Madonna—'Me main girl Madonna ere says it's cool'.

me Tarzan, you Jane

Supposed by many to be from the first sound Tarzan film, *Tarzan the Ape Man* (1932), the words were not actually spoken by Johnny Weissmuller in the film or in any of the other Tarzan films he starred in from 1932 to 1948. Nor does the line appear in the original *Tarzan of the Apes* (1914) by US writer Edgar Rice Burroughs. In fact, the fictitious ape-man is rather more articulate in Burroughs' book, saying to Jane: 'I am Tarzan of the Apes. I want you. I am yours. You are mine' (Chapter 18). Tarzan and his partner Jane went on to be featured in films, comic strips, and television series.

It is not quite certain where the phrase came from, but it was attributed to Weissmuller after he was quoted saying it in the June 1932 issue of *Photoplay Magazine*. According to some sources, 'Me Tarzan, you Jane' was a quip Johnny Weissmuller made to Maureen O'Sullivan (Jane in the 1932 film) in the movie studio parking lot. Seeing her struggle to lift her heavy suitcase into the trunk of her car, Weissmuller jokingly uttered these famous words as he effortlessly swooped up the case and tossed it into the car. Several members of the cast and crew were nearby and found it so amusing that the quip (and its intended chauvinistic tone) became forever associated with Johnny Weissmuller.

meathead

An insult suggesting stupidity or idiocy, similar to blockhead, knucklehead, or numskull—denoting the absence of any brains. It is what intolerant blue-collar worker Archie Bunker (Carroll O'Connor) repeatedly calls his hippie son-in-law on the US TV sitcom *All in the Family* (1971–83). The offensive, uninformed Archie would complain loudly and animatedly about the 'chinks', 'hebes', 'polacks', and 'jungle bunnies' taking over his neighbourhood, much to the dismay of his enlightened daughter Gloria (Sally Struthers) and her husband, Mike 'Meathead' Stivic (Rob Reiner). (See also 'stifle yourself!')

medium is the message, the

Coined by Canadian sociologist and communications theorist Marshall McLuhan in the first chapter of *Understanding Media: The Extensions of Man* (1964)—'The medium is the message. This is merely to say that the personal and social consequences of any medium...result from the new scale that is introduced into our affairs by each extension of ourselves or by any new technology'. McLuhan became famous in the 1960s for his theories on the role of the media and technology in society, and is particularly known for claiming that the world had become 'a global village' in its electronic interdependence, and that 'the medium is the message', because it is the characteristics of a particular medium rather than the information it disseminates which influence and control society.

melts in your mouth, not in your hand

An advertising slogan for M&M's chocolate candy, coined by Bates USA and launched in 1954. M&M's were already becoming a household name in America by the 1950s, but in 1954 the famous slogan and the brand characters (animated versions of the various types and colours of candy) were featured in the brand's first TV advertising campaign. The full slogan was 'The milk chocolate melts in your mouth, not in your hand'. As a catchphrase, the 'milk chocolate' could be substituted with other edibles.

Meredith, we're in!

Associated with writer and music-hall actor Fred Kitchen who said it repeatedly in Fred Karno's stage sketch *The Bailiff*, first performed in 1907, to comically stress moments where he seemed to have gotten away with something. Fred Kitchen, with his slow speech and a shambling walk in enormous boots, featured in Karno's first comic play, *His Majesty's Guests*, produced in 1902. Fred Karno, who became one of the world's greatest impresarios and showmen, transformed the music-hall by creating a riot of laughter out of chaos, originating the custard pie in the face. He decided how Kitchen would dress and move and Karno's 1902 play shot Kitchen to stardom.

midnight, and the kitties are sleeping

An amusing play on the word 'kiddies' that was popularized by US comedian David Letterman, as host of *Late Night with David Letterman* (1982–). The line provided an appropriate tone for much of the late-night silliness this popular TV talk show was known for.

mind how you go

The phrase, meaning be careful/look after yourself, has been common in the UK since the 1940s. It was popularized by the BBC TV police series *Dixon of Dock Green* (1955–76) where it became the sort of phrase one would expect and hope to hear from the average, caring policeman. (See also 'evening (evenin') all'.) The warm, avuncular PC George Dixon, played by Jack Warner, would often use the concerned caution, increasing the programme's homeliness and setting it apart from the 'realism' of later British police series such as *Z Cars* and *The Bill*.

mind is a terrible thing to waste, a

Advertising slogan (and motto) for the US United Negro College Fund, which was founded in 1944 to provide financial support at historically black colleges and universities. The slogan, with occasional help from basketball's Michael Jordan, has helped raise over $1 billion for the College Fund/UNCF. The UNCF has financially helped more than 300,000 African Americans to graduate.

The slogan gained a different type of publicity in May 1989, when the then vice president Dan Quayle, speaking to an audience from the United Negro College Fund, maimed that organization's familiar slogan by saying: 'What a waste it is to lose one's mind, or not to have a mind is very wasteful.' Admitting to the mess he made of the phrase, Dan Quayle wrote the following in his memoir *Standing Firm*: 'Yes, I did mangle the United Negro College Fund's slogan ("A mind is a terrible thing to waste")...I'll admit it: "mangled" isn't enough. I fractured, scrambled and pureed the slogan.'

mind my bike!

Spoken by Jack Warner on the hugely popular wartime BBC radio series *Garrison Theatre*. The series was devised by Charles Shadwell and was based on his experiences during the First World War while serving in the West Yorks Regiment as an Entertainment Officer. Among the troops featured was 'Private' Jack Warner, whom the show made a star. Warner would enter ringing a bell and crying 'mind my bike!'; he would also engage in back-chat with Sergeant-Major Filtness, and deliver comedy Cockney monologues. The show was transferred to the stage, an excerpt being broadcast on 6 August 1940.

missed it by that much!

One of the most enduring catchphrases from the US TV comedy series *Get Smart* (1965–70), a James Bond spoof scripted by Mel Brooks and Buck Henry. Usually uttered by Agent 86, Maxwell Smart (Don Adams), when he was just a little bit off in his aim, guesswork, or goal. It was first used in *The Day Smart Turned Chicken*, in which an enemy KAOS agent was attempting to jump from a window into a truck filled with mattresses. When he jumps Max looks out the window, turns back to the room and utters this phrase.

mission impossible

A pessimistic remark often used jocularly when a situation is difficult or time constraints are tight. From the title of the US TV spy series which ran from 1966 to 1972 and 1988 to 1990, and more recently re-popularized by the films *Mission: Impossible* (1996) and *Mission: Impossible 2* (2000), both starring Tom Cruise. The expression may have been derived from 'mission accomplished', a military phrase or formula that was current in the US and the UK by the mid-1940s. (See also 'this tape will self-destruct in five seconds'.)

M'm! M'm! Good!

What most cooks would like to hear from guests after serving a dish, it is an advertising slogan for Campbell Soup Co., used on and off since the 1930s. When Campbell's, the world's No. 1 soup maker, was struggling at the end of the 1990s to overcome poor domestic soup sales and disappointing earnings, several different advertising campaigns were initiated to try to boost sales, but none of them worked. In the end, the company decided to bring back its old, highly recognizable 'M'm! M'm! Good!' advertising slogan. The old tagline stresses the wholesome goodness of the product, and the new television advertisements, which began airing in 2000 and featured the slogan, predictably claimed various health benefits of eating soup.

Mmmm . . . sacrelicious

Associated with Homer J. Simpson in the award-winning animated TV series *The Simpsons* (1989–   ). Homer, the slightly slow-witted head of the Simpson household, who tends to give bad advice to his children (as when he tells his daughter Lisa that it is acceptable to steal things 'from people you don't like'), precedes many a comment or simple observation with 'Mmmm . . .', making this sound his best-known catchphrase. Some other frequently used combinations are: 'Mmmm . . . beer', 'Mmmm . . . chocolate', 'Mmmm . . . donuts', and 'Mmmm . . . free goo'.

One instance in which this version, which conveniently crosses 'sacrilegious' with 'delicious', crops up is in the episode entitled 'Homer Loves Flanders':

Homer: Oh, Lord! Why do You mock me?
Marge: Homer, that's not God. That's a waffle Bart stuck to the ceiling. [Marge prises the waffle off the ceiling.]
Homer: Lord, I know I shouldn't eat Thee, but . . . [munch munch munch] mmm . . . sacrelicious.
Homer: Mmmm . . . beer.

moi

The use of 'moi'—in the place of 'I' or 'me'—will forever be associated with Miss Piggy on *The Muppet Show* (1976–80), created by puppeteer Jim Henson for US television. Miss Piggy is the quintessential classic Hollywood-style star and seductress. Whenever she speaks her main focus is invariably on 'moi', 'moi', and 'moi', or, 'moi' in relation to Kermit the Frog (for whom she has a soft spot) or to a potentially camera-grabbing celebrity. This expression, meant to be a sign of her high level of sophistication (which would necessarily include a command of French) and her ingrained suavity, makes an appearance in almost all her lines. This example is from an episode which featured Babe, star of the eponymous 1995 film, as one of its guests:

Kermit: So, without further ado...the number one pig star—BABE!!!!! YAAAAAY—um—gulp.
Miss Piggy: Oh, Kermie, dear...Um, did moi just hear you refer to that—that common swine as 'the number one pig star?' Hmmmm?!!!
[Babe appears on stage...]
Miss Piggy: *THAT* is the number one pig star?! Kinda scrawny if vous ask moi...

1998 saw the launch of a 'seductive new fragrance inspired by the Divine Swine' herself. In honour of her favourite expression, the perfume was called 'Moi', and its slogan was: 'At the End of the Day, There is Only Moi'. The bottle of Moi features an elegant rendition of Miss Piggy's unmistakable profile, right down to her signature single strand of pearls.

mon capitaine

Associated with the seemingly omnipotent being known as 'Q' (John de Lancie) on the US TV series *Star Trek: The Next Generation* (1987–94), created by Gene Roddenberry. The words, directed at Captain Jean-Luc Picard (Patrick Stewart), commander of the Starship *USS Enterprise-D*, and referring to his distant French origins, is annoyingly tagged on at the end of Q's sentences, as in 'As you wish, mon capitaine', or, more ominously, 'Oh, but you are a Borg, mon capitaine'. 'Q' is the United Federation of Planets designation for an impudent, self-superior and often hostile being from the otherwise mysterious Q Continuum. Beginning in 2364, the alien, known for his juvenile humour, literally began to pop up in Federation space to tease, torment, and try Starfleet officers, and Captain Jean-Luc Picard in particular.

morning

A greeting that was associated with Minnie Bannister (Spike Milligan) on the BBC comedy radio *Goon Show* (1952–60). The elderly Miss Minnie Bannister, 'Spinster of the Parish', lives with the equally senile and decrepit Henry Crun (Peter Sellers), with whom she can usually be heard arguing. She bumbles about and turns up mostly as assistant to Crun, often heard humming some 'sinful modern type music'. Thanks to her surname, her presence or arrival on a scene often leads to jokes, such as 'Didn't I see you on the stairs?' (See also 'you can't get the wood, you know'.)

most illogical

Associated with Mr Spock (played by Leonard Nimoy) on the US TV series *Star Trek* (1966-9). Spock, as a half-Vulcan, lives utterly by logic and is frequently brought to utter this remark whilst observing the emotion-driven actions and reactions of his wholly human shipmates as well as of other beings from other planets. It is spoken without feeling, or with only perhaps a touch of surprise in its tone, as though he was intrigued; a scientific utterance produced by a being ruled almost entirely by uncluttered reason. In fact, the simple comment is also used to note the inexplicable technical malfunctions caused by aggressive outsiders attempting to sabotage or destroy the Starship *Enterprise*, on which he is second in command. However, Spock also struggles with his human half and, his observation 'most illogical' at times indicates an inner desire to comprehend or share what is sadly beyond his reach. Spock also frequently uses a slight variation on this response—'highly illogical'.

move 'em on, head 'em up (or head 'em up, move 'em on)

Now a humorous way to encourage others to move along, or get going, the line was from the theme song to the US TV western series *Rawhide* (1959-66), which was taken from the longer, classic Frankie Laine song. The show centred around a long, hazardous cattle drive, featuring drovers and their daily problems, as well as the many characters they meet on their way. Charles Marquis Warren, writer, producer and director (especially of westerns)—who had been asked by CBS to come up with an idea for a western series that could compete with the many shows already saturating TV in 1958—created the line, 'move 'em on, head 'em up'. It became one of the most famous lines in television history, and the catchphrase of the early 1960s. The series went on to become a major hit, giving stars Clint Eastwood (who played Rowdy Yates) and Eric Fleming (the leading, rough trail boss Gil Favor) their career breakthroughs.

The refrain from *Rawhide*'s theme song was:

Move 'em on, head 'em up,
Head 'em up, move 'em on,
Move 'em on, head 'em up,
Rawhide!
Head 'em out, ride 'em in,
Ride 'em in, let 'em out,
Cut 'em out, ride 'em in,
Rawhide!

Mum won't like it, Uncle Arthur!

Popularized by the BBC TV comedy series *Dad's Army* (1968–77), the phrase was spoken by Private Frank Pike, Walmington-on-Sea's junior bank clerk (played by Ian Lavender), to Sergeant Arthur Wilson, the bank's chief clerk (John Le Mesurier). It had a comic twist as viewers had been led to suspect that 'Uncle Arthur' and Mrs Pike, a young widow, had a relationship, and that Pike was possibly Wilson's illegitimate son.

music, maestro, please

An expression used to prompt musicians (most often an orchestra) to start playing, but also spoken sarcastically to point out and interrupt an overly romantic or melodramatic moment. It became a stock phrase among bandleaders during the late 1930s, the Swing Era, and had, by the late 1940s, become almost a cliché. The line was often used in musicals (both stage and film) as a dramatic punctuation, to introduce and ease in to the next musical number, and was also a favourite among US bandleaders on TV shows during the 1950s and 1960s. Its earliest use was as the title and lyric of a song (words by Herb Magidson, music by Allie Wrubel) made famous by Tommy Dorsey and his orchestra, recorded in 1935. This popular Swing number was sung by Edythe Wright. In the UK, the line was popularized by the British bandleader Harry Leader, for whom it became a signature tune in the early 1940s.

must be American-made

A comment—intended to be amusing by mocking American assumptions of efficiency and skill—popularized by the 1990s 3D

Realms computer game *Shadow Warrior*, where it is spoken by the player's character, Lo Wang, known as the Shadow Warrior. Lo Wang, who has been a master ninja assassin for 20 years, is known to players for his wisecracks, which add to the overall fun of the game. This remark, often preceded by an 'Oh', or a 'Huh', is his favourite response when, for example, a Caterpillar (construction vehicle) is blown up, or upon examining a faulty forklift, and is meant to both offend and amuse.

my arse

Remark popularized by Jim Royle (played by Ricky Tomlinson) on the popular BBC TV comedy series *The Royle Family* (1998–2000). The slovenly king of couch potatoes employs these words on countless occasions, finding many instances and reasons to doubt the integrity or honesty of just about anyone. Tomlinson has become so thoroughly associated with this catchphrase that he complained in an interview in August 2000 of being tired of people hounding him in the street with the phrase. Bus drivers—particularly in his home town—are his worst tormentors—'In Liverpool, whenever they go past, they all beep and go "My Arse"'. On one occasion, when Jim is checking the phone bill, he says 'Ninety-eight quid...It's good to talk my arse', managing to combine his catchphrase with another, very popular, one (see 'it's good to talk').

my boys can swim!

The proud, yet fearful, words spoken by George Costanza (Jason Alexander) on the US TV sitcom *Seinfeld* (1989–98), when he learns that he might be a father. In an episode entitled 'The Fix-Up', George (a short, balding man who has never been successful with women) goes on a blind date with Cynthia (a neurotic, bulimic friend of Elaine's who is looking a man who could 'appreciate being with me because he's so desperate'). George promptly—and proudly—saddles Cynthia with a pregnancy scare. Although the phrase was not repeated over other episodes it became a national catchphrase. However, 'my boys' as the nickname for Costanza's sperm did continue, and was also used by both Jerry Seinfeld and his next-door neighbour Kramer (Michael Richards) as a nickname for their genitalia. *My Boys Can Swim!: The Official Guy's Guide to Pregnancy* is the title of a book by Ian Davis published in 1999.

my goodness. My Guinness

An advertising slogan for Guinness Brewery, devised in 1931 by the advertising agency S. H. Benson, which was vaguely reminiscent of the 'Guinness is good for you' slogan (see above) launched in 1929, while making no health-related claims. The memorable phrase became famous throughout the UK. But, aside from being a slick line, the advertising campaign was made memorable by the illustrations of the Guinness drinker seeing his pint under some sort of threat (perched on the nose of a performing seal, for example). It invoked a wry smile and a tinge of sympathy on the part of the audience at the potential loss if the Guinness was dropped.

my husband and I...

Associated with Queen Elizabeth II who first used it to begin her 1953 Christmas Message broadcast from New Zealand. This form thereafter became a regular feature of her delivery. However, by the 1960s it became clear that this familiar formula was becoming a standing joke, and she began to use 'Prince Philip and I...' instead. The Queen herself joked about her association with this catchphrase in a speech delivered at the Guildhall, London, on her 25th wedding anniversary in 1972: 'I think everybody really will concede that on this, of all days, I should begin my speech with the words "my husband and I".'

my name is — How can I help you?

Part of a 1980s advertising slogan for Citibank (preceded by: 'Greetings from Citibank'), which quickly caught on in the US as a parody of the customary telephone greetings required of employees by large companies. Many Citibank employees were still using the slogan as a greeting when answering the phones in the late 1990s.

my wife will explain

One of the enduring catchphrases associated with Basil Fawlty (John Cleese) on the BBC TV situation comedy series *Fawlty Towers* (1975–9), based on a real-life hotel in the English seaside resort of Torquay. The awkward, snobbish Basil is forever coming up against the dreaded wrath of his wife, Sybil (Prunella Scales), when he's not expressing his contempt for the 'riff-raff' making up a large proportion of the hotel's guests. When caught in a tight situation, Basil would often pass on the task of explaining (usually necessitating a lie or cover-up) to his wife who could charm and deal with the guests more successfully than him. Aside from shifting the responsibility off his shoulders, there was a certain pleasure to be found in annoying his wife by putting her on the spot.

Sybil, an overdressed gossip, has no sympathy for Basil's feelings, and is continually losing patience with him and his ineptitude. But, unlike him, Sybil is quite practical and has the ability to be both tactful and soothing when dealing with their guests. Much of the humour in the series turns on their relationship: Basil describes Sybil as 'a rancorous coiffeured old sow' while she calls him 'an ageing brilliantined stick insect'.

Nn

nanoo nanoo

Catchphrase spoken by Robin Williams, a then little-known comedian, as the alien Mork from Ork on the US TV sitcom *Mork and Mindy* (1978–82). Mork is sent from his home planet of Ork to Boulder, Colorado, to study earthlings and their unusual concept of 'emotions'. He manages to befriend Mindy and take up residence in her attic; she becomes his guide to earthlings' emotions and to their customs, which turn out to be the direct opposite of Orkan customs. Mork's Orkan expressions 'nanoo, nanoo', a way of saying hello, and 'shazbot', a all-purpose Orkan profanity, entered the American vocabulary when the show was at the height of its popularity during its first couple of seasons.

Robin Williams's character Mork, and his catchphrase, first appeared in a February 1978 episode of the US TV series *Happy Days* (1974–84), entitled 'My Favorite Orkan'. In this episode, Mork pays Richie Cunningham (Ron Howard) a visit, planning to kidnap him. Williams's unique comic performance, highlighting his skills as a manic improviser, instantly won over audiences. The network therefore decided to give Mork his own spin-off series later that year. The show was resurrected for one season in a cartoon format.

naughty but nice, (it's)

From a TV advertisement in the UK for cream cakes in the early 1980s, and also used by the National Dairy Council in the late 1980s to promote cream. The slogan's appeal sprang from the basic paradox facing most consumers. Even though many of us are well aware of the best 'lifestyle choices' for good health—plenty of exercise and fat-free food—we still often opt for the less healthy path. The 'Naughty but Nice' advertising campaign for cream cakes accepted that most people know exactly what they're doing when they eat or drink unhealthily and gave consumers permission to enjoy themselves—it implies one should be permitted to break the rules for the sake of pleasure.

British comedian Larry Grayson (1923–95), known for his camp, deliciously naughty humour, appeared in the advert for cream cakes with this slogan, adding this to his many other well-known catchphrases (see 'shut that door!' and 'what a gay day'). The slogan was coined by British author Salman Rushdie, who worked as a humble advertising copywriter during the 1980s. It was also the title of two US films: one released in 1927, starring Colleen Moore and directed by Millard Webb (in which Loretta Young made her film debut), and a 1939 musical, starring Dick Powell, Gale Page, and Ann Sheridan. More recently, an article in the *New Statesman* referred to the Spice Girls as 'naughty but nice, with a vote-winning dash of cosmetic militancy' (21 February 1997).

never-ending battle for truth, justice, and the American way, the

Often used to describe corny plots or endings in books, films, etc. The phrase forms the ending to the opening signature to *Superman* on the US radio serials (1940–51) and the TV series (1953–7), which recounted the adventures of the superhero, featured in comic books since 1938. *Superman* was the creation of writer Jerome Siegel and artist Joseph Shuster, and although he was not an earthling, he had been brought up on Earth the 'All-American way' with wholesome morals and values. His superhuman powers, famously listed in the voiced-over opening to the radio and TV episodes (see 'faster than a speeding bullet' above), are merely the tools needed in his conscientious fight against evil and wrong-doing: 'Superman—who can change the course of mighty rivers, bend steel with his bare hands, and who, disguised as Clark Kent, mild-mannered reporter for a great metropolitan newspaper, fights the never-ending battle for truth, justice, and the American way.'

never give a sucker an even break!

Spoken by US actor and screenwriter W. C. Fields in the 1936 film *Poppy*. It became Fields's catchphrase after he reportedly said these words in the musical comedy of the same name (1923), although the phrase does not occur in the libretto. He was well known in show business for his ad-libbing and complete disregard for prepared scripts, and undoubtedly ad-libbed these famous words in the 1923 stage musical. Once he said that the only lines he followed truly were those of Charles Dickens. *Never Give a Sucker a Break* was the title of a major W. C. Fields film in 1941, which was also his last starring role in a feature-length film. The phrase has also been attributed to US dramatist Edward Francis Albee, but generally became associated with Fields and his special brand of off-beat humour.

The famous utterance, meaning look after number one and don't have too many scruples about coming out ahead of the next person, probably had its origins at the dog race track. Dog owners, betting on the speed of their hounds when chasing the hare, had to make sure they started at exactly the same time, that they had an even break. 'Even break' came to refer to all dog and horse races, meaning a clean start that was fair to all competitors. W. C. Fields was saying: don't ever pass up the chance to give yourself a head start.

never mind

Words of apology uttered sheepishly by Emily Litella, a *Saturday Night Live* character played by Gilda Radner in the late 1970s. The spinsterly, half-deaf media analyst Emily Litella appeared periodically on the US TV show's regular 'Weekend Update', and would embark on a long-winded discourse, which was based upon a complete misunderstanding of the situation at hand. When she finally ended her tangent and was informed of the subject actually being examined, Emily would say: 'Oh. That's very different. Never mind'. One example of this was when she spoke at length against *busting* children (December 1975). When she begins to list the problems facing children in jail, anchorman Chevy Chase interrupts her apologetically to point out: 'The editorial was on *bussing* schoolchildren. Bussing. Not busting.' Emily Litella predictably replies with: 'Oh. I'm sorry. Never mind.' Radner revealed that Litella was based on her nanny, Dibby.

Other Radner characters featured regularly on *Saturday Night Live* who also contributed catchphrases to the 1970s and 1980s slang lexicon were Geek Queen Lisa Lupner ('That was so funny I almost forgot to laugh') and bushy-wigged, heavily accented newscaster Roseanne Rosanna-Danna ('It just goes to show you, it's always something').

nice 'ere, innit?

A conversation starter or filler that makes comic reference to a late 1970s British ad for Campari, in which an attractive, sophisticated-looking girl on a Venetian balcony suddenly destroys the illusion of elegance she presents by blurting out this line. The advertisement starred Cockney actress Lorraine Chase, who went on in 1979 to release a single entitled 'It's nice 'ere innit'. Chase was also responsible for putting Luton Airport on the map, by appearing in a second Campari ad where a clearly enamoured gentleman asks her, 'Were you truly wafted here from paradise?' to which she replies with the unexpected 'Nah...Luton Airport'.

nice guys finish last

Generally ascribed to Leo Durocher, manager of the Brooklyn Dodgers baseball team from 1951 to 1954, suggesting ruthless tactics are a far better guarantee of success than kindness. The concept is not a recent one, as the saying, 'More nice than wise', included in John Ray's proverb collection of 1670, illustrates. However, the particular wording of this catchphrase suited the fiery style Durocher was famous for and which earned him the nickname 'The Lip'. You need to be tough to win in baseball, in other sports and, presumably, in life. In *Nice Guys Finish Last*, his 1975 autobiography, Durocher is quoted as saying 'Take a look at them. All nice guys. They'll finish last. Nice guys. Finish last' (6 July 1946, with reference to the New York Giants).

According to Ralph Keyes in *'Nice Guys Finish Seventh': False Phrases, Spurious Sayings, and Familiar Misquotations* (1992), Leo Durocher never actually said 'Nice guys finish last'. What he did say, before a 1946 game with the New York Giants was: 'The nice guys are all over there. In seventh place.' Durocher's words, however, lacked pizzazz, so sportswriters perked them up, and gave America one of its most familiar misquotations. Whether or not it is a misquotation, it has become the saying for which Durocher is most famous and, as such, very much a part of American lore and language.

nice little earner, a

A small, but by no means negligible, source of profit or income. Used by Arthur Daley (played by George Cole) in the BBC TV series *Minder*

(1979–94), the phrase became a part of everyday speech in Britain. Originally created as a vehicle for ex-*Sweeney* star Dennis Waterman (who played ex-boxer Terry McCann), *Minder* gave viewers Arthur Daley, one of the most memorable characters in British television history, the man whose name became synonymous with dodgy goods and shady deals, and who knew a 'nice little earner' when he saw one. The series became a British institution in the 1980s and 1990s, reaching over 18 million viewers in the UK.

nice one, Cyril!

From a 1972 UK TV ad for Wonderloaf in which two Wonderloaf bakers—one of whom is called Cyril—are discussing loaves as though they were individually made (not mass-produced), and the phrase is simply a compliment that implied one could actually tell which loaves were produced by Cyril.

Tottenham Hotspur football supporters strengthened their already impressive musical repertoire further in 1973 by adding the very successful and catchy 'Nice One Cyril', recorded by the Cockerel Chorus. Although the song peaked at 14 in the charts, its success was not mirrored on the pitch. Fullback Cyril Knowles was the inspiration for the chant, 'Nice One Cyril, Nice One Son, Nice One Cyril, Let's Have Another One'.

nice to see you, to see you nice

A catchphrase belonging to Bruce Forsyth, as host of the BBC TV game show *The Generation Game* (1971–8 and 1990–5). *The Generation Game* was devised from a Dutch show called *Een Van De Acht* (One From Eight) which was put together by a housewife who had been inspired by other game shows of that time. When Forsyth was given charge of the BBC's new show on 2 October 1971, he walked on stage, threw his catchphrase—'Nice to see you, to see you nice'—at the audience and instantly made *The Generation Game* an integral part of British Saturday night television. Forsyth was famous for cajoling his contestants, which was actually part of his charm, and the contestants were in any case protected by Anthea ('Give us a twirl') Redfern. For more than ten years the show dominated the weekend ratings and at its peak had 26 million viewers. The show continues to be broadcast, hosted by Jim Davidson since 1996.

no, I'm|we're with the Woolwich

A British slogan from an advertising campaign for the Woolwich Building Society since 1970s. The line, expressing a form of loyalty and sense of security, quickly became a national catchphrase, and was also given as a response (with a humorous twist) to the query 'are you with me?' meaning are you following or understanding me? The slogan has become so thoroughly identifiable with the Woolwich, that the building society has chosen to stick with it in the 21st century.

no offence!

A catchphrase of the pompous Captain George Mainwaring (Arthur Lowe), leader of the bungling Home Guard platoon, featured in the BBC TV comedy series *Dad's Army* (1968–77). As Walmington-on-Sea's bank manager, the hard-working, self-made Mainwaring prides himself on knowing better than most, and will use this phrase out of politeness before going on point out the mistakes of others.

no one likes us, we don't care

Line sung at matches by fans of London's Millwall football club, to the tune of 'Sailing' by Rod Stewart. Rivalries between teams, and especially between London teams, are often expressed in song. The songs tend to be witty chants, usually set to the tune of a popular song, as in Millwall's case. Millwall fans have revelled in their tough reputation expressed by their signature tune, which has been adopted by groups and teams of workers in different walks of life. According to a report published by the Institute for Public Policy Research, a leading thinktank, 'Local councillors are so disenchanted with their jobs that they are taking on the "No one likes us, we don't care" mantra of Millwall football club'. (*Guardian*, 3 May 2001). *No One Likes Us, We Don't Care: the Myth and Reality of Millwall Fandom*, by Garry Robson was published in 2000.

no one's a bigger idiot than me

What George Costanza (Jason Alexander) repeatedly claims on the popular US TV sitcom *Seinfeld* (1989–98). A man with numerous shortcomings, which he is always quick to admit to, George is quite happy to hold what seems to be almost a 'title' in this field. In one episode Jerry (Seinfeld), his best friend, says 'You may THINK you're an idiot, but with all due respect, I'm a much bigger idiot than you are'. To which George replies fervently 'Don't insult me my friend. Remember who you're talking to. No one's a bigger idiot than me.'

no problem!

A common expression (meaning 'don't worry, I can take care of whatever has gone wrong') that became associated with Alf, the extraterrestrial star of the US TV comedy series *ALF* (1986–90), who was stranded on Earth and had to move in with the Tanner family. The furry, wise-cracking alien is always getting into trouble, and his frequent use of this phrase comes in handy, though it usually is a blatant understatement. (See also 'Ha, ha, ha, I kill me!' and 'hey, Willie'.)

no, sir, I don't like it

A phrase expressing distinct displeasure that was popularized by Mr Horse (voiced by John Kricfalusi) on the US TV comedy animated series *The Ren & Stimpy Show* (1991–5). The insanely energetic Nickelodeon show featured the exploits of Ren and Stimpy, a Chihuahua and a cat, and a pack of bizarre creatures including Mr Horse, the bad-tempered fish Muddy Mudskipper, and The Royal Canadian Kilted Yaksmen. See also 'happy happy joy joy'.

no soup for you!

Catchphrase belonging to the gruff soup store operator (Larry Thomas), featured on a 1994 episode of the US TV sitcom *Seinfeld* (1989–98). Despite his sour demeanour, the man, nicknamed 'The Soup Nazi' by the show's characters, made some of the best soup in New York City and fans would queue around the block to wait for his savoury creations. But if he didn't like the way a customer behaved, as when George (Jason Alexander) asked for bread, 'The Soup Nazi' would yell over the soup counter 'No soup for you, Next!' and throw him or her out. 'No soup for you' has also become a popular catchphrase in baseball, used when a pitcher strikes out a batter.

The character was based on Ali 'Al' Yeganeh, owner of the International Soup Kitchen in New York City. Yeganeh did not appreciate the humour of the episode and threatened to sue the programme if they used the character again. Meanwhile, Soup Nutsy, a soup kitchen modelled on the one in *Seinfeld*, has opened near to the International Soup Kitchen, and has been visited by hordes of customers, many of whom actually wanted to be abused. Capitalizing on the notoriety of the *Seinfeld* episode, the owners of Soup Nutsy planned to go nationwide, opening a chain of 500 Soup Nutsys.

no such thing as a free lunch, there ain't|is

Colloquial saying from economics, popular since the 1960s, and largely associated with US economist Milton Friedman, who used it as the title of his 1975 book. The source of the phrase is not known, though it has been dated to the 1840s when it was used in saloons where customers were offered free snacks. In the epilogue of *America* (1973), Alistair Cooke ascribes the saying to an Italian immigrant outside Grand Central Station, New York City. However, its use in the field of economics dates to the early 1950s, at the latest. A 1952 article in the journal *Ethics*, about nationalizing industries, attributes the saying to Professor Alvin Hansen in his 'famous TINSTAAFL formula—"There is no such thing as a free lunch" '. (Professor Hansen was a prominent economist and professor at Harvard University.) It was also recorded in the form of 'there ain't no such thing as a free lunch' from 1938, which gave rise to the acronym TANSTAAFL in Robert Heinlein's *The Moon is a Harsh Mistress* (1966).

nobody doesn't like . . . Sara Lee

Sara Lee Bakery's familiar advertising slogan that played on the warm feelings the US company has tried to cultivate. Although television advertising was doing well in the 1960s, Sara Lee decided it needed something more. In 1968, Mitch Lee, creator of the Broadway musical, *Man of La Mancha* wrote the jingle 'Nobody Doesn't Like Sara Lee', which became the core of all the company's new ads, even appearing on all Sara Lee-owned lorries. The words of the simple jingle were: 'Everybody doesn't like something, But nobody doesn't like Sara Lee.' It quickly became a format phrase as well, with 'Sara Lee' being replaced with other names or things.

—, not!

As in 'I really like you—NOT!' Popularized by the US films *Wayne's World* (1992) and *Wayne's World II* (1993) starring Wayne (Mike Myers) and Garth (Dana Carvey), the eternal teenagers with a taste for Heavy Metal. The characters were created by Canadian comic Myers and developed into a comedy sketch on US TV comedy series *Saturday Night Live* on a 1989 show hosted by David Letterman. Living in Aurora, Illinois (a suburb of Chicago), Wayne and Garth express the views of 1990s media-oriented, white middle-class youth, strongly influenced by television shows, commercials, and MTV, and characterized by its own special lingo, social behaviour, and body language. The best example of this is their use of the word 'not' (pronounced 'naht!'), which provided the youth of America with an unusual linguistic device.

not a lot!

An expression associated with British magician Paul Daniels, and popularized by its use on his BBC TV show which ran from 1981 to 1996. It usually formed part a longer form of introduction to a stage—usually the final one—in the build-up to one of his famous conjuring acts; 'you're going to like this...not a lot...but you'll like it!' (see below). Daniels made his television debut in 1970 on *Opportunity Knocks*.

not gonna do it!

A line popularized by US comedian Dana Carvey as George Bush senior on the live TV comedy series *Saturday Night Live*, during his term in office from 1989 to 1993. For many Americans the 'kinder and gentler' Bush is remembered best from Carvey's imitation of him as an inarticulate preppie-president saying, 'Not gonna do it. Wouldn't be prudent'. Carvey also used his hands to express this phrase, flailing his arms around. *Saturday Night Live* has always included political satire, and many of the series' signature skits have targeted the nation's political leaders. For example, Chevy Chase's Gerald Ford falling down stairs was one of the first season's most recognizable images. And, in 1990, the show's ratings unsurprisingly went up after Dana Carvey's George Bush became the standard impersonation of the president.

not many people know that! (or not a lot of people ...)

A catchphrase of British stage and film actor Michael Caine,
who at times uttered it in his films. It was the title of his
1984 memoirs, and a 1986 collection of facts put by the
actor was entitled *Not Many People Know That!: Michael Caine's
Almanac of Amazing Information*. As Peter Sellers pointed out,
after imitating the well-known catchphrase during an interview
on a BBC TV chat show in 1972, Caine had a habit of gleefully
offering information garnered from *The Guinness Book of Records*,
concluding with his famous remark.

not that there's anything wrong with that

A phrase associated with comedian Jerry Seinfeld on the US
TV comedy series *Seinfeld* (1989–98), most famously uttered in an
episode in which Seinfeld is denying that he is gay, while not
wanting to be seen as anti-gay. In 'The Outing', George (Jason
Alexander) and Jerry, while dining in a restaurant, convince a
reporter that they are gay. Their fumbling efforts to then
repudiate any significant relationship—'We're not gay!'—was
perfectly and memorably captured by this politically
correct catchphrase, which implies a comic, potentially
politically incorrect, sense of embarrassment.

not tonight, Josephine!

A refusal or rejection, usually given because of fatigue or
disinterest, believed to be Napoleon Bonaparte's legendary reply to
the Empress Josephine. Although the phrase does not appear in
contemporary sources, according to accounts, Josephine found
Napoleon offhand when he got back from battle in October 1809,
and discovered he had ordered the doors between their
apartments at Fontainebleau to be blocked up. This could have
been when the famous rejection was issued. Two months later
they were divorced. In any event, the phrase was current by the
late 19th century and popularized in music hall sketches during
the early 20th century. A song called 'Not Tonight, Josephine' was
sung by music hall performer Florrie Forde in 1915. On her 1996
album, *Boys For Pele*, Tori Amos croons 'Not Tonight Josephine' on one
of the tracks.

not until after six o'clock!

From the popular BBC radio comedy series *Ray's a Laugh* (1949–61), starring Ted Ray in domestic situations. One of the show's rich collection of catchphrases, this was spoken by the glamour girl—the 'Mayfair Girl'—who would do anything, but 'not until after six o'clock!' Played by Patricia Hayes, a team regular who provided the voice for many parts, the 'Mayfair Girl' would inevitably reply to any question from Ray with 'Yes, but not until after six o'clock!'

nothing comes between me and my Calvins

A slogan from a Calvin Klein jeans advertising campaign of the 1970s, that was first spoken by Brooke Shields and then by other models and celebrities. The slogan was quite controversial at the time, and not only because Brooke Shields was only 12 years old, but because it contains a double entendre intended to attract viewers on at least two levels. The double meaning is obvious here, especially when the slogan is coupled with the picture of an attractive, young girl.

now cut that out!

One of US comedian Jack Benny's trademark lines. Already a familiar item on his popular radio programme *The Jack Benny Show*, which ran from 1932 to 1955, the phrase became a national catchphrase when the programme was produced for television from 1950 to 1965. Jack Benny, owed much of his success to his perfect timing and rueful demeanour, and his ability to make the most of the direct rapport he enjoyed with his audiences. Not only would he use the live audience as a sounding board for timing, but he also used the intimacy of that crowd to introduce much of the surreal humour and bizarre content of his shows. His 'Now cut that out!' was in fact an aside to the audience which let them know that he also found the show's content odd and ridiculous. This live interaction generally had the effect of rendering the strange subject-matter more palatable for mainstream audiences. Although this catchphrase had become a predictable cliché within the programme's format, it never failed to produce laughs.

now isn't that special?

Also 'Well, isn't that special!' Catchphrase belonging to 'The Church Lady', one of the original characters played by US comedian Dana Carvey in skits on the live TV comedy series *Saturday Night Live* in the late 1980s. Carvey's sassy Church Lady hosted a religious talk show, interviewing celebrities and public figures (played by members of the *SNL* cast) such as Jim and Tammy Bakker, Donald Trump, and his then girlfriend, Marla Maples. Bespectacled, dressed in prim and proper knit suits, and topped with a grey wig, the Church Lady twitched and puckered her lips to show her disdain for her guests' very public sins, often suggesting that Satan may well be behind their wrongful ways. Her moral outrage was openly vented when O. J. Simpson and Madonna appeared on her show; she called him O. J. sinner, slicer, and stabber, and Madonna a slut. After reading a letter sent in to the show asking how she knows she is 'God's Favourite', she says: 'Well if I am not God's Favourite, let me explode right now.'

now it's garbage

A classic line, delivered with acid, by Oscar Madison in a hilarious scene in Neil Simon's 1965 hit play *The Odd Couple*, when Oscar insists on calling the linguine Felix has cooked 'spaghetti' (Felix: It's not spaghetti, it's linguini!'). It ends with Oscar, who becomes increasingly impatient and peeved, throwing the pasta at the wall and declaring 'Now, it's garbage!' The line was popularized by its inclusion in the 1968 film version, starring Walter Matthau as Oscar and Jack Lemmon as Felix Ungar, and then the TV series (1970–5).

now then, now then

A phrase associated with ex-radio DJ Sir Jimmy Savile, whose television show *Jim'll Fix It*, aimed mainly at children, received a viewing audience of 19 million in the late 1970s. The 'Fix Its' he was asked to embark on included blowing up a cooling tower, flying with the RAF, burning one million pounds, and going to the set of *Fawlty Towers* to meet the mistreated Manuel. Savile was often being impersonated by famous comedians of the time, and, aside from 'Now then, now then, boys and girls,' his much parodied catchphrases included 'Howzabout that then' and 'What have we got here then'. He was also well known for his gold jewellery and cigars, as well as his charity work.

now we do the dance of joy!

A whacky outburst popularized by Balki Bartokomous (Bronson Pinchot) on the US TV comedy series *Perfect Strangers* (1986–93). According to the naive, sheep-rearing Balki, this physical expression of elation (the dance of joy) was a well-established custom on his home island of Mypos, distant as that may seem to the ways of his new home, Chicago. (See also 'don't be ridiculous'.)

now, we'll do some cooking, but first we must WASH OUR HANDS!

A catchphrase from the unconventional, youth-oriented, short 'cookery-for-the-people' programme *Get Stuffed* (1991–4), shown late nights on ITV. Using shaky camera work, shouting, hand-drawn illustrations on cardboard, and comedy songs in the background, the shows would attempt to demonstrate how to make quick, simple, cheap, but tasty, meals using basic ingredients. The show would feature a different pair of hosts each time, invariably a male and a female, looking like typical university students. Once the ingredients for the dish had been purchased and assembled in the kitchen, the show's inimitable catchphrase would, without fail, be announced. The show and its catchphrase was parodied by comedians of the time, notably by comedy writers Graham Linehan and Arthur Matthews in Channel 4 comedy sketch series from the late 1990s, including *Sorted!* and *The Day Today*.

nudge nudge, wink wink

A means of hinting and insinuating something, usually to draw attention to an innuendo, especially a sexual one, in a conversation. The phrase was popularized by a salacious character played by Eric Idle in the BBC TV cult comedy series *Monty Python's Flying Circus* (1969–74) and became associated with the show. It first appeared in a 1969 sketch, and was often followed by 'say no more!' or 'need I say more?' The phrase is also often applied to situations of doubtful morality or legality. It was used by BBC2 *Newsnight* presenter Kirsty Wark on 23 January 2001 to describe (jokingly) the intervention of former Secretary of State for Northern Ireland Peter Mandelson in support of a British passport publication for the Indian businessman Srichand Hinduja.

Oo

obey your thirst

Tagline for Sprite soft drink since 1994, devised by the advertising agency Lowe Lintas & Partners. Before 'Obey your thirst', Sprite had emphasized its lemon-lime taste by calling itself the 'limon' drink. The current campaign, featuring ads that parody celebrity endorsements, carry the slogan: 'Image is nothing. Obey your thirst'. By combining humour, irony, and the unvarnished truth, the ads and catchy slogan appealed to urban teens.

often|always a bridesmaid but never a bride

An early 20th-century proverb expressing disappointment in always being second-best, and not the one whose dreams come true. A 1917 song entitled 'Why Am I Always the Bridesmaid?', with Charles Collins and Lily Morris, included the line 'Why am I always the bridesmaid, Never the blushing bride?' However, the saying, in what has become its most popular form—'Often a bridesmaid but never a bride'—came from an American advertisement for Listerine mouthwash. The text was written by Milton Feasley and first appeared in 1925. The advertisement was so successful that it ran for more than 10 years.

oh, Baby Gizmo! (also Garden Gizmo|Kitchen Gizmo|etc.)

A multi-purpose term for any kind of appliance or contraption advertised during the 'Chanel 9' sketches on the BBC TV comedy series *The Fast Show* (1994–7), created by Paul Whitehouse and Charlie Higson. See 'action pumpo!'

oh, calamity!

Exclamation popularized by British comic stage and film actor Robertson Hare. Hare, whose other catchphrase was 'Balderdash!', appeared in comic films and stage productions from the late 1930s until the early 1970s, and starred as the Archdeacon alongside Derek Nimmo's dithery curate in the TV clerical comedy *All Gas and Gaiters* (1967–71).

A much-loved *farceur*, Robertson Hare was always best remembered by those who saw him in the first decades of his long career (including Winston Churchill) calling out 'Oh, calamity!' whenever his trousers fell down. Hare's expletive was also familiar to former prime minister Margaret Thatcher, who wrote: 'After John [Wakeman] and Ken [Baker] had left, Norman Lamont came in and repeated the formula. The position, he said, was beyond repair. Everything we had achieved on industry and Europe would be jeopardised by victory for Michael Heseltine. Everything but Robertson Hare's "Oh Calamity" ' (*The Downing Street Years*, 1993).

oh, I say!

From the BBC radio series *The Navy Lark* (1959–77), one of the longest running comedy shows ever. It was the catchphrase of Leslie Phillips, who played the silly Sub-Lieutenant aboard HMS *Troutbridge*. The exclamation expressed the Sub-Lieutenant's characteristic, and so easily elicited, bewildered surprise.

ohhhh, lady!

A catchphrase belonging to US comic actor and director Jerry Lewis. During his time on *Saturday Night Live* in the early 1980s, comedian Martin Short repopularized the line through his impression of a slobbering Jerry Lewis who would always cry out, 'Hey Lady!'

oh, mama!

Popularized by Niles Crane (played by David Hyde Pierce) in the US TV comedy series *Frasier* (1993–   ), which portrays the everyday neuroses and perplexities in the lives of Dr Frasier Crane (Kelsey Grammer), his family and associates. Niles, Frasier's eccentric and competitive brother, is a fellow psychiatrist and is as priggish and snobbish as Frasier—if not more so. His catchphrase, uttered in response to many of the numerous mishaps, messes, and misunderstandings that spice the show's weekly episodes, appears inappropriately subdued, but by

Niles's standards is about as forceful an exclamation as he might muster. Niles is after all the antithesis of the 'macho man'.

oh my God, they killed Kenny

Popularized by the US TV cartoon series *South Park* (1997–), which sees Kenny McCormick, one of the four principal 8-year-old characters in the show, die in almost every episode. Although often spoken by Eric Cartman (the fat kid), the phrase is not exclusive to any one character, and often becomes a general refrain. Kenny wears a giant orange parka drawn tightly around his mouth so that whatever he says is completely unintelligible to all except the other boys. What viewers hear is 'mmph mmrph mmmph', etc. and this has become his 'catchphrase'. His family is dirt-poor—a fact which the boys, and Cartman in particular, continuously point out—and his parents are both drunks. In one episode Kenny won a can of string beans, but his family couldn't afford a can opener. His deaths tend to be elaborate, bizarre, and horribly painful, including being nuked in a microwave, decapitated during a football game, and pecked to death by turkeys. Conclusion: Kenny is immortal.

oh, my lord!

Words showing anxiety or astonishment spoken by Larry Appleton (Mark Linn-Baker) on the US TV comedy series *Perfect Strangers* (1986–93). Larry and his distant, sheep-rearing cousin from Mypos, Balki, regularly find themselves in trouble. The countless misadventures of this comic Chicago-set variation on *The Odd Couple* naturally lead Larry to make frequent use of his catchphrase. This example, from an episode entitled 'The Men Who Knew Too Much, Part 1', shows both Larry's use of the line as well as Balki's on-going struggle with the English language—Larry gasps 'Oh my Lord!, it's Marco Madison, he's very big in the underworld!' To which Balki replies excitedly 'Boxers or Briefs!!!'

Oh! Ohhh! Oooooohhhh!

Rochester's (Eddie Anderson) trademark exclamation on the US TV series *The Jack Benny Show* from 1950 to 1965. Rochester was Benny's valet and chauffeur, and was often clever enough to disguise a put-down with seeming subservience. Benny and his extremely raspy-voiced valet shared an unusually intimate and complex relationship in which Rochester bore the burden of tending to Benny's needs, while Benny made sure his job wouldn't be easy.

oh, what a feeling!

An advertising slogan for Toyota, introduced to launch the new front-drive Corolla in 1980. The tagline, that ran until 1985, encapsulated what the commercials showed—Toyota car owners experiencing total satisfaction, to the point of euphoria. The actors in the TV spots would actually jump for joy, being captured in freeze frame as they leapt with glee and excitement. The image rapidly became Toyota's trademark. In 2001, Toyota launched its biggest ad campaign ever, attempting to once more pump some excitement and emotion into its rather dull and sensible image. Built around the tagline 'Get the feeling', the campaign played off the familiarity of Toyota's earlier long-running slogan, while hoping to attract younger buyers. 'What a Feeling' by Irene Cara, a massive hit single from the 1983 film *Flashdance*, also summed up the sense of exhilaration many in the early 1980s seemed to be striving to for.

OK, yah!

Words signifying agreement or consent, associated with and made famous by Sloane Rangers—a sub-stratum of London's upper class, who congregate largely within an area around Sloane Square. The expression was popular among Sloane Rangers throughout the 1980s, used mostly by the female members of this social group. 'OK Yah' was eventually transformed into a label for the people who use it and is now a noun. *Yah*, is now defined as 'an upper-class person' in the *Concise Oxford Dictionary*.

okay—so I ain't neat

Admission coined by Jerry Colonna, US character actor and sidekick of Bob Hope (see 'greetings, gate!'). The zany Colonna was caricatured in many Warner Bros. cartoons, and this catchphrase, like others he popularized, was used by cartoon characters in the 1940s. Unsurprisingly, this remark on his lack of tidiness or

cleanliness, is associated with pigs—appearing at the end of
Gregory Grunts' letter of introduction in *Porky's Hired Hand* (1940), and
uttered by the dirty pig in *Farm Frolics* (1941).

old — trick, the

From the catchphrase-packed US TV comedy series *Get Smart*
(1965–70), used by the show's star Maxwell Smart (played by Don
Adams). In the series, bumbling Maxwell Smart, Agent 86 for
CONTROL, with a great deal of help from his competent partner,
Agent 99, battles the forces of KAOS. The line first appeared in
Mr Big as 'the old garbage trick', and was usually followed by 'that's
the second time I've fallen for that this month/week'. This format
phrase became quite a tongue-twister when it appeared in
Smartacus: 'The old Professor Peckinpah all purpose anti-personnel
Peckinpah pocket pistol under the toupee trick.'

ooh matron!

A cry associated with British comedian Kenneth Williams in many of
the 'Carry On' films he starred in from the late 1950s until the 1970s.
Accompanied by his flaring nostrils and camp behaviour, Williams
would deliver this line when truly shocked. Comedy actress Hattie
Jacques, who starred in 14 'Carry On' films, was famous for her role
during this film series alongside Williams as 'Matron'. A famous scene
in which this catchphrase comes up is in *Carry On Camping* (1969),
where a young Barbara Windsor is doing some morning exercises. In a
sudden thrust of excitement, her bikini top flies off, landing in the
hands of a horrified Kenneth Williams. With a cry of 'ooh, Matron,
take them away', Barbara is led away by the matronly Hattie Jacques.

ooooh yeah, DIG IT!

Euphoric remark popularized by professional wrestler Randy Savage
during televised World Wrestling Federation bouts. The showy,
exaggerated nature of the catchphrase is in keeping with the current
popular style of professional wrestling that enjoys television coverage
and is seen more as an extension of show business than serious sport.
Randy, described as the 'Macho Man', is usually accompanied by his
lovely manager and wrestling ally, Miss Elizabeth.

ooh! You bwoke my widdle!

A catchphrase of a Red Skelton character by the name of Junior, the Mean Widdle Kid, who first appeared on Skelton's radio show in the late 1930s, and then became well known to US audiences through his sketches on Skelton's TV show from 1951 to 1971. The mischievous and offensive boy used the exclamation, usually with a degree of exaggeration, to show he had been upset or wronged. It appeared in numerous Warner Bros. cartoons, including in *The Impatient Patient* (1942) and *Ain't That Ducky* (1945), generally when a small character overreacted to a physical stimulus. (See also 'he don't know me vewy well, do he?' and 'I dood it'.)

ooh, you are awful ... but I like you

Associated with British comedian Dick Emery (1917–83) who starred in the long-running TV sketch show *The Dick Emery Show* (1963–81). Emery played a range of regular characters, including Kitchener Lampwick, a wheezy old soldier, Camp Clarence (with his catchphrase 'Hello, Honky-Tonks'), and in drag, Randy Mandy, who would always say: 'Ooh, you are awful! But I like you.' The series, written by David Cumming, John Warren, John Singer, Steven Singer, Mel Brooks, and Mel Tonkin, among others, led to the production of a 1972 film entitled *Ooh, You Are Awful* (aka *Get Charlie* in the USA), directed by Cliff Owen, and starring Dick Emery as Charlie Tully.

one of these days, Alice, pow! Right in the kisser!

A recurring rancorous, yet loving, threat spoken by the loud-mouthed, blue-collar authority on matters of importance Ralph Kramden, played by Jackie Gleason, on the US TV sitcom *The Honeymooners* (1955–6). Ralph, a downtrodden but scheming bus driver, would say these menacing words to his wife Alice (Audrey Meadows), when angered by her. Alice, however, could easily defend herself—at least verbally— against her overweight husband. Although this TV series ran for only one year, it achieved cult status and has been rerun endlessly not only because it made viewers laugh, it also showed the way many lower-class people actually lived.

Setting a harsh yet realistic tone, the Kramdens yelled all the time—they *liked* yelling, and were not afraid to raise their voice and, as in this case, issue empty threats. When Ralph threw this familiar threat at Alice she would just look at him serenely, judgmentally, and fearlessly, because she knew he was far more fearful and fragile than she. Ralph and Alice really loved each other, despite their bickering, and Ralph would always apologize for his inexcusable conduct at the end of each episode, telling Alice 'Baby, you're the greatest'.

one ringy-dingy

Spoken by one of Lily Tomlin's characters on the gag-a-second US comedy TV series *Rowan and Martin's Laugh-in* (1968–73). The sarcastic, nasal telephone operator Ernestine would say 'one ringy-dingy, two ringy-dingy…' while punching in calls. The character was so comic and the words were soon so familiar that the telephone company AT&T attempted to hire Tomlin to feature in their commercials using her routine, but she declined. Comedienne Lily Tomlin and others who were practically unknown when they first appeared on *Laugh-in*, such as Goldie Hawn and Richard Dawson, went on to have successful film careers.

open the box!

What most of the audience would shout when contestants were given the choice of opening the box or taking the money on the British TV quiz *Take Your Pick* (1955–68). Hosted by Michael Miles—the 'quiz inquisitor'—contestants were put through a series of minor obstacles, including the infamous 'Yes-No' qualification game, and then the fast-talking Miles would enter into some cash bidding for the keys to the box selected by the players; three out of thirteen boxes contained booby prizes. Box 13 contained a mystery prize, not known even to Miles, and then there was the treasure-chest of money and 'tonight's star prize', which would be greeted with an exaggerated crescendo of oohs from the audience. The show's other catchphrase was 'There's the keys, take your pick'. A 1990s version, that was very similar to the original show, was hosted by Des O'Connor and ran from 1992 to 1998.

other pill, the

The other essential, daily requirement; not to be missed. This was an advertising slogan for One-A-Day Multiple Vitamins Plus Iron, that made an obvious reference to the contraceptive pill (commonly referred to as 'the pill'), which, when it was launched in 1967, would have raised a few eyebrows.

overpaid, (overfed,) oversexed, and over here

A gibe at the expense of the US army in Europe during the Second World War. By January 1944 almost a million American troops were crammed into southern and southeast England. The standard of living enjoyed by GIs astounded some and irritated others among their hosts, and the popularity of the GIs among the female population caused some Britons to characterize their American allies as 'overpaid, oversexed, and over here'. It was popularized by British comedian Tommy Trinder on his stage and radio shows in the form of 'overpaid, overfed, oversexed and over here'.

In the claymation film *Chicken Run* (2000), Rocky, a flying rooster (or so it would appear), arrives on the scene, feeding the chickens' hopes of escape. Rocky (voiced by Mel Gibson) claims to be a professional. However, he is also an American, which draws some scepticism— 'Overpaid, oversexed and over here', one hen comments.

'ow do, 'ow are yer?

A casual Yorkshire salutation that was popularized by Wilfred Pickles as presenter on the BBC radio quiz show *Have a Go* (1946–67), in which he would speak with and question ordinary people, giving away modest cash prizes for correct answers to simple questions. Pickles travelled over 400,000 miles around the country in the 1940s and 1950s, presenting his popular radio series, with regular audiences of twenty million hearing him ask: ''Ow do, 'ow are yer?'—the catchphrase with which he opened each show.

Pp

....

pass!

I don't know, 'I give up'; associated with BBC TV's *Mastermind* quiz show (1972–97) hosted by Magnus Magnusson. In Round One of the show, each of the four contestants went up to the famous black chair one by one, and would be asked 'Name?', 'Occupation?', and 'Specialized subject?' Each contestant would then be subjected to two minutes of quick-fire questions about their subject. Contestants could pass if they wished—hence the catchphrase—although in the event of a tie these were taken into account. Round Two was played similarly to Round One, but with general knowledge questions instead. 'Pass' answers would be given at the end of each round.

pass the sick bag, Alice

Used by *Sunday Express* columnist Sir John Junor to denote disgust. He admitted using the phrase once, referring to a canteen lady at the old *Express* building in Fleet Street, who conveyed plates of egg and chips to journalists at their desks (in the *Guardian*, 'Notes and Queries', 1991). The phrase was then popularized during the mid-1980s when Junor's opinion column was regularly parodied by the satirical magazine *Private Eye*.

password confirmed. Stand by

Words associated with the computer on *Babylon 5*, a US science fiction TV series that ran from 1994 to 1998, and four two-hour TV movies shown during 1998 and 1999. The first series is set in the year 2257, when the Earth Alliance is preparing to place its Babylon 5 station into operation. The purpose of the Babylon Project is to serve as a kind of interplanetary 'United Nations', a place where representatives of the major races of the Galaxy can meet to resolve conflicts and work for their worlds' mutual benefit. As a port of call for refugees, smugglers, businessmen, diplomats, and travellers from a hundred worlds, Babylon 5 could be a dangerous place. For obvious security reasons, the station's soft-voiced computer must clear all arrivals.

people's —, the

Used to describe a public figure held dear by a nation; someone the general public can identify with. The expression dates to the early 19th century and, by the late 1860s, the British Liberal prime minister William Gladstone had become known as 'the people's William'. Thornton Leigh Hunt, editor of the *Daily Telegraph* until his death in 1873, had frequently described Gladstone in this way in his newspaper. More recently, it became associated with Diana, Princess of Wales, whose popularity with the British people had led many to consider her 'a queen in people's hearts', even though she had relinquished the title of 'Her Royal Highness' and any future claims to the British throne in 1996. The special title was however popularized by Prime Minister Tony Blair who, on hearing of her death on 31 August 1997, said: 'She was the people's princess, and that is how she will stay ... in our hearts and in our memories forever.'

Pepsi ... the choice of a new generation

An advertising slogan for Pepsi Cola, introduced in 1984 as a continuation and development on Pepsi's earlier 'Come alive! You're in the Pepsi generation' slogan (see above). The most popular entertainer of the time, Michael Jackson, starred in the first two commercials of the new campaign, turning the two spots into 'the most eagerly awaited advertising of all time'. Various other stars were featured in the campaign, including Tina Turner, Lionel Ritchie, Billy Crystal, and sports hero Joe Montana. In 1989, 'The Choice of a New Generation' theme was expanded to categorize Pepsi users as 'A Generation Ahead!'

By the end of the 1980s, the slogan had become embedded in the public consciousness, and has become a popular catchphrase/format phrase, with a 1999 article about an automatic rifle in *Soldier of Fortune* magazine bearing the title 'MP5—The Choice of a New Generation', while *Maitreya: The Choice of a New Generation* (2000) is the title of a book about Buddhism by Tessa Laird. Viagra has also been a favourite filler/substitute in this format phrase.

perfick!

'Perfect', as pronounced by characters with a Kentish accent in the rural books of H. E. Bates, and particularly by Sidney 'Pop' Larkin in Bates's 1958 collection of short stories *The Darling Buds of May*, which was dramatized for TV (1991–3). The period comedy drama series featured stories of the permanently optimistic Larkin family in an ever sunny 1950s. Perfick…everything is just perfick according to Pa Larkin: 'Larkin by name and Larkin by nature'.

The phenomenally popular show starred David Jason as the quick-eyed, kindhearted junk dealer 'Perfick' Pop Larkin, and made a star of Catherine Zeta Jones as his beautiful daughter, Mariette Larkin. He and Ma Larkin (played by Pam Ferris) enjoy their rural life and six children. Daughter Mariette's concern that she might be pregnant, and not sure who the father is, does nothing to dampen the family's overall good spirits. Nor, for example, does the arrival of a Tax Inspector, Mr Charlton. As his income is all spent, Pop doesn't see that he is required to pay taxes.

permission to speak, Sir!

Popularized by the BBC TV comedy series *Dad's Army* (1968–77), set during the early years of the Second World War, and featuring the diverse characters comprising the fictitious Walmington-on-Sea's Home Guard platoon. The phrase was associated with Lance Corporal Jack Jones (Clive Dunn), Walmington-on-Sea's elderly butcher and ever-keen Boer War veteran. 'They don't like it up 'em', was another of his favourite catchphrases. (See also 'don't panic'.)

phone a friend

Phrase popularized by Chris Tarrant, as host of the popular UK TV quiz show *Who Wants to Be a Millionaire?* (1998– ; US 1999–), which has become synonymous with 'ask for help'. Contestants on the show are provided with three 'lifelines' in case they can't answer a question (which happens frequently). The lifelines are '50:50', 'ask the audience', and 'phone a friend'. '50:50' takes away two wrong answers out of the four answers to choose from leaving the right answer and the one remaining wrong answer. 'Ask the audience' asks the live audience to vote on what they think is the correct answer, revealed as a statistical bar chart, while 'Phone a friend' means the contestant can phone a friend and tell them the question. The friend then has 30 seconds to give the contestant a correct answer. This is often the safest of the three, as friends are naturally selected for their erudition and trustworthiness (unlike the audience).

The catchphrase was used in the title of an article—'Blair sets up "phone a friend" link with Bush'—to describe the kind of relationship the two world leaders plan to cultivate. The special report on New Labour in government, in the *Guardian* (21 February 2001), begins: 'Tony Blair last night served notice on Britain's European allies and his own party that he intends to make a "pick up the phone" friendship with President George Bush a major priority as the new Republican administration settles down in Washington'.

phone home

A phrase popularized by ET, the wrinkly, plump, rubber-necked, and completely endearing alien creature featured in Steven Spielberg's 1982 multi-million-pound box office hit *ET the Extra-Terrestrial*. ET, mistakenly left behind on Earth, is found by a young boy, Elliott (Henry Thomas), who hides him in his home. Their friendship grows and changes both their worlds forever. Elliott and ET become so close that they share emotions; as ET becomes ill, so does Elliott. Ultimately, despite the ease of American suburban life, ET feels lonely and wants to go home (three million light years away). He tries to communicate with his family through a makeshift umbrella-satellite, then struggles to explain what he is hoping to do to Elliot, saying, 'ET phone home'.

The phrase quickly entered the lexicon of the 1980s, and resurfaced in 1999 when ET and his famous words appeared in British Telecom's (BT) advertising campaign (coinciding with the re-release of the film). The series of TV commercials starred the model of the alien which cost Spielberg £750,000 to create, using the talents of special effects wizard Carlo Rambaldi. BT claimed that the advertising campaign was aimed at letting people know that—with the age of multi-media—ET can do quite a bit more than simply phone home and would encourage people not to be daunted by 'space-age' technology.

play it again, Sam

Famous misquotation, and now an established catchphrase, associated with Rick Blaine (Humphrey Bogart) in the 1942 film *Casablanca*. What he actually said was 'If she can stand it, I can. Play it!' Earlier in the film, Ilsa Lund (Ingrid Bergman) makes a request to Sam (Dooley Wilson) the piano player, saying 'Play it, Sam. Play "As Time Goes By" '. Some have suggested that Jack Benny, on his radio show in 1943, might have popularized this incorrect version. In a parody of *Casablanca*, he played a character called 'Ricky Bogart' who, in one show, becomes increasingly inebriated and repeatedly pleads with Sam (Eddie Anderson) to 'Sing it, Sam'. He finally exclaims: 'Sam, Sam, play that song for me again, will you?'

Play It Again Sam was the title of a 1972 Woody Allen film in which movie buff and film writer Allan Felix (Allen) is left by his wife and allows his best friends to try to fix him up with various women. Coaching him in the fine art of seduction is the ghost of Humphrey Bogart (Jerry Lacy), who does his best to boost Allan's self-confidence and dispense tough-guy wisdom about women ('I never saw a dame yet that didn't understand a good slap in the mouth or a slug from a .45'). The phrase, meaning once again or even again and again, became a fitting advertising slogan for the New York State Lottery.

please don't squeeze the Charmin

An advertising slogan for Charmin toilet tissue that was made a household phrase in America by Mr Whipple (aka 'George the Grocer'), played by Dick Wilson, in more than 500 commercials over 20 years. The slogan was introduced in 1964, with George Whipple as the grocer who guarded Charmin's apparently irresistible softness (or 'squeezability'). In a 1978 poll, Mr Whipple was named the third best-known American—just behind former President Nixon and Billy Graham. In 1999, Wilson, aged 82, came out of retirement to star in new TV commercials to introduce the then 'new' Charmin.

point Percy at the porcelain, (I must go and)

A colourful way for a man to say he must urinate, popularized by the *Private Eye* cartoon strip 'Barry Mackenzie' about an Australian innocent with a unique vocabulary abroad in London, which ran from 1964 to 1974. The strip was drawn by Nicholas Garland and formulated by the then unknown Australian comedian Barry Humphries. This is one of many euphemisms for male urination involving names for the penis, including 'train Terence at the terracotta', 'aim Archie at the Armitage', or 'Dennis at the Doulton'.

pork—the other white meat

An advertising slogan devised by America's National Pork Council in 1986, that changed the way Americans thought about pork and had, by 2000, increased pork sales by 37 per cent. While it was clever in its appeal, the slogan was a little confusing to some. White meat is any meat that comes from an animal that has wings, so pork is considered red meat. The bases for the ad were: first, when cooked, fresh pork is white; and secondly, pork's nutrient content is more like chicken than beef. Most importantly, due to the high demand for less fatty foods, pigs have been bred to be leaner and meatier, so they now are closer to white meat than red meat. Whether or not it can pass for 'white meat', whenever pork is now offered to guests (with or without a hint of humour) as the 'other white meat', they will at least know what they're getting.

power to be your best, the

An advertising slogan for Apple, which the computer company introduced in 1990 and used for several years. The catchy, highly positive slogan was further popularized when *Saturday Night Live* parodied the phrase with a 'commercial' called 'The Power To Crush The Other Kids'. In the satire, a schoolchild produces a report about dinosaurs on the family personal computer. At school the next morning, he notices a classmate's report looks better than his own, including not only attractive typefaces and formatting, but images of actual dinosaurs. When he asks the classmate 'How did you make that?' he replies: 'On my Macintosh', and the lettering on the black screen at the end of the commercial reads, 'Macintosh. The Power To Crush The Other Kids'.

priceless

Conclusive remark popularized by an advertising campaign for the
MasterCard credit card company since 1997. The word forms a
judgement towards the conclusion of a series of commercial spots
which depict sentimental episodes of people together, while one
person assigns a monetary value to a variety of goods and services. The
items all add up to an intangible event, like 'a day where all you have
to do is breathe', or an emotional moment like 'Watching her play
with the cardboard box', which are then labelled 'priceless'. The ads
conclude: 'There are some things in life money can't buy. For
everything else, there's MasterCard.'

The catchword has been parodied by a number of comedians and
shows, including Jay Leno and *Saturday Night Live*. However, when in
Autumn 2000 the Green Party presidential candidate Ralph Nader
created an ad that parodied the credit card giant's ad campaign,
MasterCard sued him, seeking upwards of $5 million in damages. The
Nader ad was an almost exact duplicate of the MasterCard ad format,
but instead focused on the role of special interests in the presidential
campaign. The ad shows video clips of Republican presidential
nominee George W. Bush and Vice President Al Gore, while an
announcer says 'Grilled tenderloin for fund-raiser: $1,000 a plate.
Campaign ads filled with half-truths: $10 million. Promises to special
interest groups: over $10 billion'. The ad then cuts to a shot of Nader
working, with the voice-over concluding: 'Finding out the truth:
Priceless. There are some things money can't buy. Without Ralph
Nader in the presidential debates, the truth will come in last.'

promise her anything, but give her Arpège

When Arpège, a commercial perfume for women, was created by
Jeanne Lanvin in 1927 this advertising slogan was used to launch it.
It became an advertising classic as memorable as the scent itself.
The lyrics of 'Promise Her Anything (But Give Her Love)', a song by
Roy Alfred, recorded by Dean Martin in 1957, suggested that
whatever luxuries men might promise their women, whether
diamonds or furs (or perfume), what they should always give them
ultimately is love. This variation on the phrase naturally became
popular during the late 1950s and the 1960s, but the slogan,
which became a useful format phrase in which Arpège has been

substituted with everything from Belgian chocolates to a punch,
is still recognized as the original.

psst! Hey, buddy

Words used Sheldon Leonard to get Jack Benny's attention, and
hopefully convince him to buy whatever he's selling, on Benny's radio
comedy show that ran from 1932 to 1955. Later known as a comic
tough guy character actor, Sheldon Leonard's career had its
beginnings in his regular appearances with Jack Benny on radio and
then in films. Leonard's 'Psst. Hey Buddy, come 'ere' always got laughs.
His 'tout' character and others he played on the Jack Benny
programme would make comments about 'The big chief, bud! It's a
real sleeper!' His line was also parodied in Warner Bros. cartoons of
the late 1940s and 1950s.

pukka

A British slang expression used to describe something of quality—'the
real thing'—popularized by the young, thick-tongued, Cockney
celebrity chef Jamie Oliver. In one of his cookbooks (and videotape),
entitled *Pukka Tukka* (2000), 'pukka' is equated with the trend
showing people turning away from easy, pre-prepared meals in
favour of fresh ingredients. The Food Network's web site,
FoodTV.com, provides recipes from *Naked Chef* episodes (Jamie
Oliver's BBC TV cooking series, 2000–), and, as an added bonus,
includes a 'Naked Chef Slang Dictionary', where one can learn that
'pukka' means 'excellent'. An episode of the TV cooking show,
broadcast in November 2001, showed the chef preparing a curry in an
Indian restaurant, where the owner confirmed that 'pukka' was
a word used by Indians to mean authentic, the way it should
be—'the real thing'.

punky power!

A catchphrase from the US TV series *Punky Brewster* (1985–9), starring
Soleil Moon Frye as Punky Brewster, George Gaynes, and Brandon the
Wonder Dog. Punky was an orphan who, along with her dog Brandon,
was discovered living in an abandoned apartment by old, irascible
apartment manager Henry (Gaynes). Henry quickly grows fond of

Punky, decides to take care of her, forming the basis for the adventures that followed. An animated version, called *It's Punky Brewster* ran from 1985 to 1987, with the new addition of a magical creature named Glomer, who would magically transport Punky and friends to faraway places. 'Punky power', which had to do with the girl's ability to solve problems and make things work out, began to fade, along with the show's popularity, by the end of the 1980s.

put a tiger in your tank!

Advertising slogan for Esso petrol in the US, from 1959. This popular and catchy phrase, meaning get some real power or energy into your car (or yourself), also inspired numerous jokes and cartoons. The company that is now Exxon began using the tiger as its promotional symbol in the mid-1930s. In 1959, when the company was Standard Oil of New Jersey and its subsidiaries were marketing Esso and Enco brands of gasoline, an advertising copywriter in Chicago, Illinois, came up with what would become one of the most famous slogans of the 1960s. The cartoon version of the tiger, alongside the slogan, originated in 1964. Exxon registered its tiger with the US Patent and Trademark Office in 1965.

The Esso Tiger first appeared in the UK on a poster for Esso Extra in 1952. The slogan was translated into many languages and was mimicked in a series of advertising slogans for other products. In the 1990s, the tiger campaign and slogan—with its seductive imagery of endangered mammal, fast car and petroleum industry—started to take on an audaciously un-PC message. New themes were adopted, such as 'Rely on the Tiger', and in 1995, ExxonMobil began to contribute towards helping to save the tiger from extinction; in the late 1990s, Exxon made the largest single contribution ever to the Save The Tiger Fund.

put that light out!

Fearsome cry popularized by Chief ARP Warden William 'Bert' Hodges, played by Bill Pertwee, on the BBC TV comedy series *Dad's Army* (1968–77). Hodges, Walmington-on-Sea's greengrocer, was Captain Mainwaring's greatest adversary, doing whatever he could to anger him and to try to push out Mainwaring's Home Guard in favour of his beloved ARP Wardens, except, of course, when any real danger presented itself. As the village's chief air-raid warden, Hodges was responsible for ensuring its inhabitants adhered to the black out rules, and would habitually strike fear into the villagers with his cry of 'Put that light out!' (See also 'hooligans!')

Qq

quality is Job 1

A slogan from a 1970s advertising campaign created by Wells, Rich, Greene advertising agency for Ford Motor Company. The phrase—a claim that would impress, if not satisfy, any customer—quickly became a popular expression, and one which has continued to be used by all manner of businesses.

queen for a day

An expression used by or about a woman to mark an occasion of unusual pampering or special treatment. It was the title of a US radio show, hosted by Jack Bailey, that ran from 1945 to 1955. Bailey then went with the show when it moved to television, from 1956 to 1964, and would begin every show with, 'Do YOU want to be…QUEEN…FOR…A…DAY?' It was one of US daytime television's most popular tear-jerkers. Each day, four women chosen from the studio audience would appear on stage one at a time, and each woman would talk about the great tragedies and misfortunes in her life. At the end of each programme whoever was in the worst shape—as assessed by the audience 'applause meter'—was crowned 'Queen for a Day'. She would be literally draped in a sable-trimmed red velvet robe, have a jewelled crown placed on her head, and be showered with gifts. According to the show's producer, Howard Blake, 'Five thousand Queens got what they were after. And the TV audience cried their eyes out, morbidly delighted to find there were people worse off than they were, and so they got what they were after.'

quicker picker upper, the

An advertising slogan for Bounty kitchen towel, that was popularized by the 'pinafored' Rosie (Nancy Walker) in a series of TV commercials in the late 1970s. Actress, singer, and comedienne Walker had a rather nasal voice and a sarcastic, self-deprecating manner, bringing a lot of humour to an ad for what was a particularly mundane type of product/activity. The slogan was already memorable, to some degree, because of its association with tongue-twisters. It was also rich in—and perhaps best-loved for—its potential sexual innuendo. It is now often used with reference to the drug Viagra, and appears on one of US comedian and talk show host David Letterman's top ten lists, as one of the 'Top Ten Slogans For The New Wonder-Bra'.

Rr
··········

racialist

Generally any offensive, prejudiced, or racist action or person, as used and popularized by the politically incorrect Ali G (Sacha Baron Cohen) on Channel 4's comedy series *The 11 O'Clock Show* (1998–) and *Da Ali G Show* (2000–1). Ali G, an uneducated 'black' interviewer and TV show host, cleverly manages to get politicians and celebrities to take deliberately ignorant questions seriously, often employing 'racialist' as a term describing anything from racist to simply wrong. For example, when Ali interviewed Admiral Stansfield Turner about the CIA, he asked what the acronym stands for, and then whether intelligence was a prerequisite for employment. When Turner replies that a college degree is required, Ali interrupts with 'Ain't that a bit racialist though that you have to be intelligent?'

The character of Ali G, the creation of a white, well-educated man, has offended some people, notably a group of black comedians who complained that Ali is racist (or as he would say, 'racialist'). Sacha Baron Cohen has refused to answer accusations of racism or impropriety. Little is known about the comedian, other than that he has completed a thesis on racism at Cambridge.

radiant, sir, radiant

Habitual response given by one of the two exuberantly lascivious tailors (Paul Whitehouse), when asked how he is, on the BBC TV comedy sketch series *The Fast Show* (1994–7). Always accompanied by his fellow lecherous partner, played by Mark Williams, Whitehouse would utter this line with an exaggerated wide-eyed expression and neck-craning. (See also 'did she want it, sir? Did she want it?' and 'suits you, sir'.)

reach out and touch someone

Connect and share with someone who is physically distant; often spoken with a melodramatic tone, parodying the syrupy heart-warming advertisements for AT&T telephone company (now Bell System) that used this slogan from 1979 to 1984. The ads were aimed at showing how phone calls could keep families together, with a woman trying to speak to her grandchild (who can only gurgle back), or grandparents hearing about their grandchild's first steps. The tagline was created by communications scholar Marshall McLuhan, who thought of the telephone as an extension of the human voice, and believed that the voice's isolation from all the other senses, as we experience it on the telephone, highlights the fact of our most deprived sense: touch.

— refreshes the parts that other — cannot reach

A well-established format phrase often employed to point out or stress the efficacy of a person or thing, derived from an advertising slogan for Heineken beer from 1975: 'Heineken refreshes the parts that other beers cannot reach', coined by Terry Lovelock. An article commenting on America's use of 'PR wizardry to sell its message' concerning the fight against terrorism across the globe incorporates this familiar format, doubly apt because of its instant connection to advertising—'As the United States struggles to persuade the world that bombing Afghanistan is the best way to fight the war on terrorism, the Bush administration is turning to marketing wizardry to reach parts that old-fashioned political propaganda apparently cannot reach' (*Independent*, 7 November 2001).

remember the —!

A format phrase popular in the US, where it has been used either as a battle cry or as a means of making sure certain battles and attacks will not be forgotten. One of the best known is 'remember the Alamo!'—the battle cry at San Jacinto, 21 April 1836, traditionally attributed to General Sidney Sherman. This is now often said jokingly, by way of simple warning. 'Remember Pearl Harbor!' was another slogan with a popular political message, which came into use soon after the 1941 attack. More recently, following the attacks on 11 September 2001, T-shirts went on sale in the US bearing the message 'Remember 9/11/2001' combined with the US flag and the words 'Support America'.

resist or serve

From the US TV series *The X-Files* (1993–2002), about two FBI agents, Fox Mulder (David Duchovny) and Dana Scully (Gillian Anderson), who work with the 'X files', cases that have unexplainable elements often involving the paranormal. This motto replaced 'The Truth Is Out There' as the tagline in the episode *The Red and the Black*, and is, in a nutshell, where humans must stand in the face of the alien colonists, the on-going battle against which is the focus of this episode.

The perfidious double agent Alex Krycek (Nicholas Lea) employs the phrase when he tries to warn Mulder in the same episode that there is 'is a war raging', against a planned invasion and colonization of the planet 'by an extraterrestrial race'. Mulder, ever suspicious of Krycek, does not take him seriously at first, but then Krycek mentions three sites already being investigated by Mulder and Scully, claiming they are 'all alien lighthouses where the colonization will begin, but where now, a battle's being waged. A struggle for heaven and earth. Where there is one law: fight or die. And one rule: resist or serve.' Mulder replies 'Serve who?' to which Krycek replies: 'No, not who. What.'

resistance is futile

Catchphrase belonging to the alien beings known as the Borg on the US TV series *Star Trek: The Next Generation* (1987–94), issued as a warning before they assimilate the culture and technological components of a civilization. Set in the 24th century, about 80 years after the time of Captain James Kirk, many threats to the security of citizens of the United Federation of Planets still exist. However, the Borg, human/machine creatures, soon present themselves as the Federation's greatest threat. They spread by absorbing any civilization they encounter—'assimilating' other species into the collective—and their other catchphrase is 'you will be assimilated'. The Borgs' catchphrase was reminiscent of an earlier retort, 'resistance is useless' favoured by the Daleks, the mutant monster robots from the planet Skaro intent on destroying or subjugating all other species on the BBC TV series *Doctor Who* (1963–89). (See 'Exterminate! Exterminate!') More recently, anti-capitalist protesters have modified this slogan to 'resistance is fertile'.

The Borg and their catchphrase appeared again on the 1996 film *Star Trek: First Contact* in which they travelled back in time to enslave the Earth, and also returned to confront the crew of the Spaceship *Voyager* as they travelled through the Delta Quadrant on the TV series *Star Trek: Voyager* (1995–2001).

ride the punani, ride the punani

A euphemism for having sex, in hip-hop slang, frequently used by Ali G, a 'black gangsta' character created by British comedian Sacha Baron Cohen, on Channel 4's comedy series *The 11 O'Clock Show* (1998–) and *Da Ali G Show* (2000–1). 'Punani', which means female genitalia in rap and hip-hop slang, is also the name of a Jamaican dance involving pelvic gyration, but can also be used—as it sometimes is by Ali G himself—to mean a good looking, sexy woman.

ring my chimes

One of the memorable catchphrases springing from the US comedy TV series *Rowan and Martin's Laugh-in* (1968–73). Not associated with a particular character, this phrase—a product of developments in the flourishing lexicon of 1967's 'Summer of Love'—was repeated by various performers. The words, quickly popularized by the series, entered common currency to mean please me or push (or press) my button. Its many slang variations, also popular at the time, included 'turn me on', 'float my boat', and 'rattle my chain'.

rooby, rooby, roo

Catchphrase of Scooby, the Great Dane who, along with four teenage detectives, stars in the US TV cartoon series *Scooby Doo* that premiered in 1969 (see also 'scooby-doo').

Roxanne, who do we have now?

Phrase popularized by US radio and TV personality Bud Collyer, as host of the stunt-oriented game show *Beat the Clock* (1950–61), and directed at his charming co-hostess. During the show's heyday, Collyer and his beautiful blonde co-hostess Roxanne (show name of Dolores Rosedale) reigned as television's first popular game show couple, and the line became a part of the American lexicon of the time. Unfortunately, with their popularity came rumours that Collyer had grown jealous of Roxanne's fame. Whether or not those rumours were true remained a subject of debate for years afterwards. In 1956, Roxanne was replaced by Beverly Bentley who was then replaced by Nancy Kovack, who joined Collyer when the show transferred to ABC in 1958.

Ss

same Bat-time, same Bat-channel!

A jocular way of setting an appointment, or reminding someone
of the next in a series of regular meetings or events; the sign-off
line ending each episode of the US TV series *Batman* (1966–8). The
closing voice-over (William Dozier) would urge viewers to tune in
again for the next episode, and usually came at a suspenseful
moment in the adventures of the caped hero Batman (Adam
West) and his sidekick, Robin the Boy Wonder (Burt Ward).
(See also 'holy —!')

sapristi knuckoes|knockles|nadgers!

'Sapristi', followed by a variety of words (though most often by
'knuckoes', 'knockles', or 'nadgers'), is a recurring exclamation used
by Count Jim Moriarty (Spike Milligan) on the surreal BBC comedy
radio *Goon Show* (1952–60). A Frenchman who gets to do all the dirty
jobs and likes to say 'Ow' a lot, Moriarty is the constant sidekick of
Hercules Grytpype-Thynne (Peter Sellers). Both 'nadgers' and
'knuckoes' or 'knockles' are British slang for testicles. The Goons
were working within a strict BBC censorship policy and it was their
delight to get forbidden phrases past their often comparatively
unworldly producers. 'Nadgers' also appears in an episode of the BBC
TV science fiction sitcom *Red Dwarf* (1988–92), in which Arnold J.
Rimmer has suddenly grasps his genital area and shouts 'Oh! Me
nadgers!', and on the BBC radio comedy series *Round the Horne*
(1965–9).

  In 'The Flea', a show first broadcast on 20 December 1956 (written
by Spike Milligan and Larry Stephens), when Seagoon says 'A German
diplomat is always welcome in England', the French arch villain
Moriarty responds, using his trademark expletive: 'What? Sapristi
knockles! Hairy insult! You insult me, a Frenchman! We must fight a
duel'. Moriarty was the name of the villainous Professor introduced

by Sir Arthur Conan Doyle as Sherlock Holmes's major opponent in *A Study in Scarlet* (1887), his first story about Holmes. He was an evil genius and a kind of doppelgänger of Holmes. Although obviously boasting a far lesser intellect, Milligan's Moriarty might also have aspired to be 'the greatest schemer of all time, the organizer of every deviltry' as Holmes describes the Professor in *The Valley of Fear*.

say hey!

An exclamation popularized by US baseball star Willie Mays, who used it repeatedly during his career playing with the New York (later San Francisco) Giants from 1951 to 1972 and the New York Mets in 1973. Mays has actually become known as the 'Say Hey Kid', a nickname for which *New York Journal* American sportswriter Barney Kremenko has claimed responsibility. Kremenko has said that in Mays' rookie season, the reticent Mays 'would blurt "Say who," "Say what," "Say where," "Say hey." In my paper, I tabbed him the "Say Hey Kid." It stuck.' In 1954, 'Say Hey' (the Willie Mays song) was recorded by the Treniers, with Mays singing background and Quincy Jones directing the orchestra.

say it with flowers

Advertising slogan in the US, used to promote floral gifts by the Florists Telegraph Delivery Association (FTDA). The FTDA was founded in 1910 by a group of 13 florists, meeting during a recess at the Society of American Florists (SAF) convention in Rochester, New York. The famous slogan, still used today, was coined in 1917 by a Major Patrick O'Keefe for Henry Penn, chairman of the National Publicity Committee of the SAF. Suggesting that the nicest way to express your sentiments is with a gift of flowers, the popular slogan was later used in several songs. The phrase was used in the UK by Interflora.

say kids, what time is it?

Opening question asked by Buffalo Bob (Robert Smith) at the beginning of each episode of the popular US TV children's programme *The Howdy Doody Show* (1947–60), which combined puppets and humans. The exhilarated resounding answer would always be: 'It's

Howdy Doody Time!' Each episode would end with 'It's time to say Goodbye, Goodbye, until some other day when we may be with you again'.

schwing!

An exclamatory (slang) term meaning or implying an instantaneous erection, caused by the presence of, or thought of, an arousing sexual stimulus, such as a beautiful 'babe'. The juvenile term was popularized by Wayne Campbell (Mike Myers) and Garth Algar (Dana Carvey), as co-hosts of 'Wayne's World', a basement metalhead community access cable show on *Saturday Night Live* in the late 1980s and early 1990s. As might be expected, on one 1991 *SNL* show, on which Wayne and Garth did a countdown of 'Wayne's Top Ten Babes of All Time' (leading to guest star and no. 1 babe, Madonna), 'schwing', accompanied by the appropriate crotch-raising, crops up several times. When Garth's Mom is named as no. 3, much to Wayne's embarrassment and Garth's disgust, Wayne admits: 'I'm sorry, I know it's your Mom, but I'm afraid she's a babe—[raises crotch] Schwing! Sorry.'

scooby-doo

Best known as the title of a US (Warner Bros.) TV cartoon series featuring a Great Dane called *Scooby-Doo* (1969–86), one of the most popular cartoon series in history. The meaningless syllables actually came from back vocals on Frank Sinatra's hit 'Strangers in the Night', which in turn came from scat singing, a popular form of jazz singing with nonsense syllables, using the voice as an instrument, which was begun by trumpeter Louis Armstrong in the 1920s. In the context of jazz and scat singing, these syllables are usually components of a longer sequence, such as 'scooby-dooby-doo-wap-de-wah'.

The Hanna-Barbera show was originally going to revolve around four teenage detectives who travelled the country in a van, called the Mystery Machine, solving mysteries in dangerous situations. A Great Dane accompanied the foursome but was not a prominent character, and the show was known as *Who's Scared?* At the last minute, CBS rejected the show, claiming it was too frightening. Fred Silverman, the show's creator, immediately flew back to Los Angeles, and while listening to Frank Sinatra singing 'Strangers in the Night' on the flight, the phrase 'Scooby-dooby-doo' struck him so much that he returned, saying: 'We'll call the show *Scooby-Doo, Where Are You?* and we'll make the dog the star of the show'. And that was how Scooby-Doo was created with the other characters supporting him. Another catchphrase from the show was 'those meddling (or pesky) teenagers and that dog of theirs', uttered by the culprit whose identity is invariably uncovered by the teenagers at the end of each episode.

scorchio

Hot, scorchingly hot; from the 1990s BBC TV comedy series *The Fast Show*, created by Paul Whitehouse and Charlie Higson. One of the show's most popular catchphrases, 'scorchio' was a simple (and silly) English/pseudo-Spanish hybrid word spoken mainly by weather girl Poula (Caroline Aherne) while presenting the forecast on the programme's regular sketch featuring a TV news studio set in a fictitious South American country. Aherne would gesture gracefully with her arms and hands to show viewers a map littered with large images of the sun and smilingly produce this single word; the sub-sketch would last less than a minute. The word 'Scorchio' was used by an ad agency for Sol beer, to which Whitehouse and Higson responded on the show by flashing up the slogan 'Scorchio' at the end of a spoof ad for a beer called 'Pissi'.

screw you, hippy!

One of Eric 'Beefcake' Cartman's recurring phrases on the US TV cartoon series *South Park* (1997–   ). The overweight, obnoxious and foul-mouthed Cartman is one of the popular show's four central 8-year-old characters. Cartman is also terribly opinionated, despite being far from well informed. He absolutely loathes hippies (a group of which appear to be living and/or taking drugs in the woods surrounding South Park), who he equates with vermin and the dregs of society.

see you later, alligator

Words of farewell, originating in US 'jive' of the 1930s, that became particularly popular during the 1950s and 1960s, after the release of the song by that title by rock and roll legends Bill Haley and the Comets. As in the song, the spoken response would always be: 'in a while, crocodile.' The song, written by Robert Guidry, soared in popularity after it was featured in the 1956 film *Rock Around the Clock*, which starred Haley and the Comets, and was the fictionalized rags to riches story of the band's rise to fame. The film co-starred the Platters, Freddie Bell and the Bellboys, and Alan Freed.

seems like a nice boy

A potentially camp remark that was popularized by British comedian and television compère Larry Grayson. Grayson became very well known for his catchphrases, such as 'What a gay day' and 'Shut that door!', as well as his camp innuendos. On one occasion, when he was recording *The Generation Game* (which he hosted from 1978 to 1981), gay activists demonstrated outside the studio in Shepherd's Bush about his stereotyping of gay men while at the same time being closeted himself.

selecta

A late 1990s dance music term used as a simple exclamation denoting approval and/or pleasure. Often preceded by 'bo', as in Artful Dodger and Craig David's 'When the crowd say bo selecta' on their 1999 'Re-Rewind' single. The expression reached an even larger audience through its frequent use by Ali G, the black hip-hop character created by Sacha Baron Cohen, on Channel 4's comedy series *The 11 O'Clock Show* (1998–) and *Da Ali G Show* (2000–1). When he interviewed Madonna in 2000, Ali G opened with: 'Selecta! I is ere wiv none uver dan da Queenie Mum of pop muzic, Madonna. Check it!'

seriously though, he's doing a grand job

Used by David Frost in the BBC satirical TV show *That Was The Week That Was* (1962–3), as a sarcastic comment when someone's (generally a politician's) performance was clearly shown to be far from satisfactory. A scathing profile of Home Secretary Henry Brooke, describing him as 'the most hated man in Britain', ended, 'If you're Home Secretary, you can get away with murder'. David Frost would often follow such an attack with the line 'Seriously though, he's doing a grand job'. Frost's profile had insinuated, amongst other things, that Brooke's intractability in an immigration case had led to the murder of the subject. Brooke, who had also famously deported American comedian Lenny Bruce in 1963, was so thoroughly ridiculed by the programme that the BBC decided to cancel it in case it affected the result of the 1964 General Election.

In the early 1960s, before the Profumo scandal, the show became the voice of an emergent young generation that was appalled by the Macmillan government, and provided a lot of the impetus for *Monty Python* and Peter Cook and Dudley Moore. The immensely popular satirical comedy series, which was the first to take pot shots at the establishment, was both influential and disliked by the government. The young David Frost, the show's host, went on to become one of the first celebrity interviewers who were actually more famous than their guests.

sex, drugs and rock 'n' roll

Phrase now popularly (and sometimes nostalgically) used to describe the 1960s and 1970s. It is derived from the title of a 1977 song by Ian Dury and The Blockheads that became a pop anthem, thanks to its punk disco sound and abrasive lyrics. A review of the film *Still Crazy* (21 January 1999; cnn.com) states: 'The 1960s and 1970s are known as the era of sex, drugs, and rock 'n' roll, and it's been said that if you can remember that period you weren't really there.'

shaken, not stirred

A trademark phrase proffered by James Bond, British Secret Service agent 007, in Ian Fleming's suspense novels, and their many successful film versions, featuring the tough laconic ladies' man. The line, along with his other famous catchphrase 'Bond...James Bond', with which he characteristically introduces himself, have become synonymous with this familiar fictional character, regardless of the actor playing him. It refers to the preparation of 007's favourite drink—the vodka martini, a recipe that results in what, as Ian Fleming once wrote, 'should taste like a silver cloud'.

The line first appeared in Fleming's *Dr No* (1958): 'A medium vodka dry Martini—with a slice of lemon peel. Shaken and not stirred, please. I would prefer Russian or Polish vodka.' *Dr No* was also the first James Bond film, released in 1962, starring Sean Connery as James Bond, and Ursula Andress as Honey Ryder. Andress, widely considered the ultimate Bond girl, shot to stardom when she first appeared in the film, emerging from the sea wearing a white cotton bikini. CNN (online version, 12 January 2000) described the famous article of clothing as 'The white bikini that left James Bond shaken and stirred in one of the most memorable scenes from the British spy film series. . . .' The famous martini recipe perfectly encapsulated the character's self-assured sophistication, and became well known even to the 'baddies' Bond would invariably vanquish. They liked to show they had done their research before offering their foe a drink— usually as an aperitif or prelude to a description of his imminent death as well as disasters on a more global scale.

Although literally only a cocktail-making direction, the catchphrase has come to be used more generally to mean slightly disturbed/ moved/affected, but not terribly or significantly, as in this Reuters headline: 'Connery shaken, not stirred, by his Bond roles' (19 February 2001). The article begins: 'Fans might consider him the greatest British film star ever, but Scottish film legend Sean Connery would rather watch anyone else play the role that made him famous.'

she knows, you know

Catchphrase belonging to English comedienne Hylda Baker, one of the biggest variety stars in the 1940s and 1950s. She would say this phrase with reference to Cynthia, who appeared in sketches with Baker but never uttered a word and was actually a man in drag. *She Knows You Know* was the title of a play by Jean Fergusson which explores Baker's life—from her music-hall days to touring the country as a stand-up comedienne, her eventual 'star' status and her television and film work—and featuring her classic act along with her favourite songs. Her other well-known catchphrase was 'you big girl's blouse'.

she's gotta have it

A phrase used to describe a woman's determination or 'empowerment', popularized by the title and storyline of Spike Lee's feature film. Lee's 1986 film centres on the life of Nola Darling (Tracy Camila Johns), an independent and sexy, young African-American woman, and her simultaneous romantic entanglements with three men. *She's Gotta Have It* was also the title of a Channel 4 fashion show, aimed at women only.

shome mistake, shurely?

Slurred, possibly drunken, catchphrase associated with the British satirical magazine *Private Eye*, in which it appeared repeatedly during the 1980s magazine. Simply a comical way of pointing out what must obviously be an error.

show me the money!

Don't make promises and exaggerate the complexity of things, just come up with what is expected or required. The exuberant slogan was shouted by the loud and demanding footballer Rod Tidwell (Cuba Gooding Jr.) in the 1996 film *Jerry Maguire*, and it quickly became a national catchphrase, with variations on it popping up in monologues, magazines, and newspaper headlines across the US Cameron Crowe, writer and director of *Jerry Maguire*, put the phrase in his movie after hearing a real-life football player use it. And it took off—'It hit me when I was watching the Westminister Dog Show,' said Crowe. 'When they managed to work "Show me the money!" in a dog show, I knew it was all over. We were in the mainstream and flying.'

An article in the *New York Post* (12 January 2001), reporting on a rally by the city's policeman (under the headline 'Singing the NYPD Blues'), begins 'Chanting, "show us the money," and blasting Mayor Giuliani, thousands of off-duty cops gathered at City Hall yesterday for a noisy but peaceful rally calling for a wage hike'.

shut that door!

Catchphrase of British entertainer and TV comedian Larry Grayson, uttered originally because he could feel a terrible draught while on stage in 1970. It also reflected his apparently constant hypochondria that was a theme of his patter: 'Ooh! I've got it all down this side.' The first television show Grayson hosted was called *Shut That Door* and ran from 1972 to 1973. (See also 'seems like a nice boy'.)

Shuttlecraft to Enterprise ... request permission to come aboard

Spoken by Commander Spock (Leonard Nimoy) and others on the cult US TV series *Star Trek* (1966–9). When members of the Starship *Enterprise* crew or their guests, whether invited or uninvited, were not 'beamed' aboard by ship's transporter, they would return or arrive in a shuttle which would need to dock and its passengers be given leave to enter the mother ship. The hugely popular series, with its memorable, yet simple, special effects that included 'phasers', 'cloacking devices', and 'photon torpedoes', was often not far from real developments in the world of space science, and the US space shuttle programme even named one of its shuttles *Enterprise* in its honour.

silly moo

Variation on the British slang insult directed at women, 'silly cow', that was popularized by the bigoted and racist Alf Garnett (Warren Mitchell), who would direct it at his wife, Elsie (Dandy Nichols) on the BBC TV sitcom *Till Death Us Do Part* (1966–74). Created and written by Johnny Speight, the series satirized working-class manners, breaking many taboos while showing a darker side of British society. The monstrous Alf Garnett would treat all within hailing range to his substantial prejudices and bouts of blame-laying. His favoured topics were race, permissiveness, feminism, and the monarchy. He would become particularly vitriolic when it came to 'coons', the shortcomings of incumbent Prime Minister, Harold Wilson, as well as in the face of his own family—his son-in-law (with his irritatingly long hair) was a 'Scouse git', and his wife invariably a 'silly moo'.

The series attracted numerous complaints, from viewers as well as from the Church and the British broadcasting standards campaigner Mary Whitehouse, who failed to see that Garnett was anything more than an ironic portrait of bigotry. However, although the character had been created to air and discredit views and opinions shared by ordinary people, many viewers missed the point, either identifying with Alf or pleased to see a man who spoke his mind, free of liberal attitudes. By 1974, many felt that Speight had created a monster that did as much to feed as to expose the problems, and the series came to an end. The show's format was sold to the US, where it was toned down to a less provocative version called *All in the Family* (1971–83), in which Archie Bunker (Carroll O'Connor) replaced Alf Garnett's 'silly moo' with 'dingbat' (see above).

sit on it!

Popularized by Joanie Cunningham and others on the US TV series *Happy Days* (1974–84), set in 1950s Middle America. Although not initially a big hit, the show's producer kept tinkering with the programme's elements throughout the first year and soon the show climbed into the Nielsen top ten. 'Sit on it!', similar to 'leave it be' or 'shut up', became a national catchphrase.

sixty-four thousand dollar question, the

The crucial issue, the dilemma or difficult question we'd all like an answer to. This idiomatic phrase comes from a catchphrase originating on the popular quiz show *Take It or Leave It* (1940–8) on the CBS radio network. The show's questions became progressively more difficult, and the value of a right answer kept doubling: 1, 2, 4, 8, 16, 32, and then its highest prize of $64. The phrase '$64 Question' gained some currency, but the current catchphrase became familiar after the idea was later adopted in televised quiz shows on both sides of the Atlantic (e.g. *Double Your Money* in the UK). The 1950s television version upped the ante a thousandfold, giving rise to the catchphrase 'the sixty-four thousand dollar question'.

smarter than the average bear

What cartoon-film character Yogi Bear says about himself to his companion and accomplice Boo-Boo (a cautious cub) in the US cartoon series (1958–92). The famous cartoon series *Yogi Bear* was created for television by US animators William Hanna and Joseph Barbera, and first appeared as part of the *Huckleberry Hound Show* in 1958. Yogi soon emerged as a star in his own right, quickly spinning off to his own syndicated series, which began in 1961 and continued, in different incarnations, into the 1990s. The smiling, cheeky Yogi, being what he called a 'smarter than the average bear', eschewed normal bear-type hunting techniques, such as swatting at fish, in favour of hunting for pre-made food found in tourists' 'pic-a-nic' baskets. Stealing picnic baskets from tourists and generally creating mischief for Mr Ranger in Jellystone Park were his main activities. Always at his side was the diminutive Boo Boo, who constantly pointed out the evil of Yogi's basket-stealing ways. The phrase appears in the *Yogi Bear Show* theme song, including its opening lines: 'Yogi Bear is smarter than the average bear/Yogi Bear is always in the Ranger's hair.'

smeg, or smeghead

'Smeg' was a catchall word featured in insults, like 'smeghead', 'smeg off', 'smeg for brains', 'treat me like smeg', etc., favoured by Dave Lister ('the last human alive'), played by Craig Charles, in the BBC TV science fiction sitcom *Red Dwarf* (1988–92). By the end of the first series, these words had been introduced to the English language. The cult series centres on a 24th-century earth mining ship, *The Red Dwarf*, which has its entire crew wiped out, except for space technician Dave Lister, who is lost in space with only a hologram of his bunk-mate, the ship's computer, a mad android servant, and a part cat/part human hybrid. Smeg was also the name of Dave's younger self (in a parallel universe), fronting his first band, Smeg and the Heads.

The series was created by Rob Grant and Doug Naylor, the chief writers of the hugely popular satirical TV puppet series *Spitting Image*.

smile, you're on Candid Camera!

Uttered when someone is caught unawares after he or she has involuntarily become part of a prank-like or embarrassing situation. The remark was the catchphrase of Allen Funt on *Candid Camera*, the TV show he created, produced, directed, and hosted (1948–53; 1960–7; syndicated 1974–8; 1989–90). Thanks to Funt, who made it the show's trademark way of informing the persons being unwittingly recorded by a hidden camera—after they had made a big enough fools of themselves—that they were on *Candid Camera*. The TV programme had been born of Funt's *Candid Microphone*, a 1940s radio show he originated after his army service in the Second World War.

smoke me a kipper, I'll be back for breakfast!

Associated with Ace Rimmer (Christopher Barrie) in the cult BBC TV comedy series *Red Dwarf* (1988–92). The most popular sub-character of the series, Commander 'Ace' Rimmer is from an Alternate Dimension. His life was the same as Arnold Judas Rimmer (now dead, but on board the Red Dwarf mining ship as a hologram) until the age of 7. Ace, using a dimension-jumping spacecraft, crosses into Red Dwarf's dimension and comes face to face with his counterpart Rimmer. Described by Arnold as a 'smug, self-satisfied git', Ace is just the type of 'cool guy' who would come out with this sort of 'space-macho' line.

snap, crackle, and pop

Part of an advertising slogan for Kellogg's Rice Krispies breakfast cereal in the US from around 1928. Rice Krispies was introduced in 1928, and its earliest advertising campaigns focused on the noise that the cereal makes when combined with milk. Kellogg's chose 'Snap! Crackle! Pop!' to describe the sounds (an earlier version had been: 'It Pops! It Snaps! It Crackles!'). The three-word slogan first appeared on the front of the package in 1932.

The three sounds were represented, on the cereal box, by three gnomes wearing differently coloured hats. Apparently, they never changed these signature sartorial trademarks, except during the Second World War, when they posed with guns, tanks, and ships that urged consumers to 'Save time, save fuel, save energy'. The hats of the cereal box heroes were important not only to differentiate the three of them, but to reinforce the Rice Krispies slogan, as a corporate history explains: 'In 1949, Snap! Crackle! and Pop! changed drastically from gnomes with huge noses and ears and oversized hats, to more human creatures with boyish haircuts, proportional features, and smaller hats. They continued to evolve as fashions changed, appearing with longer or shorter hair, rounder eyes, and different costumes. Their hats have changed least.'

so farewell, then

Frequent opening of poems, usually obituaries, by 'E. J. Thribb' in the satirical magazine *Private Eye* from the 1970s. Obituary writer E. J. Thribb was in fact one of Peter Cook's inventions. The English satirist Peter Cook founded the Establishment clubs in London and New York in 1960, and both financed and wrote for *Private Eye* (from 1963). The magazine marked its proprietor's death in its 13 January 1995 issue with a cover picture of Cook, holding a drink and cigarette in his right hand, under the caption 'So. Farewell then...'

A poem-obituary by E. J. Thribb, in memory of Kenneth Wood, 'inventor of the "Kenwood" Mixer and the Reversible Toaster', published in *Private Eye* (31 October 1997), honours its subject by taking the form of a 'Reversible Poem'. It begins 'So. Farewell then' and ends 'Then farewell. So'.

so stupid he/she can't chew gum and walk straight at the same time

An American saying that was in use by the 1960s, and appears in this form in John Braine's *The Pious Agent*, published in 1975. It was about this time that it was popularized as a comic description of Gerald Ford, who became president in 1974 when Nixon was forced to resign following the Watergate scandal, and quickly became notorious for his clumsiness. Chevy Chase's impersonation of Ford falling down stairs on the US TV comedy series *Saturday Night Live* (1975–) became one of the first season's best-loved and most recognizable sketches. Former president Lyndon B. Johnson said of Ford, soon after his inauguration, 'so dumb he can't fart and chew gum at the same time'. This variation on the catchphrase became even more popular.

sock it to me

Popularized by Judy Carne in sketches on the US comedy TV series *Rowan and Martin's Laugh-in* (1968–73). Carne became famous around the world for her frequent declaration of 'Sock it to me!', which would often lead to a bucket of water being hurled at her. The furiously fast-paced satirical show attracted an array of guest stars but, rather than appearing in several skits, these celebrities would make very brief cameo appearances. One of the most memorable of these cameos was a shot of President Richard Nixon declaring solemnly 'Sock it to me' in 1968.

The phrase, meaning make a forceful impression on me, be 'straight' with me or 'give me your all', was already known as the repetitive, rhythmic background chorus to Aretha Franklin's 1967 hit single 'Respect'. The phrase had also been employed by US writers, including Mark Twain, and formed part of the jargon of black jazz musicians in which it carried a sexual innuendo.

softly, softly, catchee monkey

An early 20th century proverb that suggests a cautious, quiet approach is the one most likely succeed, especially in the apprehension of a thief. It was adopted as the motto of the Lancashire Constabulary Training School, and *Softly, Softly* was consequently chosen as the title of a BBC TV police drama series that ran from 1966 to 1976. Lord Thomas of Macclesfield, speaking in the House of Lords on 23 March 1998, in favour of a cautious approach to the introduction of a minimum wage said: 'My third argument is that the essential part of this Government's policy in this Bill is that they propose a softly, softly, catchee monkey approach to see what happens to unemployment, costs and wages whenever they change the minimum rate.'

s'OK? S'awright?

Words of approval, or approval-gauging, popularized by master ventriloquist Señor Wences, who often appeared, with Johnny (created with his hand) on US TV programmes, including *The Ed Sullivan Show* (1948–71). The trademark remarks were made possible by his strong Spanish accent, which was an integral part of the charm of his act. (See 'deefeecult for you; easy for me!')

sold (to) American!

A slogan, based on the expression 'sold to —', commonly heard at auctions, that was featured in radio commercials for Lucky Strike cigarettes, which were manufactured (and still are) by the American Tobacco Company. In many of the commercials in this campaign, Speed Riggs, a tobacco auctioneer, would launch into a high-speed sales talk, concluding with 'Sold American!' Several 1940s Warner Bros. cartoons included gags based on the commercial.

some like it hot

Some like things to be passionate and fiery, usually said with reference to sex or jazz. The expression was popularized as the title of the 1959 comedy film classic, starring Tony Curtis, Jack Lemmon, and Marilyn Monroe, in which both sex and jazz are principal concerns. Although in a completely unrelated context, the line appears in 'Pease Porridge Hot', an 18th-century nursery rhyme—'Some like it hot/Some like it cold/Some like it in the pot/Nine days old'.

some of our best men are women

Advertising/recruitment slogan for the US Army during the late 1970s, obviously targeting women while trying—perhaps unsuccessfully—to satisfy the then fast-growing American feminist movement. It was really only a short-lived 'sub-campaign' aimed at increasing the relatively small proportion of women that normally find a career in the armed forces an appealing prospect.

Many of the recruitment slogans created for the US Army have become familiar in their time, if not catchphrases. 'An Army of One', which debuted in January 2001, was the fifth generation of Army advertising campaigns in nearly 30 years. The first campaign of the all-volunteer Army was 'Today's Army Wants to Join You'. In 1973, the Army introduced 'Join the People Who've Joined the Army'. This campaign evolved into the short-lived 'This is the Army'. The Army introduced the more catchy 'Be All You Can Be' in January 1981.

sorry about that chief

One of Maxwell Smart's (Don Adams) staple phrases on the US TV comedy series *Get Smart* (1965–70). Max, CONTROL's ever-bumbling Agent 86, came out with this line on many of the frequent occasions in which he has clearly blundered. Directed at his boss, Chief of CONTROL spy network (played by Edward Platt), the phrase was first used in *The Day Smart Turned Chicken*, and gained real currency after one of the *Apollo* astronauts used it when he made a mistake in late 1965.

space—the final frontier

From the preamble to the US TV series *Star Trek* (1966–9): 'Space—the final frontier. These are the voyages of the Starship *Enterprise*. Its five-year mission: to explore strange new worlds, to seek out life and new civilizations, to boldly go where no man has gone before'. The original *Star Trek* series features the adventures of the crew of the Starship *Enterprise* sent out by the United Federation of Planets (a peaceful alliance of democratic worlds of which Earth is a member) on its five-year mission to explore and patrol the 'final frontier' of space.

The five-year mission lasted only three Earth-years, but the series, with its familiar characters and catchphrases, became an integral part of Western culture. In syndication, the series spawned a cult following—individual fans are called *Trekkers* or *Trekkies*—that numbers in the millions. From the founding series has sprung an animated series, three television series, numerous feature films, and hundreds of novels and merchandise/products. In 2002, the original series was still being broadcast regularly in over 100 countries around the world.

stand by your man

Title of a 1968 song by country singer Tammy Wynette and of a 1981 film about her life and career. 'Stand By Your Man' (lyrics and music by Billy Sherrill and Tammy Wynette) became almost an anthem in parts of America, selling more than one million copies in 1968, the most then sold by a woman in country music. Wynette is primarily known for two songs, 'Stand By Your Man' and 'D.I.V.O.R.C.E.', though her huge catalogue includes 20 US country number 1 hits, mostly dealing with these two subjects.

Wynette clearly saw the limitations of the maxim conveyed by her popular song as she herself married five times. When the song had reached its initial success, her marriage to guitarist Don Chapel disintegrated and, after witnessing an argument, country star George Jones eloped with her. Unaware of the turmoil in Wynette's own life, American feminists in 1968 condemned Wynette for supporting her husband, right or wrong, in 'Stand By Your Man', but she maintained, 'Sherrill and I didn't have women's lib in mind. All we wanted to do was to write a pretty love song'. During a televised interview (on *60 Minutes*, January 1992) Hillary Clinton attempted to justify her decision to continue to stick with and support her husband, while pointing out that 'I am not standing by my man, like Tammy Wynette'.

stifle yourself!

Hush now, or be quiet! An order issued by the bigoted blue-collar worker Archie Bunker (Carroll O'Connor) on the US TV sitcom *All in the Family* (1971–83), pronounced 'stifle yah self'. His catchphrase would be directed either at his squealing wife, Edith (Jean Stapleton), or other members of his family, all of whom he found completely frustrating much of time. The series brought a harsh sense of reality to TV, especially through its portrayal of loud-mouthed, reactionary, and racist Archie Bunker. It was also the first US sitcom to deal openly with racism, bigotry, gender roles, religion and politics, as well as taboo subjects, including abortion, menopause, impotence, homosexuality, rape, and anti-war sentiments. While satirizing Archie and his racist and generally uninformed views, the series showed viewers a character who was also quite familiar to the average American. And ultimately, he was portrayed as a caring and devoted husband, father and grandfather. As Rob Reiner, who played Archie's son-in-law, Mike Stivic, notes '*All in the Family* shows that people can be ignorant and still have loving, human qualities'.

stop it, you saucebox!

An admonishment in the face of men's advances popularized (and possibly coined) by Crystal Jollibottom, played by comic British character actress Patricia Hayes, on the popular BBC radio comedy series *Ray's a Laugh* (1949–61). Miss Jollibottom was a strange lady who would cry out her catchphrase in a high-pitched cockney-accented voice.

suits you sir (or Oooh! Suits you, sir. Ooh)

From the popular BBC TV comedy sketch series *The Fast Show* (1994–7), written by Paul Whitehouse and Charlie Higson. The phrase was popularized by Whitehouse and Mark Williams playing a pair of slightly 'dodgy' tailors whose speech is steeped in sexual innuendo. The duo and their repetitive, suggestive catchphrase were featured in a television advertising campaign for Holsten Pils beer (2000).

survey says!

Suspenseful words spoken by Richard Dawson, lively host of the US TV game show *Family Feud* (1976–85), before revealing the results of

'A survey of 100 people'. On the show, two groups, each composed of five members of the same family, would compete against each other to come up with answers that match with the results of a survey. As the players needed to guess the most correct answers to win, Dawson's phrase was associated with some of the programme's most exciting moments, and has since become a household expression in America.

Tt

....

take a walk on the wild side (hey babe,)

Take a chance, an adventure, stray from the path of conformity. *A Walk on the Wild Side* is the title of a 1956 novel by US writer Nelson Algren, but the variant of the phrase that turned it into an enticement, and made it especially popular, was from the lyrics of Lou Reed's song, 'Walk on the Wild Side', on his 1972 album *Transformer*.

take me to your leader

A catchphrase that was traditionally spoken in science fiction cartoons and stories during the 1950s. It soon became the predictable, but humorous, line spoken by aliens encountering their first earthlings or vice versa.

takes a licking and keeps on ticking

A superior mechanism or product; denoting durability. The catchy expression comes from an advertising slogan for Timex watches that was introduced in 1956.

ta-ta for now (or TTFN)

Farewell, goodbye for now; also common in its shortened, abbreviated form (acronyms having been particularly popular during the Second World War, see 'it's that man again!'). The phrase, in both forms, was popularized in the 1940s by the light-hearted char woman Mrs Mopp, a character played by Dorothy Summers on the popular BBC radio comedy series *ITMA* (1939–49). (See also 'can I do you now, sir?')

tell Sid

The £40 million 'Tell Sid' campaign, devised by Young & Rubicam, was used by the British government to promote British Gas share sales when the utility was privatized in 1986. It was the most famous of the Thatcher government's privatization campaigns, and the name Sid became synonymous in the financial world with small, poorly informed, private shareholders. Sid, the star of the series of advertisements, has come to be a lasting symbol of the Thatcher years, and the 'shorthand version of the Thatcher years, as retold in the Iron Lady's memoirs, and on the after-dinner circuit—where she earns an estimated £1.5m a year—is that Britain was changed from the land of Red Robbo and wildcat strikes to the land of "Sid" and the share-owning democracy' (in the *Guardian*, 22 November 2000).

thank God it's Friday (or TGIF)

An expression of relief, spoken in anticipation of a hard-earned weekend break, associated in the US by the 1950s with schoolteachers in particular, but now common among members of all professions. *Thank God It's Friday* was the title of a 1978 disco-film starring Donna Summer, and of the film's best-selling soundtrack album.

that guy could make his own gravy

Remark associated with, and possibly coined by, US comedian David Letterman, host of the TV talk show *Late Night with David Letterman* (1982–   ). Letterman, nick-named 'The Big Man', seems to use the phrase to suggest the person referred to is overweight and/or angry or nervous. Letterman uses 'gravy' to mean a number of things (such as money and even plain old gravy) and it has come up in different contexts, including his regular and extremely popular 'Top Ten Lists'. For example, number one on his 'Top Ten Signs You've Eaten Too Much' is 'You're sweatin' gravy', while 'Hot and cold running gravy' was number one on his 'Top Ten Other Changes President Clinton Has Made at the White House'.

The word 'gravy' is generally used to mean money or pleasure, and according to David McKie ('All aboard a gravy train ', in the *Guardian*, 11 November 1999) 'gravy trains' first originated in the US in the 1920s, 'though gravy in the sense of coming by riches and luxuries you do not deserve and have done nothing to earn goes back to the early years of this century. "Stick him for all you can. You're a hard worker, and you mustn't let someone else git the gravy."—*Saturday Evening Post*, 1910'. But, over time, 'gravy' has come to have multiple types of usage. In the 1994 movie *Ace Ventura: Pet Detective*, Ace uses 'Gravy!' to show acknowledgement of something (similar to 'bingo!'). And by the late 1990s, it seems the word had come to be used in many different contexts giving rise to a number of interpretations, and could denote pleasure, anger, or confusion, or be placed within phrases such as 'Hold that Gravy' to mean 'Now, just hold on a minute', or 'How's the Gravy?' to mean 'How are you?'

that is quite illogical, captain

A recurring remark of the consistently calm half-Vulcan Commander Spock (Leonard Nimoy), on the US TV series *Star Trek* (1966–9), directed at Captain Kirk (William Shatner). Possessing the highly logical, rational mind of a Vulcan, Spock will rarely be able to refrain from noting this observation in the often bizarre and emotion-driven situations Captain Kirk and his crew continuously find themselves. This is one of several catchphrases associated with Mr Spock, relating to the United Federation of Planets' startling lack of logic. (See also 'most illogical'.)

that'll do nicely, sir

A servile, and potentially sexually charged, assent forming the concluding line in a series of TV commercials for American Express in the late 1970s. The career of 'Bond girl' Cassandra Harris (*For Your Eyes Only*, 1981) was launched by her lucrative role of the American Express girl saying 'That'll do nicely' and trying to convince Amex cardholders that their custom is welcome almost everywhere.

that's all, folks

Pronounced 'Th-uh-th-uh-That's all Folks!', this was the trademark stammering sign-off delivered by Porky the Pig (voiced by Mel Blanc) at the end of the Looney Tunes cartoons produced by Warner Bros. When Mel Blanc starred in a TV commercial for American Express in 1975, he indirectly made it clear that this was one of the best-known cartoon catchphrases. The ad begins with Blanc saying, 'Do you know me? Would you believe I'm the voice of Bugs Bunny. But in here [a restaurant] they don't care if I'm Daffy Duck. Desthpicable' and, finally: 'Why without this [indicating Amex card], the only way I'd get any attention is by saying, "Th-uh-th-uh-that's all, folks!"'

that's your actual French

Remark popularized by Sandy, a character played by British comedian Kenneth Williams, on the BBC radio comedy series *Round the Horne* (1965–9). Sandy and Julian (Hugh Paddick) appeared together in weekly sketches, and the two effete ex-chorus boys were by far the most popular characters on the show. Sandy's line came up frequently, to highlight and draw attention to his use of the French language, no matter how well known the French expression might be (e.g. pied a terre). In one sketch, Sandy says 'Mr [Kenneth] Horne—we are in the forefront of your Nouvelle Vague. That's your actual French'. Julian then adds: 'It means we are of the New Wave', and Horne quips, 'And very nice it looks on you, too'. (See also 'I'm Julian, and this is my friend Sandy'.)

there is no alternative

The unofficial slogan of the British Conservative government under Margaret Thatcher from 1979 to 1990, that has become a political catchphrase favoured by those wishing to show that they are tough and decisive. The words, first used in a speech by the then prime minister to the Conservative Women's Conference in May 1980, became so famous that the acronym, TINA, was, within a year, both a national watchword and Margaret Thatcher's combative nickname.

A more recent example of this catchphrase being used within a political context, was when Carmen Pate, President of Concerned Women for America (CWA), was quoted on the CWA website on 7 January 1999 as using the phrase to summarize the CWA's stance and her 'decisive statement to US Senate Majority Leader Trent Lott about the presidential impeachment trial'. Ein Bereirah, which means 'there is no alternative' in Hebrew, was also used as a slogan by a Israeli group on the margins of the political spectrum during the 1970s.

there's a lot of it about

Associated with British comedian Spike Milligan, the phrase was the title of a 1982 BBC TV series of his in which the line was repeatedly used. Reportedly, Spike Milligan wanted to call this programme *Q10*, following on from *Q5*, *Q6*, *Q7*, *Q8*, and *Q9*. But BBC chiefs objected, pointing out that he had already made a number of programmes with very similar names. Presumably as a reaction to such comments, Spike decided to call the programme *There's A Lot Of It About*. In spite of the rather 'different' programme name, however, this is very much a continuation of the Q sequence of programmes. As with the earlier programmes, each episode consisted of a rapid succession of sketches which varied considerably in quality.

there's gold in them thar hills

There's profit to be made, it is just a matter of having the stamina and perseverance needed to go after it. It is likely that the phrase had its origins in the gold rush days in America in the mid-19th century, and was later popularized, in the 1930s and 1940s, through films portraying stories of those times and of the Wild West. Thanks to the films, the catchphrase was also became known in the UK by the 1930s. The phrase became more popular after 'There's gold in them thar hills', a song by country singer Frankie Marvin was released in the 1930s.

there's no answer to that

Reply associated with Eric Morecambe in the late 1960s and during his performances on the 1970s BBC TV *Morecambe and Wise Show*. Used mainly as a means of avoiding the creation of any sexual innuendo, as when he had to find a reply to Casanova's (played by Frank Finlay) 'I'll be perfectly frank with you—I have long felt want'. *There's No Answer to That—An Autobiography by Morecame and Wise*, by Eric Morecambe and Ernie Wise, with Michael Freedland, was published in 1981.

there's no place like home

Line from the 1939 US film *The Wizard of Oz*, starring Judy Garland as Dorothy, a young girl who finds herself lost in Oz and longing for home. She visits the Wizard, who gives her a task that she must perform (killing the Wicked Witch) before he will help her. When she and her friends accomplish this task, Dorothy comes back to the Wizard, only to discover that he's a charlatan with no more powers than she. He is, however, wise enough to know and tell Dorothy that she has had the power to go home all along—within her. All she has to do is click her ruby slippers together saying, 'There's no place like home'. Although spoken only a few times during the film, the phrase carried one of the film's most important messages, and the one that probably had the most impact on young viewers. It quickly entered the American lexicon, and remains current, whether uttered with longing or with sarcasm.

they're greeeeaaaat!

An advertising slogan for Kellogg's Frosted Flakes breakfast cereal introduced in the early 1950s, and spoken by cartoon character Tony the Tiger. The slogan, especially effective as delivered by the product's 'spokestiger', came at a time when America's baby-boomers were entering elementary school, and the company was developing cereals meant to appeal to their younger tastes. The slogan and Tony the Tiger both became registered trademarks, ones that also became, over time, imprinted on the general public's consciousness. (See also 'best to you each morning, the'.)

this is a local shop, we'll have no trouble here

Words of warning given by Tubbs and Edward (Steve Pemberton and Reece Shearsmith), Royston Vasey's psychotic, inbred local shop owners on the BBC TV comedy series *The League of Gentlemen* (1999–2000). The two weird and dark characters are brother and sister, as well as man and wife, and have a pathological hatred of anyone who either wants to purchase something from the shop, or is not 'local'. Their aversion to non-locals is not merely intense, it is actually homicidal, making them two of the most sinister characters to inhabit the show's fictional northern town of Royston Vasey. The couple and their shop were based on a shop Pemberton and Shearsmith came across on a trip to Rottingdean on England's south coast.

The League of Gentlemen, with a cast of four, arrived on television screens for the first time in 1999 after a highly successful debut on Radio 4. Their stage show, *A Local Show for Local People* opened in London's West End in 2000.

this is Funf speaking

Spoken obviously by Funf, a character created and played by Jack Train on the BBC radio show *ITMA*, the most famous British radio comedy of the war, that aired weekly from 1939 to 1949. Funf, the elusive German spy, would phone in repeatedly, introducing himself with this phrase. The line became so well-known that it began to work itself into many private telephone conversations over the show's first few years, helping to make the German propaganda machine seem little more than a wireless joke.

this tape will self-destruct in five seconds

Words at the end of a taped message (followed only by 'good luck...') given to secret agent Daniel Briggs (Steven Hill) and later James Phelps (Peter Graves) at the beginning of each weekly episode of the US TV spy series *Mission Impossible* (1966–72; 1988–90). The tape-recorded message (voice of Bob Johnson) would detail the mission in question. Reflecting advances in technology, the self-destructing recorded instructions given to the members of the IMF (Impossible Missions Force) were on laser disc when the series was revived from 1988 through 1990. The introductory sequence to the films *Mission: Impossible* (1996) and *Mission: Impossible 2* (2000), both starring Tom Cruise, include the TV show's trademark scene and catchphrase, but otherwise distanced themselves significantly from the trademark characteristics which made the series quite unique.

this week I 'ave been mostly eatin'... (bourbon biscuits|yogurt|taramosalata|etc.)

Popularized by comedian Mark Williams playing the weary country bumpkin 'Jesse' on the popular BBC TV comedy series *The Fast Show* (1994–7). He would come out of a building, shed, or outhouse, say his line and then turn around and go back inside.

this week's deliberate mistake

Usually 'did you' or 'have you spotted this week's deliberate mistake?'; the catchphrase became a means of covering up what was in fact an unintentional error or product of ineptitude.

It originated on the 1930s BBC radio series *Monday Night at Seven* (1938–9; later *Monday Night at Eight* 1939–48), after an incorrect answer was accidentally allowed by the presenter of 'Puzzle Corner'. He used the phrase jokingly after listeners phoned in to correct him, and it then became regular feature of the programme. Richard Murdoch (1907–90) presented 'Puzzle Corner' from 1946 to 1948.

though knowin' my luck

Catchphrase of Unlucky Alf, a regular character played by Paul Whitehouse, on the BBC TV comedy sketch series *The Fast Show* (1994–7). As his nickname sugests, Alf is cursed with unrelenting bad luck, to the point that he has become accustomed to being able to predict it, inserting this phrase repeatedly in his monologues to show he fully expects yet another disaster to befall him. A miserable old pensioner with a thick Northern accent, Unlucky Alf tries not to look for trouble, enjoying—if he can make it there—a visit to the British Legion Club for a game of cards or dominoes. But no matter how hard he tries to escape his bad luck, things always go wrong. As in a sketch in which he has a ticket to the F.A. Cup final, but decides to stay in and watch the match on TV with a glass of beer, explaining 'Though knowing my luck, they'll prrob'ly cancel t' game. So ah've decided not t' risk it'. He then presses a button on the remote control, and the TV promptly blows up.

Thunderbirds are Go!

From the BBC TV cult science fiction series *Thunderbirds* (1965–6), which always began with Barry Gray's distinctive theme music: 'Five! Four! Three! Two! One! Thunderbirds are Go!' Written by Gerry Anderson, who made his name as producer of science fiction puppet series in the early 1960s, *Thunderbirds* featured an ex-astronaut, Jeff Tracey, and his five sons, each with his own Thunderbird rocket ship, who formed the anonymous International Rescue organization to aid mankind. They were aided by their genius house guest, Brains (voiced by David Graham), and the high-class Lady Penelope (Sylvia Anderson). Also the title of a 1966 feature film written by Gerry Anderson and directed by David Lane.

time for bed

Closing line from the BBC TV children's programme the *Magic Roundabout* (1965–77), which became a television legend. The five minute slot just before the early evening news reached a large and mixed audience, and the seemingly innocent children's animation series included witty commentary for the adults. With its laid-back, heavy 1960s flavour and often surreal view of life, the series soon achieved a cult status. Zebedee, an eccentric bouncing character who would make his arrival known with a 'boing', would deliver the standard closing line, sending millions of children to sleep every evening.

today —, tomorrow —

A boastful claim, indicating bigger and wider aspirations and often spoken with a degree of irony. Originally a political slogan, which had, according to Nigel Rees in the *Bloomsbury Dictionary of Popular Phrases*, been used in the early 1930s by the German Nationalist Socialist Press in the following form: 'Today the press of the Nazis, tomorrow the nation's press', while 'For today Germany belongs to us/And tomorrow the whole world' formed the closing lines of a Hitler Youth song written in 1932. However, it was as the all-powerful, conquering slogan 'Today Germany belongs to us—tomorrow the world' which may have been spoken by Hitler, that became the basis for countless similar versions that cropped up in films, books, the media, and the business world since 1939.

Tomorrow the World, a successful drama staged on Broadway in 1943, was the basis for the 1944 film by the same title, starring Frederic March and Agnes Moorehead. It was about an orphaned member of the Hitler Youth who comes to America to live with his uncle.

tonight's the night

A phrase expressing certainty that something important or highly desired is about to finally happen, usually something of a sexual or romantic nature. The phrase was first popularized in 1915 as the title of a song and musical comedy by the English composer Paul Reubens. There have been numerous songs entitled 'Tonight's the Night', and cover versions thereof by artists over the years, from The Shirelles (1960) to Neil Young (1975), Rod Stewart (1976), and Janet Jackson (1999).

trust no one

A basic, well-worn tenet more recently associated with FBI Special
Agent Fox Mulder (David Duchovny), one of the two leading characters
on the US cult TV series *The X-Files* (1993–2002). It is the second most
important motto in Mulder's life, neatly capturing his distrust of his
superiors, the government, and just about anyone he encounters. It
replaced 'The Truth Is Out There' (see below) as a tagline for the
episode *The Erlenmeyer Flask*, an episode in which these words are
FBI informant Deep Throat's dying words. And according to
Little Green Men, an episode from the conspiracy series' second
season, 'trustno1' is Mulder's computer password.

truth is out there, the

The tagline appearing at the beginning of most episodes of the US cult
TV series *The X-Files* (1993–2002). It is associated with one of the series'
two leading characters, FBI Special Agent Fox Mulder (David
Duchovny), and is perhaps the phrase which best describes his
attitude to life and his job—the truth is out there, hidden beneath all
the red tape, the reams of documents that convey lies all stamped with
an official seal, and he is committed to unearthing it. Such
commitment often puts his life in danger, but he makes certain not to
risk fellow agent Dana Scully's life in the process. As Scully (Gillian
Anderson) herself tells Mulder in one episode, 'the truth is out
there but so are lies'. And then again, in another episode and with
a touch of humour, Scully says: 'You're in the basement because
they're afraid of you, of your relentlessness and because they
know that they could drop you in the middle of the desert, and tell
you the truth is out there, and you'd ask them for a shovel!'
Mulder's response: 'Is that what you think of me?' Scully: 'Well, maybe
not a shovel. Maybe a backhoe.'

turn on, tune in, and drop out

From a 1966 lecture given by US psychologist Timothy Leary,
published in *The Politics of Ecstasy* (1968). The phrase, which became a
slogan of the 1960s, originally appeared in this context: 'My advice to
people today is as follows: If you take the game of life seriously, if you
take your nervous system seriously, if you take your sense organs
seriously, if you take the energy process seriously, you must turn on,

tune in, and drop out.' As the man who popularized LSD during the 1960s, Timothy Leary inspired a whole generation with this infamous catchphrase. Leary's experiments with mind-altering drugs finally led Harvard University to dismiss him from his position of professor of psychology in 1963.

Twilight Zone, the

The unknown, a fantasy world where anything can happen. From the title and preamble to the critically acclaimed US TV series *The Twilight Zone* (1959–64), written, created, and narrated by Rod Serling: 'There is a fifth dimension beyond those known to man. It is a dimension vast as space and timeless as infinity. It is the middle ground between light and shadow, between the pit of his fears and the summit of his knowledge. This is the dimension of the imagination. It is an area called the Twilight Zone.' The series, and particularly the concept and term 'The Twilight Zone', quickly entered the lexicon of popular culture.

Once the character(s) and rudiments of the story were introduced, Serling's voice would return to sum up the episode's basic idea and end with a line like 'They have just entered the Twilight Zone' to mean the ordinary laws and rules of reality no longer applied. For this reason, phrases such as the latter and 'You are now entering the Twilight Zone' and other variations, have also become catchphrases and are often accompanied by imitations of the show's distinctively eerie and haunting theme music. The familiar Twilight Zone theme by Marius Constant was be introduced with the series' second season. All episodes were introduced and narrated by Serling, who thereby became a TV star in his own right. Serling often used the series to tackle a number of socio-political issues, protecting himself from censorship by writing in a fanciful, metaphorical fashion. The success of *Twilight Zone: The Movie*, released in 1983, led to a revival on ABC of the original TV series.

Uu

'ullo,'ullo, 'ullo! (what's this?)

A catchphrase of the loudmouthed Mr (or 'Pa') Glum (Jimmy Edwards), a regular on the BBC radio comedy series *Take It From Here* (1948–58). The series reached the peak of its popularity in the early 1950s with the introduction of The Glums. Boorish Mr Glum presided over a household consisting of his ever-absent wife, occasionally heard from a distance (Edwards), his son Ron, a complete idiot (Dick Bentley), and Ron's fiancée Eth (June Whitfield), whose famous catchphrase was a plaintive 'Oh Ron!' Time after time, just as she seemed to have coaxed Ron into some more or less gallant display of wooden affection, and was possibly about to kiss her, Pa Glum would burst in with his ''Ullo, 'Ullo, 'Ullo . . .?'

V v

veeery interesting (...but stupid!)

One of the most popular catchphrases to come out of NBC's gag-a-second comedy TV series *Rowan and Martin's Laugh-in* (1968–73), spoken with a German accent by Arte Johnson. Johnson, with a helmet that was always precariously tilted and wire-rimmed glasses, played a German soldier who spied on the show's progress from behind a potted palm while muttering 'veeeery interesting.' *Very Interesting...But Stupid!* was the title of a 1980 book on catchphrases from the world of entertainment by Nigel Rees.

Ww

· · · · · · · · · · · · ·

wait and see

We should bide our time and allow events to run their course; an
expression first recorded in Daniel Defoe's *Robinson Crusoe* (1719):
'We had no remedy but to wait and see'. In Britain the phrase
became associated with Prime Minister Herbert Asquith, who used
the phrase repeatedly in speeches during 1910, referring to the
rumour that the House of Lords was to be flooded with new
Liberal peers to ensure the passage of the Finance Bill. He said it
so often that he became known as 'Old Wait and See'.

walk a mile for a Camel, I'd

Something that is really special, that I would go out of my way to
obtain. The famous advertising slogan for Camel cigarettes, was
introduced in 1921 by R. J. Reynolds Tobacco Company.
R. J. Reynolds spent millions of dollars on the Camel campaign,
and, by 1923, Camel had captured 45% of the US market. By the
1980s, when one in three billboards in the US advertised tobacco
products, Joe Camel and the 'I'd walk a mile for a Camel'
slogan well suited the flash impressions and memorability that the
billboards so effectively embedded.

we are not amused

Words attributed to Queen Victoria, spoken when confronted with
something she found to be undignified or improper. Probably her best-
known line, 'We are not amused', seems to fit well with the stern,
unsmiling photos and portraits of her. However, there is no actual
proof of her uttering this famous phrase; on the other hand, she is
known to have said 'I was very much amused'. The well-known
remark was attributed to the Queen in Caroline Holland's *Notebooks of
a Spinster Lady* (1919; ch. 21, 2 January 1900).

Queen Victoria Was Amused (1977) by Alan Hardy, sets out to dispel the image of Queen Victoria associated with this catchphrase—of a puritanical old lady who seldom smiled or laughed—and revealing the gayer, light-hearted side of the Queen.

we did it once at Bannockburn

Used by Scottish music hall performer Alec Finlay during the 1940s and 1950s. Known as 'Scotland's Gentleman', Finlay's comedy was entertaining and kindly, with recognizable studies of the Oldest Inhabitant, the Postman, and above all, the Kirk Elder. Another of his principal characters was a Scots Home Guard Sergeant who would always pull out this catchphrase (referring to the Battle of Bannockburn in 1314 in which Robert (I) the Bruce of Scotland defeated the English under Edward II) whenever the abilities or prowess of his company were questioned. The Scots could not be doubted—if they did it then, when they were so heavily outnumbered, they could certainly do it again.

we have ways (and means) of making you talk

Associated with 1930s Hollywood villains and Nazi characters, namely the Gestapo or SS officers, featured in films and television series after 1940. Spoken in a menacing mock-German accent—'ve haf vays...', the phrase quickly became a cliché and a caricature of itself. No longer seriously associated with imminent torture, it was more recently popularized on the catchphrase-packed NBC TV comedy series *Rowan and Martin's Laugh-in* (1968–73). It perhaps had its origins in evil Mohammad Khan's line 'We have ways of making men talk' in the 1935 classic film *Lives of a Bengal Lancer*.

we're getting there

Slogan for British Rail during the 1980s that instantly became the butt of bitter humour from weary commuters, forever finding faults in the service, and later came to serve very well as a neat shorthand for successive governments' approach to transport and other issues. British Rail's advertising tagline, interpreted as an apologetic, but patently untrue, statement was mercilessly picked on by satirists.

The catchphrase came up during a House of Commons question time clash between Prime Minister Tony Blair and William Hague 12 July 2000, when its use—this time by the Labour government—again seemed to equate it with an admission of failure. The Tory leader, looking for an indirect way to substantiate his claim that the government was intentionally concealing crime figures and 'their utter failure on crime', said that the Prime Minister had that day 'attempted the third re-launch of his Government in a single month under the inspiring slogan of "We're getting there"—a slogan last used by British Rail when it was not getting anywhere'.

we was (or wuz) robbed

An exclamation uttered when someone has been tricked or outwitted, often in sports when one has been unfairly or unexpectedly denied a victory. The phrase is attributed to boxing manager Joe Jacobs, who made the remark after Jack Sharkey beat Max Schmeling (of whom Jacobs was manager) in the heavyweight title fight on 21 June 1932.

weak will perish, the

Ominous statement associated with the evil, fearsome life form known as 'Species 8472' on the US science fiction TV series *Star Trek: Voyager* (1995–2001). They communicate with telepathy, possess highly advanced and deadly weapons, and are simply intent on 'destroying everything'. Although quite evil-sounding, their catchphrase is not considered by many *Star Trek* fans to be nearly as chilling or original as the Borg's 'resistance is futile' (see above).

wee-eed weee-eed

What Little Weed, friend of Bill and Ben, the Flowerpot Men, said on the 1950s BBC children's programme *The Flowerpot Men* (see 'flobbadob'). Little Weed, also referred to as 'Ipple Weeb', would let Bill and Ben know when was safe to come out and play and warn them when the gardener was returning by uttering this glass-shattering modulated whine, the only thing it could say. In a new, updated version that began in 2001, Little Weed has a larger role, wears sunglasses, and has learnt to speak.

we-e-e-l-l-l, Daaaisy June!

A catchphrase of country yokel Clem Kaddidlehopper, a creation of US comedian Red Skelton, and later used by Warner Bros. cartoon character Daffy Duck. (See 'heere I Yaaam!')

weekend starts here, the

Slogan for the Friday TV pop show *Ready, Steady, Go* (1963–6), co-hosted by Keith Fordyce and demure, mod Cathy McGowan. The first live acts on the series were Billy Fury and Brian Poole and The Tremeloes, performing in front of about 200 teenagers on a studio disco set. Manfred Mann provided the theme tune, '5-4-3-2-1'. The phrase has since been used by a wide array of Friday evening radio and TV programmes. It was also the title of a track on Fatboy Slim's (Norman Cook) 1997 album *Better Living Through Chemistry*.

welcome to Marlboro Country

See 'come to where the flavour is'.

well, ex-cuuuuuse me!

Exclamation popularized by comedian Steve Martin during the late 1970s and 1980s, when he frequently guest-starred on the US TV comedy sketch series *Saturday Night Live* (1975–   ). Martin's trademark one liner asking for pardon, without really meaning it, always brought laughter to the studio audience, as well as to many home viewers.

well, I'll go to the foot of the stairs!

An old northern English expression meaning 'I'm astonished' and similar to the US 'I'll be darned!' It was popularized by the Liverpudlian comedian Tommy Handley who used it frequently on the wartime BBC comedy radio series *ITMA* (1939–49), as well as in his earlier stage shows.

well, that wasn't very good, was it, Ted?

Phrase—usually an understatement—spoken frequently by Father Dougal McGuire (Ardal O'Hanlon) to Father Ted Crilly (Dermot

Morgan) on the Channel 4 TV comedy series *Father Ted* (1995–8). The two priests, together with Father Jack Hackett (Frank Kelly) are charged with the care of parishioners on Craggy Island, a small island off the west coast of Ireland. Father Ted, no matter how hard he tries to remain sane in the circumstances, always manages to mess up any activity he tries to organize or supervise, or any problem he sets out to solve. His disaster-prone endeavours inevitably result in his complete embarrassment. It was often at these moments that the blissfully inane Father Dougal—the youngest and very much the most junior of the three priests—would often proffer what he believed to be a judicious comment. His catchphrase also came in handy as a judgement of some of his own notorious faux pas.

what did you do in the Great War, Daddy?

Slogan featured on a British First World War recruiting poster (by Saville Lumley, 1917) that depicted a man sitting in an armchair and his son standing by the armchair asking this question. The guilt tactics propagandists were using were apparently quite successful, and the question 'What did YOU do in the Great War?' quickly became a popular catchphrase. There were also various, sometimes subversive, responses, such as 'Tried to stop the bloody thing, my child' attributed to Bob Smillie, Scottish miners' leader. The phrase was also the title of a 1966 US film.

what do you think of it|the show so far?

Line habitually used by Eric Morecambe on the 1970s BBC TV comedy *Morecambe and Wise Show*, and guaranteed to raise some laughs, particularly after the audience had replied with a roaring 'Rubbish!' Still a favourite among live entertainers.

what I want, what I really really want, (I'll tell you)

From the 1996 hit single 'Wannabe' by British pop band the Spice Girls, on their first album *Spice*. *Spice* became an instant hit, and 'Wannabe', their first single, shot to no. 1 in 22 countries. 'Wannabe', an infectious blend of hip-hop grooves, R&B harmony vocals, and bubble gum pop hooks (like the 'tell me what you want, what you really really want' line), set the tone for their style and their celebration of the virtues of what they called 'girl power', introducing the phrase that expressed all this to the dialect of international youth. During this time, the Spice Girls also acquired the individual nicknames that would become their calling cards when they were invented by British reporters during a press conference: Baby, Ginger, Posh, Scary, and Sporty.

what larks, Pip!

Derived from the novel *Great Expectations* (1861) by Charles Dickens, although the exact phrase is never used in the novel. It came to be considered a typical phrase of the blacksmith Joe Gargery, who does on several occasions say 'what larks' to Pip. In the novel, Philip Pirrip (Pip) is brought up by his sister and her husband, Joe Gargery. The exclamation of joy and good fortune, together with the name of the novel's central character, eventually became as popular as Gargery's true words, if not more so. The 1946 classic film, *Great Expectations*, directed by Sir David Lean and starring John Mills, Jean Simmons, and Alec Guinness, helped to popularize the phrase even though, again, it was not spoken in this form. Joe Gargery (played by Bernard Miles) does use the expression 'what larks', but never follows this with his brother-in-law's nickname.

what the well-dressed — is wearing

Originally from a tailor's or couturier's slogan, probably early 20th century, which would have had 'gentleman' or 'man about town' as its subject and target. In recent decades it has been used sarcastically, with the subject slotted in often being the last person one would want to emulate, like 'clown' or 'bag lady', while an advertising slogan for Jockey Shorts in 1971 read: 'what the well-dressed man is wearing this year'. More recently, an article in the Autumn 1999 issue of *Scientific American* bore the title 'What the Well-Dressed Warrior Will Wear'—'Clothes that generate power and change appearance, new battlefield rations and tiny robotic scouts may assist the well-equipped soldier of the next century.'

what, what, what, what, what, what, bok, bok, bok, bok, bok, bok

Spoken very quickly, this was Neddy Seagoon's (Harry Secombe) catchphrase on the surreal BBC comedy radio *Goon Show* (1952–60). Seagoon, who was prone to patriotism, was usually the main character in the series' episodes, which often consisted of his falling foul of an evil plot concocted by Hercules Grytpype-Thynne (played by Peter Sellers). Seagoon's other nonsensical catchphrases were 'yingtong, iddle i po' and 'needle, nuddle, noo'.

what's it all about (, Alfie)?

What does life (and love) really amount to and mean? The question was popularized by the 1966 film *Alfie*, starring Michael Caine as the eponymous Cockney womanizer, and by the hit theme song 'What's It All About, Alfie?' by Burt Bacharach and Hal David. On the one hand, Alfie was a light, comical character, but on the other, there was also a cynical ('nobody don't help you in this life') side to him. Ultimately, he comes across as a selfish anti-hero who by refusing to take responsibility for anything he's ever done makes a mess out of both his own and everybody else's life, while thoroughly mistreating all the women he becomes involved with. In his 1992 autobiography, entitled *What's It All About?*, Caine revealed: 'Alfie's intention to make love to as many women as possible caused the most incredible amount of fuss. I was treated like Jack the Ripper.'

what's it matter what you do as long as you tear 'em up!

A catchphrase belonging to one of Jon Pertwee's most memorable radio characters, the Postman, on the BBC radio comedy series *Waterlogged Spa*, which had followed in 1948 from *HMS Waterlogged*, a segment on the forces radio show *Merry Go Round* (1943–8). It was in this series that Pertwee first began to indulge his flair for accents, and making the most of radio's potential for surrealism, gave life to many catchphrases that became part of the nation's common speech, such as this one which, coldly dissected, meant little or nothing even at the time.

what's new, pussycat?

A 'cool', confident, often predatorial greeting that became popular in the late 1960s, following the release of the 1965 film *What's New, Pussycat?*, starring Peter Sellers, Peter O'Toole, Romy Schneider, and Paula Prentiss. The theme song, of the same title, by Tom Jones did much to popularize the phrase further. Written by Woody Allen, the title had been chosen because it was associated with US actor Warren Beatty, a well-known smooth womanizer, who had originally been chosen for the lead role, but was in another project at the time.

what's up, Doc?

Bugs Bunny's running gag (written by US animator Tex Avery) in the Looney Tunes/Merrie Melodies cartoons by Warner Bros. (1940–64). Although the popular cartoon rabbit character, voiced by Mel Blanc, made his debut in 1937, he was not given his name and his famous catchphrase until 1940 when he made his first solo appearance in *A Wild Hare* with Elmer Fudd, the doctor referred to in the line. Elmer, who referred to Bugs as that 'Silly Wabbit', devoted himself to hunting Bugs, but was always unsuccessful in his attempts to destroy the 'wiseguy' rabbit. The catchphrase was originally 'What's cooking?' but was soon changed 'What's up, Doc?' usually preceded by 'Eh', and followed by some serious carrot-crunching. The phrase, like all of Bugs's lines, was spoken in a Brooklyn accent and with a superior, tough guy attitude. The phrase was also to title of a 1972 comedy film starring Barbra Streisand and Ryan O'Neal.

whatchoo talkin' 'bout?

Popularized by child star Gary Coleman, who starred in the US TV series *Diff'rent Strokes* (1978–86). The story revolved around Arnold (Coleman) and Willis Jackson (Todd Bridges), two poor black kids from Harlem who are taken in by a wealthy gentleman living with his naive young daughter. Coleman, who was made an instant star at the age of

10 when *Diff'rent Strokes* debuted on NBC in 1978, played smart-mouthed, chubby-cheeked Arnold Jackson for the sitcom's entire eight-year run. He has since rejected the fame he enjoyed in connection with this role, claimed he no longer watches television, and does not even like talking about his time on the small screen; at the end of 1998, he placed a moratorium on reporters' questions about the show, stating he definitely will not, if asked, say 'Whatchoo talkin' 'bout?'

whazzup?

[Also: 'whassup', 'wassup'.] From a series of TV commercials for Budweiser beer, forming part of the brand's 'True' advertising campaign. The highly publicized commercials successfully captured ways in which a large number of American males relate to each other (while always cradling a bottle of Bud), with 'whazzup' forming the principal means of communication. Featuring a group of young black friends, they also allowed Budweiser to break away from its traditional conservative white user base, and aim for a younger, black minority. The idea for the ads actually began as an independent short film by director Charles Stone III, who was then contracted by Anheiser-Busch (makers of the beer) to create the series of commercials. The commercials created a degree of controversy, as many viewers felt they had negative connotations, picking on different aspects of group culture, from the male view of women, to the black minority view of the white middle/upper class. The campaign nonetheless won many awards in the advertising industry, and created a cultural phenomenon with the catchphrase 'Whazzup?!'

The series of commercials, combining a balanced, subtle mix of ironic self-parody, humour, and base inanity, became one of the most popular advertising campaigns in recent television history. And aside from creating one of the most popular catchphrases in years, it also inspired a new kind of art form: the viral parody. Budweiser has discovered over 70 parodies of its 'Whazzup?' ads, scattered on sites across the Web. 'Wasss-Up?!!' had been popularized, though to a lesser extent and a different context, by Detroit shock-radio-show host Martin Payne (Martin Lawrence), who would greet listeners calling in to his show on the US TV sitcom *Martin* (1992–6).

when the going gets tough, the tough get going

Attributed to US tycoon and diplomat Joseph P. Kennedy, father of
President John F. Kennedy. Although Kennedy is quoted in *Honey Fitz*
(1962), by J. H. Cutler, as saying these words, it is not certain that he
did in fact coin the saying, and it has also been ascribed to American
football coach Knute Rockne. The axiom nonetheless became strongly
associated with Kennedy, probably because its ethos of action and
endurance was so well suited to the life and achievements of the self-
made millionaire and original patriarch of the Kennedy clan.

The saying was more recently popularized as the advertising slogan
and title of the theme song of *The Jewel of the Nile*, a 1985 film starring
Michael Douglas and Kathleen Turner. 'When The Going Gets Tough
(The Tough Get Going),' which has the catchy saying as its refrain,
was sung by Billy Ocean and was a no. 1 hit in 1986. A cover version
by the popular boy band Boyzone reached no. 1 in 1999.

when you've got it, flaunt it

Popularized as an advertising slogan in the US for Braniff Airline in a
series of TV commercials in 1969. The adverts featured flashy or
eccentric celebrities, including Andy Warhol, Sonny Liston, and the
rock group Vanilla Fudge. The line was probably derived from its
repeated use by Zero Mostel in Mel Brooks's 1968 film *The Producers*.
Mostel's character shouts the oft-quoted line in the film, 'If you've got
it, flaunt it baby, flaunt it!', into the ear of Gene Wilder.

where have all the — gone?

Format phrase expressing nostalgia for better, usually purer, things
and times; it is based on the title of the ballad 'Where Have all the
Flowers Gone?' by US folk singer and songwriter Pete Seeger. The
1961 ballad was popular throughout the 1960s, becoming a
hippie anthem because it highlights the loss of a simpler, more
'natural' past.

where's the beef?

An advertising slogan that turned into a political catchphrase,
meaning where's the substance, the 'filling' that really matters/that
we're paying for? The line was first used in a highly popular

1984 TV commercial produced by the Wendy International hamburger chain which featured three elderly, and quite comical, ladies. The ad campaign launched Wendy's from a distant third in the hamburger wars to the leadership position. Unfortunately, their tenure in the number one position was short-lived because of difficulty in delivery. The line was then used by former vice-president Walter Mondale, running for the Democratic presidential nomination in 1984, referring to his rival Gary Hart's policies in a televised debate. After losing the 1984 presidential election to Ronald Reagan, Mondale retired from national politics.

who he?

An ungrammatical, but quick-paced remark aimed at getting a quick simple answer. It was popularized in Britain by its use in the satirical magazine *Private Eye* during the 1980s. The interjection had been taken directly from Harold Ross, editor of the *New Yorker*, who had the reputation of being a man who stood no nonsense, and would scribble in the margins of the scripts and proofs at the newspaper: 'Who he?' whenever an unexplained or unfamiliar name cropped up.

who killed Laura Palmer?

A classic extended whodunnit teaser from the cult US ABC TV series *Twin Peaks* (1989–91), created and written by Mark Frost and David Lynch and directed partly by David Lynch, and Lynch's 1992 film *Twin Peaks: Fire Walk with Me*. Renowned for his dark portrayals of small-town America in films such as *Blue Velvet* (1986) and *Wild at Heart* (1990), Lynch formed a partnership with Mark Frost, a television writer and producer of the hit drama *Hill Street Blues* (1981–7), with the goal of creating a possible screenplay, and came up with the image of a girl's body wrapped in plastic and washed up on a beach. This simple idea (the girl was Laura Palmer) grew into a phenomenon of its time, eventually ending up as a thirty-episode TV series for ABC and a feature film.

Thanks to the slower development of themes and narrative made possible by the TV series medium, the question of who killed Laura Palmer became a national event, Lynch and Frost producing subtle signs and 'red herrings' to feed the viewers' imagination. The series came quickly to an end when, due to pressure from ABC, the killer's identity was revealed and Lynch played less of a part in its creation. The initial premiss was of a soap opera/drama centred on the murder of 17-year-old homecoming queen Laura Palmer (Sheryl Lee) committed by her father Leland (Ray Wise). His identity was to be kept secret for some time, along with the fact that he is possessed by a horrific evil spirit named 'Bob'. The investigation of the crime by an FBI agent named Dale Cooper (Kyle Maclachlan) gradually introduces the town and its strange inhabitants to the audience.

A very similar national frenzy was provoked 10 years earlier, in the summer of 1980, when, rather strangely, *Time Magazine* and BBC1's Evening News concerned themselves with a soap opera plot line. Clearly showing the impact of the US TV series *Dallas* throughout the world, the big question being dealt with was 'Who shot JR?' In the UK, in 2001 and on a slightly smaller scale, a substantial number of TV viewers were asking 'Who shot Phil Mitchell?' as BBC1's most popular soap opera *EastEnders* teased fans over a number of episodes.

who loves ya, baby?

Greeting or chat-up line popularized by the outspoken and streetwise New York police lieutenant, played by Telly Savalas, on US TV police drama series *Kojak* (1973–8 and 1989–90). Theo Kojak had a cynical sense of humour and was determined to get his way, regardless of what his superiors in the New York Police Department said, and was not above stretching the limits of the law if it enabled him to solve a case. Location filming was done in New York and Kojak could be seen all over the city with his trademarks lollipops sticking out of his mouth. In 1989, the 65-year-old Savalas returned to his role and the streets of Manhattan to make some new *Kojak* television films for the *ABC Mystery Movie* series. This time an Inspector, lollipops and 'who loves ya, baby?' were once again featured elements in this new 'hipper' edition of *Kojak*. Telly Savalas recorded a single entitled 'Who Loves Ya, Baby?' in 1975.

will the real —, please stand up?

Famous line from the US TV game show *To Tell the Truth* (1956–69; syndicated 1969–   ) originally hosted (1956–69) by Bud Collyer.

A game of bluffing, the CBS show presented three contestants to be grilled by a celebrity panel. One of the contestants had an unusual experience or life story; the other two were impostors that had been briefed by the 'real' person. The impostors were free to tell the truth if they wished, but only the real one was forced to tell the truth (under threat of forfeiture of winnings). Each celebrity panellist had about two minutes to question the three contestants on their background and what they had done, trying to trip up the impostors or glean information that would reveal who was actually telling the truth. Each of the four panellists would then cast a vote as to who they thought was telling the truth. At that point, the host would ask 'Would the real [insert name here] please stand up?', thus revealing the truth-teller.

A British version, called *Tell the Truth*, was shown on ITV from 1955 to 1959, hosted by McDonald Hobley. There were several versions since 1959, and the show was last revived in the 1980s.

win one for the Gipper!

A catchphrase used by Ronald Reagan as a political slogan. It was based on a quotation from US footballer George Gipp—'Tell them to go in there with all they've got and win just one for the Gipper'. Reagan felt comfortable appropriating the line as he had played Gipp in a 1940 film *Knute Rockne, All American* and the public could easily make the association. Reagan used the phrase so often that it eventually took the form of 'win just one more for the Gipper!'

winning isn't everything, it's the only thing

A maxim used in sport as well as in the political and business worlds, frequently misattributed to US football coach and manager Vince Lombardi. What Lombardi did say in a 1962 interview was 'Winning isn't everything, but wanting to win is'. The famous line was in fact penned by Henry 'Red' Sanders—'Sure, winning isn't everything, It's the only thing'—in *Sports Illustrated* (26 December 1955).

without hesitation, deviation, or repetition

Words of instruction given to speakers on the BBC radio panel game *Just a Minute* (1967–   ), devised by Ian Messiter. The show, a revamped version of *One Minute Please*, was chaired by Nicholas Parsons. Quick-talking personalities had to speak for one minute on a surprise topic 'without hesitation, deviation, or repetition'. Participants on the first programme were Beryl Reid, Derek Nimmo, Clement Freud, and Wilma Ewert, but later Kenneth Williams joined and virtually took over the show. Although the show was intended primarily as a game, it quickly became more of a comedy, mainly because of the way Nimmo and Freud, and later Kenneth Williams, turned on the chairman.

More than anyone else Williams made the show what it became, and after his death in 1988, many of the show's loyal listeners wondered whether it could continue. Fortunately, stand up comic and writer Paul Merton (a long time fan) began participating on the show, alternating with Nimmo, Freud, and Peter Jones and other younger names. Merton, with his slightly anarchic style, helped turn the show once more into a venue for young comedians. The show continues to be popular, featuring comedy stars like Graham Norton, and versions of the game have been played in over 50 other countries.

works for me

Ready retort popularized by Detective Sergeant Rick Hunter (Fred Dryer) on the US TV police series *Hunter* (1984–91). Hunter would utter the line, meaning it 'convinces me' or 'I'll go with it', when he agreed with something, often directing at his partner, Sergeant Dee Dee McCall (Stephanie Kramer). The officers were homicide investigators with the Los Angeles Police Department, who often had to go undercover to apprehend a variety of L.A.-style villains.

world is your lobster, the

A comic twist on 'the world is one's oyster', if not a minor malapropism, popularized by the ever-dodgy Arthur Daley (played by George Cole) on the award-winning British TV series *Minder* (1979–94). Hired originally as ex-boxer Terry McCann's (Dennis Waterman) bodyguard or 'minder', Daley in fact became the one finding most of the trouble. The two of them ducked and dived through the criminal world, while Daley pursued his latest get-quick-rich scheme.

would you believe —?

Probably the best known of Maxwell Smart's (Don Adams) many catchphrases on the US TV comedy series *Get Smart* (1965–70). Many of the mannerisms and sayings of Maxwell Smart, including this famous line, actually came from Don Adams and his stand-up work. The phrase in fact predated the spy spoof series, appearing in a routine Don Adams and Bill Dana recorded called 'The Bengal Lancers', in which he plays Lieutenant Faversham trying to convince the villainous Mohammed Khan that he is surrounded by British forces. Finding his first attempt fails to alarm Khan in the least, Faversham asks 'Would you believe the First Bengal Lancers?' to which Khan simply replies 'No'. An exasperated Faversham then retorts: 'How about Gunga Din on a donkey?'

would you buy a used car from this man?

Its coinage has been attributed to different American comedians, including Lenny Bruce, but has never actually been ascribed with certainty to any individual. It was in use in the USA by the 1950s and was most famously used with reference to President Nixon from 1968. The 'used-car salesman' has long been a cliché in American culture for a predatory merchant and 'Would you buy a used car from this man?' was an obvious metaphor that questions a person's honesty. The catchphrase became a slogan used by the Democrats to underscore the 'Tricky Dick' character of the Republican candidate during the 1968 presidential campaign (unsuccessfully). By destroying the American people's trust in the nation's highest office, Nixon's role in the Watergate cover-up did much to reinforce his association with this phrase.

Yy

● ● ● ● ● ● ● ● ● ● ●

yabba-dabba-doo!

Most probably originating with scat singing, a popular form of jazz singing with nonsense syllables, it has become known as Fred Flintstone's trademark cry of glee on the Hanna-Barbera TV cartoon comedy series *The Flintstones* (1960–6). The series featured Stone Age caveman Fred Flintstone and his diminutive thick-headed neighbour and pal, Barney Rubble, together with their wives, Wilma and Betty, leading 20th-century-style lives in the suburban town of Bedrock. A 1994 film using real actors, entitled *The Flintstones*, starred John Goodman in the role of Fred.

yada yada yada

Similar to 'blah-blah-blah', meaning 'so on and so forth', 'whatever' or 'etcetera, etcetera'. The term was popularized by characters on the US TV comedy series *Seinfeld* (1989–98), who used it to cut the rough-and-dirty out of a story. An example of how Elaine (Julia Louis-Dreyfus), might use the expression would be 'I went to the bar and came home late, and yada yada yada I had sex with the guy'.

Yehudi

A running gag associated with US character actor and comic Jerry Colonna (see also 'greetings, gate!'), which became part of the American lexicon of the 1940s. A reference to the classical violinist Yehudi Menuhin, the name itself—outside any real context—can sound like a question in itself. It became part of Colonna's routine and eventually a popular song. Apparently, Colonna did not know who Yehudi Menuhin was, and when he asked the cast of Bob Hope's radio show—'Who's Yehudi?', it turned out they didn't know either, though they found the question hysterical. The search for the mythical Yehudi thus became an on-going joke. As with many of Colonna's catchphrases, this one quickly transferred to several Warner Bros. cartoons of the 1940s, including *Hollywood Steps Out* (1941), in which an invisible figure is sitting next to Colonna, and is identified by Jerry (of Tom and Jerry) as Yehudi, and in *Farm Frolics* (1942) where an owl hoots 'Who's Yehudi?'

yes, we have no bananas today

A nonsensical, but cheerful, contradiction, first popularized in the US as the title of a 1923 song by Irving Cohn and Frank Silver, that began: 'Yes, we have no bananas, We have no bananas today'. The catchphrase was then revived in 1939, with the release of *Only Angels Have Wings*, a film directed by Howard Hawks, in which The Kid (Thomas Mitchell) quips: 'Yes, they have no bananas'. It had caught on in Britain as well by the 1920s, thanks to the catchy, carefree song, and then was revived during the war-time and immediate post-war food shortages from 1940 to 1946, aimed at making light of the hardships many then faced.

you ain't heard nothin' yet

Famous multiple negative heralding better or more striking things to come, attributed to US singer Al Jolson (Asa Yoelson). The first record of Jolson's use of a version of the phrase was in a café in 1906, when he had to compete with the din from a neighbouring building site and said 'You think that's noise—you ain't heard nuttin' yet!' (*The Real Story of Al Jolson* (1950) by Martin Abramson). Then, in 1918, he notoriously blurted out the expression on stage during a concert organized in aid of First World War soldiers at the Century Theatre, New York City, when, following a rousing rendition of 'Over There' by Enrico Caruso, he ran on to the stage before the applause had died down, threw out his arms and called out: 'Folks, you ain't heard nothing yet.' The phrase's popularity truly took off, however, with the release of Jolson's 1919 song 'You Ain't Seen Nothing Yet', and subsequently as an aside by Jakie Rabinowitz (Jolson) in the 1927 film *The Jazz Singer* (1927)—'Wait a minute, wait a minute, you ain't heard nothing yet. Wait a minute I tell you. You ain't heard nothing yet. Do you want to hear "Toot, Toot, Tootsie"?'

you ain't seen nothin' yet

A version of Al Jolson's 'you ain't heard nothin' yet', that was popularized by former US president Ronald Reagan when he turned it into a kind of slogan in his 1984 re-election campaign. The phrase was carefully chosen to taunt his political opponents, while striking a colloquial or popular note. It is also a promise that can apparently cross partisan boundaries. Al Gore's presidential election campaign in 2000 did not have one official song, but used a collection of 1970s and modern hits, including 'You Ain't Seen Nothing Yet', a 1974 hit by Bachman Turner Overdrive. In the case of this song, Gore's campaign focused on the chorus, which says, 'Here's something that you're never gonna forget—baby, you ain't seen nothing yet'.

you and your education

A disparaging remark popularized by US character actor and long-time sidekick of Bob Hope, Jerry Colonna. These words were said by the wind-up toy son of Daffy Duck to Porky at the very end of the 1941 Warner Bros. cartoon *A Coy Decoy*.

you are the weakest link ... Goodbye

Anne Robinson's catchphrase on *The Weakest Link* (2000–), which became the BBC's most successful quiz show. In Anne Robinson's case, an intonation alone has achieved the status of an identifying characteristic. The show requires a team of contestants to answer rapid-fire questions from host Anne Robinson. After each round of questions, the teammates vote to eject one of their number, until the team of nine has been reduced to two, who then vie for the final jackpot. As each player is banished, Robinson callously dismisses the spurned player with her signature put-down: 'You are the weakest link. Goodbye'. The loser is marched off in a 'Walk of Shame' and then questioned about how it feels to be rejected and where things went wrong. Robinson's dismissive catchphrase became immediately popular and was even used by Prime Minister Tony Blair during a question time session with Conservative Party leader William Hague. 'Labour MPs roared with approval as, rounding on Hague, he said: "We know he is very keen on summing up policies in six words: you are the weakest link—goodbye." ' (*Times*, 7 December 2000).

you bastards!

Popularized by Kyle Broslowski, the smart kid, on the satirical US TV cartoon series *South Park* (1997–   ). Kyle is the only one of the four main 8-year-old characters in the series who does well at school. He is also the only Jewish one (his father is a rabbi). This line is usually hurled at his own 'buddies'.

you bet your sweet bippy

One of a series of popular catchphrases spouted by the gifted cast of NBC's comedy TV series *Rowan and Martin's Laugh-in* (1968–73) that quickly became a vital part of the American vocabulary. Rather than being associated with a particular character, this was one of the show's few phrases that were repeated by various performers. The flamboyant US pianist Liberace, guest-starring on one of the shows, found himself roaring with laughter after saying 'I bet my sweet bippy and lost!' A silly, yet priceless, variation on the familiar idiomatic phrase 'you can bet your boots' (or 'bottom dollar' or 'life'), meaning you can be absolutely certain.

The show, which earned high ratings during its five-year run, spawned a 1969 film entitled *The Maltese Bippy*. This unsuccessful attempt to combine horror movie clichés with the lightweight double entendre humour of *Laugh-in*'s comic duo, did nothing to extend the careers of Rowan and Martin, who sank into obscurity when *Laugh-in*'s run ended.

you big dummy!

What Fred Sanford, played by Red Foxx, calls anyone who disagrees with him, but most often his son, Lamont (Demond Wilson), in the US TV comedy series *Sanford and Son* (1972–7). The widowed Fred Sanford is a 65-year-old Los Angeles area junk dealer, who is grudgingly assisted by Lamont. While feeling obligated to remain a partner in his father's junk business, Lamont is always looking for a way out. The series focuses mainly on the conflict between father and son and their differing opinions on how to run both the business and their lives. An opinionated old man, Fred is full of get-rich-quick schemes and often meddles in the affairs of his son, but Lamont ultimately cares for his father too much to leave him. Lamont therefore puts up with his brash and pushy (and comical) father, as well as the verbal abuse—including years of being called a dummy. The series was a US remake of the successful BBC TV situation comedy *Steptoe and Son* (1962–5/1970–4), about a cockney junk dealer and his offspring.

you cannot be serious!

Exclamation associated with US tennis player John McEnroe whose audacious and often hot-tempered behaviour on court was a major feature of the men's game in the early 1980s. Although McEnroe won the men's singles title at Wimbledon three times, the US Open three times, and collected a total of 10 Grand Slam doubles titles in a professional career that lasted from 1978 to 1992, he is ultimately best known for is his fiery outburst of 'you cannot be serious'. For most people, the phrase will almost certainly spring to mind before any title win or great match.

The line was said during the 1981 Wimbledon tournament, when McEnroe was playing Tom Gullikson in the first round, and had just seen chalk fly up from a serve of his which was called long. The infamous four words were part of a memorable tirade by the US pro which also included his other well-known catchphrase, 'You've got to be the pits of the world'. The umpire agreed that, 'there was chalk, but it was chalk which had spread beyond the line'. Having been given a warning, the 'pits' insult generated a point penalty, and then McEnroe really did lose his temper. He demanded to see the referee, and told him: 'We're not going to have a point taken away because this guy is an incompetent fool'. McEnroe got his way and went on to beat Bjorn Borg in the final and win his first Wimbledon title.

you can't get the wood, you know

Associated with Peter Sellers's Henry Crun character on the BBC comedy radio *Goon Show* (1952–60), famous for its blend of surreal humour, insanity, and catchphrases. Crun is an elderly, senile, fumbling, methodical, rather dim, craftsman inventor of the old school. He usually turns up as an inventor or caretaker of a major element of a *Goon Show* episode, e.g. in some he is the caretaker of a fort. Crun lives with his companion, the almost kinky and just as elderly and senile Minnie Bannister, played by Spike Milligan, and most episodes contain an extended scene with just him and Minnie talking nonsense. His catchphrase is often used to bring an end to these seemingly pointless discussions, and is a handy saying to indicate an old timer's acceptance of whatever is lacking or missing.

you dirty old man!

A disparaging expression, usually implying sexual misbehaviour (more often contemplated than actually committed). Popularized by Harold (Harry H. Corbett) in the extremely popular BBC TV situation comedy *Steptoe and Son* (1962–5/1970–4). In the successful series, Harold Steptoe, a middle-aged rag-and-bone man, yearns to break away from the clutches of his elderly, mean, cantankerous, and quite disgusting, father, Albert (Wilfred Brambell). However, no matter how much Harold wants to escape from his father and make a life of his own, Albert is always prepared to go to any lengths to prevent him from reaching those aims. His father's generally uncouth behaviour frequently provokes Harold to utter what is the series' only catchphrase: an exasperated 'You dirty old man!'

you dirty rat!

Attributed to the US film actor James Cagney who is often associated with gangster roles, as in *The Public Enemy* (1931) and *White Heat* (1949), but however, never uttered these exact words. The phrase is actually a popularized form of 'You dirty, double-crossing rat', spoken by Cagney in the 1931 film *Blonde Crazy*. He also used another version, 'you dirty, yellow-bellied rat', in *Taxi*, released in 1932. The phrase became a favourite of impersonators, who tried to reproduce the actor's unusual physical intensity and staccato vocal delivery. In his autobiography *Cagney by Cagney* (1976), the actor vehemently denied ever saying the shortened version that became such a popular catchphrase.

you dirty rotten swine, you

Associated with Bluebottle, played by Peter Sellers, on the 1950s BBC radio *Goon Show*. Bluebottle, an East Finchley boy scout who, famously, got 'deaded' every episode (pre-dating Kenny, and his recurring deaths, on the US animated TV show *South Park*, by 50 years). Whoever 'deads' him is greeted with the catchphrase 'you dirty rotten swine, you', followed by his 'YE HE HE' laugh. His other swine-related catchphrases were 'you rotten swines. I told you I'd be deaded' and the variant 'you filthy swine!'

you got it, dude

Phrase coined by Michelle Tanner (played by twins Mary-Kate and Ashley Olsen) on the US sitcom *Full House* (1987–95). Michelle is the youngest of three sisters being brought up by their father Danny, assisted by his brother-in-law and his best friend, after their mother's death. The very 'cutesie' little Michelle came up with several popular expressions. (See also 'you're in big trouble mister'.)

you look mahvelous

Catchphrase belonging to Billy Crystal's Fernando character on the US TV series *Saturday Night Live*, during its 1984–5 season. The vain, white-haired Fernando of 'Fernando's Hideaway' used to say, 'As you all know, it is better to look good than to feel good . . . and you look mahvelous!' The singer and actor Fernando Lamas, originally from Argentina, was the real-life Latin lover who inspired Crystal's routine. Aside from the wildly popular Latin lover, Fernando, Crystal scored with several other memorable characters during his time as a member of the *Saturday Night Live* ensemble, including an impressive interpretation of Sammy Davis Jr., and an inadvertently masochistic moron, whose catchphrase was 'I hate when that happens!'

you might very well think that. I couldn't possibly comment.

The chief whip's habitual, and often quite annoying, response to questioning in the classic BBC TV series *House of Cards* (1991), spoken almost teasingly to the camera. The series, which was recently voted one of the top 100 TV programmes of all time by the British Film Institute, is an adaptation of Michael Dobbs's novel of political back-stabbing and murderous intent. The line, however, does not occur in the novel. In the television version, Ian Richardson dominates proceedings with his portrayal of chief whip Francis Urquhart, an aspiring Tory politician who'll do anything to get to the top and ends up doing just that. *House of Cards* gives a broad picture of the underhanded dealings at Westminster, while focusing on the ruthless methods that Urquhart employs to become prime minister.

you plonker!

A Cockney insult meaning penis or idiot, fool, and what 'Del Boy' Trotter (David Jason) considers his younger brother Rodney (Nicholas Lyndhurst) to be much of the time on the BBC TV comedy series *Only Fools and Horses* (1987–). (See also 'lovely jubbly'.) Del Boy's easily misled 'plonker' brother is always getting unwittingly caught up in Del's scams. It is the relationship between Del Boy and Rodney that has maintained the series' success, veering as it has from conflict and petty deceptions to pathos and genuine warmth and reliance upon one another.

you talkin' to me?

Line now used playfully, but never without reference to its famous appearance in Martin Scorsese's 1976 film *Taxi Driver*, in which Robert De Niro, as the deranged taxi driver Travis Bickle, taunts himself in a mirror, repeating, with a psychotically belligerent tone, 'you talkin' to me?, I said are you talkin' to me?' Travis Bickle is trying to become a 'tough guy', a somebody, and becomes a crazy person. The classic film quote has become the mainstay of every De Niro impression—good or bad—one might encounter.

you rang?

The words spoken by Lurch, played by Ted Cassidy, on the US TV series *The Addams Family* (1964–6). Lurch was the seven-foot monosyllabic, Frankenstein look-alike, family butler. He would intone his words of enquiry—'You rang?'—with such a deep and powerful voice that the sound of him was often just as frightening as his looks, to 'normal' visitors to the Addams family home. The show's episodes usually revolved around the outside world's attempts to make sense of the family's offbeat customs and the family's general ignorance of the fact that they were considered strange by others.

This ABC sitcom began its life in 1937 as a series of macabre, mostly wordless one-panel cartoons drawn by Charles Addams, which became one of the *New Yorker* magazine's most popular features. The cartoons featured a ghoulish-looking family indulging in their very particular ideas of family entertainment, such as baking cookies in the shapes of bats and snakes. The television series gave the family members names and identities: Gomez was the head of the extended family, a lawyer with aristocratic bearing who loved to fence. Morticia, his wife, was graced with a deathly pallor, languid movements, and a deadpan look, and could drive her husband into romantic rapture by speaking a few words in French ('Tish! You spoke French!'). To complete their nuclear family unit were two creepy children, Pugsley and Wednesday.

you silly twisted boy

A running gag in the BBC comedy radio *Goon Show* (1952–60), written by Spike Milligan. The phrase was first used in 'The Dreaded Batter Pudding Hurler' episode, which was aired on 12 October 1954. The recurring words of reproach belonged to Hercules Grytpype-Thynne (Peter Sellers), a cad usually found plotting, along with his hapless French accomplice, Moriarty (Milligan), to steal money or belongings from Neddy Seagoon (Harry Secombe) or others.

you stupid boy, Pike

From the highly popular BBC TV comedy series *Dad's Army* (1968–77) which features the comic ineptitude of a Home Guard platoon in the imaginary seaside resort of Walmington-on-Sea, on the south coast of England. The phrase is spoken repeatedly by the self-important Captain George Mainwaring (Arthur Lowe) to Private Frank Pike (Ian Lavender).

you too can have a body like mine

Slogan for 'Charles Atlas' body-building courses which became almost synonymous with muscle-building from the 1930s. The Charles Atlas ads often appeared in comic books, illustrating how muscle-building 'made a man out of Mac'. Charles Atlas, who won the title of 'The World's Most Perfectly Developed Man' in 1922, soon became the most famous and most recognizable name in all body-building. Atlas himself had been a 'skinny, timid weakling of seven stone' before developing his particular method of body-building.

Born Angelo Siciliano, Atlas started a mail-order course with little success until 1928 when Charles P. Roman joined the company as campaign director and suggested the company advertise in comic books. The plan worked, and the Charles Atlas course named

'Dynamic Tension' sold millions of copies and continues to be advertised in comic books today.

you're despicable!

Cartoon character Daffy Duck's popular, spitty catchphrase, pronounced 'you're desthpicable!' The black duck with a white ring around his neck starred in a number of Looney Tunes cartoons produced by Warner Bros. beginning with *Porky's Duck Hunt* (Tex Avery, 1937). His sloppy lisp was said to have been based on that of producer Leon Schlesinger, who, legend has it, not only did not recognize the source, but enthused about 'the funny voithe'.

you're extinct

Used repeatedly by Austrian-born US film actor Arnold Schwarzenegger in the 1982 sword-and-sorcery film *Conan the Barbarian*, an observation/threat that goes a step beyond the already established Americanism 'you're dead'. One look at Schwarzenegger's rippling muscles would presumably be sufficient for the person or creature being addressed to abandon all hope.

It was this film that turned Schwarzenegger into a global superstar. Conan, the pulp hero created by Robert E. Howard in the 1930s, was at the height of his popularity in the late 1970s and early 1980s. During those years, the sword-and-sorcery genre was experiencing a boom (partly due to the growth of a new role-playing game called 'Dungeons & Dragons') aided by the arrival at book shops of a dozen 'original' paperbacks detailing Conan's exploits (compiled by Howard, L. Sprague De Camp, and Lin Carter), several new novels, and at least three Conan comic books.

you're going to like this … not a lot … but you'll like it!

A line employed by British magician, entertainer and game show host Paul Daniels during his conjuring acts, especially on his weekly BBC TV show which ran from 1981 to 1996. Daniels made his television debut in 1970 on *Opportunity Knocks* on which he came second, and was soon given the chance by Granada to launch what became an extremely successful television career. Almost overnight, his catchphrase—'You'll like it, not a lot, but you'll like it'—became a household saying. Appealing to live and television audiences around the world, Daniels made his performances complete by adding to them a particular comedy style, perfectly illustrated by his famous catchphrase.

you're in big trouble mister

Phrase popularized by Michelle (played by twins Mary-Kate and Ashley Olsen) on the US sitcom *Full House* (1987–95). Created by Jeff Franklin, *Full House* is about a father (Danny Tanner), who gets help from his brother-in-law (Jesse) and his best friend (Joey), raising his three young daughters DJ, Stephanie, and Michelle, after Pam, Danny's wife, died. Michelle is the youngest Tanner girl and the one with the 'oooh so cute' factor who is responsible for the sitcom's most popular sayings. Aside from 'You're in big trouble, mister', Michelle is known for her 'puh-lease', 'Oh nuts', and 'You got it dude!' Most of her antics revolve around cookies, cake, and ice cream.

you're never alone with a Strand

A British advertising slogan for brand of cigarettes (1959 and early 1960s) which became a classic. Devised by John May of S. H. Benson for the W. D. & H. O. Wills tobacco company, the ad campaign attempted to attract the youth market by identifying the brand with a moody loneliness embodied in a character who was reminiscent of both a young Sinatra and James Dean, in hat and trench coat, played by Terence Brook.

The character became a popular figure, standing on a damp, fog shrouded city street or leaning against the parapet of a deserted London bridge, and 'The Lonely Man' TV ad theme tune even became a hit. However, the ads failed to increase sales and it seems that the advertising ended up leading consumers to equate the brand with loneliness, rather than with the antidote to loneliness. Despite being one of the best-remembered ads, the campaign sounded the death knell for the brand and it soon disappeared from the market. *You're Never Alone With* is the title of an album released in 2000 by The Rapiers, which features 1960s numbers, including successful reproductions of the early 1960s sound of Cliff Richard and The Shadows.

you've come a long way, baby

Slogan for Virginia Slims cigarettes that gained considerable currency in the US during the late 1960s and 1970s, as part of an advertising campaign that focused on women smokers. It suggested that women had made a great deal of progress, becoming far more assertive and independent than the subservient women portrayed in many of the ads' insets, which depicted recreated, early 20th-century settings. Virginia Slims were tailor-made for women—so long and slender that no man would probably be seen dead smoking one. The ads featured some of the world's sexiest and most fashionable models dressed in the latest fashions, proving that Virginia Slims were the cigarettes chosen by independent, confident, solvent American women who preferred to make their own choices. The slogan was first used in the mid-1960s, but without 'Baby'. The full line 'You've Come A Long Way, Baby' was first used in 1969 and last appeared in 1995. 'You've Come A Long Way, Baby' was also the title of a techno-dance album by Fatboy Slim released in 1998.

you've never had it so good

Political slogan associated with, though not coined by, Harold Macmillan, British Conservative Prime Minister (1957–63). The slogan won him the 1959 election, but what Macmillan actually said, in a speech given at a garden fête in Bedford on 20 July 1957, was: 'Let us be frank about it: most of our people have never had it so good.' 'You Never Had It So Good' had already been used as the Democratic Party slogan during the 1952 US election campaign, and was attributed to the American labour leader George Meany.

The slogan, a triumphal celebration of economic prosperity promising voters a continuation of the 'good things in life', is still a highly valued one on both sides of the Atlantic. It was chosen as an early favourite slogan for Jean Chrétien's Liberals hoping to secure a third majority government in summer 2001 polls in Canada. It also figured in the US presidential election campaign of 2000, which seemed to be echoing earlier campaigns. According to University of Virginia political scientist Larry Sabato, quoted in *The Dallas Morning News* (3 September 2000), 'From a historical perspective, the whole election will boil down to two time-tested slogans: The Democrats will run on "You've never had it so good." And the Republicans [will] run on "It's time for a change." ' As in 1952, the slogan failed to keep the Democrats in government. While in Britain, the *Guardian* (16 August 2000) states 'Labour is expected to walk this election because, its much-publicised public sector troubles aside, it is a Macmillan-style "You've never had it so good" election'.

your country needs you

Recruiting slogan during the First World War appearing on the famous poster by Alfred Leete, featuring a portrait of Lord Kitchener pointing at the viewer. British field marshal Horatio Herbert Kitchener, who was Secretary for War from 1914 to 1916, raised an army of 70 divisions with the aid of his famous slogan-carrying recruiting poster. The words soon became an established catchphrase to encourage or cajole a person into doing something they less than relish the thought of. The poster was later imitated in the United States where the army and navy came up with recruitment posters with pointing figures (Uncle Sam and an alluring woman respectively) and slogans beginning 'I want *you* ...'

Zz

· · · · · · · · · ·

zis is KAOS, ve don't — here!

Catchphrase associated with Siegfried, Vice-President of Public
Relations and Terrorism for KAOS, on the US TV comedy series *Get
Smart* (1965–70). The cunning, ruthless Siegfried (Bernie Kopell),
was the foe faced most often by Maxwell Smart (Don Adams) in
the series. A stickler for detail, he usually uttered this line to
silence his assistant KAOS agent, Shtarker (King Moody). Siegfried
first used the line without the first part in *A Spy For A Spy*: Max
says 'Couldn't you have just shushed him?' to which Siegfried
replies 'Ve don't Shush here!' The full format phrase was first
used in *Closely Watched Planes*, after KAOS has captured Max and
Agent 99 and Shtarker is preparing to gun them down (making
the sound of a machine gun firing), Siegfried says 'Shtarker, zis is
KAOS, ve don't Dududu here'.

zoinks

Sound of surprise, popularized by Shaggy, the beatnik teenager,
and member of the 'meddling' foursome on the US (Warner Bros.)
TV cartoon series *Scooby-Doo* (1969–86), featuring a Great Dane
called Scooby. The cowardly Shaggy, who was also Scooby's
best friend, would often use this expletive to inform the
others of yet another peril as in 'Zoinks! It's the one-legged
zombie again!'

Source Information

The following descriptions are for TV shows, films, or books that have three or more catchphrases in the book.

Absolutely Fabulous

A BBC television comedy series broadcast from 1992 to 1996, and 1994 to 1997 in the US. The series centred around the life of the manic, desperately trendy Edina Monsoon (Jennifer Saunders), her conscientious, prudish daughter Saffron (Julia Sawalha), and outrageous best friend Patsy Stone (Joanna Lumley). Other regular characters are Edina's mother (June Whitfield) and Edina's assistant, Bubble (Jane Horrocks). A new series of *Absolutely Fabulous* was broadcast in 2001.

ALF

A US TV comedy series, starring a furry, wise-cracking extraterrestrial called Alf (Alien Life Form), transmitted from 1986 to 1990 on NBC. Stranded on Earth after his spacecraft went out of control and landed on a suburban garage (his home planet of Melmac had also just blown up), Alf becomes a part of the Tanner family. Alf, with his distinctively big, ridged snout, was highly popular with children. The trouble-making alien was played by a puppet in stationary scenes, and by actor Micah Maestros in walking scenes. The furry diminutive creature successfully disrupted the Tanners' formerly boring life while commenting sarcastically (voice by the show's co-creator Paul Fusco) on the faults and shortcomings of earthlings.

Da Ali G Show

A British comedy/talk show hosted by Ali G, a notoriously politically incorrect TV personality created and played by British comic Sacha Baron Cohen, transmitted on Channel 4 from 2000 to 2001. Ali G, an uneducated 'black gangsta' from Staines dressed in trademark yellow FUBU track-suit, wrap-around shades, chunky gold jewellery, and Tommy Hilfiger hat, first became a popular television figure as a sketch on Channel 4's satire comedy series *The 11 O'Clock Show* (1998–). *Da Ali G Show* included absurd interviews with prominent politicians and personalities conducted by Ali G and reports from a visiting journalist from Kazakhstan (also played by Cohen), researching English customs.

All in the Family

A US TV sitcom that focused on the blue-collar household of Archie Bunker (Carroll O'Connor) and his slightly vacuous but well-meaning wife, Edith

(Jean Stapleton), and was transmitted on CBS from 1971 to 1983. The series was one of the first to bring a harsh sense of reality to TV, especially through its portrayal of its bigoted and openly racist star, Archie Bunker, and dealt with a number of issues that had previously been considered taboo on prime-time television, such as abortion, menopause, impotence, homosexuality, and rape. The series was based on the BBC sitcom *Till Death Us Do Part* (1966–74).

'Allo, 'Allo

Broadcast on BBC1 from 1984 to 1992, this successful BBC television comedy series began as a spoof version of the BBC drama series, *Secret Army*, which was broadcast from 1977 to 1979. The series was set in a café in the small town of Nouvion in occupied northern France in 1940, focusing on café owner René Artois (Gordon Kaye) and his dealings with the German officers stationed in the town, with members of the French Resistance trying to smuggle downed British airmen back to England, and with his willing young waitresses, while keeping his cantankerous wife, Edith (Carmen Silvera) at bay.

The Archers

Britain's longest-running radio soap opera, this serialized 'everyday story of country folk', has run on BBC radio since 1950. The series tells the stories of the Archers, working and residing at Brookfield Farm, and others in the village of Ambridge, in the fictional county of Borsetshire. Despite numerous character and cast changes, the serial's consistent realism has helped it maintain a loyal following over the decades, still drawing 4.5 million listeners after over 50 years.

Are You Being Served?

A BBC TV comedy series broadcast on BBC1 from 1973 to 1983, written by David Croft and Jeremy Lloyd, creators of *Dad's Army* and *It Ain't Half Hot Mum*. Set in an old-fashioned department store called Grace Brothers (based on Simpson's in London's West End), the series follows the misadventures of the Ladies' Fashions and Menswear floor's eccentric staff. The success of this single-set, farcical sitcom was based on its flow of double entendres and its outrageous characters—including the gay Mr Humphries (John Inman) and the octogenarian 'Young' Mr Grace (Harold Bennett), the store's owner.

The A-Team

A US action/adventure/comedy TV series broadcast on NBC from 1983 to 1987, about four Vietnam veterans and their underground adventures as mercenaries assisting those in need. During each episode, the team—each member of which possessed specialized skills or strengths—would complete one of a series of impossible tasks, emerging victorious. Led by former Army Colonel John 'Hannibal' Smith (George Peppard), the members of the A-Team were wanted by the government for a crime they did not commit, and therefore worked secretly as formidable soldiers of fortune.

Bandwagon

A regular weekly comedy and music BBC radio series that was aired from 1938 to 1939, and was co-hosted by resident comedian Arthur Askey and compère Richard Murdoch. Askey, whose background had been mainly in music-hall, and Murdoch provided the comedy spots that came to dominate the show. This popular weekly radio show was the first comedy show to be designed specifically for the radio, and the first of its kind to make considerable use of catchphrases, helped along by the studio audience's enthusiastic response. Among the series' recurring features were sketches in which Askey and Murdoch shared a top floor flat in Broadcasting House, 'Mr Walker wants to know' (in which Sid Walker played an old Cockney junkman), lavish musical numbers, and the popular 'Bandwagon Crash' (sound effect) which followed Askey's frequent falls off a ladder and other accidents.

Being There

A novel by Jerzy Kosinski, published in 1971, and the title of a 1979 film adaptation starring Peter Sellers and Shirley MacLaine. *Being There* is a satirical fable about Chance (Sellers), a reclusive, simple-minded gardener who has lived all of his life inside the walls of an elegant Washington town house, and whose only knowledge of the outside world is through watching television. When the master of the house dies, the household staff is disbanded, and Chance, impeccably dressed in his employer's tailored suit, wanders out into the city. He manages to then stumble into America's political and social upper crust, and is immediately mistaken for Chauncey Gardiner, an aristocratic businessman. Due to a series of mistaken assumptions, Chance's simple, TV-informed utterances are mistaken for profundity, and are taken very seriously by Washington D.C.'s influential political circles, and the president himself.

Blackadder

A BBC TV historical comedy series broadcast on BBC1 from 1983 to 1989, starring Rowan Atkinson as Lord Edmund (also known as The Black Adder) and spanning from the 15th century (*The Black Adder*) to the First World War (*Blackadder Goes Forth*). Written by Richard Curtis, Ben Elton, and Rowan Atkinson, the series featured many of Britain's best-known comedians, including Stephen Fry, Hugh Laurie, Robbie Coltrane, Rik Mayall, and Adrian Edmondson.

Dad's Army

A BBC TV comedy series broadcast from 1968 to 1977 on BBC1, set during the Second World War and featuring the comic inadequacies of a Home Guard platoon in the fictional south-coast resort of Walmington-on-Sea. Written and produced by Jimmy Perry and David Croft, the series' many comic moments sprang from the relationships between the very diverse group of persons within the platoon—often represented through the very English class tensions that would normally separate them, and their inept attempts to protect the locals. Among the show's principal stars were Arthur Lowe (Captain Mainwaring), John Le Mesurier (Sergeant Wilson), Clive Dunn (Lance Corporal Jones), and John Laurie (Private Frazer).

Dixon of Dock Green

The longest-running police series on British television, *Dixon of Dock Green* began on BBC Television in 1955 and ran until 1976. PC George Dixon (Jack Warner) was the chief character in this enormously popular series set principally in a suburban police station in the East End of London. Focusing on the routine tasks and relatively petty crimes dealt with by the station's police officers, the series was more interested in portraying the moralizing influence of Dixon and the community-based concerns of those at the station than the more realistic and harsh aspects of police work that came to characterize later British and US police series.

Doctor Who

A BBC television science fiction series that began in 1963. *Doctor Who*, created by Sidney Newman and Donald Wilson, followed the exploits of the unusual eponymous science-fiction hero as he travelled in his space vehicle, the Tardis, combating all sorts of alien enemies, including the famous robot-like Daleks. As the world's longest-running science fiction TV series, cast changes were at first necessary, if not inevitable, and then became a natural part of the developing story-lines. In all, seven actors have played the Doctor: William Hartnell, Patrick Troughton, Jon Pertwee, Tom Baker, Peter Davison, Colin Baker, and Sylvester McCoy.

Educating Archie

This highly popular BBC radio show, scripted by comedian Eric Sykes, ran from 1950 to 1958, transferring to television (1958–9) (ITV). Surprisingly, for a radio show, the stars were a ventriloquist's dummy called Archie Andrews and his operator, Peter Brough. Other members of the original cast were Robert Moreton as Archie's tutor, Max Bygraves as an odd-job man, Hattie Jacques in various supporting roles, and Julie Andrews, then only 13, as the resident singer. Tony Hancock later took over as tutor; Beryl Reid, Harry Secombe, and Benny Hill, among other up and coming comedians, appeared in later series. The television version of the series, scripted by Marty Feldman and Ronald Chesney, starred Archie Andrews with ventriloquist Peter Brough, Irene Handl as the housekeeper Mrs Twissle, and Dick Emery as the opportunist Mr Monty.

The Fall and Rise of Reginald Perrin

A BBC television comedy series broadcast from 1976 to 1979, following the ups and downs of Reginald Perrin, played by Leonard Rossiter. The series begins with the bored middle-aged executive Perrin, working for Sunshine Desserts. On the verge of a breakdown, Perrin eventually fakes his own suicide and sets off to start a new life. But, disguised as his non-existent best friend Martin

Wellbourne, Perrin returns to attend his own memorial service, eventually starts up a relationship with his own wife Elizabeth (Pauline Yates), and returns to work at Sunshine Desserts, before his true identity is eventually revealed. In the second series, Perrin sets up his own business, opening a shop called 'Grot' specializing exclusively in completely useless goods. The highly successful venture soon spawns a growing chain of 'Grot' shops, making him a millionaire. In the third series, Perrin sets up a 'community' for disenchanted middle-class people, much like his original self. And, in fact, he ends up realizing that he is very much in the same position he first tried to escape from.

The Fast Show

A BBC television comedy series transmitted on BBC2 from 1994 to 1997. Written by Paul Whitehouse, Charlie Higson, and others, this fast-paced sketch show was based on the idea of keeping sketches, with their recurring characters and catchphrases, short, and cramming as many of them as possible into each programme. The often zany and bizarre sketches featured Paul Whitehouse, Charlie Higson, Mark Williams, John Thomson, Simon Day, Caroline Aherne, and Arabella Weir. It also appeared in the US, renamed *Brilliant!*

Fawlty Towers

A BBC television situation comedy series written by John Cleese and Connie Booth and broadcast in 1975 and 1979. Set in a guest house in the seaside resort of Torquay, England, the two series comprising 12 episodes followed the flow of mishaps produced by Basil Fawlty (Cleese), the hotel's awkward and abusive manager, and his relations with his overbearing wife Sybil (Prunella Scales), the relatively calm and sane Polly (Booth), who helps out at the hotel, and Manuel (Andrew Sachs), the comically stereotypical Spanish waiter on whom Basil vents most of his frustration and anger. *Fawlty Towers* has been shown throughout the world and became the BBC's best-selling programme overseas during the late 1970s.

Frasier

US TV comedy series *Frasier* that premiered on NBC in 1993. The show follows the lives and loves of the rather neurotic and pompous radio psychiatrist Dr Frasier Crane (Kelsey Grammer) and his immediate family and work associates. The other principal characters are his snobbish, highly sensitive brother and fellow psychiatrist Niles (David Hyde Pierce), his live-in father Martin (John Mahoney), an unsophisticated ex-cop, who brought with him his English home-care provider and physiotherapist Daphne Moon (Jane Leeves) and his expressive Jack Russell terrier Eddie (Moose), and at work, his often morally questionable producer Roz Doyle (Peri Gilpin).

Full House

A US sitcom, created by Jeff Franklin, broadcast on ABC from 1987 to 1995. The series was about a widowed father (Danny Tanner), raising his three young daughters DJ, Stephanie, and Michelle, with some help from his brother-in-law (Jesse) and his best friend (Joey). Michelle (played by twins Mary-Kate and Ashley Olsen), the youngest and very 'cutesie' Tanner girl, was responsible for much of the sitcom's popularity.

The Generation Game

BBC television game show hosted by Bruce Forsyth from 1971 to 1978. Forsyth was replaced as host in 1978 by Larry Grayson but returned to host the show again from 1990 to 1995. Since 1996, Jim Davidson and Melanie Stace have co-presented the show—renamed *Jim Davidson's Generation Game*. *The Generation Game*, which had its origins in a Dutch show called *Ein Van De Aacht* (One From Eight) that was put together by a housewife, involved pairs of contestants who had to be both related and of different generations and were given tasks to complete, including acting out a wildly farcical sketch. It was the first show featuring ordinary contestants on which the public was given an opportunity to perform on prime time Saturday night television.

Get Smart

A US TV comedy series that ran from 1965 to 1970 on both NBC and CBS. In 1995, FOX attempted to bring the series back with some changes, but it was unsuccessful and lasted only one month. Essentially a cold war James Bond satire, the series was about a spy who worked for an ultra top-secret government organization. The spy, Maxwell Smart aka Agent 86 (Don Adams) receives his orders from the Chief of CONTROL and, with a great deal of help from his competent partner Agent 99, battles the forces of KAOS thus preserving the free world. The wacky show, featuring unlikely gadgetry such as sandwiches that turn out to be telephones, was conceived by producer Dan Melnick and writers Mel Brooks and Buck Henry.

The Goon Show

A half-hour comedy programme aired on BBC radio from November 1952 to January 1960. Famous for its blend of surreal, if not insane, humour and catchphrases, most of the episodes were written by Spike Milligan. Milligan also performed many of the series' characters along with Peter Sellers, Harry Secombe, and for the first two series Michael Bentine. Wallace Greenslade became a regular announcer in 1953, and also played some parts. The show did not have a single theme or on-going plots until the third series, when the episodes began to normally consist of Neddy Seagoon (Secombe) being duped by the dastardly Hercules Grytpype-Thynne (Sellers) and his French accomplice Moriarty (Milligan), or the interactions between naive schoolboys Bluebottle (Sellers) and Eccles (Milligan).

Happy Days

US TV series broadcast on ABC from 1974 to 1984. The show led the way in capitalizing on the mid-1970s' nostalgia craze for the 1950s by presenting an updated version of teenage life in mid-1950s America. Set in Milwaukee, the heart of middle-class America, the series told the story of the Cunningham family, originally centring on the eldest son, Richie (Ron Howard) and his friend Warren Webber (Anson Williams), better known as 'Potsie'. But it was the motorcyling, leather-jacketed Arthur 'Fonzie' Fonzarelli, aka the Fonz (Henry Winkler), who soon became the show's most popular character and its true star after taking on a 'big brother' role towards Richie and his pals.

Have a Go

A BBC radio quiz show, presented by Wilfred Pickles, that ran from 1946 to 1967. On the series, Pickles would speak with and question ordinary people across the country, giving away modest cash prizes for correct answers to simple questions. Pickles travelled over 400,000 miles in the 1940s and 1950s, visiting factories, hospitals, and other venues around Britain. The popular radio series had regular audiences of twenty million, making Pickles, with his Yorkshire accent, a household name.

The Hitchhiker's Guide to the Galaxy

Created and written by Douglas Adams, it was a successful BBC radio science-fiction comedy series prior to its transformation into a novel in 1979, and was then serialized for BBC television by Alan J. Bell in 1981. The series is about an 'average' Englishman, Arthur Dent, whose planet is destroyed to make way for a hyperspace bypass, and is rescued by his friend, Ford Prefect, actually an alien from a small planet near Betelgeuse, and follows his attempts to make it back home again, while searching for 'The Answer to the Great Question...Of Life, the Universe and Everything'. The series was re-run on BBC 2 in 2001, following the death of Douglas Adams.

ITMA

A popular wartime BBC comedy radio series that ran from 1939 to 1949, and starred Tommy Handley assisted by a team of regulars, including Jack Train, Dorothy Summers and Horace Percival. Ted Kavanagh, who devised the show in 1939, and Tommy Handley decided to name the new show after a catchphrase associated with Hitler and his mounting territorial claims that was then appearing in newspaper headlines: 'It's That Man Again'. As abbreviations or acronyms such as the RAF, the ARP, ENSA, and others were already very popular, it became *ITMA*. The show, relying heavily on its absurd characters and many catchphrases, became an important part of wartime British society, providing much needed comic breaks in stressful times.

The Jack Benny Show

A US comedy/variety TV series from 1950 to 1964 on CBS and from 1964 to 1965 on NBC (and weekly on radio from 1932 to 1955). The show's success was based on its successful transition from radio to television; the show's format (which included occasional musical interludes and celebrity appearances), and Benny's personality as a notorious cheapskate quickly became a TV fixture. His stinginess, vanity (perpetually claiming to be 39 years old), the wreck of a Maxwell he drove, and other comic characteristics, all projected the blustering ego that had made him a favourite with radio audiences since the early 1930s. Regulars on the radio show also became fixtures on the TV series, including Rochester Van Johnson, Benny's gravel-throated valet, announcer Don Wilson, Mary Livingstone (Benny's wife), singer Dennis Day, the incredibly rude Frank Nelson, and Benny's violin teacher Professor Le Blanc (Mel Blanc).

Kojak

A US TV police drama series that ran from 1973 to 1978 and from 1989 to 1990 on CBS. The series followed police Lieutenant Theo Kojak, played by Telly Savalas, as he investigated crimes, often disregarding the wishes and advice of his superiors in the New York Police Department. Filmed on location in New York City, the series' portrayal of crime and police work was often considered gritty and realistic for its time.
Kojak's cynical sense of humour and strong determination added individuality to a screen personality that became both familiar and endearing.

Late Night with David Letterman/The Late Show with David Letterman

US TV talk show *Late Night with David Letterman* was broadcast on NBC from 1982 to 1993. After being passed over as the replacement for the retiring Johnny Carson on *The Tonight Show*, comedian Letterman accepted a multi-million dollar offer from CBS to switch networks. He and his band leader/sidekick Paul Shaffer moved to CBS, where *The Late Show with David Letterman* has been running opposite *Tonight with Jay Leno* with since 1993. Both Letterman's shows followed the main familiar elements of late night formats, with the host's opening monologue, followed by two or three guests in between which the host delivers a comedic skit or recurring item involving the audience. Letterman's shows, however, have differed from others in content, style of delivery and rapport both with guests and the audience. Among his regular instalments are 'Stupid Pet Tricks', 'Stupid Human Tricks', and one of the most popular items in his repertoire, the 'Top Ten List', announced nightly by Letterman.

Minder

A Thames Television drama/comedy series broadcast from 1979 to 1994 on ITV that combined tough realism with a cutting humour. The series starred George Cole as the ever-dodgy Arthur Daley and Dennis Waterman as the ex-boxer and ex-convict Terry McCann. Daley, hired originally as McCann's bodyguard, or 'Minder', was in fact the one finding most of the trouble, getting both of them involved with the criminal world while he pursued his latest get-quick-rich scheme. It was the comic partnership between Daley and McCann that ensured the series' success both in Britain and abroad.

Monty Python's Flying Circus

A BBC television comedy series broadcast from 1969 to 1974. These non-traditional, free-form, satirical, and often anarchic, shows made fun of most of the conventions affecting British life and society, including television. It was written by and starred Graham Chapman, John Cleese, Eric Idle, Michael Palin, and Terry Jones, and also featured animation by Terry Gilliam. The series was considered groundbreaking in many ways, with its innovative haphazard nature, often featuring sketches that are seemingly abandoned before reaching a satisfactory conclusion. Of the series' 45 episodes, the first 39 were called *Monty Python's Flying Circus*, while the last six, created without John Cleese, were entitled *Monty Python*. The series was first shown in the US on PBS in 1974. Its popularity soon grew to cult status and ABC purchased the rights to air the fourth and final series.

Much-Binding-in-the-Marsh

One of the most popular BBC radio comedy series originating during the war years. The programmes aired from 1944 to 1954, and were written by and starred Kenneth Horne and Richard Murdoch. Following on from *ITMA*, and its tradition of relying on a stream of catchphrases, *Much-Binding-in-the-Marsh* began as an RAF station, but by the early 1950s the RAF station had become inoperative and its former staff ran a newspaper called the *Daily Bind* instead. Other contributors included Maurice Denham, who played the upper class Dudley Davenport, and Sam Costa, who represented the rank and file.

The Muppet Show

A comedy children's series, created by puppeteer Jim Henson, that was first broadcast on the now-defunct ITV company ATV from 1976 to 1980 and quickly became a favourite among adult audiences around the world. Kermit the Frog and the other Muppet characters, including Miss Piggy and Fozzie Bear, quickly became popular figures, if not celebrities, among both young and adult audiences in 100 countries. The show, which also featured top celebrity guests, began in 1976 with the backing of British television mogul Lord Lew Grade, and ran for five years, becoming one of the world's most widely seen TV programmes.

The Navy Lark

A BBC radio comedy series that ran from 1959 to 1977, presenting a light-hearted satire on the Senior Service. The programmes were all set aboard HMS *Troutbridge*, and followed the capers and pranks of the ship's crew as it sailed from port to port. The original cast included Dennis Price as the Number One (replaced by Stephen Murray after the first series), Leslie Phillips as the Sub-Lieutenant, and Jon Pertwee, playing Petty Officer

Pertwee. Others later joined the cast, including Ronnie Barker as (Un)Able Seaman 'Fatso' Johnson, and Lieutenant-Commander Standon.

Perfect Strangers

A US TV sitcom about Balki (Bronson Pinchot), a goofy, fun-loving shepherd from the Mediterranean island of Mypos, who moves to Chicago, turning up unexpectedly at the apartment of his distant cousin, Larry Appleton (Mark Linn-Baker). The sitcom focuses on their adventures as flatmates—including Balki's wide-eyed, gullible discoveries *vis-à-vis* the 'American way of life' and the near-total disruption of Larry's life—and eventually, best friends. A slapstick comedy, the series revolved around Balki's misadventures as he sought to comprehend America, gain employment (and citizenship), while chasing girls with his American cousin.

Private Eye

Independent and influential satirical news fortnightly co-founded by Willie Rushton and Christopher Booker in 1961. With its comprehensive attack on the establishment, who were presented as running England in the manner of a private club, *Private Eye* pioneered a style of satire that was to become fashionable in the early 1960s. When the magazine was hit by financial difficulties in 1962, British satirist Peter Cook quickly stepped in and bought controlling shares, initially creating 'offices' in the waiters' changing room at the Establishment Club in London. Aside from its humorous articles and comic strips, *Private Eye* also excelled at investigative journalism, breaking the Profumo scandal and generally attacking the government, media, and the like—a tradition it continues to this day.

Ray's a Laugh

A popular BBC radio comedy series, starring Ted Ray, that ran from from 1949 to 1961. The programmes centred on Ray in domestic situations with his wife, played by Kitty Bluett, interspersed with his conversations with his conscience, office scenes, and encounters with a number of unusual characters (each with their own catchphrase), played by Peter Sellers, Kenneth Connor, Kitty Bluett, and Patricia Hayes, among others. Beginning its life as more of a sketch show with a large cast, the long-running radio series was the direct successor to *ITMA*, which had ceased broadcasting because of the death of its star, Tommy Handley, in 1949.

Red Dwarf

A BBC TV science fiction sitcom that ran on BBC2 from 1988 to 1992. This humorous extension of many elements associated with traditional sitcoms became the cult series of the late 1980s, and still boasts a relatively large following. Its five series star Dave Lister ('the last human alive'), played by Craig Charles, and centre on a 24th-century earth mining ship, *The Red Dwarf*, which has had its entire crew wiped out, except, of course, for space technician Lister. Lister is lost in space with only a hologram of his dead bunk-mate (and not his favourite person), the ship's computer, a mad android servant, and a part cat/part human hybrid.

Round the Horne

A radio comedy series aired on BBC radio from 1965 to 1969, written by Barry Took and Marty Feldman and starring Kenneth Horne, Kenneth Williams, Hugh Paddick, Bill Pertwee, and Betty Marsden. As its title implies, the BBC sketch show featured the proper and civil Kenneth Horne (who played himself) around whom revolved a collection of characters who came out with atrocious puns and double entendres. Among the show's main characters were the outrageously gay Julian and Sandy (played by Paddick and Williams), agony aunt Daphne Whitethigh (Marsden), and folk singer Rambling Syd Rumpo (Williams).

Rowan and Martin's Laugh-in

A wild and experimental US comedy TV series that sprang from the social and entertainment revolution of the late 1960s, and ran on NBC from 1968 to 1973. The catchphrase-packed series relied on a combination of topical satire and shtick, and comic routines. Within the furiously fast-paced show, performers continuously repeated their trademark mannerisms and catchphrases, becoming part of viewers' consciousness. The cast comprised over 40 regulars appearing in the series. Although these cast members changed frequently throughout the show's five-year run, the two hosts—Dan Rowan and Dick Martin, Ruth Buzzi, and announcer Gary Owens were constant features.

The Royle Family

A BBC television comedy series broadcast on BBC1 and BBC2 from 1998 to 2000. Written by Caroline Aherne, Craig Cash and Henry Normal, this sitting room sitcom features highly realistic characters who never stray far from the lounge of their working-class Manchester home. The Royles consist of slovenly, overweight Jim (Ricky Tomlinson), his wife Barbara (Sue Johnston), their two children, teenage Antony (Ralf Little) and Denise (Caroline Aherne), who is married to Dave Best (Craig Cash). Occasionally making it into the kitchen, but mainly glued to the settee, the Royles receive visits from neighbours and non-live-in family members such as 'Nana' (grandmother), played by Liz Smith, amid the over-sized furniture and general clutter, overflowing ashtrays, constant mugs of tea, and bacon butties (sandwiches).

Saturday Night Live

A live US comedy variety programme that debuted on NBC in 1975 and has remained popular viewing for over a quarter of a century. It originally featured the then members of 'The Not Ready for Prime Time Players'—Dan Ayckroyd, John Belushi, Chevy Chase, Jane Curtin, Garrett Morris, Laraine Newman, and Gilda Radner. The show's 90-minute format had as its basis a series of comedy sketches presented by these regulars with breaks provided by guest musicians, and all hosted by a different celebrity guest each week. The highly successful show produced several consecutive generations of US comics.

Scooby-Doo

A US (Warner Bros.) TV cartoon series transmitted on CBS from 1969 to 1986, featuring a Great Dane called Scooby and four teenage detectives who travel the country in a 'groovy' painted van, called the Mystery Machine, solving mysteries in dangerous situations. Guest stars, such as Mamma Cass, the Globetrotters, Sonny and Cher, and Don Knotts (all playing themselves) appeared on shows during the mid-1970s, helping the odd fivesome solve more mysteries. *Scooby-Doo*, one of the most popular cartoon series in history, was named by Fred Silverman, the show's creator, after listening to Frank Sinatra singing 'Strangers in the Night', which includes, the phrase 'Scooby-dooby-doo'

Seinfeld

A US TV hit sitcom, described as 'a show about nothing', shown on NBC from 1989 to 1998. The series follows the lives of the title star, comedian Jerry Seinfeld (who satirizes himself) and his three friends—George Costanza (Jerry's childhood friend and perpetual loser), Cosmo Kramer (a wild and wacky neighbour who inexplicably has access to both cash and beautiful women), and Elaine Benes (Jerry's ex-lover and rather shallow, but good friend). The series followed the four friends as they experienced everyday aspects of the social world of New York City and dealt with just about everything: sex, parents, baked goods, blind dates, rental cars, parking spaces, impotence, and anything else the writers found funny.

The Simpsons

The Simpsons, which premiered on Fox as a half-hour Christmas special in 1989 and began as a regular series in January 1990, became the longest-running cartoon on US prime-time network television. The award-winning series delivers solid, and often controversial, messages about society, family, and the environment, while chronicling the adventures of Homer Simpson and his wildly dysfunctional family, residing in the fictional community of Springfield.

South Park

A controversial US TV cartoon series transmitted since 1997 on NBC. Created by Trey Parker and Matt Stone, the show features the antics of four 8-year-olds—Cartman, Kyle, Kenny, and Stan—as well as the rest of South Park's inhabitants, including their equally dubious parents, the town's mayor, their school teacher, chef, bus driver, and many more. Often touching on sensitive issues, such as homosexuality, religious tolerance, and the handicapped, the show has been criticized by some as lacking in taste or tact, and its frequently foul-mouthed characters are definitely aimed at adult audiences. It was first shown in the UK on Channel 4 and Sky in the summer of 1997.

Star Trek

The original *Star Trek* TV series, set in the 23rd century and featuring the adventures of the crew of the Starship *Enterprise* as it explores and patrols the 'final frontier' of space on its five-year mission, ran from 1966 to 1969. Although the original series, with its collection of familiar characters headed by Captain James T. Kirk (William Shatner) and Spock (Leonard Nimoy), is still regularly broadcast in over 100 countries around the world, *Star Trek* has continued to evolve over three subsequent series. The crew changes with each new starship and series, but the show's ideas and premisses, originally created by Gene Roddenberry, continue to hold older audiences while still drawing new, younger ones.

Steptoe and Son

A BBC television situation comedy broadcast from 1962 to 1965 and 1970 to 1974 on BBC1, featuring a father and son team of 'totters', or rag-and-bone men. Albert Steptoe (Wilfred Brambell), a cantankerous old widower, lives with his middle-aged son, Harold (Harry H. Corbett), and together they carry on the business of Steptoe and Son that he inherited from his father. Harold, who does most of the work, yearns to break away from the clutches of his mean and unsophisticated father. But, no matter how much Harold wants to escape from his father and make a life of his own, Albert always outwits him and finds a way to ruin his plans.

To Tell the Truth

A US TV game show transmitted on CBS from 1956 to 1968 (syndicated from 1969 to 1977 and 1980 to 1981), originally hosted (1956 to 1969) by Bud Collyer. The show presented three contestants all claiming to be the same person. After an affidavit, describing the life, unique activities, and experiences of the person all three contestants are claiming to be, was read out the contestants would be grilled by a celebrity panel, hoping to determine which one is telling the truth and which two are lying. Each panellist would then cast a vote as to who they thought was telling the truth. Incorrect answers were worth money to all three contestants, who split the winnings equally.

Twin Peaks

A US soap opera/drama series transmitted on ABC from 1989 to 1991. The largely surreal series, created and written by Mark Frost and David Lynch and directed partly by David Lynch, reached cult status, with millions of viewers frequently discussing the show when they weren't compulsively watching its every episode. The idea for the screenplay started with the image of a girl's body wrapped in plastic and washed up on a beach. The scene with the murdered girl grew, eventually ending up as a thirty-episode TV series for ABC and a feature film. The series centred on the murder of 17-year-old homecoming queen Laura Palmer (Sheryl Lee), committed by her father Leland (Ray Wise). His identity was kept secret for some time, along with the fact that he was possessed by a horrific evil spirit named 'Bob'. The investigation of the crime by FBI agent Dale Cooper (Kyle Maclachlan) gradually introduces the town and its bizarre inhabitants to the audience.

The Weakest Link

The BBC's most successful quiz show to date, transmitted on BBC1 since 2000; a US version began running on NBC in 2001. The show requires a team of nine contestants to answer rapid-fire questions from dragon-lady host Anne Robinson over a time limit which starts at three minutes and gets 10 seconds lower after each round. For each correct answer they get a 'link' in the 'chain' that begins at zero and gradually goes up to a thousand pounds through nine links, the values between each link becoming higher each time, with a thousand pounds maximum to be won in each round. If a teammate answers incorrectly the chain is broken and they have to start again from the bottom. After each round of questions, the teammates vote to eject one of their number, until only two contestants are left, who then compete for the final jackpot.

Who Wants To Be A Millionaire?

Highly popular TV quiz show that began in the UK in 1998, hosted by Chris Tarrant and shown on ITV. It has since had its format exported around the globe, with 80 countries and an estimated 100 million viewers regularly following successive would be millionaires. The US version was first aired in August 1999, hosted by Regis Philbin. At the beginning of each show, a contestant who will play for the £1 million top prize is chosen from ten qualifiers via a timed question. The contestant must then answer 15 multiple-choice questions correctly in a row to win the jackpot, but may choose to quit at any time and keep their earnings. For each question, they are shown the question and four possible answers in advance before deciding whether to play on or not. If they do decide to offer an answer, it must be correct to stay in the game. If at any stage they answer incorrectly, they fall back to the last 'guarantee point'—either £1,000 or £32,000—and their game is over. They are also provided with three 'lifelines' in case they cannot answer a question— '50:50', 'ask the audience', and 'phone a friend'.

The X-Files

A cult US TV paranormal crime series that ran on Fox from 1993 to 2002. The series follows the exploits and investigations of two FBI agents, Fox Mulder (David Duchovny) and Dana Scully (Gillian Anderson), who work with the 'X files', cases that have unexplainable elements often involving the paranormal. Mulder and Scully work in the Bureau's Violent Crimes section, specializing in cases that defy scientific explanation and which the government is generally anxious to cover up, in spite of all their agents' efforts. Special Agent Mulder began hunting the causes of paranormal goings-on after his sister was abducted by aliens when she was a child. Scully, a conscientious scientist, tends to start by thinking his fantastical theories are exaggerated or ill-founded, but most often sees them turn out to be true.

Source Index

TV and radio shows, Films, Books, Computer Games

Note: Sources are listed alphabetically and followed by their relevant entries in the main part of the dictionary.

Advertising Slogans

Women's Institute
  all Jam and
  Jerusalem
Wonderloaf
  nice one, Cyril!

Woolwich Building
  Society
  no, I'm/we're
  with the
  Woolwich

Y

Yellow Pages
  let your fingers do
  the walking

Oxford Paperback Reference

The Concise Oxford Dictionary of English Etymology
T. F. Hoad

A wealth of information about our language and its history, this
reference source provides over 17,000 entries on word origins.

'A model of its kind'

Daily Telegraph

A Dictionary of Euphemisms
R. W. Holder

This hugely entertaining collection draws together euphemisms from all
aspects of life: work, sexuality, age, money, and politics.

Review of the previous edition
'This ingenious collection is not only very funny but extremely
instructive too'

Iris Murdoch

The Oxford Dictionary of Slang
John Ayto

Containing over 10,000 words and phrases, this is the ideal reference for
those interested in the more quirky and unofficial words used in the
English language.

'hours of happy browsing for language lovers'

Observer

OXFORD